AF539422

Women, Education and Empowerment

INTERNATIONAL ENCYCLOPAEDIA OF WOMEN-2

WOMEN, EDUCATION AND EMPOWERMENT

By

Dr. Digumarti Bhaskara Rao
Chairman

&

Mrs. Digumarti Pushpa Latha
Executive Member
Care Welfare Society, Guntur–522 006
Andhra Pradesh
(India)

DISCOVERY PUBLISHING HOUSE
NEW DELHI-110002

Edition-2003
Reprinted-2011

ISBN 81-7141-495-8

Published by

DISCOVERY PUBLISHING HOUSE
4831/24, Ansari Road, Prahlad Street,
Darya Ganj, New Delhi-110002 (India)
Phone: 23279245 • Fax: 91-11-23253475
E-mail:dphtemp@indiatimes.com

Printed at:
Sachin Printers, Delhi

Contents

Foreword

Women and men are equal in every human concern in this World. They are equally competing in almost all spheres of work and power and are equally achieving the set goals. Culture, economy and polity may be barriers to women in certain parts of the globe, still women are marching ahead with great conviction and confidence to keep themselves on par with their counter parts in every affair..

This International Encyclopaedia of Women is touching every area concerned to women. Volume 1 explains the status of the world's women, Volume 2 discusses the role of education in women's empowerment, Volume 3 discusses the challenges and advancement of women, Volume 4 outlines the family health, and Volume 5 presents the details of the international instruments applicable for the development of women.

This Encyclopedia will meet the requirements of planners, researchers, educationists and activists.

Dr. Digumarti Bhaskara Rao
Mrs. Digumarti Pushpa latha
R.V.R College of Edication
Nagarjuna University,
Guntur 522006 (India)

Acknowledgements

We are thankful to the United Nations and its various commissions, agencies, divisions and departments, the UNESCO, Paris, the UNESCO Institute for Education, Hamburg, the United Nations Centre for Human Rights, Geneva, the UNESCO, Dakar, the International Institute for Population Sciences, Bombay, the Organisation of African Unity; and the United Nations Information Centre, New Delhi for extending their kind cooperation in providing us with the necessary material on our request for the preparation of this International Encyclopaedia of Women.

Volume 1 of the Encyclopaedia contains the material taken from *The World's Women 1995: Trends and Statistics*, United Nations. We thank Prof. Ann Marie Erb-Leoncavallo, Associate Information Officer, Department of Public Information, United Nations, New York for sending the above cited material along with some other valuable documents with the necessary permission to cite material with due credit.

Volume 2 contains the material obtained from Carolyn Medel-Anonueva, ed., *Women, Education and Empowerment: Pathways Towards Autonomy*, UNESCO Institute for Education, Carolyn Medel-Anonueva, ed, *Women Reading the World: Policies and Practices of Literacy in Asia*, UNESCO Institute for Education, Namtip Aksornkool, *Daughters of the Earth*, UNESCO; Cynthia Guttman, *In Our Own Hands*, UNESCO; *The African Conference on the Empowerment of Women through Functional literacy and the Education of the Girl Child*, Kampala: We thank Prof. Cendrine Sebastiani, Publications Department, UNESCO Institute for Education; Prof. Francoise Pinzon, Global Action Programme on Education For All, UNESCO; The Organisers of the African conference on the Empowerment of Women for sending the material for use in our work.

Volume 3 contains the material obtained from *Worldwide Facts and Statistics About the Status of Women*, Committee for the '95 World conference on Women, *Women: Challenges to the Year 2000*, United Nations; *Fourth World Conference on Women, The Advancement of Women: Notes for Speakers*, United Nations, etc. We are thankful to the concerned Personnel of United Nations Department of Public Information, New York, United Nations Information Centre, New Delhi; Committee for the '95 World Conference on Women, New York; and East- West centre, Honolulu for their kind material support.

Volume 4 contains the material obtained from International Institute for Population Science, *National Family Health Survey (MCH and Family Planning) India, 1992-93*, IIPS. We are thankful to the IIPS, Bombay, Government of India; East-West Centre, and Population Research Centres in India for their valuable cooperation.

Volume 5 contains the material taken from *The International Bill of Human Rights*, United Nations, *Discrimination Against Women: The Convention and The Committee*, UN Centre for Human Rights, Geneva, *Harmful Traditional Practices Affecting the Health of Women and Children*, UN Centre for Human Rights, *The Nairobi Foreword-Looking Strategies for the Advancement of Women*, United Nations (as adopted by the World Conference to Review and Appraise the Achievements of the United Nations Decade for Women: Equality, Development and Peace, Nairobi, Kenya, 15-16 July 1995), and *The Flatform for Action*, United Nations, We are thankful to the United Nations for using these international instruments on women.

We are also thankful to many scholars, researchers, teachers, administrators and friends working on women around the globe who helped us in gettings the necessary information and material on women to prepare this International Encyclopaedia of Women.

Dr. Digumarti Bhaskara Rao
Ms. Digumarti Pushpa Latha

OVERVIEW OF THE WORLD'S WOMEN

Issues of gender equality are moving to the top of the global agenda but better understanding of women's and men's contributions to society is essential to speed the shift from agenda to policy to practice. Too often, women and men live in different worlds—worlds that differ in access to education and work opportunities, and in health, personal security and leisure time. *The World's Women 1995* provides information and analyses to highlight the economic, political and social differences that still separate women's and men's lives and how these differences are changing.

How different are these worlds? Anecdote and misperception abound, in large part because good information has been lacking. As a result, policy has been ill-informed, strategy unfounded and practice unquestioned. Fortunately, this is beginning to change. It is changing because advocates of women's interests have done much in the past 20 years to sharpen people's awareness of the importance of gender concerns. It is changing because this growing awareness has, by raising new questions and rephrasing old, greatly increased the demand for better statistics to inform and focus the debate. And it is changing because women's contributions—and women's rights—have moved to the centre of social and economic change.

The International Conference of Population and Development, held in Cairo in 1994, was a breakthrough. It established a new consensus on two fundamental points:

—Empowering women and improving their status are essential to realizing the full potential of economic, political and social development.

—Empowering women is an important end in itself. And as women acquire the same status, opportunities and social, economic and legal rights as men, as they acquire the right to reproductive health and the right to protection against genderbased violence, human well-being will be enhanced.

The International Conference on Population and Development drew together the many strands of thought and action initiated by two decades of women s conterences. It was also the culmination of an active effort by women's groups to lobby international forums for women's issues. At the United Nations Conference on Environment and Development in Rio de Janeiro in 1992, nongovernmental organizations pushed for understanding the link between women's issues and sustainable development. At the World Conference on Human Rights in Vienna in 1993, women's rights were finally accepted as issues of international human rights.

At the Population Conference and later at the World Summit for Social Development, held in Copenhagen in 1995, the terms of discourse shifted. Not only were women on the agenda—women helped set the agenda. The empowerment of women was not merely the subject of special sessions about women's issues. It was accepted as a crucial element in any strategy seeking to solve social, economic and environmental problems. And building on the advances made in the recognition of women's human rights at the World Conference in Vienna, women's human rights became a focus of the debate in Cairo. The rights approach, advanced by women's groups, was added to the core objectives of development policy and the movement for women's equality.

To promote action on the new consensus, this edition of *The World's Women* builds on the first, presenting statistical summaries of health, schooling, family life, work and public life. Each has to be seen in proper context, however. Yes, there have been important changes in the past 25 years and women have generally made steady progress, but it is impossible to make sweeping global statements. Women's labour force participation rates are up in much of the world, but down in countries wracked by war and economic decline. Girls' education is improving, but there are hundreds of millions of illiterate women and girls who do not complete primary schooling, especially in Africa and southern Asia.

It is also important to look at a range of indicators. Women's political participation may be high in the Nordic countries, but in employment Nordic women still face considerable job segregation and wage discrimination. Women's higher education may be widespread in western Asia, but in many of those countries there are few or no women in important political positions and work opportunities are largely limited to unpaid family about.

It is also important to look at a range of indicators. Women's political participation may be high in the Nordic countries, but in employment Nordic women still face considerable job segregation and wage discrimination. Women's higher education may be widespread in western Asia, but in many of those countries there are few or no women in important political positions and work opportunities are largely limited to unpaid family labour.

The World's Women presents few global figures, focusing instead on country data and regional averages (see the box on regional trends). There are myriad differences among countries in every field and *The World's Women* tries to find a meaningful balance between detailed country statements and broad generalization. Generalizations are primarily drawn at the regional and subregional levels where there is a high degree of uniformity among countries. For all the topics covered, *The World's Women* has tapped as many statistical sources as possible, with detailed references as a basis for further study. Specialized studies are used when they encompass several countries, preferably in more than one region, so as to avoid presenting conclusions relevant in only one country.

Indicators relevant to specific age groups are crucial to understanding women's situation. The Programme of Action of the International Conference on Population and Development identified equality for the girl-child as a necessary first step in ensuring that women realize their full potential and become equal partners with men. This edition of *The World's Women* responds to this concern by highlighting the experience of the girl-child. Evidence of prenatal sex selection and differences in mortality, health, school enrolment and even work indicates that girls and boys are not treated equally.

The experience of the elderly is more difficult to describe from the few available data. Although elderly people constitute a valuable component of societies' human resources, data on the elderly are insufficient for regional generalizations. Considering that the number of elderly are growing rapidly in all regions, this gap needs to be addressed.

Regional trends

Latin America and the Caribbean

* Fertility has declined significantly—dropping 40 per cent or more over the past two decades in 13 of the region's 33 countries. The total fertility rate has fallen from 4.8 to 3.2. But adolescent fertility remains high—13 per cent of all births are to mothers below age 20. In Central America, 18 per cent.

* Maternal mortality has declined in most countries of Latin America but the incidence of unsafe abortion in South America is the highest in the world.

* Literacy has reached 85 per cent or more across most of the region, and girls outnumber boys at both secondary and tertiary levels of education.

* Latin America's recorded labour force participation rate for women (34 per cent) is low, but in the Caribbean it is much higher (49 per cent).

* Latin America's and the Caribbean are as urbanized as the developed regions, with 74 per cent of the population in urban areas. But the rate of growth is much higher—2.5 per cent a year compared with 0.9 per cent—which strains housing, water and sanitation and other infrastructure.

Sub-Saharan Africa

* Minimal progress is seen in the basic social and economic indicators. Health and education gains have faltered in the face of economic crises and civil strife. Literacy remains the lowest in the world, 43 per cent of adult women and 67 per cent of adult men, and the difference between women's and men's literacy rates is the highest.

* Fertility is the highest in the world at about six children per woman.

* Women's labour force participation has dropped throughout the past two decades—the only region where this occurred.

* Urban areas are growing at a rate of 5 per cent a year, but with new housing and economic growth at a standstill, many live in poverty and squalor. Africa's urban migrants are predominantly male, shifting the sex ratio in rural areas to 106 women per 100 men.

* Estimated HIV infection rates continue to soar, and unlike any other region, the per centage of women infected with HIV is estimated to be as high if not higher than the per centage of men. In Uganda and in Zambia, the life expectancy of both women and men has already declined because of the disease, and eight other countries are beginning to see similar effects.

Northern Africa and western Asia

* In the past two decades, many countries in the region have invested in girl's education—bringing the primary -secondary enrolment ratio for girls to 67 in northern Africa (from 50 in 1970) and 84 in western Asia, and raising women's literacy to 44 per cent in the region. But women's illiteracy in northern Africa remains high, and girls' enrolment still lags behind boys."

* Women are entering the labour force in increasing number—up from 8 per cent in 1970 to 21 in 1990 in northern Africa and from 22 to 30 per cent in western Asia. Still, these numbers are the lowest in the world. Also low is women's share of decision-making positions in government and business.

* Marriage among girls aged 15--19 has declined significantly in northern Africa and to a lesser degree in western Asia—from 38 per

cent to 10 per cent in northern Africa and from 24 per cent to 17 per cent western Asia. Teenage fertility, however, remains fairly high.

* Fertility—which was traditionally high—has declined significantly in the past 20 years, especially in northern Africa. It remains high (with total fertility rates over 5) in several countries in western Asia. These countries also have low female literacy.

Southern Asia

* Many health and education indicators remain low. Although it has risen by 10 years in the past two decades, life expectancy remains lower in southern Asia than in any other region but sub-Saharan Africa—58 for both women and men. Equal life expectancies are also exceptional—in all other regions, women have an advantage of several years.

* One in 35 women dies of pregnancy-related complications. Maternal mortality has declined but still remains high.

* Nearly two thirds of adult women are illiterate and the per centage of girls enrolled in primary and secondary levels of schooling is far below all other regions except sub-Saharan Africa.

* Women continue to marry early—41 per cent of girls aged 15-19 are already married—and adolescent fertility remains high.

* More women are counted in the labour force but most are still relegated to unpaid family labour or low-paying jobs. Although women's representation at the highest levels of government is generally weakest in Asia, four of the world's 10 current women heads of state or government hold office in this region.

Eastern and South-eastern Asia

* Development indicators continue to improve. Infant mortality has declined significantly in south-eastern Asia in the past two decades.

* Literacy is nearly universal in most countries for men but not for women. However, girls and boys now have nearly equal access to primary and secondary education.

* Adolescent marriage rates in eastern Asia are the lowest in the world—only 2 per cent of women and less than 1 per cent of men aged 15-19 are married—and household size is shrinking.

* Eastern Asia reports the largest average decline in fertility, from 4.7 to 2.3, and its contraceptive use now exceeds that of developed regions. Fertility has also declined in south-eastern Asia, but is still generally higher than in eastern Asia.

* Women's participation in the labour force is as high as in developed regions—approximately 55 per cent.

Developed regions

* Basic health and education indicators generally indicate high levels of well-being but in eastern Europe some show signs of deterioration. Currently, women in 13 countries have a life expectancy of 80 years of more and 11 more countries are expected to reach that level after the year 2000. Men's life expectancy has increased little during the past two decades in eastern Europe, however, partly due to a rise in death rates for middle--aged men. Women's life expectancy in eastern Europe has increased much less than in other regions.

* Fertility continues to fall—from 2.3 in 1975 to 1.9 in 1995. But teenage pregnancy is relatively high in some countries—Bulgaria, the Republic of Moldova, Ukraine and the United States.

* Traditional family structure and size are changing. People are marrying later or not at all, and marriages are less stable. Remarriage rates have dropped—especially for women—and single parent families now make up 10—25 per cent of all families. The population is ageing and becoming increasingly female as it does.

* Women's labour force participation increased significantly for regions outside of eastern Europe from 38 per cent in 1970 to 52 per cent in 1990. In eastern Europe, where women's labour force participation was already 56 per cent in 1970, the increase was small (to 58 per cent).

* Women continue to earn less than men—in manufacturing, women's average wage is three quarters that of men's. And women and men tend to work in different jobs—women in clerical, sales and services, and men in production and transport. And men commonly do work which is accorded higher pay and status. For example, the majority of school administrators are men while most teachers are women, and the majority of hospital consultants are men while most nurses are women.

* Women work longer hours than men in the majority of these countries—at least 2 hours longer than men do in 13 out of 21 countries studied. Much of the unpaid work is done by women—for example, women contribute roughly three quarters of total child care at home.

Education for empowerment

In the Programme of Action of the International Conference on Population and Development, education is considered one of the most important means to empower women with the knowledge, skills and self—confidence necessary to participate fully in development processes. Educated women marry later, want fewer children, are more likely to use effective methods of contraception and have greater means to improve their economic livelihood.

Through widespread promotion of universal primary education, literacy rates for women have increased over the past few decades—to at least 75 per cent in most countries of Latin America and the Caribbean and eastern and south—eastern Asia. But high rates of illiteracy among women still prevail in much of Africa and in parts of Asia. And when illiteracy is high it almost always is accompanied by large differences in rates between women and men.

At intermediate levels of education, girls have made progress in their enrolment in school through the second level. The primary—secondary enrolment ratio is now about equal for girls and boys in the developed regions and Latin America and the Caribbean and is approaching near equality in eastern, south—eastern and western Asia. But progress in many countries was reversed in the 1980s, particularly among those experiencing problems of war, economic adjustment and declining international assistance—as in Africa, Latin America and the Caribbean, and eastern Europe.

In higher education enrolments, women equal or exceed men in many regions. They outnumber men in the developed regions outside western Europe, in Latin America and the Caribbean and western Asia. Women are not as well represented in other regions, and in sub—Saharan Africa and southern Asia they are far behind—30 and 38 women per 100 men.

The Framework for Action to implement the World Declaration on Education for All states that it is urgent to improve access to education for girls and women—and to remove every obstacle that hampers their active participation. Priority actions include eliminating the social and cultural barriers the discourage—or even exclude—girls and women from the benefits of regular education programmes.

Seeking influence

Despite progress in women's higher education, major obstacles still arise when women strive to translate their high—level education into social and economic advancement. In the world of business, for example, women rarely account for more than 1 to 2 per cent of top executive positions. In the more general category of administration and management including middle levels, women's share rose in every region but one between 1980 and 1990. Women's participation jumped from 16 to 33 per cent in developed regions outside Europe. In Latin America, it rose from 18 to 25 per cent.

In the health and teaching professions—two of the largest occupational fields requiring advanced training—women are well represented in many countries but usually at the bottom levels of the status and wage hierarchy.

Similarly, among the staff of an international group of agriculture research institutes, women's participation at the non—scientific and trainee levels is moderate, but there are few women at management and senior scientific levels.

The information people receive through news papers, radio and television shapes their opinions about the world. And the more decision—making positions women hold in the media, the more they can influence output—breaking stereotypes that hurt women, attracting greater attention to issues of equality in the home and in public life, and providing young women with new images, ideas and ideals. Women now make up more than half of the communications students in a large number of countries and are increasingly visible as presenters, announcers and reporters, but they remain poorly represented in the more influential media occupations such as programme managers and senior editors.

In the top levels of government, women's participation remains the exception. At the end of 1994 only 10 women were heads of state or government; of these 10 countries only Norway had as many as one third women ministers or subministers. Some progress has been made in the appointment of women to ministerial or subministerial positions but these positions are usually tenuous for them. Most countries with women in top ministerial positions do not have comparable representation at the subministerial level. And in other countries, where significant numbers of women have reached the subministerial levels, very few have reached the top. Progress for women in parliaments has also been mixed and varies widely among regions. It is strongest in northern Europe, where it appears to be rising steadily.

Missing from this summary is women's remarkable advance in less traditional paths to power and influence. The importance of the United Nations Decade for Women and international women's conferences should not be underestimated, for these forums enabled women to develop the skills required for exercising power and influence, to mobilize resources and articulate issues and to practise organizing, lobbying and legislating. Excluded from most political offices, many women have found a voice in non—governmental organizations (NGOs) at the grass roots, national and international levels. NGOs have taken issues previously ignored— such as violence against women and rights to reproductive health—and brought them into the mainstream policy debate.

Since the women's conference in Nairobi in 1985, many grass—roots groups have been working to create new awareness of women's rights, including their rights within the family, and to help women achieve those rights. They have set agendas and carved out a space for women's issues.

And as seen in recent United Nations conferences, NGOs as a group can wield influence broad enough to be active partners with governments in deciding national policies and programmes.

Reproductive health-reproductive freedom

With greater access to education, employment and contraception, many women are choosing to marry later and have fewer children. Those who wait to marry and begin child—bearing have better access to education and greater opportunities to improve their lives. Women's increased access to education, to employment and to contraception, coupled with declining rates of infant mortality, have contributed to the worldwide decline in fertility.

The number of children women bear in developed regions is now below replacement levels at 1.9 per women. In Latin America and in most parts of Asia it has also dropped significantly. But in Africa women still have an average of six children and in many sub—Saharan African countries women have as many or more children now than they did 20 years ago.

Adolescent fertility has declined in many developing and developed countries over the past 20 years. In Central America and sub—Saharan Africa, however, rates are five to seven times higher than in developed regions. Inadequate nutrition, anaemia and early pregnancies threaten the health and life of young girls and adolescents.

Too many women lack access to reproductive health services. In developing countries maternal mortality is a leading cause of death for women of reproductive age. WHO estimates that more than half a million women die each year in childbirth and millions more develop pregnancy—related health complications. The deteriorating economic and health conditions in sub—Saharan Africa led to an increase in maternal mortality during the 1980s, where it remains the highest in the world. An African woman's lifetime risk of dying from pregnancy-related causes is 1 in 23, while a North American woman's is 1 in 4,000. Maternal mortality also increased in some countries of eastern Europe.

Pregnancy and childbirth have become safer for women in most of Asia and in parts of Latin America. In developed countries attended delivery is almost universal, but in developing countries only 55 per cent of births take place with a trained attendant and only 37 per cent in hospitals or clinics. Today new importance is being placed on women's reproductive health and safe motherhood as advocates work to redefine reproductive health as an issue of human rights.

The Programme of Action of the International Conference on Population and Development set forth a new framework to guide government actions in population, development and reproductive health—and to measure and evaluate programmes designed to realize these objectives. Instead of the traditional approach centered on family planning and population policy objectives, governments are encouraged to develop client—centered management information systems in population and development and particularly reproductive health, including family planning and sexual health programmes.

Fewer marriages—smaller households

Rapid population changes, combined with many other social and economic changes, are being accompanied by considerable changes in women's household and family status. Most people still marry but they marry later in life, especially women. In developing regions, consensual unions and other non-formal unions remain prevalent, especially in rural areas.

As a result of these changes, many women— many more women than men—spend a significant part of their life without a partner, with important consequences for their economic welfare and their children's.

In developed regions, marriage has become both less frequent and less stable, and cohabitations is on the rise. Marriages preceded by a period of cohabitations have clearly increased in many countries of northern Europe. And where divorce once led quickly to remarriage, many postpone marriage or never remarry.

Since men have higher rates of remarriage, marry at an older age, and have a shorter life expectancy, most older men are married, while many older women are widows. Among women 60 and older, widowhood is significant everywhere—from 40 per cent in the developed regions and Latin America to 50 per cent in Africa and Asia. Moreover, in Asia and Africa, widowhood also affects many women at younger ages.

Between 1970 and 1990 household size decreased significantly in the developed regions, in Latin America and the Caribbean and in eastern and south—eastern Asia. Households are the smallest in developed regions, having declined to an average of 2.8 persons per household in 1990. In eastern Asia the average household size has declined to 3.7, in south—eastern Asia to 4.9. In Latin American countries the average fell to 4.7 persons per household, and in the Caribbean to 4.1. In northern African countries household size increased on average from 5.4 to 5.7.

In developed countries the decline in the average household size reflects an increase in the number of one—person households, especially among unmarried adults and the elderly. In developing regions the size of the household is more affected by the number of children, although a shift from extended households to nuclear households also has some effect.

Household size remains high in countries where fertility has not yet fallen significantly—for instance, in some of the African and western Asian countries.

Work—paid and unpaid

Women's access to paid work is crucial to their self—reliance and the economic well—being of dependent family members. But access to such work is unequal between women and men. Women work in different occupations than men, almost always with lower status and pay.

In developing countries many women work as unpaid family labourers in subsistence agriculture and household enterprises. Many women also work in the informal sector, where their remuneration is unstable, and their access to funds to improve their productivity is limited at best. And whatever other work women do, they also have the major responsibility for most household work, including the care of children and other family members.

The work women do contributes substantially to the well—being of families, communities and nations. But work in the household—even when it is economic—is inadequately measured, and this subverts policies for the credit, income and security of women and their families.

Over the past two decades, women's reported economic activity rates increased in all regions except sub—Saharan Africa and eastern Asia, and all of these increases are large except in eastern Europe, central Asia and Ocean. In fact, women's labour force participation increased more in the 1980s than in the 1970s in many regions. In contrast, men's economic activity rates have declined everywhere except central Asia.

The decline in women's reported labour force participation in sub—Saharan Africa stands out as an exception—dropping from a high of 57 per cent in 1970 to 54 per cent in 1980 to 53 per cent in 1990.

In 1990 the average labour force participation rate among women aged 15 and over ranged from a high of 56—58 per cent in eastern and central Asia and eastern Europe to a low in northern Africa of 21 per cent. The participation rates of men vary within a more limited range of 72—83 per cent. Because so many women in developing countries work in agriculture and informal household enterprises where their contributions are underreported, their recorded rates of economic activity should be higher in many cases. The estimated increase in southern Asia—from 25 per cent of women economically active in 1970 to 44 per cent in 1990—may be due largely to changes in the statistical methods used rather than to significant changes in work patterns.

Although work in subsistence production is crucial to survival, it goes largely underreported in population and agricultural surveys and censuses.

Most of the food eaten in agricultural households in developing countries is produced within the family holding, much of it by women. Some data show the extent of women's unreported work in agriculture. In Bangladesh, India and Pakistan, government surveys using methods to improve the measurement of subsistence work, report that more than half of rural women engage in such activities as tending poultry or cattle, planting rice, drying seeds, collecting water and preparing dung cakes for fuel. Direct observation of women's activities suggests that almost all women in rural areas contribute economically in one way or another.

The informal sector—working on own -account and in small family enterprises—also provides women with important opportunities in areas where salaried employment is closed or inadequate. In five of the six African countries studied by the Statistical Division of the United Nations Secretariat, more than one third of women economically active outside agriculture work in the informal sector, and in seven countries of Latin America 15-20 per cent. In nine countries in Asia the numbers vary—from less than 10 per cent of economically active women in western Asia to 41 per cent in the Republic of Korea and 65 per cent in Indonesia.

Although fewer women than men participate in the labour force, in some countries—including Honduras, Jamaica and Zambia—more women than men make up the informal sector labour force. In several other countries, women make up 40 per cent or more of the informal sector.

In addition to the invisibility of many of women's economic activities, women remain responsible for most housework, which also goes unmeasured by the System of National Accounts. But time—use data for many developed countries show almost everywhere that women work at least as many hours each week as men, and in a large number of countries they work at least two hours more than men. Further, the daily time a man spends on work tends to be the same throughout his working life. But a woman's working time fluctuates widely and at times is extremely heavy—the result of combining paid work, household and child—care responsibilities.

Two thirds to three quarters of household work in developed regions is performed by women. In most countries studied, women spend 30 hours or more on housework each week while men spend around 10 hours. Among household tasks, the division of labour remains clear and definite in most countries. Few men do the laundry, clean the house, make the beds, iron the clothes. And most women do little household repair and maintenance. Even when employed outside the home, women do most of the housework.

Efforts to generate better statistics

The first world conference on women in Mexico in 1975 recognized the importance of improving statistics on women. Until the early 1980s women's advocates and women's offices were the main forces behind this work. Big efforts had not yet been launched in statistical offices—either nationally or internationally.

The collaboration of the Statistical Division of the United Nations Secretariat with the International Research and Training Institute for the Advancement of Women (INSTRAW),—beginning in 1982—on a training programme to promote dialogue and understanding between policy makers and statisticians, laid the groundwork for a comprehensive programme of work.

By the time of the world conference in Nairobi in 1985 some progress was evident. The Statistical Division compiled 39 key statistical indicators on the situation of women for 172 countries, and important efforts at the national level included the preparation of *Women and Men* in Sweden, first published in 1984 and with sales of 100,000.

Since Nairobi numerous developments have stregthened and given new momentum to this work. The general approach in development strategy has moved from women in development to gender and development. The focus has shifted from women in isolation to women in relation to men—to the roles each has, the relationships between them and different impacts of policies and programmes.

In statistics the focus has likewise moved from attention to women's statistics to gender statistics. There now is a recognition, for example, that biases in statistics apply not only to women but also to men—in their roles as husbands and fathers and in their roles in the household. That recognition reaches beyonds the disaggregation of data by sex to assessing statistical systems in terms of gender. It asks:

—Do the topics investigated on statistics and the concepts and definitions used in data collection reflect the diversities of women's and men's lives?

—Will the methods used in collecting data take into account stereotypes and cultural factors that might produce bias?

—Are the ways data are compiled and presented well suited to the needs of policy makers, planners and others who need such data?

The first World's Women: Trends and Statistics, issued in 1991, presented the most comprehensive and authoritative compilations of global indicators on the status of women ever available. The book's data have informed debates at international conferences and national policy meetings and provided a resource to the press and others. Its publication greatly contributed to the understanding of data users and created, for the first time, a substantial global audience for statistical genderbased information. This

1

THE INTERNATIONAL SEMINAR ON WOMEN'S EDUCATION AND EMPOWERMENT

Carolyn Medel-Anonuevo and Bettina Bochynek

Introduction

Since the "UN Declaration of the Decade of Women'" in 1975, attention and action on women's concerns have steadily increased and education, whether it be the form of consciousness-raising or skills acquisition, was one of the areas women's organizations, government agencies and international donor agencies focused on. The underlying assumption was that if women understood their conditions, knew their rights and learned skills traditionally denied to them, empowerment would follow. Eighteen years have passed and there are different views as to whether such assumptions about increasing access to education and training have resulted in the tilting of the power balance in favor of women.

The International Seminar on Women's Education and Empowerment therefore was convened amidst the discussion on the relevance of women's education in improving the situation of women, in the short term, and in emancipating women, in the long run. Furthermore, the Seminar took place during a crucial phase at the UNESCO Institute for Education, where women's non-formal education is going to be a key concern.

In view of the "World Conference on Women" to be held in Beijing in 1995, the seminar meant to be one of many actions and activities relevant to women's issues which will be initiated, organized and/or supported by the Institute. The promotion of action-oriented research and the improvement of cooperation with various institutions focusing on women's education needs will be one of the priorities of the Institute in the coming years. In fact, the partnership of UIE and the UNESCO

Principal Regional Office for Asia and Pacific (PROAP) in undertaking this seminar is an example of how continuing cooperation has been a crucial factor in the success of joint projects.

The key role of education must be underlined and investigated on a continuous basis. Despite the progress in this area, much remains to be done. The Seminar, as it progressed, was able to provide a sense of what different organizations were doing and how this could be improved. It was agreed that this could be a starting point for assessing the extent to which education has empowered women.

Objectives

The general objectives of the seminar were:

1. to exchange experiences in promoting the empowerment of women through different educational programmes, both formal and non-formal;
2. to discuss the theoretical issues arising from the practice of the education of women;
3. to develop research designs on women's education and empowerment for possible collaboration in selected areas; and
4. to explore ways and means of operationlizing the term "empowerment."

By the end of the seminar, the following outputs were expected:

- a definition of and a conceptual framework for understanding women's empowerment;
- an indicative list of indicators and processes or mechanisms of empowerment; and
- initial proposals/ recommendations for future action, focusing on effective procedures and mechanisms of empowerment.

Participants

Given the diversity of work in women's education, researchers, educators and activists from different regions of the world were invited to take part in the Seminar. The objective was to bring these women together in a forum where they could discuss the whole range of activities they are involved in and cull important lessons not only for improving their work but also for assessing the impact of their programmes and/or projects.

To facilitate the exchange of experiences, the participants were each requested to prepare a background paper describing their education-related activities. It was further meant to stimulate the discussion on major problems in the field of women's education as well as to explore ways and means of carrying out efficient and innovative programmes for empowering women. The participants were likewise asked to reflect on the relevant theoretical issues and practical concerns regarding the empowerment of women through education.

To focus the discussions on theoretical and conceptual issues around empowerment, three participants were tasked with writing case studies which delved into the empirical and theoretical basis for empowerment.

A total of 16 participants from different regions in the world (Africa, Asia, Arab States, Caribbean, Europe, North America and South America) attended the Seminar. Some were university-based researchers and educators, others were working in women's organizations and non-governmental organizations (NGOs) dealing with education, a few were working in UN agencies while one came from a government agency.

As a number of them were involved in the women's movement as well as peace movements, health, literacy and development work in their respective countries, the women brought in a variety of experiences.

Highlights of the Seminar

Give the objcctives of the seminar, the sixday meeting was divided into three parts.

The sharing of the participants' experiences was scheduled for the first two days while the reflection of the theoretical and conceptual implication of the term "empowerment" was to follow in the next two days. The remaining period was used for planning and coming up with concrete proposals.

To ensure maximum participation, the participants were divided into smaller groups in some parts of the programme. The main points of the group's discussion were then presented during the plenary sessions.

Context of Education Work

In terms of government policies on women's education, it was observed that while there is no explicit discrimination by gender in most places, neither is there a real commitment to provide sustainable programmes for women. There is such a perceived gap between the rhetoric and policies of decision-makers that many of the women considered the policies as simply paying "lip service" to women's concerns. Even in developed countries, the proportion of resources that is being allocated to women's needs is small considering the many diverse needs of the women. The fact that many of the decision-makers are men also constrains their appreciation of these needs.

The actual working and living conditions of women also prevent many of them from meaningful participation in women's education programmes/projects. The increasing impoverishment of women makes it necessary for them to focus on income-generating activities simultaneous with the performance of household chores. This, therefore limits their time and energy to get involved in education programmes.

Many of the women that have been projected to be beneficiaries of development programmes are illiterate, so the issue of literacy as a women's development concern is likewise a priority.

In spite of the above-mentioned problems, the participants agreed that, in order to promote women's empowerment, it is necessary to create an environment in educational programmes and share the benefits. It was therefore emphasized that while there is a need to set up specific education programmes for women, there is also a necessity to develop forms of education that will sensitize people towards gender discrimination and will raise their acceptance of women's promotion.

The discussion on the relationship between the women's movement and the different areas (peace, health, literacy) of involvement of the participants likewise raise the important issue of how feminist concerns are integrated in these. While a few women related the problems of doing so, others shared their successful strategies in mainstreaming. It was observed that there is a tendency for some to look at women's only programmes as "marginalization" or "ghettoization" but there was consensus that such programmes have their specific contribution to improving the women's situation just as integrative programmes do.

This implies that the structures of society have to be taken into account. The approach to women's empowerment must be holistic in the sense that, apart from educational measures for women, other factors such as a) men being the decision-makers and b) the influence of popular culture and mass media must be taken into consideration.

The participants also compared notes as to how education programmes (whether they be women only or integrative) can empower. It was pointed out that one of the key determinants of successful programmes is the extent to which they had taken the multiple roles of women into account and how they helped in alleviating the burden.

Given these, among the suggested components are:

- promotion of gender awareness;
- lessons on health and nutrition;
- integration of technical, entrepreneurial, cultural and communal aspects;
- information and lessons on politics; and

- provision of planning and thinking skills.

It was also necessary to clarify the goals of women's education. The participants agreed that the more important objectives are:
- to eliminate illiteracy;
- to develop self-esteem and self-confidence;
- to have knowledge about their bodies and sexuality;
- to have the ability to make their own decisions and negotiate;
- to raise the women's awareness of their civil rights;
- to provide skills for income generation;
- to make participation in community/society more effective; and
- to prepare them to be good women leaders.

Crucial to education work are other complementary activities such as those in the areas of legal reform, transformation of international economic and political relations, action-oriented research and networking. It was stressed that it is equally important to convince men that better education of women will be beneficial to the entire family and the society as a whole.

The Concept of Empowerment

There was consensus among the participants that "empowerment" has become one of the most widely used development terms. Women's groups, non-governmental development organizations, activists, politicians, governments and international agencies refer to empowerment as one of their goals. Yet it is one of the least understood in terms of how it is to be measured or observed. It is precisely because this word has now been one of the fashionable concepts to include in policies/programmes/projects that there is a need to clarify and come up with tentative definitions. Furthermore, the particular implications of empowement of women is an area that needs to be discussed.

1. *Definition*

The nature of empowerment renders it difficult to define. On the one hand, it is often referred to as a goal for many development programmes/projects. On the other hand, it can also be conceived as a process that people undergo, which eventually leads to changes. Nelly Stromquist, for instance, defines empowerment as "a process to change the distribution of power both in interpersonal relations and in institutions throughout society" while Lucy Lazo describes it as "a process of acquiring, providing, bestowing the resources and the means or enabling the access to a control over such means and resources."

Given the above, the term is therefore more relevant to the marginalized groups the poor, the illiterates, the indigenous communities-and of course, cutting across these categories, the women.

From the discussion, it was also clear that empowerment can be observed at different levels. The above-mentioned definitions already point to interpersonal relations and institutions as possible sites of empowerment. Namtip Aksornkool looks at the individual level when she cites Paz's definition of empowerment as "the ability to direct and control one's own life". But it is clear from Ms. Aksornkool's presentation that such an individual empowerment of women is attained in relationship to the larger society. Citing Depthnews, she writes that "it is a process in which women gain control over their own lives by knowing and claiming their rights at all levels of society at the international, local, and household levels. Self-empowerment means that women gain autonomy, are able to set their own agenda and are fully involved in the economic, political and social decision-making process."

To add to the already complex nature of empowerment, it was also pointed out that it is difficult to come out with a general definition since it can be somehow determined by the respective cultural contexts. The relativity of empowerment, although in a different sense, is one of the important features discussed in Ms. Lazo's paper. She argues that "empowerment is a moving state ; it is continuum that varies in degree of power. It is relative... One can move from an extreme state of absolute lack of power to the other extreme of having absolute power."

As articulated in some of the papers, empowerment can have four components: cognitive, psychological, economic and political.

According to Ms. Stromquist, the cognitive component would include the "women's understanding of their conditions of subordination and the causes of such conditions at both micro and macro levels of society. It involves acquiring new knowledge to create a different understanding of gender relations as well as destroying old beliefs that structure powerful gender ideologies". The psychological component, on the other hand, would include the "development of feelings that women can act upon to improve their condition. This means formation of the belief that they can succeed in change efforts".

These two components are exemplified in Ms. Anita Dighe's presentation of the Nellore experience, where a literacy campaign contributed to the anti-drinking campaign. She writes that "women have picketed the arrack (local liquor), marched unitedly to the district collector's office and organized a "dharna" to ensure that auctions are not allowed to take place, they have become strengthened in their conviction that it is only such united action that can bring any change".

The economic component "requires that women be able to engage in a productive activity that will allow them some degree of autonomy, no matter how small and hard to obtain at the beginning" (Stromquist). The case study of Ms. Lazo demonstrates how socio-economic aid (through granting of revolving funds, marketing assistance and product development) has helped in the setting up of micro-enterprises run by women. In contrast, Ms. Digh's presentation stresses that while the cognitive and psychological components of empowerment are evident in the Nellore experience, the economic component might be more difficult to demonstrate as "income-generating activities, however, are difficult to implement because they are risky, time-consuming and hard to sustain."

The political component would encompass the "ability to organize and mobilize for change. Consequently, an empowerment process must involve not only individual awareness but collective awareness and collective action. The notion of collective action is fundamental to the aim of attaining social transformation" (Stromquist).

It follows from the above components that empowerment allows women to have choices, which in turn means relative strength and bargaining power for them. While it is clear that women can be empowered individually, the feminist vision is one where women are able to articulate a collective voice and demonstrate collective strength.

It was also stressed that incorporating the feminist perspective in the concept of empowerment implies a long-term redesigning of societies that will be based on democratic relationships. The paper of Ms. Dighe talks about empowerment as dealing with strategic rather than practical gender needs.

2. *Indicators of Empowerment*

Understanding that empowerment is a complex issue with varying interpretations in different societal, national and cultural contexts, the participants also came out with a tentative listing of indicators.

At the level of the individual woman and her household:

- participation in crucial decision-making processes;
- extent of sharing of domestic work by men;
- extent to which a woman takes control of her reproductive functions and decides on family size;
- extent to which a woman is able to decide where the income she has earned will be chanelled to;

- feeling and expression of pride and value in her work;
- self-confidence and self-esteem; and
- ability to prevent violence.

At the community and/ or organizational level:

- existence of women's organizations;
- allocation of funds to women and women's projects;
- increased number of women leaders at village, district, provincial and national levels;
- involvement of women in the design, development and application of technology;
- participation in community programmes, productive enterprises, politics and arts;
- involvement of women in non-traditional tasks; and
- increased training programmes for women; and
- exercising her legal rights when necessary.

At the national level:

- awareness of her social and political rights;
- integration of women in the general national development plan;
- existence of women's networks and publications;
- extent to which women are officially visible and recognized; and
- the degree to which the media take heed of women's issues.

3. *Facilitating and Constraining Factors of Empowerment*

Empowerment does not take place in a vacuum. In the same way that Ms. Lazo talks about women's state of powerlessness as a result of "a com bination and interaction of environmental factors," one can also discuss the condition/factors that can hasten or hinder empowerment. As above, the listing is a preliminary one based on the discussions.

Facilitating factors

- existence of women's organizations;
- availability of support systems for women;
- availability of women-specific data and other relevant information;
- availability of funds;
- feminist leadership;
- networking;
- favorable media coverage;
- favorable policy climate.

Constraining factors

- heavy work load of women;
- isolation of women from each other;
- illiteracy;
- traditional views that limit women's participation;
- no funds;
- internal strife/militarization/wars:
- disagreements/conflicts among women's groups;
- structural adjustment policies;
- discriminatory policy environment;
- negative and sensational coverage of media.

Strategies for the Future

Empowerment through education is ideally seen as a continuous holistic process with cognitive, psychological, economic and political dimensions in order to achieve emancipation. Given the complexity of political, societal and international interrelations, one has to systematically think about the strategies and concrete proposals for future action if one hopes to achieve such a goal.

A set of strategies on education, research/documentation, campaigns, networking, influencing policies, training and media was developed by the participants. As can be seen from the listing, the strategies are interrelated to each other.

a. Education

The formal and non-formal education systems would need to be considered. It would be important to analyze the gender content and to ascertain the manner in which it is addressed/ not addressed in the educational system. On the basis of the analysis, curriculum changes would need to be brought about. Likewise it would be important to reorient the teachers on gender issues so that overall gender sensitization in the educational system could be brought about.

In concrete terms, this would mean:

- reorienting and reeducating policy makers;
- securing equal access for boys and girls in education;
- holding workshops/seminars for teachers;
- revising teaching materials;
- producing materials in local languages;
- implementing special programmes for women in the field of Adult Education;

- incorporating issues such as tradition, race, ethnicity, gender sensitization, urban and rural contexts in the programmes;
- raising awareness on the necessity for health care;
- politicizing women to show them how macro level mismanagement is responsible for their loss of jobs; and
- focusing on parents as role models.

b. Research/Documentation

The importance of doing participatory and action research was underscored. It was considered important to organize workshops to train grassroots women to conduct participatory research where they could develop skills to critically analyze their existing conditions. This will facilitate their organizing for collective action.

While participatory research was considered to be important, it was recognized that traditional quantitative research was also necessary. The guiding principle, however, was to share the results with the women in a language and manner that was understandable to them.

Research as a strategy would therefore entail:

- disseminating information;
- producing and disseminating information leaflets regarding women's rights;
- referring to women in all national and UN statistics;
- collecting oral history of women;
- documenting and analyzing successful and failed programmes of the women's movements;
- analyzing successful advocacy cases in order to learn about the arguments that persuade policy makers;
- collecting cross-cultural case studies;
- constantly evaluating research; and
- involving women as agents (instead of objects) of research.

c. Campaigns

If one is to have an effect in society, it is important to undertake campaign and lobby activities that will put the issue of gender in the minds of the legislators, policy-makers and the large public. This will therefore mean:

- pushing for a dialogue between stake holders;
- raising gender issues within the national policy arena;
- pressuring to upgrade women's bureaus (which are a result of the UN Decade for Women) into ministries of women's affairs;
- lobbying for sex-equity and affirmative action legislation;

- lobbying for "counter structural adjustment policies";
- organizing pressure groups (like "Greenpeace");
- using consumer power for boycotts;
- securing access to information;
- demanding child care centers; and
- producing video and CDs, T-Shirts etc.

d. *Networking*

Through networking, it would be possible to share experiences and learn from one another. In this manner, understanding and solidarity among women's organizations, development organizations (governmental/ non-governmental) and multilateral agencies could be forged. This would therefore entail networking at the national, regional and international levels. Moreover, at the international level, South-South linkages were considered to be particularly important.

- organizing at least one meeting a year of gender sensitive organizations;
- bringing together donor agencies, governments and NGOs;
- setting up a north-south dialogue and collaboration;
- setting up a south-south cooperation and exchange;
- linking women's movements all over the world;
- establishing alternative credit schemes that offer women access to funds.

e. *Training*

In our societies, there is a gender division of labor which dictates the kind of training one acquires. If one talks about women's empowerment, it is important that women have access to the different training opportunities previously denied them. This therefore means:

- preparing for jobs that are usually not open to them;
- providing income-generating projects that are market-oriented (not welfare-oriented projects); and
- training capable female leaders at all levels.

f. *Media*

Considering the attitudinal barriers in traditional societies and the role which the mass media play in reinforcing them, the following strategies were advanced:

- organizing mass media campaigns to raise awareness;
- creating a social climate friendly to women's issues;
- resisting the tendency to send women back to the kitchen; and

- disseminating information about conferences that will take place in the coming years.

EVALUATION OF THE SEMINAR

As reflected in the preceding discussion, the seminar moved step by step to meet the objectives set out from the beginning. The participants were not only able to learn from each other's experience but also collectively reflected on the concept of empowerment. Furthermore, they were also able to identify concrete proposals that they can take back to their organizations and implement, as well as to identify possible areas of collaboration with others.

The seminar also left the participants with the feeling that they were not alone in their work and, in fact, are part of a larger movement whose combined efforts can push for women's empowerment worldwide.

In terms of the conceptualization of empowerment, some participants would have preferred that a more concrete definition of empowerment and its indicators were ready to be taken back. They commented that the concept of empowerment has not yet been completed. Others, instead, were glad that a simplistic definition of empowerment had been avoided and that the discussion of the issue will be further elaborated when they get back to their organizations.

2

THE THEORETICAL AND PRACTICAL BASES FOR EMPOWERMENT

Nelly P. Stromquist

Empowerment has become a widely used word. In spheres as different as management and labor unions, health care and ecology, banking and education, one hears of empowerment taking place. The popular use of the word also means that it has been overextended and applied in circumstances that clearly do not involve much power acquisition beyond some symbolic activity or event.

Empowerment in its emancipatory meaning, is a serious word—one which brings up the question of personal agency rather than reliance on intermediaries, one that links action to needs, and one that results in making significant collective change. It is also a concept that does not merely concern personal identity but brings out a broader analysis of human rights and social justice.

To gain a greater understanding of the concept, it might be helpful to look into its origins among popular movements. It emerged during the U.S. civil rights movements in the 1960s, after substantial work took place in civil disobedience and voter registration efforts to attain democratic rights for Afro-Americans. Displeased with the pace and scope of the changes, several black leaders (headed by Stokeley Carmichael) called for "black power", which they defined as:

> a call for black people in this country to unite, to recognize their heritage, to build a sense of community. It is a call for black people to begin to define their own goals, to link their own organizations, and to support those organizations (Carmichael and Hamilton, 1967, p. 44).

Empowerment began to be applied within the women's movements in the mid 1970s. The similarities among oppressed groups are considerable because they face the common problem of limited willingness by those in control to see the seriousness of their condition and to work to solve it. Under the circumstances, the oppressed must themselves develop power for change to occur; power will not be given to them for the asking.

Applied to gender issues, the discussion of empowerment brings women into the political sphere, both private and public. Its international use probably began with the appearance of the book by Sen and Grown, *Development, Crisis, and Alternative Visions: Third World Women's Perspectives* (1985), prepared for the Nairobi Conference at the end of the U. N. Decade for Women in 1985. In this book, a section on "Empowering Ourselves" clearly identifies the creation of women's organizations as central to the design and implementation of strategies for gender transformation.

Women and men are placed in bipolar categories by numerous institutions in society. These institutions, through day-to-day practices embedded in long-standing beliefs, construct male and female subjects who face strong forces to conform. Family practices, religious myths, the social division of labor, the sexual division of labor, marriage customs, the educational system, and civil laws combine to produce hierarchies, internalized beliefs, and expectations that are constraining but at the same time "naturalized" and thus seldom contested.

In this context, empowerment is a process to change the distribution of power, both in interpersonal relations and in institutions throughout society. Traditionally the state has interpreted women's needs to suit its own preferences. The typical and enduring consideration that women have received from the state has been in their capacity of mothers and wives. Women therefore need to become their own advocates to address problems and situations affecting them that were previously ignored. Empowerment ultimately involves a political process to produce consciousness among policy makers about women and to create pressure to bring about societal change.

There is an additional point to be made. Empowerment is a process which should center on adult women for two central reasons: first, their adult lives have produced many experiences of subordination and thus they know this problem very well, although they have not labeled it as such and second, the transformation of these women is fundamental to breaking the integrational reproduction of patriarchal authority.

Defining Empowerment

The subordinate position of women in society, even though this position is somewhat attenuated in higher social classes, has well-known manifestations: limited representation in the formal political system, a large share of the economy's informal sector and other types of labor with reduced financial rewards, almost exclusive responsibility for family and children, and the more subtle signs of narrow career aspirations and low self-esteem. Not infrequently, subordination is also manifested in unwanted pregnancies and wife-beating.

Women in many societies, particularly in Latin America, have relied on "networks of reciprocal exchange" (Lomnitz, 1977) that provide information and assistance from family, friends, and neighbors to obtain basic services such as health, childcare, food, and even services such as loans and job procurement. These networks operate within all social classes, the poor as well as the elite (Lomnitz, 1977 and 1984). At one level, these informal networks constitute a valuable source of assistance for women. But at another level, these structures create mechanisms of social control through the maintenance of notions of femininity and masculinity, and through deference to authoritarian, patriarchal rule.

If subordination has many facets, so has empowerment. Empowerment is a sociopolitical concept that goes beyond "formal political participation" and "consciousness raising". A full definition of empowerment must include cognitive, psychological, political, and economic components.

The cognitive component refers to women's understanding of their conditions of subordination and the causes of such conditions at both micro and macro levels of society. It involves understanding the self and the need to make choices that may go against cultural and social expectations, and understanding patterns of behavior that create dependence, interdependence, and autonomy within the family and in the society at large (Hall, 1992). It involves acquiring new knowledge to create a different understanding of gender relations as well as destroying old beliefs that structure powerful gender ideologies. The cognitive component of empowerment involves knowledge about their sexuality beyond family planning techniques, for taboos on sex information have mystified the nature of women and men and provided justification for men's physical and mental control of women. Another important cognitive area involves legal rights. In most countries, including democratically advanced nations, legislation for gender equity and women's rights is well ahead of practice; women therefore need to know which legal rights already exist in order to press for their implementation and enforcement. A more comprehensive and articulated type of knowledge needed for empowerment concerns elements that shape conjugal dynamics such as control of wives' fertility, sexuality, child bearing and rearing, companionship, feelings of affection and rejection, unpaid domestic work, and household decision-making. As Beneria and Roldan observe, these elements constitutes wives' duties under the "marriage contract" (1987, pp. 137-139); therefore, they are the most vulnerable to patriarchal control.

The psychological component includes the development of feelings that women can act at personal and societal levels to improve their condition as well as the formation of the belief that they can succeed in their change efforts. The sex role socialization of women has inculcated attributes of "learned helplessness" within women. Through the repeated experience of uncontrollable effects, many women come to believe that they cannot modify their environment or personal situations and thus their persistance in problem-solving is diminished (Jack, 1992). Attributions of helplessness preclude opportunities for mediation and compromise and often women respond by complying with female stereotypes of passivity and self-sacrifice. Clearly, not every women succumbs to the dominant sex-role socialization forces and several are able to question and even reject them. But, in general, it is a well known fact that many women, particularly those in low-income household, develop very discernible low levels of self-esteem.

One cannot teach self-confidence and self-esteem; one must provide the conditions in which these can develop. Empowerment cannot be developed among "beneficiaries" of programs but only by "participatns'. Empowerment requires involving women directly in planning and implementation of projects (Rao et al., 1991). Activities that seek empowerment must involve women in all stages of any specific project, though not necessarily with the same intensity at all times. Women must participate in problem definition, the identification of concrete solutions to problems, the implementation of these solutions, and the assessment of the efforts undertaken. That this may involve some inefficiencies and trial and error, is a strong possibility. But experts also make mistakes. And women must be given opportunities to assert themselves. In the long run, advantages outnumber disadvantages because the skills gained through these collective, participatory approaches are transferable to a variety of social situations.

The psychological element is important but it needs to be strengthened with economic resources. Even though outside work for women often means a double burden, the empirical evidence supports the notion that access to work increases a woman's economic independence and with it a greater level of general independence is created. As Hall (1992) notes, economic subordination must be neutralized for women to be empowered. The economic component of empowerment requires that women be able to engage in a productive activity that will allow them some degree of financial autonomy, no matter how small and hard to obtain at the beginning. Income generating programs are difficult to implement because they are risky, time-consuming, and inefficient in the initial phases. But they can improve over time if accompanied by such necessary skills as marketing, accounting and sufficient funding. The problem or income-generating projects is not that they are not a good solution but rather that they have resulted in failure because they have been poorly designed, implemented and funded. There is the know-how to turn income-generating activities into successful commercial ventures. Absent is the commitment to use them in a meaningful way.

The political component of empowerment entails the ability to analyze the surrounding environment in political and social terms; it also means the ability to organize and mobilize for social change. In consequence, an empowerment process must involve individual awareness, and collective action is fundamental to the aim of attaining social transformation. As Griffin observes:

> Redistribution strategies depend for their success on mobilizing the population for grassroots development, on exploiting the myriad opportunities at the local level for small-scale projects and on organizing the various groups in the community around effective institutions so that they can articulate their demands, establish priorities and work together for the common good (p.63).

We noted earlier that there are persons who have used the concept of "empowerment" to mean only superficial advancement. Conversely, there are persons who used other terms and yet come quite close to our definition of empowerment. One such individual is Joke Schrijvers, who sees "autonomy" as "a fundamental criticism of the existing social, economic, and political order" (1991, p.6). She defines autonomy as: "an anti-hierarchical concept, which stimulates critical and creative thinking and action. What I personally like best in it, is that it expresses an inner attitude of strength, an attitude which makes room for transformation, Transformation which comes from within, which springs from inner resources of one's own as an individual or a collectivity, which moves bottom-up and goes against the unwanted domination [on the part] of others (Schrijvers, 1991, pp. 5-6).

I think that autonomy, as defined by Schrijvers, is not dissimilar to empowerment. Rather, it seems to emphasize the psychological facet of the concept. Her definition is useful because it highlights that power "from within" is very important before women may exert any power "over" other segments of society, particular the state.

Creating Empowerment

The prime target of empowerment must be adult women and, in the context of social justice and transformation, they must be low-income adult women. Within this group, authoritarian behaviours by husbands in the home make families and households in general a terrain that serves the maintenance rather than the transformation of unequal gender relations.

A prerequisite to empowerment, therefore, necessitates stepping outside the home and participating in some form of collective undertaking that can be successful, thus developing a sense of independence and competence among the women. The creation of a small, cohesive group, with which its members may identify closely is paramount. We know that because of the small scale and voluntary nature of these associations many members gain valuable experience and confidence in both leadership and membership tasks. The central activity of the group could vary; it could be literacy activity, income-generation, mutual basic needs support, etc. Whatever the objective, the group activity should be designed so that its process and its goal-attainment foster the development of a sense of self-esteem, competence, and autonomy.

Empowerment will go through a series of phases. Awareness of conditions at the personal and collective levels will lead to some public action, however small. Following from this beginning there should occur a renegotiation of family conditions. As women become more available for public action, they should be able to place more demands upon the state. Expressed in a diagrammatic way, the sequence presented in Figure 1 is anticipated.

Women can attain empowerment through different points of departure: emancipatory knowledge, economic leverage, political mobilization. While many poor women work outside the home to support their families and the tasks they perform are exhausting and meagerly rewarded, access to income improves their authority in the home. Working women, regardless of how inferior there position and small their income, have a greater sense of control over their lives and more power and control over resources within the family than nonworking women (for a detailed ethnographic study comparing working and nonworking women in six communities in the Dominican Republic, see Finlay, 1989). A study of 140 women homeworkers in Mexico City by Beneria and Roldan (1987) found that while no simple relationship existed between women's economic resources and decision making, paid work increased the women's self-esteem and wives who made a considerable contribution to household expenditures (more than 40 per cent) had augmented their domestic and conjugal decision making.

Mothers' clubs make possible the creation of free and socially accepted spaces for women. Although many of their activities do not seek transformational objectives, the clubs can provide fertile ground for empowering processes. The crucial point about these mothers' clubs, usually created under religious auspices in Latin America and Africa, is that they represent a large number of the collective spaces already occupied by women.

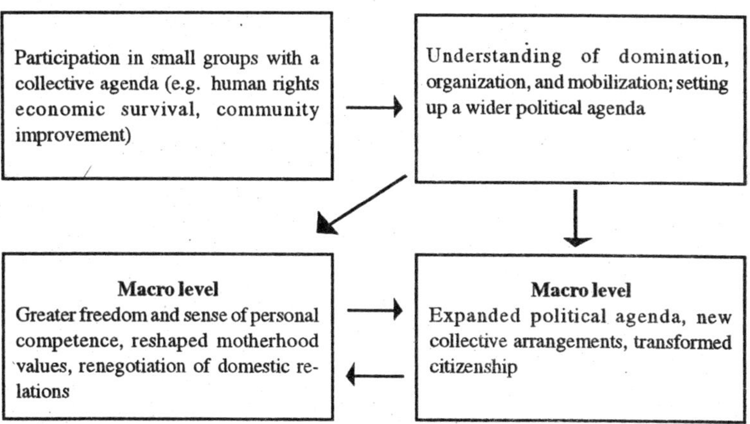

Figure.1 *Theorized Chain of Events in the Empowering Process*

Literacy skills can also be empowering, but they must be accompanied by a process that is participatory and a content that questions established gender relations, features that, unfortunately, do not characterize the great majority of literacy programs. Nonetheless, evidence from Asia and Latin America indicates that women with newly acquired literacy skills have moved into self-help organizations ranging from neighborhood soup kitchens to public health groups (Bown, 1990; Stromquist, 1993).

A description of two successful empowerment projects for women in Latin America might be helpful. The first project took place in Chile through the Rural School of Women, which functioned in three rural sites. The school provided working rural women with a consciousness-raising experience in the areas of family and work; it was organized so that the women spent several days together over a period of six months as part of their training. This project relied on in depth interviews to produce life histories of these working women that were later used in group discussions. The women's increased awareness of gender asymmetries culminated in the drafting of demands specific to nine occupations filled by women in rural areas. These demands were later disseminated among labor unions, farmers' cooperatives, and women's groups, thereby increasing knowledge about these working womens' conditions and needs.

The second project involved action-research activities in Sao Paulo, Brazil. Women in a total of 94 mothers' clubs engaged in a process of collective history and understanding of the functions, strengths, and weaknesses of their organizations. The investigation, which lasted two years, resulted in the production of widely popular play, audiovisual materials, and reports that were disseminated among all the other clubs. The knowledge and experience produced through this project led many of its leaders to organize the first national feminist meetings on "popular education and the women's movement" in Brail in 1986. (For a more detailed account of these experiences, see Stromquist, 1993a).

The Chilean and the Brazilian projects provides evidence that through authentic empowerment women will acquire a better understanding of their world, a clearer sense of their ability to change it, and resources to develop leverage. In the immediate term they will not change the world-hierarchies and centers of power will remain for a while -but gradually these empowered women can erode the traditional power and redefine it.

The Pedagogical Rationale for Empowerment

The creation of critical minds requires a physical and reflective space where new ideas may be entertained and argued, and were transformational demands may occur outside the surveillance of those who may seek to control these changes.

Sara Evans, an experienced member of the feminist movement in the U.S., reviewing the social roots of feminism in the 1950s and 1960s, included that prerequisites to an "insurgent collective identify" are the following:

1. social spaces within which members of an oppressed group can de-

velop an independent sense of worth in contrast to their received definitions as second class or inferior citizens;

2. role models of people breaking out of patterns of passivity;
3. an ideology that can explain the sources of oppression, justify revolt, and provide a vision of a qualitatively different future;
4. a threat to the new-found sense of self that forces a confrontation with the inherited cultural definitions —in other words, it becomes impossible for the individual to "make it on her own" and escape the boundaries of the oppressed group; and finally
5. a communication or friendship network through which a new interpretation can spread, activating the insurgent consciousness into a social movement. (1979, pp. 219-220; see also Freeman, 1975, pp. 44-70).

The need for a social space, a "free institutional space," for people with a shared condition was first discovered by people in the U.S. movement of the political left of the 1970s. Interestingly, recent findings from organizational behavior support this strategy.

Organizational theory and empirical evidence support the notice that knowledge is socially constructed. A process of mobilization and collective action develops a shared cognitive system and shared memories. These forms of organizational cognition, which call for the understanding of events, open the opportunity for social interpretation as well as the development of relatively dense interpersonal networks for sharing and evaluating the information, thus creating effective learning systems:

> Organizational learning can be relatively low level or single loop, involving only minor adjustments and fine tuning of existing organizational images and maps. Conversely, it can be reflected in the alternation of existing norms, assumptions, and values that govern action. Such learning is referred to as high-level or double-loop learning (Cousins and Earl, 1992, p. 401).

This collective learning, which draws upon the theory of social learning of Albert Bandura, has been argued to be one of the greatest benefits from participatory evaluations in education (Cousins and Earl, 1992). In my view, the rationale of learning that occurs in women's groups is the same.

Empowerment can succeed only if it is a mode of learning close to the women's everyday experiences and if it builds upon the intellectual, emotional, and cultural resources the participants bring to their social space. In the Chilean and the Brazilian projects mentioned earlier there was a clear focus upon knowing the experience of the women in their everyday life; there was an equally strong focus on making those experiences collective. This discussion of everyday life has a number of consequences. When women talk to other women about their personal experiences, they validate it and construct a new reality. When women describe their own experiences, they discover their role as agents in their own world and also start establishing connections between their micro realities and macrosocial contexts. It should be clear that the discussion of personal lives; of needs and dreams, necessitates of a friendly, receptive social space. Here, the task of a group facilitator becomes essential because this person must create a participatory process which provides constant encouragement and support to the members. The role of the facilitator is not an easy one; training to create and maintain an empowerment process is necessary.

Schrijvers proposes four criteria to assess an existing degree of women's autonomy:

1. women's control of their own sexuality and fertility; forms of shared mothering, between women or between women and men;
2. a division of labor which allows women and men equal access to, and control over the means of production;
3. forms of cooperation and organization of women which will enable and help them to control their own affairs; and
4. positive gender conceptions which legitimate women's sense of dignity and self-respect, and their right to self-determination (Schrijvers. p.3).

These criteria approximate to the notion of multi-faceted empowerment. But they need to be toned down to address the concrete form in which empowement is likely to take place, that is, within a specific project or program that is organizationally bounded. In this case, empowerment should be assessed by the number of facets the project addresses (cognitive, psychological, economic), the changes it brings in terms of women's individual understanding and collective action, the strength and stability of their organization, the renegotiation of authority it enables at the household and community levels, and the range of objectives it identifies for future action.

Empowerment and Education

In talking about empowerment activities I have focused exclusively on adult women and therefore considered only nonformal education.

Does it means formal education has no empowering role for girls?

Formal education has substantial contributions to make to an improved gender identity through the removal of sexual stereotypes in textbooks, the fostering of positive gender identities through the curricula, the retraining of teachers to be gender sensitive, and the provision of nonsexist guidance and counseling. These elements, in my view, are crucial antecedents of empowerment, not empowerment itself. I prefer to reserve the concept of empowerment for behaviors that tie understanding to a clear plan of action to vindicate the rights of women. If the concept of empowerment is freely applied to changes that are only cognitive or psychological, empowerment would not necessarily have to be translated into a collective dimension. And in the case of women's transformation, it is imperative that social structures be rearranged.

Barriers to Empowerment

While it is clear that many benefits may derive from collective action, it must also be remembered that participation in groups with a serious purpose of vindication will demand sustained involvement.

Poor women are busy women. Not only do they spend much time and energy responding to family needs, but they also face conditions such as rigid authoritarian spouse control, violence at home, social expectations regarding motherhood, and unsafe community environments that limit their physical mobility. Under these conditions, participation is fraught with obstacles and only a few will find it possible to become available for participation. The per centages women that will participate under these circumstances is not well known, but judging from rates of participation in related activities, particularly literacy groups which call for prolonged involvement, this proportion may be less than five per cent of the possible population. Projects working on empowerment will be small in their beginnings and take a substantial amount of time to mature and solidify. Ambitious expectations of quick and mass appeal have no basis in fact. How to make it possible for women to engage in empowering activities while they face a critical everyday survival is a real challenge.

The increased interest in empowerment comes at a time when structural adjustment policies are being implemented in many of the developing countries. There is strong evidence that these policies have had a negative impact on women in multiple dimensions of their lives, including education (see Commonwealth Secretariat, 1989, and UNICEF, 1987). In fact, the Commonwealth Secretariat report concluded that,

> the types of stabilization and adjustment policies followed in the 1980s have brought to a standstill many of the practical advances which women made earlier, and have actually reversed some of the most fundamental of them like education and health (p. 105).

To break some of the barriers in empowerment, the work of three sets of actors will be needed: grassroots and feminist groups to do the outreach and work with marginalized women who need support; women in development and international institutions who can provide the funds necessary to create projects and programs with empowerment features; and women in academic circles, who will contribute theoretical analysis of how gender is created and how it can be modified in society.

Avoiding the Mirage

Empowerment is needed to break a number of real dichotomies affecting women: personal/collective, domestic/public, material/ideological. Women who are empowered should be able to stop the undesirable, to transform ongoing practices, and to create new vision. While several governments and institutions are including the word empowerment in their discourse, much less often is there evidence of developing and funding activities that identify empowerment as a genuine goal.

This evidence is coming through acts of both omission and commission. NGOs, puritanically women-run NGOs, are the organizations most likely to work on empowering women. As important elements of the civil society, they are groups where democratic practices can begin to develop. Yet, the financial support they receive from the state and from even progressive donor agencies is miniscule compared to their needs and their potential for expansion.

In the prescriptions for structural adjustment in many of the developing countries, scant attention is paid to the burdens that the diminution of social services by the state brings upon poor women. In a related matter, the macro economic forces that create underdevelopment and inequality and that ultimately affect the social and sexual division of labor are not a significant part of any ongoing international negotiation.

Evidence by omission comes from recent efforts to make the world more democratic. Policy initiatives by USAID (AID, 1990a and 1990b) and a blue-ribbon committee study on the problems of democracy in Latin America (The Aspen Institute, 1992) recognize the importance of working with public institutions but offer only a weak acknowledgment of the need to work with women's groups so that they can develop their autonomy and advance their agenda.

A key document in education, the World Declaration on Education for All, drafted at the international conference in Jomtien in March 1990, acknowledges the need for women to benefit from educational opportunities and considers that the "most urgent priority is to ensure access to, and improve the quality of, education for girls and women, and to remove every obstacle that hampers their active participation" (Inter-Agency Commission, WCEFA, P. 45). Its plan of action calls for new partners, including the role of "non-governmental and other voluntary associations" (Inter-Agency Commission, WCEFA, 1990, p. 58). Yet, it is not clear how much support will be forthcoming for women-run NGOs, nor to what extent emancipatory, empowerment-producing educational projects for adult women will be supported past a few that may involve literacy. A sign that EFA will not pay significant attention to adult women is reflected in the agenda of the Second EFA Forum, to be held in late 1993. The forum will focus on four factors: early childhood development, assessment of learning, financing, and educational content (UNESCO, 1992, p. 6). These issues address mostly formal education, much less questions of empowerment.

Some important recommendations that move us beyond the definition and conceptual framework of empowerment must be considered if the concept is to become a reality. The commonwealth Secretariat's report cited earlier (1989) has clear recommendations for new funding for women. They suggest the use of "structures markets" or the allotment of a certain proportion of credit, foreign exchange, and public expenditures to women (p. 106). This report also suggests strengthening Women in Development (WID) units and funding directly women's organizations, from trade unions to cooperatives (pp. 128-129). These recommendations are concrete and sound. They should be heeded; otherwise, women's empowerment will remain a concept in search of true supporters.

References

The Aspen Institute (1992) *Convergence and Community: The Americas in 1993.* A Report of the Inter-American Dialogue. Washington, D.C.: The Aspen Institute

Beneria, Lourdes and Roldan, Martha (1987) *The Crossroads of Class and Gender.* Chicago: The University of Chicago Press.

Bown, Lalage (1990) *Preparing the Future. Women, Literacy, and Development.* Action Aid Development Report No. 4. Sommerset: ActionAid.

Carmichael, Stokely, and Hamilton, Charles (1967) Black Power: *The Politics of Liberation.* New York: Random House.

Commonwealth Secretariat (1989) *Engendering Adjustment for the 1990s. London:* Commonwealth Secretariat.

Cousins, J. Bradley and Earl, Lorna (1992) The Case for Participatory Evaluation. *Educational Evaluation and Policy Analysis* 14 (14): 397-418.

Evans, Sara (1979) *Personal Politics.* New York: Alfred Knopf.

Finlay, Barbara (1990) The Women of Azua: *Work and Family in the Dominican Republic.* New York: Praeger.

Griffin, Keith (1988) Development Thought and Development Strategies. Riverside: University of California, mimeo.

Hall, Margaret (1992) *Women and Empowerment. Strategies for Increasing Autonomy.* Washington, D.C.: Publishing Corporation.

Inter-Agency Commission, WCEFA (1990). *Final Report. World conference on Education for All: Meeting Basic Learning Needs.* New York: Inter-Agency Commission, WCEFA.

Jack, Raymond (1992) *Women and Attempted Suicide.* Hove, U.K.: Lawrence Earlbaum Associates, Publishers.

Lomnitz, Larissa (1977) *Networks of Marginality: Life in a Mexican Shantytown.* New York: Academic Press.

Lamnitz, Larissa (1984) Posicion de la mujer en la gran familia, unidad basica de solidaridad en America Latina. In CEPAL (ed.), *La Mujer en el Sector Popular Urbano.* Santiago: Commission Economica para America latina y el Caribe.

Rao, Aruna, Feldstein, Hilary, Cloud, Kathleen, and Staudt, Kathleen (1991) *Gender Training and Development Planning: Learning from Experience.* Conference Report. Bergan: The Chr. Michelsen Institute.

Schrijvers, Joke (1991) Women's Autonomy: From Research to Policy. Amsterdam: Institute for Development Research, University of Amsterdam, mimeo.

Stromquist, Nelly (1988) Women's Education in Development: From Welfare to Empowerment. Convergence 21 (4): 5-17.

Stromquist, Nelly (1993b) Education for the Empowerment of Women: Two Latin American Experiences. In Vincent D'Olyey and Adrian Blunt (eds.), *Development and Innovation in Third World Education.* Vancouver: Pacific Education Press.

Stomquist, Nelly (1993b) Women's Literacy and Empowerment in Latin America. In Carlos Torres (ed.), *Education in Latin America.* Albert Park, Australia: James Nicholas Publishers.

UNESCO (1992) EFA 2000 No. 9. Paris: UNESCO.

UNICEF (1987) *The Invisible Adjustment. Poor Women and the Economic Crisis.* Santiago: UNICEF Regional Office for the Americas and the Carribean.

USAID (1990a) *Family and Development.* Washington, D.C.: USAID, December.

USAID (1990b) *The Democratic Initiative. Washington,* D.C.: USAID, December.

Note

1. *This section draws in part from my previous work (Stromquist, 1988).*

3

SOME REFLECTIONS ON THE EMPOWERMENT OF WOMEN

Lucita Lazo

Let me begin by thanking the UNESCO for giving me the opportunity to think aloud with a group who shares a common interest—the empowerment of women. There are more of us now thinking about the subject but still not enough. I have been asked to talk about empowerment in the light of my practical experiences in Southeast Asia where with the support of the DANIDA (Government of Denmark) and with the International Labour Office as the implementing agency, we are making efforts to upgrade the working and living conditions of women workers in the putting out system.

I have been assigned to address two objectives:

a) to have a definition of and a conceptual framework for understanding women's empowerment;
b) to have a tentative list of indicators (manifestations) and processes or mechanisms of empowerment.

My task is obviously to abstract from my practical and concrete experiences and help crystallise the concept of empowerment. For this reason I shall be moving from the concrete to the abstract and from the particular to the general from time to time.

To make my own thinking process easier, I thought three basic questions can and should be asked: what is empowerment, why empowerment, and how does one go about the business of empowerment?

Let me go about my assigned task by giving you a brief background of what I do in the field. Hence my discussion will be in two parts. Part I presents what I do in the field. Part II will be an attempt to interpret those experiences, learn from them and help clarify and understand the notion of empowerment.

Women's Empowerment In the Making

The Case of Women Workers in the Putting Out System.

Ka Lilay weaves sawali or palm leaves for a subcontractor in her remote village in the Philippines. But she is not paid by her employer, who happens to be a subcontractor/trader for an exporter. Unable to deliver on time for reasons of his own, the subcontractor/ could not collect his fees. Then, he decided not to pay thirty sawali weavers working for him on the pretext that their products are of poor quality. Can Ka Lilay and her co-workers complain and file a case in court and have their wages paid?

Ibu Hassana has been embroidering traditional costumes in a far-flung village in Indonesia since she was twelve. At thirty-five, her eyes are blurred from her day to day threading and stitching. Too poor, she could not buy a pair of glasses, least of all, consult an eye doctor. Can she ask her employer to give her glasses or to foot her doctor's bill?

There are many more of such cases. The common denominator is that the victims are mostly women who work under subcontracting or putting out arrangements. Putting out is a system whereby traders and middlemen, with little investment on their part, collect orders for the production of a good or service and assign the jobs to women in the villages or urban slums of many developing countries in Southeast Asia such as Thailand, Indonesia and the Philippines. In turn the women produce the goods or services from their homes or nearby premises, making them known as homebased workers.

Lacking the legal status of a worker due to the absence of formal employer-employee relationship, homebased workers make goods and services under special arrangements. They work in their own homes without a written contract under the putting out system or subcontracting arrangement. Their homes are actually extensions of factories and for all intents and purposes, they are part of the factory. Yet while they are part of factory production activities, they are not counted in the benefits extended to factory workers. In this sense, they are workers in limbo. Homeworkers' working set-up is highly informal; they do not have maternity and sick leaves, and medical and social insurance and similar such benefits. Homebased workers in Southeast Asia, like their kindred in South Asia, are isolated and unorganized. There is no single unit or body of government that pays attention to their welfare.

Could they ever hope to have any form of social protection?

Against this social backdrop, the International Labour Office launched a subregional development project entitled "Rural Women Workers in the Putting Out System", hereafter referred to as the homeworkers' project. The project covers three Southeast Asian countries and is funded by DANIDA (Government of Denmark).

Purpose of the Project

The project seeks to enhance the employment and promote the working welfare of homebased women workers, especially those in the rural areas. The two-pronged project goal was to ensure jobs and humane, nonexploitative conditions of work. This is a tall order. Many times, the protection of good conditions of work jeopardises the very jobs of those being protected, especially women. In labour surplus countries, any move to increase wages could mean the potential loss of jobs.

The ultimate purpose of the project is to extend social protection to the women, without losing their jobs or source of income. This could mean a number of things such as: increasing their piece rates and wages, reducing exploitation by the middleman, reducing dependence on the middleman for job orders, affording health, housing education and other appropriate benefits.

In creasing piece rates implies having to bargain with an employer. Alone, a homeworker's chance of winning is nil given the comparative strength of the employer. Homeworkers are isolated, fragmented and unorganised. To match the strength of the employer, they would have to marshal their individual strengths into a collective. Organisation becomes necessary.

For some homebased workers, the work stops when their employers stop sending them orders. The only alternative is for them to produce and sell to the market directly when there are no such orders. But this means having the means to buy raw materials and the connection to other buyers and market outlets. Many homeworkers are poor, assetless, illiterate, and have neither marketing skills nor connections to markets and buyers. Without a collateral and a guarantor, they could not borrow from the banks and formal financial institutions. With little knowledge of markets and marketing, they could only sell on a limited scale to the surrounding villages or within their villages. Add to this their general lack of self-esteem and self-confidence, they are hard put into starting an enterprise of their own. Access and control over essential resources and social services is one obstacle in their way.

Exploitation by traders and middlemen comes in the form of paying extremely low piece rates and demanding delivery on time, sometimes penalising the women if they fail to deliver and abandonment of the obligation to pay for whatever reason. Further, miscellaneous costs of production such as electricity, work space and the like are passed on to the homeworker. However, some traders could earn huge profits by selling at high costs to the exporters and reducing as far as they can the wages of the homebased petty producers. How can the homebased workers get away from unfair treatment? With the exporter/employer located in the city and relying only upon the middleman and traders, the homebased rural women oftentimes do not even know who their employer is. Who would give them social protection?

The situation I have described thus far shows you the state of powerlessness of the women workers in the putting out system. Our concern for them arises from an underlying belief that society has a moral obligation to help the disadvantaged and to redress poverty and ensure equity. And empowerment is argued to be the appropriate mode of doing this.

The Notion of Empowerment

- Empowerment denoted a process of acquiring, providing, bestowing the resources and the means or enabling the *access to and control over such means and resources*. This implies that the individual has the potential to acquire power upon her own initiative or that another party could make it possible for her to have power. This point is vital because it identifies the potential agents of empowerment: it is the person who is to be empowered or it could be another person or agent. Empowerment could be a self-propelled and self-propelling process. If by some gift of God, it dawns on a women that her life could become better if she tried to act upon such thoughts, link up with the source of resources, then she is facilitating her own empowerment.
- Empowerment *enables* the person to gain insight and have an awareness of what is undesirable and unfavorable about her current situation, perceive a better situation, the possibilities of attaining it and realising what is within her reach and what she could do to get to a better situation. This characterisation of empowerment implies that the process could involve a *Change of perceptions* about the self, the environment, and the relationship of the self and the environment. It is a process that involves the creation of images, the generation of a "push" to act or what psychologists call motivation. Change of perceptions implies a change of attitude and a change in one's outlook in life.
- Empowerment enables women to *generate choices* and as an out-

come of having such choices, she *acquires leverage and bargaining power*. Empowered, a women would take steps to find and/or create options or find and link to the means to find the options. An external party could help women find and create such options. When one has options, one can a) choose not to follow the pressures and demands of the more powerful party; b) ask and negotiate with the other party to change the situation and make it more acceptable.

For example, women homeworkers who can link and sell to other buyers can have the possibility of refusing bad deals such as exploitative and low-paying orders from traders and middlemen. But since the Third World countries are labour surplus markets, the women's options are stunted, making for a situation of no choice for the women.

Empowerment makes a person able to choose and able to demand. It makes the person able to choose her goals, generate opportunities to reach the goals and determine the overall direction of her life. This makes the notion of empowerment a fascinating and powerful one.

In the Third World, some women have no possibility to choose their own life goals and this indicates a state of powerlessness. We are aware for instance of societies and tribes where women are committed to marriage by their parents even before they are born or ready for it. By the norm of their society, this mode of behaviour is acceptable; yet it may not always be for the betterment or happiness of the woman. Still the woman has no choice and is therefore powerless under the situation. Hers is to obey and not to protest.

- Empowerment enables a woman to gain *relative strength* as a result of having choices and bargaining power. The consequences could be reduction of invisibility as she is able to demand attention from those concerned, especially decision and policy makers, to generate the appropriate positive responses, reduction of vulnerability, reduction or elimination of exploitability, availability and use of social services and resources. Ultimately, empowerment should lead to the improvement of women's socio-economic status.
- Simply put, tautological though it may be, empowerment is the ac quisition or the bestowing of power. The variables of power are the variables of empowerment as well. Power is a complex quality that gives the person the authority and the strength to exercise control and influence. Power arises from possessing a complex combination of personal and physical resources that is being bestowed or being acquired in the process of empowerment.

Power implies a relationship. There is one individual or party who possesses (or has greater change of accessing and availing) a physical, economic, social and/or psychological resource and/or quality which becomes the basis for the exercise of control and influence over another. Conversely, in the power relationship, there is an individual or party who is the "weaker" whom the other party controls.

In layman's parlance, power means having the *capacity and the means* to direct one's life towards desired social, political and economic goals and/or status. It is the ability to influence events and control outcomes in the environment. The crux of power lies in the possession of and/or access to and control over means and resources.

Let us digress for a while and try to apply this concept to the case of the women homeworkers, and let us look at the variables of power. Women workers in the putting out system are powerless vis-a-vis their employers, the traders and middlemen. The women homeworkers' powerlessness can be traced to a number of factors. An indicative list is shown in Figure 1.

▶ Personal x	▶ Environmental/Sociological Factors	
Illiteracy	Societal conditions	
Lack of skills		
Lack of information	weak economy →	no job options
	labour surplus →	no job options
	gender ideology →	discrimination
Lack of money	no public awareness →	no government
	policy →	women's invisibility
(poverty/assetlessness)	no protective laws for women →	no social protection
Lack of awareness	Household conditions	
Low self esteem		
	female headed	
Lack of self-confidence	big family size	
Low sense of efficacy	high dependency ratio	
	Working conditions	
	isolation, fragmentation, unregistered →	invisibility
	atomisation, lack of organisation →	vulnerability,
	no work contract →	exploitability
	no clear status as workers →	no social protection
	no direct contract with	
	the employer →	dependence on middleman

***Fig. 1.** Illustrative Analysis of the Variables of Power.*

Women's state of powerlessness is borne by a *combination and interaction of environmental and personal factors*. In the case of the women homeworkers, the conditions of work in the putting out system intensify or aggravate the disadvantage they suffer like most other women in society. This makes it necessary to pay special attention to their conditions of work.

Women's powerlessness arises from their illiteracy, lack of awareness, lack of information and knowledge about markets and lack of skills, their overall lack of self-steem and self-confidence, their lack of money, their lack of job opportunities, lack of connections to those who can provide jobs and lend them money to start own small enterprise. The women's very lack of awareness and insight into their circumstances aggravate their powerlessness. They remain in a state of blissful that they cannot change their poor situation. As a result of this long-standing poverty and powerlessness the women lose their sense of control over their environment. They have low efficacy, meaning they lack belief in their own ability to control and influence the outcomes and events in their world.

That the women work individually and silently in their homes reinforces their powerlessness. They are said to be isolated, atomised and fragmented. This way they are unable to share and discuss their common concerns, problems and solutions. With little exposure to the outside world as they are preoccupied with their day to day chores, the rural women homeworkers are not aware of possibilities out there. Ignorance and lack of awareness perpetuate their powerlessness.

The women's circumstances also contribute to their powerlessness. For example, in underdeveloped and weak economies, labour exceeds job supply and limits the job options for the general populace. Coupled with the prevailing gender ideology that discriminates against women, the job options for women are even narrower. Lack of public awareness about the burdens of women and the conditions of their life and work make for benign neglect by the goverment so that there is no policy or progoramme to promote women homeworkers' welfare.

Similarly, household conditions either precipitate, perpetuate or aggravate women's powerlessness. For example, limited resources for education will given preference to education of sons than daughters. Women are then consigned to illiteracy.

The case of a woman homeworker demonstrates a situation where the working conditions keep the woman invisible to the government and policy makers because of her isolation. Her lack of a work contract, and ambiguous status as a worker, no clear cut employer-employee relationship and no direct contact with her employer altogether make her vulnerable and exploitable. She does not have the benefit of social protection —all of which are manifestations or symptoms of powerlessness.

- Empowerment is a moving state; it is a continuum that varies in degrees of power. It is relative. The diagram below visualises this concept. One can move from an extreme state of absolute lack of power to the other extreme of having absolute power. The extreme ends of the continuum are of course "idealised" states.

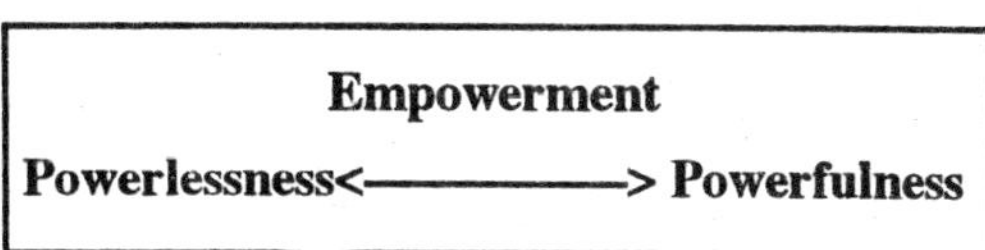

The power continuum

Now, the practical question is **how** can women be empowered?

Again, let me answer the question by telling you of what we have done in the field. Then we shall come back and extract the mechanisms and manifestations of empowerment.

Making Empowerment Happen for Homeworkers in the Philippines

The strategy is a combined and iterative process of doing studies on the situation of homeworkers, educating and training them to study and research their own situation and formulate solutions and appropriate practical actions, organising and teaching the homeworkers to organise other homeworkers. In addition, they are also trained on the productivity enhancement of their economic projects.

At the grassroots, the actions proceeded in three stages:

1) Selecting, preparing and equipping the community workers and trainers for the process of organising;
2) actual organising of the homeworkers;
3) networking and consolidating the homebased organisations and strengthening them by increasing their access to financing, markets and essential social services.

A vital feature of the project strategy is the active involvement of the target group. The homeworkers themselves, with guidance from the women academics and activists and the ILO, co-determine the direction of their development. In collecting background information at the village level, the women learn how to formulate questions, conduct interviews, collect, analyse and interpret data. This is the essence of the participatory action research approach.

At the individual level, the homeworkers' project could have short and long term impacts. Presently, the main concern is to create and establish an institution which could give the women homeworkers *collective strength and a collective voice*; in short a power base.

The practical actions consisted of education and training in organising and how to do participatory action research, development of training materials and paralegal training of the homebased workers in the various provinces. These activities prepared the women for the massive organising work to be done. Thenceforth, educating, training and organising activities continue to be pursued and the campaign for homeworkers' welfare in the Philippines was born. Over the long term, the project seeks to improve the economic and social status of the women through education, training and organisation, all of which are geared towards empowerment of the rural women. It also seeks to establish linkages with government and non-government organisations (GO-NGO), to gain increased access to services essential to homebased producers and to establish within the organisations services and facilities for women homebased workers.

In summary, the project activities revolved around three action areas:

a) Education, Training and Research of Community Workers and Women;
b) Organising of the Homebased Workers: and
c) Strengthening the Organisation and Empowerment of Homeworkers.

The Target Group

The rural women homeworkers in the Philippines mostly operate as unorganised and isolated workers. Although they are by law considered to have legal status as workers and are entitled to protection, in practice they do not enjoy the benefits which regular factory workers have. Their being isolated and unorganised make it difficult to apply and enforce the protective provisions of the law.

There is no registry of homeworkers although there is a roster of subcontractors at the Department of Trade and Industry. For the purpose of labor protection and monitoring of the application of labour laws on homeworkers, there is no practical administrative system yet.

Homebased workers have no institutional means for voicing their common concerns, influencing national policy and programmes, pressing for their rights and redressing their grievances.

Women homeworkers are *not* members of the trade unions although lately, the trade unions have become more accommodating towards them. At the international level, the International Federation of Plantation and Agricultural Workers (IFPAAW) and the International Confederation of Trade Unions (ICFTU) are both taking cognizance of the issue. However, it may take time for concrete actions at the field level to take effect.

Awareness-raising Workshops, Meetings and Dialogues

One drawback of the project was the lack of public awareness of the plight of homeworkers. To overcome this, meetings, workshops and dialogues were held. For the first time, homeworkers' concerns were publicly presented to the government and other concerned organisations. Policy recommendations and a national plan of action were accordingly formulated.

Women homeworkers listed their needs and concerns, effectively setting the direction of future practical actions. Their participation was initiated and underscored in the series of consultative meetings launched upon the initiative of a homeworker, later to become the president of the National Network of Homeworkers, locally known as *Pambansang Tagapag-ugnay ng mga Manggagawa sa Bahay*, or PATAMABA. Having attended the subregional technical meeting in Bangkok in June 1989, she hatched the idea of conducting consultations.

One hundred and eighty garments homeworkers from Bulacan province attended the consultative meetings from June to September 1989. In these meetings, the women aired, identified, discussed and documented their common problems and their issues and most important, proposed solutions.

On 1 October 1989, the National Coordinating Council of the National Network of Homeworkers was formed, the first leap forward in the homeworkers' campaign.

The women's collective recommendations were presented to the National Tripartite Workshop on 2-6 October 1989. Representatives of government, NGOs, workers and employers organisations attended the workshop.[2]

The research findings earlier mentioned were presented in the workshop and were vital in initiating the debate on what to do in order to alleviate the plight of the homeworkers. Notably, the homeworkers contribution in the debate proved highly instructive to the participants, especially those in government. The women homeworkers had a position of their own which they read before the Labour Department secretary.

Awakening of Government Consciousness

Upon the request of the Bureau of Women and Young Workers, the *Katipunanng maga Babaing Pilipina* (KaBaPa) took the Labour Undersecretary in charge of Labour Standards on a field trip to the homeworkers' sites (i.e. papier mache makers and garment sewers), prior to his attendance and chairmanship of the ILO Committee of Experts' Meeting on the Social Protection of Homeworkers in October 1990 in

Geneva. These village visits were featured in the October 1990 issue of the *Philippine Labour*, a publication of the Department of Labour.

Media Campaigns

PATAMABA printed its brochure for wider distribution in order to inform the public about the existence of the homeworkers' cause and network. With the assistance of KaBaPa, it now publishes its own newsletter called *Bahay Ugnayan* which features articles on homework-related issues. The first issue was distributed during the first national congress of homeworkers in May 1991.

Radio and television interviews as well as press releases and articles on homework have been shown and issued since the subregional project was launched. Such activities are continuously pursued along with the national workshops as well as the subregional workshop hosted by the KaBaPa-PATAMABA on 7-10 May 1991.

The subregional workshop was a forum for exchanging experiences among the participating countries in the ILO-DANIDA subregional project. The KaBaPa-PATAMABA, with the technical assistance of the Philippine Department of Labour and Employment, organised the workshop and financial sponsorship of the ILO, the Netherlands Government, the University of the Philippines' College of Social Work and Community Development and the Women's Studies Center.

Education and Training

The women were trained in participatory action research which they used as their tool for entry into the organising of the women. Using data gathered during the research, the women could determine how to approach, assemble and mobilise the women homeworkers in the community, and who should be approached.

Two three-day workshops on participatory action research (PAR) were conducted at the University of the Philippines School for Labour & Industrial Relations (UP-SOLAIR) in collaboration with the Bureau of Rural Workers of the Department of Labor and Employment. During these workshops, the participatns were also instructed on how to prepare video documentations. Fifty women homeworkers were trained in participatory research and documentation in two workshops.

The training led to the formulation of a community survey form by a team of KaBaPa officials/ leaders and the DOLE-Bureau of Women and Young Workers staff. These surveys were conducted alongside the focussed group discussions (FGDs) in the various project sites where organising was to be done. The FGD is a technique where the women homeworkers assemble in small groups and with the help of a facilitator, they express their ideas and feelings openly but they focus discussions on issues that relate to certain themes/topics such as gender issues, homeworkers' working conditions, homeworkers' needs, methods of and approaches to organising in their respective community and the like. FGDs were conducted in 18 provinces involving some 350 homeworkers. Through the FGDs, data pertinent to organising work were collected and community profiles were made. [3]

In collaboration with the UP Law Center, the KaBaPa-PATAMABA designed a paralegal training and trained twenty homeworker-members of the PATAMABA during the first course on 22 November 1990. Primers for homeworkers were compiled and the Secretary of Labour's paper on the "State of Jurisprudence on Homeworkers" and appropriate sections of the Labour Code were translated into Pilipino, the national language, to ensure that the homeworkers themselves understand the rules.[4]

Creating Legal Awareness

Thirty-five members of KaBaPa and PATAMABA from 11 provinces attended a paralegal orientation and training seminar on 22-24 November 1990 sponsored by the University of the Philippines Law Center. The concept and application of paralegal functions was introduced to the community organisers within the context of the homeworkers' campaign.

Organising and Networking

Upon the initiative of the women homeworker-members of the KaBaPa, 29 women homeworkers representing eleven (11) provinces met on 1 October 1989 in the province of Bulacan. Note that this meeting was preceded by the consultative meetings mentioned above. They then formed the national network of homeworkers which was called the *Pambansang Tagapag-ugnay ng mga Manggagawa sa Bahay*.

On 21 October 1989, the PATAMABA ad hoc national coordinating committee met to draft its two-year workplan, January 1990 to December 1991. The work programme included the creation of consciousness raising and training materials to enable the PATAMABA networkers to organise homeworkers in various provinces all over the country. The process of developing training materials was participatory—homeworkers related their living and working conditions; researchers provided data and organisers shared their experiences in organising.

On 1 October 1990, PATAMABA celebrated its first anniversary and held a conference at the UP School of Labour and Industrial Relations during which the Coordinating Committee presented a progress report. By the, PATAMABA already had amassed some 1,000 members and was organising the subcontractors. In the conference, the homeworkers decided to convene a Congress on Labour Day, 1 May 1991. PATAMABA registered itself with the Securities and Exchange Commission before its national congress in May 1991 which gave it a legal personality as an organisation. The network then spun off from the KaBaPa and now exists as an independent organisation. It also registered itself as a rural organisation with the Bureau of Rural Workers of DOLE.

The PATAMABA functions as an autonomous body though it is still being supported by the KaBaPa until it acquires adequate institutional capacity. It co-chairs the National Steering Committee (NSC), an ad hoc national committee that advocates promotion of homeworkers' welfare and empowerment in the country.

Mechanisms and Manifestations of Empowerment

1. Awareness Raising

The conscientising and media campaigns have made the women homewokers, government authorities and policy makers, the NGO sector and the general public aware of the plight of homebased workers and the exploitation in the putting out system. Through the campaigns, the homeworkers have generated sympathy, enabled the women to call attention to the Department of Labour and launch their advocacy for policy reforms. As a direct result the Labour Department has formulated and promulgated Department Order No. 5 which embodies the implementing rules and regulations of the Labor Code provisions on subcontracting.

Through this mechanism, the push for organising and networking among the homeworkers was reinforced. More women are interested in joining the network.

Outcomes/Manifestations/Indicators

- Consultations, meetings, workshops
- Media campaigns
- Field visits
- Conscientising of the women
- Enabled the women to generate public sympathy; call the attention of government, the Department of Labour in particular and pave the way for policy reforms.

Prior to 1989 when field actions were launched, there were few studies on homeworkers, the homeworkers, the homeworkers issues were hardly mentioned in the media, the Department of Labour paid no or little attention to the issue and did not consider it a priority concern. *Homeworkers are invisible no more*:

- Numerous press releases, radio-TV plugs, radio interviews of homeworkers and government officials on homeworking topics.
- For the first time, high labour department officials went to visit homeworkers in some homeworking sites.

2. Education and Training

Through this mechanism the women have acquired varied skills: how to organize, how to conduct participatory research, how to plan, how to make proposals, how to network, how to manage micro enterprises and the like. Now, there is growing self-confidence among the homeworkers.

This is demonstrated in PATAMABA's spinning off from the KaBaPa, its mother organisation in 1991. With the skills they have learned from the KaBaPa, they are now able to run their organisation and pursue programmes independently. They occasionally seek guidance from the KaBaPa and the Department of labour as well as other agencies whenever they deem necessary.

The homeworker fellow to the Self-Employed Women's Association in India has given the women ideas, particularly in setting up their own bank in the long run. The women agreed to save from their own pockets to create a seed fund for their future Women's Bank.

With their acquired skills, the women attend meetings and speak up, and no longer hesitate to voice their concerns and their expectations of government. They come forth with suggestions and solutions.

Outcomes/Manifestations/Indicators

- The women learned skills on how to organise, how to make proposals, how to conduct participatory action research, how to network, how to lobby and advocate, how to manage microenterprises and the like.
- A homework was sent as a fellow to observe the workings of the Self-Employed Women's Association in Ahmedabad, India.
- Enabled the women to train other women at the grassroots.
- Enabled the women to prepare community profiles, obtain data they need to prepare for their organising and networking activities.
- Enabled the women to prepare proposals by themselves.
- Gave the women self-confidence in approaching authorities such as government officials and donor agencies to solicit and appeal for aid.

This can be seen as a step towards access to means and resources.

- Gave the women courage to speak up, tell the authorities about their needs, declare that they have rights as workers.
- Despite limited resources, grassroots women were trained in the various skills using a Training the Trainers' approach.
- Proposals prepared by PATAMABA submitted to ILO and other donors. Grants and donations were obtained from NGOs like the OXFAM, KULU and WAND-DIWATA and private individuals.
- For the first time, a fellowship is awarded to a lowly-educated person. Most fellowships are for those with at least high school education.
- PATAMABA officials drafted a position paper which they read to the Secretary of Labour in the 1989 national workshop; formulated a Declaration of Rights.
- The fellow to SEWA persuaded her homeworker friends and members of PATAMABA to contribute some money every month to generate a seed fund for their future Women Workers' Bank. This is ongoing now.
- PATAMABA spun off from the KaBaPa its mother organisation, in 1991 and organised their second national congress in May 1992 by themselves.

3. Organising and Networking

Organising and networking are the major mechanisms for the homeworkers. PATAMABA and the Homeworkers' Center are physical evidences of the collectivisation of the women homeworkers, giving them a collective voice. Their collective strength can be harnessed and mobilised in dealing with employers and middlemen, especially the exploitative ones.

Through the organisation, the homeworkers have gained *political power*. They are able to seek representation in government organisations, public for a, national planning where policies and decisions affecting them are made.

Outcomes/Manifestations/Indicators

- The women met, discussed and consulted one another and agreed to form the national network of homeworkers locally known as the *Pambansang Tagapag-ugnay ng mga Manggagawa sa Pilipines* in October 1989.
- Go-NGO collaboration between the homeworkers' sector was

formalised with the creation of the National Steering Committee (NSC) chaired by the Under secretary of the Department of Labour and co-chaired by the PATAMABA president. KaBaPa and other government agencies are represented in the NSC.

- The Homeworkers' Center, a small rented apartment in Quezon City, was inaugurated in October 1992 and serves as the national headquarters and office of the PATAMABA.
- Enabled the women to collectivise and reduce their isolation, fragmentation and atomisation. From a small ad hoc group of 29 members that formed the network, there were more than 1,000 women homeworker members in May 1991. By August 1991, there were some 2,000 members.
- Enabled the women homeworkers to gain political power and influence the Department of Labour in its policy making and to access to programmes and services government.
- Enabled the women to have a voice and the PATAMABA is represented in many meetings and policy making fora.
- Enabled the women to have a collective vision of how their "future" could be improved.
- Enabled the women to initiate contacts with the officials of the Social Security System to explore how the home-workers could be given social protection
- Enabled the women to access to vital information and through the NSC, contacts with the source of aid and services is facilitated for them.
- *Homeworkers are officially visible and officially recognised.* The PATAMABA has a legal personality since it is registered with the Securities and Exchange Commission as an organisation and as a rural workers' organisation with the Bureau of Rural Workers of the Department of Labour.
- The Labour Department's Bureau of Women and Young Workers conducted a survey on homeworkers. The Bureau of Rural Workers of the same department has assigned a small unit to handle homeworker-related matters.
- Through the National Steering Committee's Research Group and with the help of the Labour Department, the homeworkers are seeking to be included in the labour force survey and to be classified as "workers" and not as mere unpaid family labour as happened in previous years. This is still ongoing and will hopefully eliminate the statistical invisibility of the women.
- A KaBaPa woman member is representing the sector in the updating

of the medium term development plan of the country.

- The women homeworkers attend the meetings of the Labour, Income and Employment Statistics inter-agency committee. The also attend meetings like those on Woman health, Environment.
- The homeworkers drafted a five-year plan from May 1991 to April 1996, indicative of a growing sense of efficacy among the women and continuning hope for reform and change and ultimately, improvement of their socio-economic situation.

4. Socio-economic Aid

Through the organisation, a revolving fund for socio-economic projects has been made available. The homeworker groups in various communities have gotten loans for their microenterprises. The PATAMABA has also solicited 400 US dollars for its members who were victims of the eruption of Mount Pinatubo.

Outcomes/Manifestations/Indicators

- Revolving Funds are made available to support the microenterprises of the women.
- Marketing Assistance
- Product Development
- Enabled the women to avail of loans at low interest with the least red tape possible.
- Sixteen economic project proposals were submitted by March 1991. Some of these have been granted loans. For example, the piggery project in Zambales province using a revolving fund, is reportedly working well. The piglets have been returned and additional piglets are being farmed to other homeworker households.
- Twenty five women homeworker/members of the garments of the garments cooperative in one province, Bulacan, were given a grant in early 1989. The money was used to finance the production activities of the cooperative which was formed to "fight subcontractors who exploit garment sewers and to awaken communities on the plight of homeworkers." This project was not too successful in 1989 to 1990. However, the women's group turned it around by investing their remaining funds into grain trading.
- The homeworkers have brought samples of their products at the Homeworkers' Center where they have a show nook.
- The homeworkers organised bazzars during the meetings and workshops organised by PATAMABA.
- The number of groups and women availing of the revolving fund is

increasing and loans will be further granted in 1993.

- Increases in earnings and incomes of homeworkers is reportedly occurring but there is no hard data at the moment. This will be obtained in 1993.

During the field visits to the project sites, the Evaluation Mission (in March 1991) found an "awareness among homeworkers when it comes to the importance of organising, but with respect to access to resources such as credit and marketing, the awareness among the homeworkers on how to go about it seemed to be limited."

In 1993, the socio-economic projects will be further strengthened by product and marketing consultancies. Access to such services from the government is somewhat difficult because of the limited resources of the agencies concerned. The demand for the service is great but through a special programme to be developed by the PATAMABA, access to such consultancy could be facilitated.

By making economic aid available, the women can hopefully create and make the option of self-employment work in their favor. This should reduce their exploitability and dependence on the middleman.

Summing up and Concluding Remarks

Empowerment can have overt and covert outcomes. For the latter, it can only be cautiously inferred from the actions taken by the women. The indicators of empowerment could be very subtle. For example, by all indications, the women's sense of efficacy has been awakened but this can only be inferred from their actions. Their continuing pursuit, support and commitment to the cause of the PATAMABA is evidence of this. During the inauguration of their Homeworkers' Center in October 1992, Ka Ester Tina, the PATAMABA president tearfully stated: "It is the first time in years that they can ever claim they have an office to come to when they need something or when they have problems and concerns". The tears were of extreme gladness mixed with disbelief. They never thought it could happen.

Empowerment is "enablement" by changing the person, changing structures, replacing or recreating conventional institutions and/or rearranging the environment.

Empowerment transpires over time and usually, it is not instantaneous. As the women homeworkers are empowered they move from silence to articulation, from invisibility to recognition, and from isolation to organisation.

Empowerment means building aspirations, hopes and expectations. Thus empowerment keeps the women going!

Lessons From the Field on Empowerment

The empowerment process entails building up the women's arsenal of resources—physical, economic, social and psychological. The age-old strategy of minimising or reducing weaknesses and enhancing strengths remains as valid as ever.

Empowerment means giving the women the capacity to give themselves power, even if only psychologically.

Empowerment means giving the women the means enabling the women to avail of vital resources and services.

Empowerment of women is maximised by collectivisation. Hence, organising makes a lot of good sense. Within the context of the organisation, the weakness can be reduced by complementation. Individually, one woman's strength could be the other's weakness and vice-versa. The strengths could be put together and the individual weaknesses plugged via the group or the collective.

In practical terms, women's weaknesses could be plugged by awareness raising, conscientising, organising, education and training.

Women's greatest resources are themselves-their personal capacities including their self-image. To be empowered, women must learn to respect themselves and to regard themselves as capable.

- Improvement of their self image and their self appraisals.
- Increasing their literacy.
- Upgrading their practical skills—technical, management, entrepreneurial, lobbying, advocacy, pressurising, etc.

The Input Side

Personal Capacity Building

Organising

Education and Training

Paralegal Training

Facilitating Access to Social Services and Resources

Availment of Resources and Services

Product Consultancy and Marketing

Assistance

Credit Schemes

Revolving Funds

The Output Side

Policy Reform and Advocacy—changes in the public attitudes and government policies Socio-Economic Upgradation of the Women's Status—changes in the women's skills, incomes, and conditions or work.

The Empowerment Equation

Personal Capacity (Self-esteem, technical skills management skills)	x	Physical Powerfulness (capital, facilities)

Explanatory Notes

The *Katipunan ng Bagong Pilipina* (KaBaPa) is a mass-based, activist women's non-government organisation which endeavours to promote male and female equality before the law in all fields where such does not exist; equality of economic rights, non-discrimination in employment opportunities and security of employment after marriage and equality of rights and responsibilities in the family and home. The KaBaPa was launched on March 8, 1975, by some 2,000 women, mostly from rural areas. Today, it claims membership of 28,000 women from all over the country. The organisation has been most active in educating women through its indigenous training system. It has been involved in organising children and youth, the urban poor and market vendors to whom it has extended solidarity during strikes and struggles against eviction.

The KaBaPa has many members who are homeworkers and they are spread out in the provinces. Some of them have been involved in participatory action research on homeworkers since the early 1980s.

Also, it has had substantial involvement in human resource and community development involving rural women and many of its projects are funded with aid from donors. Using its indigenous training system called *gabay*, it has trained more than 20,000 members and non-members as well as 500 trainers. The gabays are guidelines in simple question and answer format to teach women how to organise, how to be a good homemaker and community leader, how to manage projects and the like.

With minimum prodding, the KaBaPa was persuaded to focus on the homeworkers' cause instead of community-based enterprises as such. The path for the homeworkers' project was laid.

The *Katipunan ng Bagong Pilipina* saw itself as an initiator in organising homebased workers, and envisages the homeworkers' organisation developing into a independent body. Realising that organising homeworkers is a gargantuan task, KaBaPa advocates the involvement of and seeks support from non-governmental and governmental organisations. This could be done through a sustained networking process, the main strategy adopted by the KaBaPa in campaigning for the homeworkers' welfare.

References

Ang Bagong Pilipina, (English Edition), March 1990-March 1991, 4 pp.

"Asian homeworkers meet in RP May 10", News Today, Manila, Philippines, May 1, 1991, p.3.

Bahay Ugnayan, Pahayagan ng PATAMABA, INK, Mayo 1991.

Draft of the Memorandum of Agreement Establishing the National Steering Committee.

"DOLE pushes legislation for homeworkers, *Businessworld,* Manila, Philippines, April 10, 1991, p. 11.

Dole Workshop, Malaya, Manila, Philippines, 1 October 1989, p. 2.

"Drilon appeals for welfare of homeworkers", *The Manila Chronicle,* Manila, Philippines, 7 October 1989, p. 3.

"Drilon wants protection for 7M home *workers", Business World,* Manila, Philippines, October 9, 1989, p.11.

"Drilon vows to protect homeworkers", *Manila Bulletin,* Manila, Philippines, 7 October 1989, pp. 1 & 20.

"8M home-based workers grossly underpaid: DOLE", *Malaya,* Manila, Philippines, May 13, 1991, p. 2.

"Gov't, NGOs help homeworkers", *News Today,* Manila, Philippines, 6 October 1989, p. 3.

"Homeworkers: an exploited lot", *Malaya,* Manila, Philippines, May 10, 1991, p. 18.

"Help for Homeworkers sought", *The New Chronicle,* Manila, Philippines, April 10, 1991, p. 4.

"Homeworkers' Aid Sought", *Manila Bulletin,* Manila, Philippines, May 13, 1991, p. 16.

"Homeworkers Meet on", *Manila Bulletin,* Manila, Philippines, May 7, 1991, p. 5.

"Homeworkers Organise to Get Better Income", *Daily Globe,* Manila, Philippines, January 16, 1990, p. 14.

"Homeworkers as exploited class", *Businessworld,* Manila, Philippines, May 1, 1991, p. 8 and in Philippine Daily Inquirer, May 17, 1991.

"Homeworkers Widely Ignored Despite GDP Contribution", *Philippine Labor*, March 1991, p. 7.

"It's worth a try", *Philippine Daily Inquirer*, Manila, Philippines, 7 October 1989, p. 8.

"ILO cites Gov't, NGO efforts to promote homeworking", *Businessworld*, April 29, 1991, p. 12.

"Laws to protect home-based workers sought", *Manila Bulletin*, Manila, Philippines, May 19, 91, p. 12.

"Look after homeworkers' welfare, Drilon asks solons", *Daily Globe*, Manila, Philippines, 7 October 1989, p. 6.

Minutes of the Meetings, National Steering Committee for Homebased Workers' Program, July 30, 1991, 5 pp.

"Homeworkers: Vulnerable to Abuses, Insecurities", and "Home is Where the Work Is", *Philippine Labor*, Manila, Philippines: October, 1990, volume XVI, pp. 2, 8-9.

Report of the Final Evaluation Mission on the ILO/DANIDA Subregional Project (DAN/RAS/86/MO4), March-April 1991, 56 pp. plus annexures.

Resolution for the Creation of the National Steering Committee.

"The most exploited women workers", *People's Journal*, Manila, Philippines, 7 October 1989.

Ulat Ukol sa Pagkilos Para sa MB, Hulyo-Agosto 12, 1991, typewritten, 2 pp.

Ulat ng Pambansang Tagapag-ugnay ng PATAMABA, Mayo 1-Hunyo 28, 1991, typewritten report, 4 pp.

Unang Kongreso ng PATAMABA, Ink., Mayo 1, 1991, 16 pp.

Notes:--

1. Subcontractors are those who get job orders from producers or exporters and in turn, they assign the job others such as the homebased women workers.

2. The proceedings are published in the monograph, "Homeworkers of Southeast Asia: The Struggle for Social Protection in the Philippines," 1992: Bangkok, Thailand.

3. Homeworking activities in the various provinces are as follows: Isabela, sewing & embroidery; Laguna, sewing paper mache, weaving, making of wooden toys; Bulacan, sewing, embroidery, stitching of sequins & decor onto garments; Nueva Ecija, sewing & Broomstick making; Batangas, sewing; Manila, sewing & handicrafts; Pampanga, weaving of tikiw (a local fiber); Quezon, weaving of fans and baskets; Camarines Sur, sweing, hat, bag weaving, crocheting; Tarlac, clay jar making; Pangasinan, bamboo craft; Mandawe City, rattan craft; Bataan, weaving of baetong (another local fiber).

4. "Homeworkers of Southeast Asia: The Struggle for Social Protection in the Philippines", 1992.

4

WOMEN'S LITERACY AND EMPOWERMENT: THE NELLORE EXPERIENCE

Anita Dighe

Understanding Empowerment

The term empowerment has been bandied about so much in recent years that there is now a genuine danger of it being coopted as a 'development buzzword' that will meet the same fate as terms such as 'decentralization', 'people's participation' and the like. Despite this, it is important to understand what the term connotes. After attempting a review of literature, Shetty (1992) comes to the conclusion that empowerment is easy to 'intuit' but complex to define. But while it may be difficult to define it, one is able to understand its meaning when one sees the manifestation of what it implies. Thus an empowered individual would be one who experiences a sense of self-confidence and self-worth; a person who critically analyzes his/her social and political environment; a person who is able to exercise control over decisions that affect his/her life.

These are, however, not the only dimensions or facets that define empowerment. But while recognizing that empowerment is multi-faceted in nature, an attempt is made in this paper to examine how a literacy campaign has brought about women's empowerment. This is done by analyzing the anti-arrack (country liquor) agitation of Nellore district of Andhra Pradesh, which has shown how literacy played a significant role in raising the consciousness of village women so that they have now spearheaded an agitation that is fast engulfing the state of Andhra Pradesh.

In the last section of this paper an attempt is made to define some aspects/dimensions of empowerment as gleaned from the Nellore experience.

Literacy and the Anti-Arrack Agitation in Nellore District

The origin of the agitation can be traced back to the implementation of the Total Literacy Campaign (TLC) in the district two years ago. The campaign was officially launched in Nellore from January 1991 after an intensive preparation that lasted for four months. As in most TLC's, in Nellore the district collector was the official organizer and the prime mover of the campaign. Prior to launching the campaign, special efforts were made to elicit active support for the campaign by involving various political parties, bureaucrats of different development departments and organizations/ agencies/individuals representing a cross-section of people. Nellore district, with a literacy rate of 49% (national average 52.1% and state average 45.1%), had 450,000 non-literates in the 9-32 age group.

At the district level, the Collector, with a team of dedicated workers, constituted committees such as an academic committee to provide resource support to the campaign, and a cultural committee to use varied cultural forms such as song, drama, street plays, to convey to the non-literates the importance and the need for literacy.

In order to generate sufficient enthusiasm for literacy, wall writing, pamphleteering and even *padyatras* or processions were carried out. As the main purpose of the campaign was to enthuse not just the non-literates but also literates who were expected to become volunteers, *kalajathas* or cultural troupes were formed. A large number of these artists who came from the rural areas toured extensively in the district giving about 7,000 performances in an idiom and language that was understood by the village folk. The themes of the plays and songs involved problems encountered in life because of illiteracy- exploitation of labour, low wages, untouchability, powerlessness, inability to deal with social evils such as dowry, alcoholism, wife beating etc. The ideological content of the songs and plays underscored the importance of a people's movement for fighting illiteracy and of the relevance of literacy in understanding the nature of exploitation. Usually after the conclusion of a *Kalajatha* a call was given inviting volunteers to take up literacy work. Those who volunteered were asked to take an oath in the presence of the audience to work for the cause of literacy. The method became so popular that about 55,000 volunteers registered their names when the need was only for 40,000 (Shatrugna, 1992).

After creating a favourable climate for the campaign, a three-tiered training programme ensured that training of the functionaries at various levels was carried out. The literacy classes were started thereafter and an attempt was made by the volunteers to complete each of the three levels of literacy primers that were prepared for the campaign. That women's participation was high is borne out by the fact that of the 150,000 who completed the first phase of the campaign successfully, 100,000 were women. Most of them belonged to the Scheduled Castes and backward classes (Shatrugna, 1992).

As the main purpose of the campaign was not only gaining literacy skills but also development and empowerment, the post-literacy phase consisted of formation of *Jana Chetana Kendras* (Centres for People's Awareness) where the problems facing the villagers were discussed. The overall experience was that these kendras numbering 6000, were very popular with women taking a leading role in their functioning. As the women came together at the centres, they not only discussed the general problems faced by the village, but also shared their experiences and problems with one another.

The origin of the anti-arrack agitation was due to various factors. The role played by the CPI (Communist Party of India)-(ML) groups in bringing opposition to the arrack business on to the national agenda cannot be ignored. In the earlier phase of the work of the CPI (ML) groups (mainly in the Telegana districts), the focus was on reduction in the retail price of arrack. Subsequently, these groups took up the struggle to stop the arrack auctions and prevent the sale of arrack in the villages. In this effort, they received tremendous support from women who suffered daily at the hands of their inebriated husbands. But this effort of the CPI (ML) groups was 'top-down' - women's participation was elicited but they were not involved in the planning and decision-making processes. In other words, the initiative did not come from the women themselves.

What spurred the agitation was a small incident that took place in Doobagunta village in Nellore district. In this village, the women of the village stopped the vending of arrack after two men of the village had died after a bout of drinking. This incident had been preceded by a lot of discussion among the villagers (especially women) about the evils of excessive drinking. These discussions focused on how in many families the men drank all they earned and how women had to work and run the household on their earnings and get beaten daily in the bargain by their drunken husbands. The volunteers of Jana Vigyan Vedika organized by the CPI (M) cadre had played an important role in generating this consciousness (Balagopal, 1992).

In the post -literacy primer called *Chaduvu Velugu* (light of knowledge), the Doobagunta example was cited in the form of a lesson titled *Adavallu Ekamaithe* (if women unite). The text of the lesson was a story

how to cope with such revelations. I am often scared that I won't react in the best way, I think too I have been ambivalent about my role, feeling that the learners should be speaking with a counsellor trained in how to deal with such issues. Also I so badly want to change the situation for the learner that my own helplessness is tough for me to deal with -I feel so inadequate that I can not rescue her. I also discovered that by listening to a learner's account that she had not told before, I stepped into an unknown area, where the relationship of trust that has been developing is precious, but also demanding, and far beyond the limits of the literacy interaction. "[2]

Since then I had continued to tutor and have gone through many highs and lows as I tried to learn how to support this student but not rescue her, to encourage her to take up her own challenges rather than to lean on me. I have had to learn to set limits and support her in keeping them. I have had to become clear about the limits of my role, my responsibility and my time and avoid being drawn in to providing support that was beyond what I felt comfortable with. I too have had to take on the challenge to explore my own difficult childhood memories. Together we have learnt to develop a new form of relationship between tutor and student, respectful of both our needs.

This tutoring, though it often seems immensely difficult, has also been the most exciting literacy learning I have seen. I have often spoken about the value of literacy as allowing a person to read about the experience of others and write about her own experience, so finding the commonality of her own situation and distancing from her own experience to consider her own experience more fully. But I have never seen the value of this so powerfully as in tutoring focusing on experience of violence and abuse which have been hidden as a shameful secret. In community-based programmes in Toronto, most workers are adamant that we cannot work with issues of abuse because it is too difficult and too specialized an area. We are no therapists, I am often told, and should not be dabbling, and yet how can we separate literacy from this very crucial experience of so many women's lives, without denying women the "empowering' possibilities of literacy?

I feel that working in an individual tutoring situation has been invaluable for this woman who had never told anyone about the sexual, physical and mental abuse of her childhood. It has helped her build her sense of herself as someone who has a right to demand respect and she has become a vocal spokesperson for learners' rights. But I would prefer to move towards addressing these questions in a group, where women can break the isolation and find common ground. I have been exploring the possibilities of running a women's writing group jointly with a therapist from a community health centre. Neither the literacy programme nor the health centre saw this as a priority and we have not yet been able to find funds.

In Toronto, the field of work on issues of violence and literacy have remained extremely separate. I would like to explore a variety of ways of working collaboratively with women who have been abused, for example, with women working as counsellors in women's shelters, or feminist therapists, so that we can learn from their experience on how to deal sensitively, not only with the issues, but also with the relationships which develop. This could mean anything from talking with these women, to holding workshops on issues such as 'women and violence' or 'boundaries between women counselling and women being counselled', to rethinking and recorganizeing the ways and places that literacy happens.

Asking Questions About Women's Lives

During the research I carried out with women in rural, Maritime Canada, I explored the promise of literacy programmes. A link between violence and literacy became a powerful theme. In 1990 I wrote about the study:

> "Women's dependence on men, on inadequately paid work and on social service assistance is threaded through the lives of many of the women I interviewed. This dependence leads to violence: the violence of women's isolation in the household and sometime actual physical violence; the violence of the drudgery of inadequate, paid, hard, monotonous jobs; the violence of living on an inadequately paid, hard, monotonous jobs; the violence of living on an inadequate welfare income and enduring the humiliation of receiving assistance. Some of the violence is spoken of and shared, but much is endured in the silence and isolation of the home.

The illusion that illiteracy creates women's problems obscures the violence of many women's lives. Our attention is focused, not on the way women's lives are organized, but on women's failure to become literate. These women's lives are the context in which they experience the "promise" of literacy, and dream of how different their lives will be when they improve their education level. Yet for these women there is little chance that this promise will be fulfilled, particularly through many of the training programmes women are offered, which serve instead to embed them more firmly in their current lives".

I concluded the paper:

"Many of the women interviewed spoke about the importance of the challenge of an educational programme and the search for meaning in their lives, they wanted something in their minds "besides the everyday". Where programmes create space for the discussion of issues and for questioning the meaning of literacy, this can lead to exploring the unproblematic connection between education and "getting ahead". I this way the nature of the challenge of literacy can be broadened and the possibilities of social change strengthened."[3]

The importance of not simply offering women access to literacy for the sake of their children, and of helping them to do their traditional role better, is striking in Canada, as funding for women's programming is increasingly framed around "family literacy", as if literacy for women can only be justified for the sake of the children. Literacy workers are, I think, also frequently caught in the bind of wanting to justify the importance of funding for literacy programming and so inflating the promise of literacy, although workers know that for real change to happen literacy is not enough, much more needs to change in many women's lives. We do not want to destroy learners' dreams and hopes, but if women are to gain real power through literacy we must offer programmes which assist learners in understanding society rather than offering false promises.

Working on Women and Literacy

Workshops with women literacy workers under the title "women and literacy" are a place where we can explore what we are offering women learners in current literacy programmes. It has become almost obligatory at conferences and trainings to add in one session on women! Over the last few years I think my workshops on this topic have changed gradually from an emphasis simply on the needs of women learners to much more focus on the common ground and differences between women learners and workers (and of course I have been pressuring for moving away from adding women in as one session, asking whether all the rest of the curriculum is about men?). I have also begun to explore questions of feminism and literacy with broader audiences, focusing on the questions of why literacy is a feminist issue and why feminism is a literacy issue.

In one workshop women talked a lot about the conditions of their own work and the lack of "safe" places to reflect on their work with women with other women who shared some understanding. Women spoke of knowing that they must hide their feminism and sometimes also their sexual orientation for the sake of avoiding confrontation in their workplaces. One participant in this workshop said:

> " I am discouraged by the state of the social/economic context in which we work—as women, as feminists. How can we support poor women, ethnic women, ourselves as practitioners in the political scene in British Columbia? Lots of anger and frustration surfaced during this 'safe' workshop." [4]

The crucial question on how far you can support others in gaining power when your own power is limited, was raised. By the end of this conference women had decided to try to form a feminist literacy workers' network to create more safe places to discuss and develop our understanding and our practice. The Feminist Literacy Workers Network has since created a system of "wandering books" which people write in and pass on, and held one conference. Both these developments have been exciting, though perhaps not surprisingly, the conference did not always feel 'safe' to all women as there was much difference about whether everyone could identify with the concept of feminism or whether some concept of feminism or whether some people were comfortable with others' discussion about heterosexism and homophobia. The network continues, though we struggle to find the time to carry out the work needed, wanting the organization to become a place of communication where we can challenge and support each other, not become one more burden.

Training Literacy Workers

The training of literacy workers is another place for us to question our current practice in literacy programming in Toronto. Too often we design creative, innovative educational approaches for the women we work with, but ourselves participate in traditional hierarchical educational processes which can be extremely silencing and disempowering. This training course was shaped around a vision of bringing a wide variety of people together to learn from each other and look critically at our literacy work to build a stronger movement. The participants included paid workers, volunteers and adult learners, with a wide range of educational backgrounds. As the course progressed it became clear that exploring difference was one focus of the course. I sought throughout the process to create an environment of support and challenge for all participants. Before the course began the vision was described:

> "After all the research was completed we generated a vision for the course we were trying to create, building on the directions we were given in combination with our beliefs. Our goal became to create an innovative experiment in participatory education. We wanted a wide variety of people in the course who would learn from each other, from readings and from reflecting on their own experience. We wanted the course to strengthen and build the literacy movement, not simply build individual careers. We wanted to create an educational experience which could not be labelled as community college level, undergraduate, graduate or anything else. We wanted everyone to bring their knowledge, skills, experience and attitudes to the class ready to examine them critically and consider new ideas and possibilities. We hoped people would be challenged by each other, by new material from readings, tapes and lectures, and by the processes they engaged in the course. We hoped this challenge would lead them to develop their own thinking and increase their own knowledge and skills. We wanted to build a supportive environment where people would fell able to question their own beliefs and their own practices. We hoped people would take their learning in the course back to their programmes to enrich the work that is carried on there. We believed that the projects could lead to workshops, articles, radio programmes, manuals and bibliographies which would provide sources for others in the literacy movement to share in the learning. We decided to offer a certificate which described the course and indicated the amount of work required to complete it and we would ask each participant to write their own statement for the certificate so that it would be clear that each person had taken on their own challenge.
>
> We were eager for people of different backgrounds to work together in this course. We set the following criteria to make it clear who was eligible:
>
> - you have experience in literacy as a paid worker, a volunteer or a learner;
> - you want to stay involved in literacy while you are in the course;
> - you have a way to contribute to the literacy movement; and
> - you are prepared to question the ways we do literacy work and the ways we think about literacy."

We saw it as a central focus of the course to create a community which valued difference. We wanted to acknowledge differences amongst the group and encourage people to read or listen to different types of material as preparation, and to draw on and value all their varieties of experience. We wanted to break down the barriers often experienced when we assume differences based on our labels. We were trying to move away from categories of difference commonly used such as learner/tutor/graduate/dropout. We wanted to acknowledge differences of experience, skills, knowledge and approach in the class and work to avoid seeing these differences as hierarchical. We did not want to see being a learner as offering the truth about literacy or having, as one learner put it, "those big papers" as offering the truth. We had to be aware of the way these differences, and the usual prejudices in society, sometimes create barriers to good communication. Our aim in this course was to challenge the categories of difference that we usually live by and to create a situation where we would all learn to listen better and learn from the rich diversity of people in the course, which would be a " springboard for creative change within our lives" (as Audre Lorde puts it).[5] We wanted to create a climate of trust and respect where people would not assume that the usual labels told us all we need to know about a person, where we would all learn from those we do not usually look to as teachers. We did not want a group that all shared one approach. We hoped we would learn from our different viewpoints and our contrasts.

The traditional education system operates through continual streaming, though sometimes it is quite hidden. At all levels the system suggests it is possible to label one person as smarter than another, one as more advanced than another, one as having more knowledge and so able to teach one with less knowledge and so only able to learn. Traditional education ignores the fact that we all come into an educational process with different skills, experience and knowledge and it judges us only on whether we leave with the same knowledge. The many people in literacy programmes demonstrate that the hierarchical system (the way of working that says we can know who is better than another, and label everything and everybody in grades) in schooling doesn't work, or works only to tell some people that they are clever, successful, important, while it tells other that they are stupid, can not learn, have nothing to offer. In this course we wanted to demonstrate that something other than this traditional education based on so many labels and levels was possible, that we could invent new creative ways of learning together. I wanted to help everyone to take on their own challenges and to go away having learnt from the processes, the content, and many of the individuals in the course[6].

In the course we sought to challenge the traditional hierarchical notions of education and to create a microcosm of a society which did not label or categorize according to hierarchies, but which also valued our differences. It was clear during the course that many of the prevalent hierarchies and prejudices in society were still operating. I would not want to suggest that we can break them down simply through individual change. But we were able to create an environment with sufficient trust to begin to explore difference and the meaning of privilege and oppression and the categories of class/gender/race/ethnicity/ ability as well as the categories particular to the literacy movement of learner/tutor/paid worker. In this way, though we were not focusing solely on gender in this course, we were participating in a vision for a form of education which would offer challenge and support for all participants, rather than building educational privilege and strengthening inequalities.

Creating Limits

Lastly I had wanted to speak about the importance for women educators to consider our own needs and set our limits in such a way that we are not always overstretched, but to do that I would stretch my own limits! So I will end saying that when we think of women, power and empowerment we cannot afford to ignore ourselves and the model we are offering the women we work with.

In all these sites of women's education I have been exploring I would argue that we need to assess critically the detailed practice of both our literacy teaching and our teacher training. We need to reassess how to acknowledge and work with women's experience of violence within the field of literacy teaching. We must consider the value of all of this work in enabling us to envision and move towards a changed, egalitarian society.

Notes:-

1. *This was written for "Wandering Book", a project of the Feminist Literacy Workers Network. Wandering books are sent from woman to woman in the network and we each add an open letter to other women in the network. They move slowly round the network and two years later I am still waiting for the book I started to return to me!*
2. *This was also part of my Wandering Book entry.*
3. *From the problem of illiteracy and the promise of literacy, in Hamilton, M., Barton, D. & Ivanic R. (eds.) Worlds of Literacy. Clevedon: Multilingual Matters. 1992.*
4. *Workshop participant's comment from Talking about lives: Planning Programs for Women, in Literacy 2000, Make the next ten years matter. Conference Summary, ed.*

Bossort, Patty et al. New Westminster: Douglas College, 1990.

5. In *"Age, Race, Class, and Sex: Women Redefining Difference" in Sister Outsider, Essays and Speeches by Audre Lorde. Freedom, CA: The Crossing Press, 1984.*

6. *From the curriculum package for Literacy Workers' Training Course: Building the Movement, Metro Toronto Movemement for Literacy, Toronto, Canada, forhtcoming.*

8

ILLITERACY ERADICATION IN VIETNAM

PAST ACHIEVEMENTS AND ORIENTATION FOR DEVELOPMENT IN THE NEW STAGE

Cu Quang Mac

For nearly half of the century, in extremely difficult circumstances Vietnamese people have perserveringly realized literacy programmes and unceasingly sought every way to enhance the people's cultural standard. In September 1945 when the Democratic Republic of Vietnam came into being, over 90% of the population were illiterate. Today Vietnam is ranked among countries that have already achieved high literacy rate (over 88%). To appreciate the gains, this paper documents the history of the literacy efforts of the Vietnamese people as well as the challenges and prospectus they face in the future.

1. The History of Illiteracy Eradication and Achievements

The illiteracy eradication undertaking of Vietnam has undergone many different stages. In each stage, the enhancement of the people's cultural standard is always paid great attention to, even when there were so many difficulties. The raising of the people's educational level is regarded as a factor closely related to the sense of mastering one's own destiny, the ability for development, living conditions improvement and the sense of national defense of the people.

Illiteracy eradication is a long and continuous process, involving the efforts of many sectors of the people, and of them the core are the teachers and educational administrators. The movement of illiteracy eradication has overcome thousands of difficulties and won great achievements: from 95 per cent of the people illiterate in the time before August Revolution to more than 10 per cent at present.

The history of illiteracy eradication in Vietnam has passed through the following phases:

- Before the year 1945: The fight against illiteracy was linked with the movement for national salvation.
- The Domocratice Republic of Vietnam was founded (2 September 1945), the fight against illiteracy became a policy of the State and the first campaign of illiteracy eradication was launched by President Ho Chi Minh himself. This mobilization continued to develop in nine years of the resistance against the French Colonialists (1946-1954).
- In 1954, the North was completely liberated. After the Campaign on literacy (1956-1958), illiteracy was basically eradicated in the North.
- With the great victory in spring 1975, the South was completely liberated, illiteracy eradication was seen as the urgent task by the government.
- With the completion of the campaign of illiteracy eradication (1976-78), illiteracy was basically eradicated in all 21 provinces of the South.

The subsequent discussion elaborates on the context the gains of these phases.

A. Before August Revolution in 1945, Vietnam was a colony of the French, the economy was backward, and 95% of the Vietnamese were illiterate. In this setting the Association for National Language Dissemination was founded and relied on the intellectuals to launch the anti-illiteracy movement. The Association encouraged its members to collect money and organized literacy classes for the working people in the pagoda, village communal houses or schools.

At the same time, the Association developed a minimum programme necessary for the illiterate adults consisting of two kinds of classes: 'primary' and 'higher primary'.

- The objective of the 'primary class' was to enable the learners to read and writer Vietnamese script (national language) and do some simple operations such as addition and subscription.
- The objective of 'higher primary class' was to strengthen the results achieved by the learners in primary class, and consolidate the reading and writing skills, and help the learners to perform 4 operations: addition, substraction, multiplication and division, solve some simple problems and grasp some common knowledge.

Particularly, the Association created a new method for teaching Vietnamese script for the adults in order to arouse interest for them and facilitate their learning. The training for teachers on the contents and methods of teaching and organizing literacy classes was given special attention.

As the anti-illiteracy movement was strongly launched, it took root in the masses and became a voluntary action of the people. From some scattered centers at the beginning, it gradually expanded to many areas in the whole country.

Through the activists of the anti-illiteracy movement from 1939 to the beginning of 1945, the Association helped over sixty thousand people become literate and assisted over ten thousand people to receive post literacy education.

B. With the success of the August Revolution in 1945 the Democratic Republic of Vietnam was founded. In the first meeting of the Council of the government on September 3, 1945, President Hồ Chi Minh regarded illiteracy eradication as the second task after the anti-famine task. In this connection, the Government issued three decrees on September 8, 1945:

- **Decree N. 17:**
  "An anti-illiteracy campaign was launched in the whole Vietnam country",

- **Decree N. 19:**
  "In the whole country evening classes for literacy were organized for peasants and workers".

- **Decree N. 20:**
  "In the time to wait for the establishments of a compulsory primary education, the learning of Vietnamese script (national language) will be compulsory and free for all people from now on....".

Through these, illiteracy eradication was institutionalized. In October 1945, President Ho Chi Minh issued "An Appeal to the whole Vietnamese people for Illiteracy Eradication" where he exhorted that "illiteracy eradication is a task of the whole society, the literate has the obligation to teach the illiterate". Furthermore, he emphasized that "Women all the more have to learn. For the long time women were held back. This is the time for you, sisters to try to be equal with men....".

Though the famine occurred, an illiteracy eradication campaign was still launched. In addition to schools where literacy classes were organized, many pagodas, temples and private houses were used for literacy classes everywhere. With the flexible way after only one year (8 September 1945-8 September 1946), there were 95,660 people involved in teaching for 2,520,600 learners in 74,950 classes.

C. On December 19, 1946 the 9 years resistance against the French colonialists broke out. The war upset the socio-economic life and daily activities of the people therefore the Vietnamese anti-illiteracy campaign had to change its content and methods of working to be relevant with the new requirements "Resisting while Learning' in order to fulfill the duty "Eradicating illiteracy while developing education". The contents and curriculum were readjusted and supplemented according to the orientation: teaching how to read and write, teaching arithmetic and basic scientific knowledge, and how to grow vegetables and raise animals and as well as teaching how to engage in work for the resistance for national salvation.

The main area of activity of the Anti illiteracy campaign in that stage was moved to the rural areas. The force of anti-illiteracy personnel was supplemented quantitatively, including the men in the units of the armed forces who stayed in the rural areas, and personnel of government agencies and organization from central to local level. The body of teachers and personnel specialized in anti-illiteracy work still played a key role.

After nine years with great efforts and perseverance over 10 million people became literate, illiteracy was completely eradicated in 10 provinces, 80 districts, 1,424 communes and 7,248 villages.

D. In 1954, the North of Vietnam was completely liberated and there were still 3 million illiterate people in the age of 12-50. To help economic and education recovery and development the Government launched the illiteracy eradication campaign in 3 years (1956-1958). The Steering Boards for illiteracy eradication from central to provincial, district and communal levels were established to mobilize resources in order to ensure the success of the campaign.

After the war, the country was divided into two zones. Though there were so many socio-economic difficulties, the movement for illiteracy eradication reached its top at the end of 1958 particularly as a result of the concrete guidance from central to local level and perseverance of the body of teachers and administrators responsible for illiteracy eradication.

As a result of these, 2,161,362 became literate, among them 231,719 people in the mountainous areas and 1,929,643 people in the delta areas.

Up to January 1959 illiteracy was basically eradicated in the deltas and midlands of the North, 93% of the population in the age of 12-50 knew how to read and write while in the mountainous areas, the undertaking of illiteracy eradication was still conducted in the following years and closely linked with the movement of complementary education for the lower and upper secondary levels.

E. After the great victory in Spring 1975, the South was completely liberated. According to the data of the survey conducted in the beginning of 1976, there were over 3 million illiterate eradication was regarded as an urgent task to quickly eliminate the backward status, and then facilitating the economic recovery and development after the war.

The illiteracy eradication campaign was launched in all provinces of the South. The Front for Eliminating Ignorance was established under the close leadership of the Steering Board for illiteracy eradication of all levels from central to grassroots. The effective activities of this system could mobilize the whole people to take part in the campaign. Again the teachers formed the core of the movement with the dynamic and creative method of working.

Consequently, illiteracy was eradicated in all 21 provinces and cities of the South in February 1978, where 1,323,670 people became literate satisfying 94% of the objective as proposed by above mentioned campaign. When the campaign ended, there were still many illiterate people in the mountainous provinces like Tay Nguyen and some remote areas in the Mekong River Delta, so illiteracy eradication programmes are still being implemented.

F. Still in 1990, in the whole country there were over 2 million people from 15-35 years who were illiterate and 2.3 million children in the age of 6-14 who did not go to school. At that time the number of illiterate adults in mountainous areas was 747,300 and 650,639 in Mekong River Delta provinces, comprising 38% and 33% respectively of the total illiterates in the whole country while the population of these two zones are 14% and 10% as compared with that of the whole country.

To serve the socio-economic renovation of the country, education is considered of primary importance to enhance the training level of the people to become part of the workforce and as well as foster the talents. Therefore, at the end of 1989, the State established a National Committee for Illiteracy Eradication with the following objectives: in 1995 illiteracy will be eradicated for 1 million people; and in the year 2000 half of the number of illiterate people at present will be decreased.

Furthermore, the criteria for people to be acknowledged as literate was enhanced. Before the year 1980, a learner needed only to finish grade one but now he must pass grade three to be acknowledged as a literate. The contents, curriculum and learning materials were also revised to implement that policy.

As a result of the effective activities of the Steering Boards for illiteracy eradication from central to local levels from 1990-1993, nearly one million adults were mobilized to go to literacy classes, among them nearly 50% were acknowledged as literates according to the new criteria.

II. Orientations for the Illiteracy Eradication in the Years to Come

Notwithstanding all the above mentioned achievements, there is still a long way to go. For example, from 1990 to 1993, only 10-13% of the illiterates were mobilized to attend class and only 38% of those learners were acknowledged as literate, though all branches of all levels had actively coordinated with the branch of education and tried hard to eradicate illiteracy. Up to April 1994 only 15% of the provinces, 25% of the districts and 37% of the communes in the whole country were acknowledged to attain the national criteria on literacy and universalization of primary education.

One problem that needs attention is that 64% of the total of illiterates in the whole country center are in the less economically developed areas, with difficult living conditions and have problems in communication and transportation. For instance, the number of illiterate adults in mountainous provinces is 599,260 and in the Mekong River Delta provinces it is 560,000 comprising 33% and 31% respectively of the total number of illiterates in the whole country.

There are also large numbers of adult illiterates among the minority groups, with the Lolo group having 96% while H'mong has 88% and the Dao, 75%.

Finally, the illiteracy rate of women is generally higher than that of men especially in the most difficult areas as can be gleaned from the Table1.1

Table 1.1-Number of Illiterates and Per centage of Women Illiteracy in Selected Areas in Vietnam

Area	The number of illiterates	Woman illiterates	Per centage
Midlands, mountainous area	348,734	222,115	6.369%
Tay Nguyen	106,885	79,394	74.28%
Former 4th zone	121,021	68,960	56.98%
Red River Delta	84,344	47,913	56.81%

The above mentioned situation poses a challenge which requires active policies and objectives and concrete solutions. Only by carrying out universalization of primary education, literacy and post literacy education at the same time can illiteracy be thoroughly eradicated. Therefore special attention should be paid to the mobilization of children in the school age, prevention of school drop-outs and decrease of repetition rate. At the same time, favorable conditions and high priority for illiteracy eradication should be given to the force of young laborers especially women. It is also necessary to mobilize every resource for illiteracy eradication in mountainous provinces, Mekong River Deltas, Tay Nguyen and coastal communes. From now to the year 2000, eradication of illiteracy for at least 250,000 people and organization of post-literacy courses for 200,000 people are planned.

To realize the above mentioned objectives the following solutions are proposed:

- Diversification of various forms of teaching and learning by grade/level and non grade/level. Apart from the consolidation of primary schools, alternate classes and classes at home should be strengthened.
- Encourage the literate people to teach illiterate ones.
- Organize groups of volunteers for illiteracy eradication in areas with many difficulties.
- Develop programmes of literacy education with the close and effective coordination between the education sector and other organizations such as Youth Union, Women Association, Peasants Association and Association of Veterans.
- Improve the curriculum, develop and produce adequate literacy and postliteracy materials according to the direction of linking closely the teaching to read and write with the teaching of functional knowledge appropriate to each target audience (women, peasants, workers, minority groups); in order to help them generate their income and improve living conditions.
- Provide adequate teachers specializing in illiteracy eradication in communes where there are many illiterate people.
- Strengthen the training of teachers and administrators on illiteracy eradication and continuing education.
- The Ministry of Education and Training, specifically the Department of Continuing Education, should have a plan of Action for literacy and post literacy education in 1995-2000.
- Increase international cooperation for exchanging experience and learning from other countries, take advantage of the assistance of organizations and individuals for the illiteracy eradication in Vietnam.

9

THE BANGLADESH GOVERMENT LITERACY INITIATIVE:

THE INTEGRATED NONFORMAL EDUCATION PROGRAM (INFEP)

Nilufer Rahman

In order to achieve the objectives of universal primary education (UPE)/education for all (EFA), non-formal education activities have been designed to complement and strengthen the efforts in the formal education. With this end in view, in May 1992 the Integrated Non-Formal Education Programme (INFEP) was launched under the Primary and Mass Education Division (PMED). INFEP is a three year experimental project for capacity building and seeks to institutionalize a broad based system of literacy and non-formal education for children, adolescents and adults as the first step towards achieving the long-term objective of making non-formal education a complementary process in the strategy of human resources development along with formal education. This would necessitate close government-NGO collaboration and people's involvement in making millions of people, mostly living in rural areas, literate.

Under the aegis of INFEP, literacy centers have been opened in 69 thanas (sub-district) of 64 districts. Out of the total number of adult literacy centers, some of which have already closed and those which are functioning, more than fifty per cent of the centers are earmarked for women learners. It may also be mentioned here that as a part of the strategy women are given preference in running literacy centers and as supervisors of these centers. They represent 54% of literacy teachers. In the proposed strategy of total literacy movement mobilizing full support of people, women would have a greater involvement in social mobilization and programmed implementation.

involved in economic, political and social decision-making processes" (Depthnews, 1992).

Empowerment is better defined as a concept than in practical terms, which leaves many questions unanswered. This is particularly true with education for empowerment. How does one educate to empower? How does learning for empowerment differ from other programmes for women? How should learning be structured? How can its impact be measured?

This paper discusses the training programme which is part of the UNDP funded project "Expansion of Skills- based Literacy Programme of Women", better known as Educate to Empower from the title of the manual it produced. The project represents an effort to answer some of the above questions. The paper also raises some other questions related to education for women's empowerment.

The Training Programme

The experience of the training programme to be discussed arose from a series of regional training workshops. Four of the workshops produced curricula and learning materials. The others designed reading materials for women with limited reading skills.

In the first group, three workshops were run by UNESCO and funded by the UNDP as part of its project RAS/88/013, Expansion of Skills-based Literacy Programmes for Women. The fourth was financed by ESCAP and UNICEF with technical support from UNESCO-PROAP. The second group is part of UNESCO's regular programme.

Five workshops were held between July 1990 and July 1992, with 20-25 participants in each. Fourteen countries of Asia and the Pacific were represented: Bangladesh, Bhutan, China, Laos, India, Japan, Myanmar, Nepal, Pakistan, Papua New Guinea, Philippines, Sri Lanka, Thailand and Viet Nam.

All countries share a common characteristic. Their women are unable to give their best to the national development.

The resulting curricula and materials help prepare women for self-development as active members of their family, community and nation. They seek overall personal development and account for the notorious double responsibility that women shoulder as economic producers and as mothers and wives.

The above approach concentrates on imparting knowledge, skills and attitudes that help women operate as efficient and equal partners of men. It is important to stress collaboration between the sexes and to make sure that empowerment does not mean "pitting women against men."

Outcome of the Regional Workshops

1. The profile of the empowered woman.
2. A manual to train in preparing programmes for empowerment.
3. 70 curricular units complete with teaching guides, learner workbooks, posters, flipcharts, booklet etc.
4. 29 picture books for women with limited reading skills.
5. The training experience gained throughout the workshops is their invisible "benefit". The work will reach its highest point when ex-participants proceed to invest their experience in their own workshops at the national/subnational levels and build on whatever they learned.

Major Components of Training

1. Gender Issues

Participants spell out and explain their long-held values concerning the respective roles of women and men. It is a summary of the traditional view: areas of work assigned to men and women; distribution of access to resources and their control; access to and respective ways of earning and spending.

Gender issues are handled with care since they involve questioning one's own attitudes, values and beliefs, frequently the very essence of one's existence. Activities are planned to ensure that all opinions are respected. In this way, participants become open to reconsidering their values.

The nature of the activities also plays an important role in creating a non-threatening climate. Group work in which peer support is clearly present is reassuring. Well-timed questions from peers also help participants entertain new views without feeling pressured into accepting them.

Training materials are more varied, interesting and appealing than usual as they are to induce new attitudes. Audio-visuals are most effective for the purpose because they present cases in which participants recognize their shortcomings without being directly challenged.

The video, *The Impossible Dream*, produced by the United Nations' Information Office, and UNFPA's video, *Women-Key to the Future*, are two examples of effective training tools. Participants also enjoy video films produced by various countries in the region. These videos are used with discussion guidelines. Sometimes, editing is necessary to bring the contents of the video to the point.

Other exercises, such as drawing and the Agree/Disagree game, lead groups to reflect on their beliefs, are fun, and reveal a lot without threatening anyone. Peer pressure is another means to cause an individual to re-examine her ways, consider new options, and adopt or reject them.

Groups have come up with exercise models that intensify the scrutiny of gender issues by assigning a framework of action. In one case they suggest assigning their future learners to write short dialogues for well-known male and female cartoon characters caught in expressive scenes of conflict, debate, or reconciliation.

Workshops have revealed that enlightened male participants exert enormous influence on the traditional gender perceptions of other participants.

In contrast to other skills, the ability to change gender attitudes takes more time to develop and must be continuously reinforced. Gender issues are therefore interwoven with other activities for a more comprehensive and facile treatment of the new concepts.

Before participants embark on preparing their own individual curricular units (or learning programmes), they develop their own "Profile of the Empowered Women". (For the latest version of the profile, see below).

2. *Work Skills*

Work was the major focus throughout the training programme as it imparts integrity and a sense of belonging.

Experience in the region and elsewhere shows that educational programmes for women often fail because they do not include training women in lucrative skills (Dighe 1989). Sewing, embroidery, tailoring, and handicrafts alone cannot sustain women's interest for long because they are not earning them much income (Line and Foss 1990).

The programme has shifted to emphasize skills that women want and need to know. Most popular among these are agricultural skills, as confirmed by the needs analysis conducted prior to the training.

Examples of topics selected by participants are: planting apple trees (Bhutan), making century eggs for sale (China), integrated farming (Laos), rice planting (Viet Nam), selling dried fish (Myanmar), raising pigs (Viet Nam and Papua New Guinea), food catering (Papua New Guinea) and brick-making (Thailand).

Enchancing women's productive skills without lessening their other responsibilities has overburdened women. Several curricular materials dwell on promoting sharing of household responsibility between husband and wife and other family members.

Although some work skills belong in the "feminine" category, the curricular units go well beyond the mere "enabling" functions.

The new subjects on the learning list include planning, management and entrepreneurial habits. They are helpful in any work area. Building up positive self-image and strengthening of women's self-confidence also receives due attention.

In addition, the workshops emphasized that, at present, in many countries "unfeminine" skills are necessary for women to cope effectively. Among them the use of technology, particularly in farming tasks, such as water-powered units for rice pounding, plumbing and water pumps maintenance, and heating.

3. Literacy and Numeracy

The workshops promoted combined treatment of gender issues, work skills, and the three R's through exercises that ask future teachers to employ terms and concepts common to all of the above. If the skills are joined into the fabric, the real-life relevance of one reinforces that of the other. However, old habits die hard. From time to time, in a bizarre way, learners insist on using words with functional content such as "groups", "loans', "credits", and "organization" in odd combinations with words like "cupboard" or "chair". Another problem consists in linking numeracy skills to other skills in meaningful ways.

Contents

The attributes outlined below in the "Profile of the Empowered Woman" and the detailed needs analysis of the target population are two important bases on which content selection is made. The profile is important because it brings into the picture the qualities desired in women learners.

The Profile of the Empowered Woman

The empowered woman appreciates the time she spends on domestic work and outside the home. She is aware that overwork is harmful to her physical and mental condition and that health is vital. She is able to question her double responsibility and seeks help from others to have enough leisure to spend on learning and participating in the social and political life of the community.

The empowered woman appreciates the value of her contribution whether remunerated or not. She is aware that she has tremendous potential to contribute to the progress of her family, community and nation. With that understanding, she is confident of her worth, is open-minded and can appreciate others.

Aware of her productivity, she seeks to improve her skills and knowledge continuously. She has enough information sources (such as extension services, available and relevant technology) and makes sure she benefits from them. She appreciates the knowledge gained from reading and reads regularly.

The empowered woman understands that she is a human being and can control her own life. Hence, she could and should question the family and social practices which negatively affect her. She seeks to get scientific insights into superstitions, and challenges those which are unjust to women.

She has freedom of movement and expression on a par with men. She appreciates her strengths and weaknesses and seeks self-improvement.

She can lead and serve as a positive role model for other women.

The empowered woman is aware of her rights as a citizen and protects them actively. She is convinced of her equality with men. She knows which laws and legal processes treat women unfairly and seeks to use her legal knowledge to protect her own and other women's rights.

The empowered woman respects herself and dares take credit and responsibility for her contribution and action. She looks for options and makes informed decisions. She dares to be different and creative.

The empowered woman appreciates and supports other women. She is aware that organization means strength and seeks to strengthen her organizational, management and leadership skills.

The empowered woman is aware that her health is related to the number of children she has. She respects the dignity of womanhood and appreciates daughters in the same way she does sons.

The empowered woman nurtures herself. She wants everybody to understand that, as a human being, she is entitled to happiness in the same way that others are. She has a zest for life.

The training manuals, *Educate to Empower*, attempts to translate one or more of the above desirable attributes into learning content of the curricular units or reading materials.

Content Presentation

The debate on the desirable qualities of the empowered woman centers on competence, proficiency and behavior attributes. It also spells out an implicit scenario in which the woman sheds the yoke of the numerous social, cultural and economic roles.

It is possible that in a few countries, a small number of women may possess these qualities. However, these women remain a small minority in any country—so widespread, cross-nationally, are the constraints to emancipation.

Educate to Empower attaches equal importance to the productive and reproductive functions of the woman. Emphasis on one to the exclusion of the other either prevents women from being economically active or shaddles them with additional and burdensome responsibilities. Programmes developers must ensure that the contents of a programme help women raise their awareness regarding their conditions and question the asymmetrical relations within the household and society.

In the final analysis, all the knowledge, skills or attitudes promoted by a programme must be useful in providing learners with knowledge, skills and attitudes which equip them to take actions for changes which will improve their status in society and lead to their emancipation.

Monitoring and Evaluation

Monitoring is done informally. Visits to focal point and target populations offer better insights into the project realities and give an idea of improvements required and lessons learned. Informal discussion and contact with life in target areas, along with the analysis of curricular materials, help make them realistic and relevant. This reflect the quality of the national training which, in turn, echoes the degree of effectiveness of the regional training.

PROAP questionnaires went regularly to all participating countries to assess the pace of progress and provide timely assistance to implementing agencies.

Monitoring of national training often indicates that generating gender sensitive curriculum and materials is, indeed, an uphill struggle. Without proper guidance and deliberate and timely intervention, the products would have concentrated on the role of women as mothers and wives. A remedial re-orientation is often necessary to make up for omissions on other roles.

Informal reports from participants indicates the degree of their involvement in disseminating or multiplying the product of a wokshop. PROAP communicates with individuals that have had regional training to check if they play an optimal role at the national level and if any support from PROAP could enhance their output.

Multiplying Effects

Educate to Empower assumes that each participant in a regional workshop is to organize a similar workshop in their respective country. The role of the latter is to educate new groups and develop better books focused on women's empowerment.

Thus far, at least two workshops have been held in each participating country. Some have had enough resources and stamina to organize up to five worshops. At the national level, training had to be adapted to suit specific requirements.

China concentrates on a handful of skills, among them pig-raising, conservation of oranges, mushroom culture and installing heating systems. They are making plans to cover other areas considered necessary for women, such as heating and plumbing.

Bhutan, with no previous experience in non-formal education, organized two national workshops to cover a host of topics from family planning and sharing of housework responsibilities to health and agricultural technology.

Bangladesh has conducted an operational workshop to adjust existing curriculum and materials to cover empowerment.

The manual, *Educate to Empower*, which documents goals, objectives, learning activities, time and materials required, is now being translated into national languages for use as training guidelines.

Lessons Learned

Training which seeks to change long-held attitudes requires enormous sensitivity and care. A supportive climate must exist to open minds to alternative ways of thinking and make them more receptive to change.

Methods seeking attitudinal change have to be participatory and non-threatening. A built-in component should provide a setting of safety and tolerance in which participants could intelligently question their own attitude, values and beliefs.

A thorough analysis of needs must precede the get-together phase so that the product addresses priority concerns. Work skills alone do not empower women. Programmes for self-reliance have to include confidence building and other survival skills, such as communication, management and problem-solving.

To integrate work skills, developers have to draw on the latest expertise in relevant fields. To be accurate and fruitful, programmes base on rice-planting, for example, should take adequate advice from agricultural specialists.

Training programmes are better received as a package of vocational skills, reading and writing, gender orientation, and leadership training.

Numeracy and literacy must be integrated into functional contents in meaningful ways.

Extra-curricular activities fostering group solidarity are as necessary as the technical component. This takes a great deal of planning and active involvement of the group. While women enjoy priority as workshop leaders in this area, male participants with positive background and experience are very helpful in effecting a change in gender attitudes both in women and men.

The key to success in this type of training is participation. Active involvement makes the group feel the programme is their "own" creation and strengthens commitment when reproducing the workshop at the national or sub-national levels.

Empowering women and raising their status requires more than changes in women alone. The same has to happen to men's attitudes and behavior. This is why materials produced should reach both men and women audiences.

Discrepancies persist between the level of participants' background and experience. Trainers need to draw on the positive potential of this reality. Strong, advanced participants could be coaches for those who need help. Resource persons need to be particularly responsive to participants' individual needs and problems.

Discussion

Contents Selection

Experience in implementing *Educate to Empower* and in assessing educational materials leads to two important conclusions.

1. Self-reliance is undoubtedly a necessary condition for emancipation. Yet, it is by no means the only one, and certainly not a sufficient condition. Millions of poor, discriminated and marginalized women, throughout the world, live in highly unfavorable socio-economic and cultural conditions. They can survive and help their households do the same because they are already highly self-reliant. Yet, they remain victimized as far as human rights are concerned.
2. Competence in staying self-sufficient turns into proficiency when there is a will for action on the part of the learners.

The presentation technique is frequently used in a story/case history format. The stories often show a woman or woman overcome a problem, leading to an improved position. However, a very large number of such materials skim glibly over the most difficult events in the story. These are the parts which have a critical, positive impact on the woman succeeding. Such glossing-over leaves the reader with no competencies, and certainly no proficiencies, to replicate the even in her life.

An increasing volume of materials on women's education has become available in the region. Particularly since the 1980s, attempts have been made to analyze materials specially designed for women (UNESCO

1990, 1992).

More often than not, the materials, two-dimensionally presented, by themselves, are too static to bring about changes in readers' self-concept. Without carefully planned activities to complement the reading materials, e.g., guided discussion, games, shows, role-play and simulation, and under circumstances of extensive and rigid discrimination against women, the story could easily take the aura of myths-entertaining yet impossible to believe.

The following is an excerpt from an actual booklet written for women. It demonstrates shortfalls of such static materials.

> "....She expressed to her uncle and auntie her keenness to learn how to read and write. Her uncle Jagat *promised* to help her. He therefore approached the village panchayat to start a functional literacy class for women. He was informed that in order to start a functional literacy class, a proper accommodation for a Women's Center was needed, and 15-20 women and girls should be willing to join the Center. It was a difficult task to convince the other women to join the Center. However, *with the active support* of the village people, within a year, a functional literacy class was started."

The above is typical of the glossing over of the most difficult operations, such as those italicized. The uncle readily agreed! The other women were easily convinced to join the center! The village people were forthcoming! What exactly had to occur to make this happen? Surely that is of first importance for success!

Other Examples are:

She communicated the idea to the women's club. (How?)

With active support of the women, she formed a club. (How was the active support produced?)

He *convinced* the village head that literacy classes should be started. (How?)

The idea was accepted. (What made them accept?)

Women appreciated her decision. (What made them appreciate it and not castigate her?)

Beenu *convinced* her mother-in-law that a boy or a girl is of equal significance. (How?)

Left with no answers to the magic "how", the readers or learners would hardly achieve competence in replicating the "story" in their lives. The events described remain hard to believe enact in the disadvantaged scenario of a victimized woman. Fantasies do not raise self-respect. Quite the contrary!

At times, the stories indicate the formation of women's groups for action—a realistic alternative to the very rare event of a woman going it alone. But how does a group function effectively? Again a number of competencies and proficiencies are required. Also, is the "learning" or empowerment only in "storage" competencies, with none of the range of proficiencies needed to take action to remedy the disadvantaged situation of women?

Is it that the learning for empowerment only produces pent-up competence, and no proficiency is necessary to correct the situation of women?

If current materials do indeed provide for some awareness raising, then the next development of learning events, and materials to support it, may focus squarely on action, to enhance self-reliance and emancipation. In other words, empowerment has to bring about actions to correct disempowering conditions.

Clearly, the two-dimensional, static reading materials do not suffice to raise women's awareness on gender issues. Other materials and activities will need to be carefully designated to complement the materials. The materials themselves could serve as a starting point for debates, discussions, role- playing, etc.

Questions related to this will include:

1. What important information gaps need to be filled for each important topic?

Example:

What laws regulate workers' rights to paid holidays? Have there been workers who insist on these rights? How did they do it? If they failed, what are the obstructing factors? if they demand paid holidays, what would be the employer's possible reaction? What conditions are necessary for success in obtaining paid holidays?

2. Once the information gaps are identified, how can learning activities be designed to ensure that learners will want to take actions to improve the situation, i.e., to demand their rights?

3. What works best in presenting information? Should the teacher deliver the same knowledge repeatedly to reinforce the effect? Should

she use the same methods to present the same information? Or is a single presentation sufficient? What is the general practice now?

4 What are other materials to strengthen existing materials, e.g., audio-visuals, etc.?

Training Techniques

People teach as they are taught. If participants are expected to train others to empower women learners, they first have to empower themselves. Training must therefore involve them in ways that enhance confidence in further training.

Training programmes have applied the following:

- group discussion
- question and answer
- songs and games
- creative work (e.g., songs and dances, drawing, story and poem writing)
- short talks, presentations
- individual work and coaching
- case study
- analysis of sample materials
- preparation of actual materials/ curriculum.

Eighty per cent of the time goes to activities other than lectures or talks by resource persons as these are too trainer-centered. Evaluation indicates that participants enjoy activities that they describe as innovative. Nevertheless, better updates on training methodology are necessary to increase overall effectiveness in future training.

Questions related to training of trainers or adult educators will include:

What are existing training methods and practices, their strengths and weakness?

- How effective are various methods tailored to training on sensitive subjects such as gender issues?
- How could innovative approaches be used to enhance the effectiveness of training.
- Do current methods enhance women's status? How?
- How to ensure that the best methods enter general practice? What methods work best with experienced teachers? And novices?

Empowerment and Policy Makers

The term empowerment has been a nonstarter in Asia and the Pacific. Many so-called traditional societies have been vehemently nagative towards any programmes or projects claiming to focus on the empowerment approach (Ramachandran 1985). The term is interpreted to have militant overtones akin to "pitting women against men". It has evoked a great deal of antagonistic feelings among policy makers seeing this as a threat to the stability of the family institution or even the human race.

Somewhere, somehow, something went wrong. Policy makers, most of whom are men, have distanced themselves from even considering the concept. Their assumption: there cannot be empowerment of women without disempowerment of men. Some have explicity expressed concerns over men's potential loss of "control" over their wives and daughters. Others fear, genuinely, that they will not be able to respond to new demands arising from empowerment education.

Even when policy makers—indeed men in general, are supportive of the empowerment concept, their support remains largely intellectual. They do not deem it necessary to insist on actions leading to positive changes. This may be compared to what happens in many domestic situations. The husband recognizes that strictures on women are unfair. He cannot, however, give up any of the foothold he has acquired in his job or any of his pay in order to share responsibility for the children.

The question facing policy makers, with traditional values regarding the roles of women and men in society, is whether such changes are desirable and worth of support. Thus far, advocates of Education for Empowerment have failed to convince policy makers to see the value of embracing women's empowerment as one of the necessary prerequisites for advancing society. Arguably, when one examines the situation of women's education in Asia and the Pacific, it could be said that no country in the region has made substantial progress in promoting women's empowerment.

One thing is clear, empowerment education will not make a difference in women's status on a large scale without supportive political will. Pockets of successful projects will not suffice to build a critical mass of empowered women (and enlightened men) to sustain any positive changes. Winning the support of policy makers is therefore a sine-qua-non for empowerment education if the latter is to help promote women's advancement in society.

The question is: what types of arguments can one use to gain policy makers's support?

Elson (*Depthnews* 1992) is doubtful about the wisdom of the prevalent practice of the attempt to fit the women's agenda into the overall development process. She argues that "..........although women in development programmes have elements of empowerment, they are based more on the "static" rather than the "dynamic" concept of power".

Miller (1992) asserts that basing arguments on the male/female dichotomy is non-productive. Instead, she proposes that the discussion considers the new term of the "human community".

Clearly, enough groundwork must be done to establish forceful and reasonable (if not non-threatening) arguments. This is necessary before negotiation begins.

Some questions related to these issues are:

- What are effective and convincing arguments in favour of empowerment?
- Are there special programmes for advocating acceptance of empowerment?
- Does advocacy focus exclusively on policy makers or does it cover wider audience?
- Is lobbying necessary? At what intervals should it be done?
- What are effective advocacy methods, media, materials, manner and approaches?
- In what areas of public policy has advocacy been successful in affecting changes? What lessons can be learned from them?

Conclusion

Training to prepare educational programmes for women's empowerment needs to integrate the four components: gender issues, work oriented activities, literacy and numeracy skills and principles of curriculum design. It is yet too early to discuss the impact of this training programme which could only be assessed in terms of how it influences changes at the national level. What is certain is that the seed of education for learners' empowerment has been sown. Clearly, many problem areas arise. Better understanding of these issues will help improve the effectiveness of the programme which will ultimately help promote women learners as "empowered" members of their society.

References

Depthnews. Women's Feature. (1992) Wanted: A Real Women's Agenda. December.

Dighe, Anita (1989) *Conceptual framework for continuing education for women in meeting the needs of women; a report of the Regional Seminar on Continuing Education.* Sydney, Australia, 4-10 December 1989. Sydney: UNESCO/PROAP Adult Learning and Development International Network (ALADIN).

Lind, Agneta and Foss, Mark (1990) International co-operation in literacy: two good examples. *International Literacy Year: Literacy lessons*. Paris: UNESCO.

Paz Ruth (1990) *Paths of empowerment: Ten years of early childhood work in Israel*. The Hague: Bernard van Leer Foundation.

Ramachandran, Padma (1979) *Education for Girls and Women: Strategies for Future Action*. Bangkok: UNESCO/PROAP.

UNESCO Writing Workshop to Develop Reading Materials for Women with Limited Reading Skills, Chiangrai, Thailand, 1-10 October 1990. *A series of 12 booklets developed at the workshop*. Bangkok: PROAP, 1992. (Asia-Pacific Programme of Education for All).

UNESCO Writing Workshop for the Development of Reading Materials for Women's Self-reliance in Chiangmai, Thailand, 17 July-2 August 1991. *Series of 17 booklets developed at the workshop*. Bangkok: PROAP, 1992 (Asia- Pacific Programme of Education for All).

UNESCO. Principal Regional Office for Asia and the Pacific (PROAP) *A series of learning programmes on self-reliance*. Bankok: PROAP.

UNESCO. Principal Regional Office for Asia and the Pacific. (1990) *Writing for women; civic awareness*. Bangkok: PROAP.

UNESCO. Principal Regional Office for Asia and the Pacific. (1992) *Writing for women: India; analysis of reading materials to promote civic awareness among women with limited reading skills*. Bangkok: PRAOP. (Asia-Pacific Programme of Education for All).

UNESCO. Principal Regional Office for Asia and the Pacific. (1992) *Writing for women: Sri Lanka; analysis of reading materials to promote civic awareness among women with limited reading skills*. Bangkok: Praop. (Asia-Pacific Programme of Education for All).

7

THINKING ABOUT WOMEN AND LITERACY: SUPPORT AND CHALLENGE

Jenny Horsman

I am involved in the adult literacy field in Canada as a freelance worker. When I first began to think about the work I have done recently, to think about issues for women and education, I thought first of the projects that are with women only. I thought of the women's literacy group I used to run, the woman literacy learner I tutor working on reading and writing around her memories of the violence in her life, the research project I carried out with women with limited literacy skills in rural Maritime Canada, and the wide variety of workshops I have given on the issue of women and literacy.

I didn't think of the literacy work I do with mixed groups, on leadership, training and facilitation skills. I was struck by that and as I began to rethink, realized that there were many issues of "empowerment" in that work and that whether I work with women alone or in mixed groups, I work as a feminist aware of questions of gender and their interwining with race, class, and ability.

I was also, as I sat down to write, far too late to do anything but sketch out some notes, and "borrow" from things I had written before, feeling guilty—why hadn't I got to this before? Why had I gotten sick just when I had planned to do it? Of course it is a familiar story, women who are over-committed, not allowing enough time to take care of ourselves, expecting our bodies to continue on like machines even if we ignore them, and feeling guilty when we don't manage to do it all!

That reminded me that there was another theme in my life--trying to learn how to do less and respect my needs as well as other people's. This too is about challenge and support and women's education and is a project I share with many women colleagues and friends. In these noted I shall look at some of these sites of women's education, exploring some key questions they raise for me as I think about women and the power to change society.

Women Working Together

In the women's group I led for several years there were usually about six women of diverse ethnicity, age, ability, experience and literacy level. I wrote, in a letter to feminist literacy workers, about a key issue from working with this group just after I finished working with them:

> "I have been struggling with many questions from my experience of working with that group. One of the most obvious has been the difficulty the group has had in listening to each other —in creating a safe place where they can all speak- far too often they don't feel heard. The women who had widely varied experience and were of different race, ability and age often seemed to find their difference more striking than any commonality of experience. Ablism and racism created many barriers—sometimes glaring, sometimes subtle—but always there. Some of the women in the group, perhaps because they were used to being devalued as "illiterates", seemed to look to me, the facilitator, for all their support rather than the other women in the group. They often ended up competing for my attention rather than being the "group" of supportive women which I had hoped to help form. They pushed the limits of my energies over and over again, leaving me always wondering what I did wrong —how could I help the group become more self-sufficient and better able to listen to and support each other."

Thus my challenge became to find ways to help the women to learn to listen to each other, to value each other, and so to strengthen their valuing of themselves and their own words.

Working on Issues of Violence

At the same time I wrote about working on issues of violence:

> "A long while ago the women's group had a session where they talked about their childhoods and shared some of the horrendous stories of drudgery and hard work. I feel that it is really important that there are spaces for issues of violence to be spoken about, but I have often felt worried that the women sometimes don't want to speak in the group, but only to me alone, and wonder sometimes

that was written from the perspective of women of Doobagunta village—of the harassment they had suffered at the hands of their drunken husbands, of the manner in which they had discussed their problems in the literacy class, of their resolve to take collective action and of the success they had achieved by closing down the arrack shop in the village. The narration in the text was simple, direct and ended with an exhortation to the reader that if they (the women of Doobagunta) could do it, "why can't you too do it?" Think........".

As the primer with this lesson was introduced in the post-literacy centres, it had an electrifying impact on women. In several villages, women's committees were formed and citing the Doobagunta example, agitation against the sale of arrack began. First the husbands, sons and male relatives habituated to liquor were advised not to drink. As the women realized that as long as the arrack shop in the village was open, it would be impossible to prevent men from drinking, they issued a warning to the arrack shop owners to close down the shops. Due to the pressure from women's groups, arrack shops were closed either with the consent of the owner, or by force. Women formed squads in the villages and a vigil was kept round the clock to ensure that no arrack entered the village either through the arrack contractor or the excise department.

By August 1992, the anti-arrack agitation had spread through the villages of Nellore district. August is the month in which excise auctions are held and on August 11, the data fixed by the collector of Nellore for auction, there was a major demontration of women at the collector's office, forcing the auction to be postponed. Subsequently, the auction would be announced but would get postponed each time due to massive mobilization of women. Gradually, all the opposition parties, voluntary organizations, women's groups, civil liberties organizations joined the protest movement so that by the end of November 1992, the anti-arrack agitation had spread to a large number of districts of Andhra Pradesh.

But the success of the anti-arrack agitation suffered a setback when in December, 1992 the Chief Minister of Andra Pradesh branded such work as 'anti-government' and announced that strict action would be taken against those government functionaries who supported the movement and worked actively for it.

Women, Literacy and Empowerment—An Analysis of the Nellore Experience

From the nellore experience, one can begin to develop a broad conceptual framework of what empowerment means.

1. Empowerment and Marginalized Groups

The term empowerment is focused on marginalized groups—the landless, the powerless, the voiceless. In Nellore, it was the scheduled castes, and other backward caste women who took up the arrack issue and who as a result, have spearheaded an agitation that has now elicited support from middle class women and men. The anti-arrack agitation has become such a powerful women's movement and has taken such deep roots in the Andhra countryside that the yearly arrack sales have now been postponed indefinitely in Nellore district and in some other parts of Andhra Pradesh.

2. The Process-oriented Nature of Empowerment

It is clear from the Nellore experience that empowerment is not an end-of-project product or a state that can be attained within defined time-frames. Instead, empowerment is a dynamic and on-going process which can only be located on a continuum (Shetty, 1992). The total literacy campaign in Nellore had given an opportunity to women to acquire literacy skills, and as a result, to begin to feel sufficiently self-confident to function as autonomous individuals. But if acquisition of literacy became the essential step in empowering then at the individual level, the issue of arrack provided the necessary spark that united them at the collective level. If empowerment is viewed as a continuum, empowerment at the group level is essential but this cannot be brought about without empowerment at the individual level.

3. The Holistic Nature of Empowerment

Empowerment cannot be constrained by a sectoral approach. Nor can it be related to just a set of activities or inputs. Empowerment is an all-encompassing term in which a whole range of economic, social and political activities, including group organisation, agriculture and income generation projects, education, integrated health care and so on, would work synergistically towards the common goal of empowering the poor (Bhasin, 1985). In Nellore, the arrack issue was the only issue on which the women's movements was built. This was a conscious decision taken by the women themselves. But as arrack shops were closed and the men saved money for running the household, the impact of a slightly better diet on their health was immediately discernible. The debilitating effect of arrack on the health of the menfolk, and the consequent effect on their productivity, became an issue of great interest to both men and women.

4. Empowerment Deals with "Strategic' rather than 'Practical Gender Interests'

It is important to differentiate between what Molyneux (1981) terms 'the practical gender interests' and 'the strategic gender interests'. She notes that the former are short term and linked to immediate needs arising from women's current responsibilities vis-a-vis the livelihood of their families and children, while the latter address bigger issues such as sexual division of labour within the home, the removal of institutionalized forms of gender discrimination, the establishment of political equality, freedom of choice over child-bearing, and the adoption of adequate measures against male violence and control over women.

It appears from the Nellore experience that to begin with, the agitation addressed the 'practical gender interests' in so far as its genesis was due to the rural women's concern about their husbands' callous indifference to their responsibilities towards the family and to the upbringing of their children. But as the agitation picked up momentum, it appeared that it had the potential to address the 'strategic gender interests', although the women from Nellore have strategically decided to focus exclusively on the arrack issue for the present. This was made apparent from the discussions with village women in some villages during which it was categorically stated that they would first win the battle against arrack before taking up any other issue. But interestingly, power relationships between men and women within the family and outside are slowly beginning to change. Women have formed anti-arrack vigilance squads in the village to ensure that illicit arrack is not smuggled into the village. There have been instances when the women have successfully challenged the bureaucracy, the police, and the politicians. But what extent the anti-arrack agitation would be able to sustain itself, consolidate its gains and move on the other issues of concern to women is now uncertain due to the present policy of the state government, which has cracked down severely on those functionaries who support the agitation.

5. Empowerment has Cognitive, Psychological and Economic Components

According to Stromquist (1988), empowerment is a socio-political concept that goes beyond 'participation', and 'consciousness-raising'. She calls for a fuller definition of empowerment that considers cognitive, psychological and economic components. The cognitive component refers to women's understanding of their conditions of subordination and the reasons that create such conditions. The psychological component includes the development of a feeling that women can improve their condition and the belief that they can succeed in their efforts. In Nellore, as women have collectively picketed the arrack shops, marched unitedly to the district collector's office and organized a *dharna* to ensure that auctions are not allowed to take place, they have become strengthened in their conviction that it is only such united action that can bring about any change. "Now that we have come out of our homes, we will fight to the very end" is the refrain that has been echoed in village after village.

But the third component, namely the economic, has not been addressed in Nellore so far. This component of empowerment signifies that women are able to engage in a productive activity that will allow them some degree of financial independence, however small and burdensome in the beginning. Such income-generating activities, however, are difficult to implement because they are risky, time-consuming and hard to sustain.

6. Democratizing Aspect of Empowerment

A key feature of empowerment is that it elicits the widest possible community participation and is, in that sense, democratizing (Shetty, 1992). This aspect of the Nellore experience is important for the agitation has mobilized support not only from certain section of village women but also from certain sections of village men. Alongside various women's groups, political parties, unions of lawyers, doctors, etc., have lent support to the agitation. An interesting development has been that the village women took a conscious decision not to identify leaders for their agitation. It is said that their argument was that once leaders were identified, they would be 'bought' over by the politicians.

7. Understanding the Nature of Literacy that Empowers

Conceptually it is important to distinguish between literacy that empowers and literacy which domesticates. Traditionally, literacy programmes have focused on acquisition of technical skills of reading and writing. While the importance of acquisition of literacy skills should not be discounted, the fact remains that in the case of women, such a literacy oftentimes merely reinforces their domestic role and does not bring about any change in social relations either within the family or outside. Literacy that empowers, on the other hand, seeks to combine both consciousness-raising and participation so that women not only understand the causes of their oppression but also take steps to ameliorate their conditions. In Nellore, it seems that in the basic literacy skills, the emphasis was on acquisition. It was, however, in the post-literacy phase that 'awareness- raising' around issues of common concern, started taking place in a systematic manner. Consciousness raising or the development of a critical view of the micro and macro reality of individuals, is a major contribution of Paulo Freire. The events at the Doobagunta village of Nellore district were probably precipitated because of the discussions that had taken place at the post-literacy centres on the evils of excessive drinking. More importantly, it was the manner in which the Doobagunta incident was converted into a lesson in the postliteracy primer that has pedagogical relevance. The lesson in the form of a story was direct, simple and written from the perspective of the women of Doobagunta.

The other lessons in the primer dealt with issues of poverty, landlessness, minimum, wages, problems with the ration shop, health services and such other day-to-day problems of the poor. This primer evoked tremendous interest among the neo-literates.

The role of literacy in the overall process of empowerment, however, needs to be understood. Is literacy a necessary pre-condition for empowerment? That this is not necessarily so is borne out by the experience of the Women's Development Programme (WDP) in Rajasthan and of Mahila Samakhya in three other states of India. This experience has shown that even though non-literate women can become empowered, the demand for literacy does get articulated by them after some time. Literacy is then perceived not as an end in itself but as a means to enable women to have better control over their lives. Literacy becomes empowering if it enables women to gain access to the storehouse of information and knowledge that has been denied to them. But literacy skills have to be constantly honed so that as new vistas open up to women, the desire to continue beyond basic literacy becomes a felt need. In this process, literacy can also become a vehicle for creative self-expression so that stories, songs and poems are written by women themselves.

8. Context-specific Nature of Empowerment

According to Shetty (1992), empowerment can be defined only within the local social, cultural, economic, political, and historical context. Even with regard to the anti-arrack agitation, it is important to understand the contextual factors that precipitated the agitation. For ten years, the importance of the arrack has increased steadily in the state of Andhra Pradesh. Arrack consists principally of rectified spirit which is obtained by distilling fermented molasses. Over the years, despite the change in government, arrack has become an important source of excise revenue for the State Government. This has increased steadily from Rs. 39 crore in 1970-71 to Rs. 812 crore in 1991-92. This increase has not been an innocuous increase caused by changing life styles and habits but the consequence of a deliberate policy pursued by the government (Balagopal, 1992). Unwilling to collect the taxes it imposes on the urban rich and unwilling to touch the rural rich, the government has increasingly turned to liquor sales as a major source of revenue. This brazenness on the part of the government has resulted in the setting up of more and more arrack shops in the villages and in the literal bringing of arrack to the doorsteps of the villagers with, at the same time, increases in the retail price from years to years.

The manufacture of arrack is the monopoly of the government distilleries but its sole selling rights are auctioned areawise to contractors. That arrack is an extremely lucrative enterprise is evident from the fact that over the years arrack contractors have amassed great wealth and have started wielding political influence.

It is against this background that the anti-arrack agitation has to be understood. For at one level there is the political role of arrack and the difficulty of fighting it, a difficulty that was not immediately apparent to the thousands of rural women who took up what they perceived to be a just struggle. Their anguish and sense of outrage was evident when they joined the agitation and posed the following questions: "We do no have drinking water, no work, no schools, for our children and our wages are low. Nothing is available here except arrack. It is the only thing that comes to the village regularly, uninterruptedly. Why is the government so interested in supplying only arrack so religiously? Why does it not stop the supply? We will now fight to stop arrack from entering our village."

9. Sustainability is an Important Aspect of Empowerment

The direction of empowerment is that of self-reliance and withdrawal of external agents wherever the initial impetus has come from outside. Grassroots organisations, an integral part of most empowerment strategies, are thus seen as critical elements in ensuring sustainability. But the total literacy campaigns are funded by the Government. That being so, the questions to be asked are: "What is the extent of empowerment that would be acceptable? What is the 'space' that would be provided by a government-funded programme?" That the 'space' provided was not very much has now become evident from the fact that the Chief Minister of Andhra Pradesh has expressed his anger at the manner in which certain district collectors, while implementing the literacy programme, had raised 'anti-government' sentiment among the learners through the literacy primers. While ordering that such provocative lessons be expunged from the literacy primers, the Chief Minister has also ordered that government functionaries should dissociate themselves from the agitation. That the State might even resort to repressive measures is becoming a distinct possibility because of the political nature of the agitation.

On the other hand, the women's movement is gradually becoming more militant and has now become politicized because of the support it has received from all the opposition political parties. Given this conflicting scenario, the future direction of the anti-arrack agitation remains uncertain. But despite this uncertainty, there is a hope the 'the women cadres and leaders emerging from this movement will pose serious questions in future. The question that the grassroots women pose to husbands, activists and parties—to the entire civil society—will be radically different from the ones that the urban middle class women have posed so far" (Ilaiah, 1992).

References

Balagopal, K. (1992) "Slaying of a spirituous Demo", *Economic & Political Weekly* vol. XXVII No. 46, Nov. 14, pp. 2457-2461.

Bhasin, K. (ed) (1985) *Towards Empowerment.* New Delhi: FAO.

Ilaih, K. "Anti Liquor Movement in Andhra Pradesh". *Economic & Political Weekly* Vol. XXVII No. 45 Nov. 7, pp. 2406-2408.

Molyneux, M. (1981) "Women's Emancipation under Socialism: a model for the Third World". IDS Discussion Paper DP 157, Sussex: Institute of Development Studies.

Shatrugna, M. (1992) "Literacy and Arrack in Andhra". *Economic & Political Weekly* Vol. XXVII, No. 48, Nov. 28, pp. 2583-2584.

Shetty, S. (1992) *Development Projects in Assessing Empowering.* New Delhi: Society for Participatory Research in Asia, Occasional Paper Series, No. 3.

Stromquist, N. (1988) "Women's Education in Development: from Welfare to Empowerment". *Convergence* Vol. XXI, No. 4.

5

THE ORGANIZATION OF AMERICAN STATES MULTINATIONAL PROJECT ON EDUCATION AND WORK

AN EXPERIENCE OF POPULAR EDUCATION FOR WOMEN'S EMPOWERMENT IN COLOMBIA

Miryan Zuniga E.

This paper presents two Colombian adult education programmes with women, developed in the context of the Organization of American States (OAS) multinational project on Education and Work (OAS/PMET project). The analysis of these programmes points out the convergence of the principles and practices of popular education, which inspires the programmes, and the process of women's empowerment. In this direction, it suggests that indicators of empowerment could be drawn up from the main postulates of popular education.

The OAS Multinational Project of Education and Work

In 1989 the OAS decided to set up a Multinational Project on Education and Work, for the period 1990-1996, with the participation of all Latin American Countries.

This project was based on the following considerations:

- In spite of the annual economic growth of 6% experienced by Latin American countries, there are deep structural imbalances which generate conditions of poverty, marginality and unemployment.
- Incomes in Latin America fell down between 22% and 23% in the period 1980-1988.
- The high rates of unemployment in the region, were a challenge to the development strategies of Latin American countries.

Given these conditions the OAS/PMET project attempts:

1. To conceptualize the relationship between education and work more broadly, in order to set forth work as something more than employment, as a fundamental activity of human beings with social and cultural determinants. That is, relating quality of education with the needs, resources and aspirations of the population.
2. To link the design of the project not only to training for employment, but also to the development of an entrepreneurial cultural which gives rise to cooperatives and microenterpries.
3. To transform all curricula, in order to organize educational contents to facilitate the overcoming of the daily problems of life, in which work is a fundamental space of cultural and social development.
4. To promote the full realization of the human potential, facilitating individual and community participation in the design, development and evaluation of the educational programmes.
5. To give priority to peasants, ethnic minorities, women and unemployed youngsters.

The OAS/PMET Project in Colombia

Colombia decided to develop the OAS/PMET project at the level of Adult Education in view of its new focus on this type of education.

Since 1988 the government has attempted to orient adult education programmes according to the principles and practices of popular education. That is, to design programmes with the people, following their needs and interests; to design these programmes to promote organization of the popular sector of society, in order to empower them to control their own development; to develop a dialogical pedagogy, which recognizes the traditional knowledge and culture of the people; to promote direct democratic processes, in order to eliminate inequalities and to establish harmonious relationships with nature and among peoples; to consider literacy and adult education as involving more than the technical skills of reading and writing as they also concern learning to manage one's day to day life.

Since 1990, the Colombian government has set up 44 community-managed Centers of Popular Adult Education (CAEPA) where organized communities develop programmes and projects to meet their learning needs.

The OAS/PMET project was established in the context of three of these centers, located in 3 different cities: Cali, Zarzal and Villavicencio.

These programmes were designed through workshops with the students, the CAEPA Coordinating Committee, non-governmental organizations (NGOs), representatives of governmental institutions and participants from the Universidad Del Valle. The result was a participatory curriculum design of the PMET programme. The Community of the Cali Center decided to set up the programme for young and adult women who wanted to be trained to establish productive enterprises. This programme is carried out by CER-MUJER, a women's NGO. The Zarzal and Villavicencio programmes gathered men and women. However, in Zarzal a group of women, community mothers, were selected to contribute to a master's degree project conducted by a graduate student of the Valley Universities.[1]

All three programmes have in common three elements:

1. An integral curriculum structure, which includes the following components: technical (to develop knowledge and skills for production), *entrepreneurial* (to develop knowledge and skills for marketing), *cultural* (to promote cultural identity and assertiveness), *communal* (to insert the programme in a process of local development), and a component aiming to promote gender awareness.
2 A pedagogical approach which starts setting up the practical experience of a production group and continues with the systematization of knowledge. Thus, it goes from practice to theory.
3. A final purpose: to generate production groups which take into account cultural and community dynamics.

The Cali Programme

This includes a 5th curriculum component, dedicated to generating gender awareness among women participants. This component includes workshops about identity; self-esteem; women and family; women and work; women, health and self-care; relationships between men and women; sexuality and values, etc.,

It also includes the celebration of events, such as Mother's Day, Women's Day and the Non-Violence against Women Day.

This programme assumes that women have three roles to play in society; the *reproductive* role, which relegates women to the private, domestic arena, where they are mothers and wives; the *productive* role, which places women in economic production; and the *community management* role, which is related with women's participation in local affairs. Therefore, the programme attempts to empower these women, to accomplish all three roles in order to break up the structure which sustains women's subordination, and to increase women's self-confidence and internal force.

So far, the Cali programme has made possible the formation of four production groups: hand-made cards, fruit pulp, clothing, and marketing of different products.

The Zarzal Programme

This attempts to further advance the San Lorenzo Project of FUNCALCO, a Colombian NGO, with women (Zuniga 1992).

It operationalizes the concept of sustained health through a process of group production of food, cooking practices and learning about nutrition as a source of health, the development of gender identity and self-esteem, and cultural community traits of their locality.

The pedagogical model of this programme is based on a dialogue of knowledge: the traditional knowledge of the women participants (that is, their experience and world view, which provides them with ways of interpreting their lives), and the systematic knowledge of the coordinators of the programme (a nurse, a teacher, and an expert in agriculture).

The dialogue flows around the kitchen, the physical setting where these women spend most of their time, and therefore the space where they feel most comfortable. These women bring to the kitchen, where the workshops are carried on, the products they grow (vegetables and small animals such as rabbits and hens). They cook a meal and learn about its nutritional value, recognizing the needs of the human body. They they talk about cultural practices, about the feeding of men, women and children, as well as about the traditional role and potentialities of women in the family, the economy and the community.

It is expected as a result of this programme, that these women's children will be better nourished and that these women will increase their self-esteem, as compared with the control group.

Popular Education and Women's Empowerment

According to Caroline Moser (1992) there are four approaches to the planning of gender in the Third World:

1. The well-being approach, which develops programmes to provide goods to women of low incomes, because they are in charge of their families, thus helping women to help their families. This type of programme only recognizes and reinforces the reproductive role of women.
2. The *equity approach*, which promotes the reduction of discrimination against women, through policies and programmes which recognize the productive role of women in society.
3. The *anti-poverty approach*, which assumes that women's poverty is caused by their lack of land, capital, training and employment. Thus, it promotes programmes which enable women to generate income to

overcome poverty.

4. The *empowerment* approach, which recognizes that the concept of gender is a sociocultural construct and points out the social relation between men and women, in which women have been systematically subordinated.

Among the four approaches, it is the empowerment approach which recognizes the triple role of women in the family, economic production and the community, and recommends challenging the social structure and oppressive situation women have to suffer. Women have to increase their power not in terms of domination over others, but in terms of gains over their self-esteem and internal force. This means women have the right to decide about their own life and to influence social change, through their ability to gain control over crucial natural and cultural resources.

This approach is not interested in the "integration" of women in society, but in the design of a new society, where relationships between men and women are more democratic. To achieve this, it is necessary to promote organizations to accomplish legal changes, political mobilization and social consciousness.

This last approach coincides with the main postulates of popular education. According to Sime (1991), between 1970 and 1990 a paradigm of popular education was drawn up with the following perspectives:

Political: it searches for a democratic society through the full participation of all people in social life regardless of their race, social status and gender. It also looks forward for people to achieve peace, tolerance and solidarity. It promotes the empowerment of minority groups, popular and marginal sector of society, and women to be able to influence social and political decisions.

Cultural: it questions to what extent to preserve the traditional, how to relate the traditional and the modern, how to manage the racism and patriarchalism of popular groups, and how to value the plural ethnicity of many countries.

Pedagogical: it questions the authoritarian relations of teachers over students. It recognizes the traditional knowledge of people, promotes assertiveness among participants and encourages multiple ways of knowing. It does not prioritize the group above the individual, or the rational over the affective.

Ethical: it seeks congruence between means and ends. It stands for human rights, the claims of women, and against exploitation of children, injustice and corruption.

Thus, the paradigm of popular education could become an agency to promote women's empowerment. In fact, the political, cultural, pedagogical and ethical perspectives of popular education, show a way to draw a system of indicators to evaluate the extent to which a programme, like the OAS of Cali and Zarzal, is helping women to become empowered.

These indicators could be identified according to the four perspectives of popular education, but they must include what Stromquist (1993) calls the cognitive, psychological, political and economic components of empowerment. These components are related to the understanding of women's condition of subordination (cognitive); the development of feelings that women can act upon to improve their conditions (psychological); the ability to organize and mobilize for social changes (political); and the skills to obtain some degree of financial autonomy (economic).

The following set of indicators could have the potential to evaluate the process of empowerment in all of its components.

1. Political perspective

Indicator: The establishment of women's production groups and associations

Cognitive component: the understanding of traditional concepts about the location of women in the private sphere of their households.

Psychological component: the development of feelings that women could have achievements in the public sphere of society.

Economic component: the development of managerial skills to achieve financial autonomy.

Political component: the ability to promote organizations to reshape relations in the public sphere of society.

2. Cultural perspective

Indicator: the use of legal offices for women and family affairs

Cognitive component: Knowledge about women's rights.

Psychological component: Confidence in women's ability to carry on legal processes to plead for their rights, even against cultural traditions.

Economic component: Ability to find resources to carry on law suits to improve their social and economic conditions.

Political Component: Ability to improve the establishment of social institutions which support women's work towards social change in the field of gender relations.

3. Ethical perspective

Indicator: Promotion of legislation about abortion, violence against women, inheritance, and competency to control business

Cognitive component: Knowledge about the moral values of society.

Psychological component: Confidence in women's ability to make decisions about moral and business issues.

Economic component: Ability to exercise advocacy for issues which assure women's autonomy.

Political component: Ability to participate in actions to promote changes in the traditional gender relations.

4. Pedagogical perspective

Indicator: Participation in the design, development and evaluation of educational programmes for women

Cognitive component: Understanding the traditional conditions of women and their development possibilities.

Psychological component: Belief in women's ability to share the responsibility for implementing a programme.

Economic component: Ability to develop skills to achieve economic autonomy through the educational programme.

Political component: Ability to develop skills to find terms of agreement about how the programme could be set up.

According to these indicators, the OAS multinational projecy on Education and Work held in Cali and Zarzal (Colombia) has empowered some women to act upon their local political, cultural, ethical and pedagogical forces in order to change their life.

In fact, this project has enabled the women to gain insights into their traditional subordinate condition as well as into their inner strength to change such a situation. Both groups of women have been able to organize small businesses to generate income, to gain self-confidence to make economic decisions, to gain skills to negotiate about the sharing of domestic work, to develop managerial skills to participate in community programmes, and to support their ideas in public meetings.

This experience points out the relationship between popular education programmes and empowerment. But it also suggests a hypothesis about the relationship between women's access to paid work and the process of empowerment. There is, however, a need to distinguish the kinds of work that have more potential for empowerment. This is the challenge the OAS project faces.

References

Moser, Caroline O.N. (1992) "Planificacion de genero en el Tercer Mundo: enfrentando las necesidades practicas y estrategias de genero". Bogota. Mimeo.

Sime, Luis (1991) "Notas para un balance del discurso de la Educacion Popular". In Palomino, Nancy (ed.) *Los discursos y la vida.* Lima: Tarea.

Stromquist, Nelly P. (1993) "The practical and the theoretical bases for empowerment". Paper presented at the International Seminar on Women's Education and Empowerment. Hamburg: UIE.

Zuniga, M. "A post-literacy project with the women of the Indian community of San Lorenzo (Colombia)". In Malmquist, Eve (ed .) (1992) Women and Literacy *Development in the Third World.* Stockholm: UNESCO and SIDE.

Note:-

1. Ms Olga Osorio, a member of the PMET project. (cf. Osorio, Olga. A. (1992) Master's Project. Cali. Universidad del Valle.)

6

EDUCATE TO EMPOWER: AN ASIAN EXPERIENCE

Namtip Aksornkool

Introduction

Over the past decade, education for women's empowerment has been intensively discussed. The reason lies in the disappointment over the "run-of-the-mill" literacy programmes. They are described as unsatisfactory and limited to the three R's, a handful of income-raising skills and certain "life quality" components.

These programmes center on areas predetermined by women's reproductive function to the exclusion of their equally important role as economic producers. The programmes often leave women disillusioned as they quickly realize that the programmes do not help improve their lives.

Despite such programmes, learners continue to face economic hardship, double responsibility and overall social inequality.

Training for better productivity does not suffice because women need decision-making capacity and ability to organize and take part in community and national activities.

Advocates of education for empowerment have argued that education needs to go well beyond mere "enabling". It has to view women as society's active members who need education to participate, effectively and meanigfully, in any activity and as equal partners of men.

Definitions of empowerment vary but Paz is most succinct—it is "the ability to direct and control one's own life" (Paz, 1990). The report of the 1991 Seminar on the integration of women in development elaborates that it is a "process in which women gain control over their own lives of knowing and claiming their rights at all levels of society at the international, local and household levels. Self-empowerment means that women gain autonomy, are able to set their own agenda and are fully

Post Literacy Life-long Continuing Education

Continuing Education is defined as the provision of opportunities for life-long learning. The concept of the learinig society as defined by UNESCO implies that the educational processes are a function of society as a whole. All societal elements have roles to play. Life-long learning implies self-directed learning, that is men and women are the agents of their education. Agencies and resources must exist to provide the programme and the facilities needed for individuals to undertake learning projccts.

Without supporting continuing education programme, neoliterates relapse into illiteracy, negating all efforts and huge investments made in the literacy programme. Therefore, for consolidating the newly acquired skills, enabling environments are to be created for the neo-literates so that they can practice their knowledge. INFEP has taken the lead in setting up to 10 villages libraries styled "Gram Shikkha Milan Kendra" in every project thana. So, far 406 village libraries have been set up in 43 thanas. There is one librarian for each library and one supervisor for 10 libraries. Librarians comprise women as well. Separate village library hours according to their convenience are maintained for women neo-literates. Besides books there is provision also for a daily newspaper, games etc.

Cognizant of the fact that female education is key to the development of the family and society and containing population growth, special emphasis has been placed on female education. To promote female education, girl students up to Class X are provided education free of charge. Government's commitment to improve both the coverage and quality of education is evident from the increasing allocations both in the revenue and development budget in recent years. Allocation for education sector in total public expenditure increased from 11% in FY 90/91 to over 16% in 1994/95. During the Fourth Five Plan period, the share of education sector in total public expenditure has been the highest and crossed 2% of GDP in 1991/92 and 3% of GDP in the FY 94/95.

Nation-wide Female Stipend Programme

The Government of the People's Republic of Bangladesh has launched an innovative programme from January 1994 for empowerment of women through education. This is a nation-wide Stipend programme for girl student in secondary Schools and Madrashas. The programme is being implemented through four development projects with the support of World Bank, Asian Development Bank, Norwegain Agency for Development (NORAD) and GOB (Government of Bangladesh).

The short-term objectives of the nation-wide programme are:

1. to provide stipend to female students to decrease their drop-out from Secondary Schools/ Madrashas;
2. to enhance and retain female students in the Secondary stage and thereby promote female education; and
3. to reduce growth rate by providing incentives to the stipend clientele group to refrain from marriage before completion of Secondary School Certificate Examination or before attainment of 18 years of age.

On the other hand, the long-term objectives are:

(i) empowerment of women through education;
(ii) elevation of status of women in society;
(iii) provide the women with access to work and income; and
(iv) help accelerate female human resources development.

Under the programme, besides other activities, all girl-students studying in Grade VI through Grade X receive stipends at various rates. In addition, each of the girl-students studying in Grade IX gets one time a lump-sum amount of Taka 250.00 for purchase of text books and each girl-students studying in Grade X will receive lump-sum amount Taka 250.00 for S.S.C. and Dakhil (S.S.C. equivalent) examination fee. In addition, concerned schools will receive Taka 15.00 per month as tuition fee against each of the girl-students studying in Grade IX to X.

Complimentary and Supportive Measures

To complement this, the government has also undertaken other initiatives. It has launched the Food for Education programme where boys and girls of poor families will get 18 kg wheat. This is expected to increase the enrolment rate of boys and girls. The government has also decided to establish one separate secondary school for girls in each thana (sub district). Furthermore satellite (feeder) schools especially for girls have been set up.

There is also that scheme where only one girl-child of any parent will be given the opportunity to study up to university degree level free of cost. Finally at the primary level female teachers constitute 75% and there are plans for gradual replacement of the male teachers by female teachers.

10

HISTORY OF LITERACY EFFORTS AND CURRENT POLICIES ON WOMEN'S LITERACY

Rose Sese

The purpose of this paper is to share the historical path of literacy efforts in the Philippines. In the process, government efforts under the Asia-Pacific Programme of Education For All (APEAL) and under the global movement Education for All (EFA) will be dealt with. It will also touch on the current efforts on literacy skills development, the issues attendant to the full realization of the intent of these efforts and future actions that may be done to achieve EOl. A priority group in all these efforts are illiterate women and girls. Finally this paper shall try to highlight the activities of the LCC in the pursuit of the present government's goal of people empowerment.

I. History of Literacy Efforts in the Philippines

Conscious efforts at literacy skills development in the country dates back to 1906. The American colonial government wanted to find out who was literate in English and gave an examination. Those who passed were given jobs in the government as clerks, aides or assistants.

This became a motivating factor that resulted in the increased enrolment in the elementary schools. There were, however, those who for some reasons could not participate in the formal education programs. So, in 1908 the Philippine Legislature passed Act. No. 1829 requiring municipal teachers to take charge of lectures on Saturdays, Sundays or after school hours to develop literacy skills in English. In 1914, Act. No. 1829 was amended by Act. No. 2424 allowing lectures by teacher even on school days. Subject of the lectures were expanded to include laws on mining and industry, animal breeding and care, and propagation of plants and trees. There are no records, however, that show the extent of participation of farmers in these lectures.

In May 1935, the Constitution of the Commonwealth of the Philippines was ratified in a national plebiscite. Among, the provisions of this Constitution was one on adult education, embodied in Section 5, Article XIV, portion of which is quoted as follows: "Government shall provide.... citizenships training to adult citizens."

The University of the Philippines took the lead in implementing this provision by organizing the President's Committee on Literacy and Civic Education. Under this project, more than 300 faculty and alumni of the university volunteered to teach functional literacy to adults in their homes. After a year, the volunteers reported more than 1,000 adults made literate. They then opened a special course in adult education, and an adult class served as a laboratory for students.

On October 26, 1936, the National Assembly passed Commonwealth Act. No. 80 which created the Office of Adult Education under the Office of the President. Its functions, among others were to:

1. Initiate and conduct surveys to determine the extent and distribution of illiteracy among adults;
2. Enlist the interest and cooperation of organizations on adult education activities;
3. Prepare a comprehensive program for adult education;
4. Organize and supervise schools and classes for adults;
5. Disseminate cultural and vocational information; and
6. Train teachers and community organizations for adult education work.

By 1940, a number of adult literacy classes were organized in provinces utilizing the adult education workers connected with the Office of the Governor.

In 1947, the Office of the Adult Education was transferred to the Bureau of Public Schools of the Department of Education. It was in recognition of out-of-school education as one of the concerns of the education agency. After a year, the Office recorded a 52 per cent literacy rate of a total population of 19,234,182. It adopted other strategies in adult literacy education. Earliest among these was the each-one-teach-one plan where every teachers was required to make at least one illiterate adult in his/her neighborhood literate.

Initially, reports on literacy gains seemed very impressive. Lather, however, some reports were found to be inaccurate, as some adults were already literate in the dialect at least.

Through the 1950s, the Adult Education Division managed programs and projects designed to achieve literacy gains. By 1960, the Census and Statistics Office reported an increase of 20 per cent over the 1948 literacy rate. Still, the focus of educational development were child education and adult literacy. An intensive six-years literacy campaign (1966-1972) was mounted with the 15-35 age group of out-of-school youths and adults as primary targets.

The strategy in this campaign was to require every complete elementary school, to make at least 30 illiterate adults and out-of-school youths literate; every public secondary school to make literate every year at least 40 illiterate adults and out-of-school youths; and each of the seven regional teacher training colleges to organize two classes in adult literacy with an enrolment of at least 30 in each class every year for the duration of the campaign.

Various schemes were used in conducting literacy classes such as:

- Team teaching where three or more teachers of agriculture or industrial arts, health and nutrition or a municipal health nurse teamed up with a teacher of reading and writing to conduct a course for adults.
- Assignment of a teacher without a full academic load to handle adult literacy classes;
- Availing of services of teachers from outside groups in helping conduct classes and recruiting out-of-school illiterates and semi-literates to participate in the class; and
- Utilizing high school and college students undergoing off-campus training to help teach the adult illiterate.

Through the 1970s, the focus of educational development was on minimizing drop-outs anywhere in the country. In 1977, the Office of the Deputy Minister for Nonformal Education was created by virtue of Presidential Decree No. 1139. The new Office had seven major programs one of which was Functional Literacy. In all the other program areas, literacy was always a component.

By 1980, nonformal education programs were in full swing in the field. The literacy rate increased to more than 87 per cent according to NCSO figures.

Data on literacy rates over time showed a consistently high trend; 83.4% in 1970, 82.7% in 1980, and 89.8% in 1989 (NSO, October 26, 1990). However the number of nonliterate Filipinos, 10 years and above, increased in the last decade by over 450 thousand between 1980 and 1989, from approximately 5.8 million to 6.25 million respectively. Within and across regions, there were gaps in literacy rates with Region XII and

Autonomous Region of Muslim Mindanao (ARMM) accounting for the bulk of nonliterates. There were also discrepancies between the simple literacy rate and the more revealing functional literacy rates, which cover not only the ability to read and write, but also numeracy and minimum skills to carry out simple functions in life. Simple literacy rates improved in all regions from 82.7% in 1980 to 89.89% on 1989. However, functional literacy rates were lower than 75% in 10 out of 15 regions (national average was 73.2%).

Table 1.1 -Literacy of Population 15 years and above in the Philippines.

Years	Total Pop./15 yrs. up	Number of Literate	Per centage of Literate
1960	18,145,872*	13.074,748	72
1970	16,047,078	11,820,863	75
1980	24,028,291	20,950,508	87

* 1960 figures were based on population 10 years and above, for other years, it is 15 years and above; all figures from the Bureau of Census

In 1986, in response to the Asia-Pacific Programme of Education For All (APPEAL) was launched. A National Coordinating Committee was organized and this Committee held a series of field consultations to review the state-of-the-practice by analyzing the present scenario in the problem areas, identifying the concerns and issues, the present intervention programs and the linkages for integration, coordination and collaboration along the areas of universalizing primary education and enhancing relevance and efficiency in the area of APPEAL's concerns. From those leaders and practitioners' inputs a five-year program was conceived as a pilot program to provide a more research-oriented baseline for the remaining eight years towards the year 2000.

The five year program of APPEAL in the Philippines aims to pilot a research-oriented scheme for the eradication of illiteracy in the year 2000 through a design scheme, Development, Diffusion and Evaluation and a corresponding organizational structure consisting of the task (the mission and purpose); people (functions and responsibilities); a technology of delivery system (a national measures and resources) and a structure (a national network of communication mechanism).

Specifically, this five-year program aims to

- establish a national organizational structure composed of the different regions in both public and private sectors across the country;
- pilot a scheme of research, development, diffusion, implementation and continuous evaluation scheme for development towards eradica-

tion of illiteracy, universalization of primary education and providing for continuing education.

- undertake a comprehensive review and documentation of the state-of-the-practice in the three foregoing areas in this country.
- establish and maintain an organizational structure that will take care of the implementation of the proposed five-year program and the sustained enhancement of relevance, efficiency, equity and effectiveness through this program.
- maintain a continuous monitoring, evaluation and improvement mechanism within the program with a vision of providing baseline data for the subsequent program for the year 1991to 2000.
- continuously consolidate regional efforts in both government and non-government entities across the country.

APPEAL in the Philippines was vitalized with the advent of the global movement, Education For All (EFA).

In 1989, President Corazon C. Aquino issued Proclamation No. 480 declaring the period 1990 to 1999 as the "Decade of Education for All". This called for the development of the Philippine Plan of Action on Education For All (PPA), which presented the programs and projects for each of the four areas corresponding to the four objectives of EFA: Institutionalization of Early Childhood Care and Development (ECCD); Universalization of Quality Primary Education (QUPE); Development and Strengthening of the Alternative Learning Systems (ALS); which covers two subprograms: Eradication of Illiteracy (EOI) and Continuing Education and Development (CED). Under EOI, the following specific policies and strategies were formulated.

1. Integration of literacy programs with other development initiatives;
2. Mutual reinforcement among preliteracy, literacy and post-literacy programs;
3. Improvement of the internal efficiency of literacy programs;
4. Establishment of a comprehensive system of locating, identifying and monitoring the status of nonliterates in critical areas;
5. Increased emphasis on the needs of special groups of learners;
6. Active participation of institutions of higher learning in the development and promotion of literacy;
7. Mobilization of various groups in literacy programs;
8. Stronger emphasis on awareness and consciousness raising in literacy and continuing education programs as vehicles to discuss relevant topics like gender biases, environmental care, science culture, peace and development, etc.

Underlining the importance of literacy under the EFA-PPA, RA 7165 was approved into law in 1991. Also known as *an act creating the literacy coordinating council, defining its powers and functions, appropriating funds therefore and for other purposes,* the LCC serves as an overall advisory and coordinating body for all literacy endeavors in the country.

Through the initiatives of the Council, two policy insurances towards EOI in the Philippines were signed by the President of the Philippines: (1) Proclamation No. 239, declaring September 2 to 8 of every year as Literacy Week; and (2) Memorandum Circular No. 71 entitled "Strengthening the Resolve to Eradicate Illiteracy by the Year 2000". This involves the LCC, its member agencies and other GOs and the NGOs in carrying out specific responsibilities related in the eradication of illiteracy.

II. Current Efforts

A. Researches

To provide concrete program and project directions, and to improve the design and delivery of its functional literacy programs, researches have been commissioned by the Literacy Coordinating Council and the Bureau of Nonformal Education.

1. **Learning From Life: An Ethnographic of Functional literacy In Fourteen Philippine Communities.** Done by the University of Philippines-Education Research Program (UP-ERP) under the direction Dr. Ma. Luisa C. Doronila, Director of UP-ERP, the objectives of the study are

- To explore the general issues and problems leading to a clearer understanding and conceptualization of functional literacy;
- To understand the nature of community life in various community types in order to contextualize the functional literacy programs;
- To propose content areas for the development of these functional literacy programs and the relevant instructional materials;
- To provide some empirical bases for the technical considerations related to the teaching and evaluation of functional literacy, acquisition, retention and loss of literacy skills
- To propose a general framework for the planning, implementation and sustainability of functional literacy programs.

From this main study, the UP-ERP is presently pursuing nine (9) related studies that will guide project proponents in the development and implementation of literacy programs. These are:

a. *Pre-Implementation Rapid Community Assessment and Training at the Community Level.*
b. *Preparation of a package of instruments derived from the Ethnographic study to be used by implementing agencies as preparation for the implementation of the project at the community level.*
c. *Taxonomies for Functional Education and Literacy Program.* This study is expected to produce a taxonomy of functional skills by occupation and by community type, as well as additional skills needed by people to compete in the world of work and to use new technology.
d. *Community knowledge in Various Phil. Community Types* The primary objectives of the study are: (1) to expand the preliminary compendium of community knowledge from the six types of marginal communities generated through the 1993 Ethographic study on Functional Literacy in 14 Philippine Communities; (2) to validate the scientific bases of this knowledge; and (3) to classify the community knowledge according to subject areas for use of the writers of exemplar modules.
e. *Development and Field Testing of Exemplar and Instructional Materials for FELP* The principal objective of this study is to develop program materials utilizing the research outputs of the Ethnographic Study for the use of Functional Education and Literacy Program (FELP).
f. *Preliminary Inventory of Existing Literacy Materials* This study involves an inventory and assessment of relevant existing literacy materials in all regions, including those materials developed by the BNFE, Government and Non-government organizations and Higher Education Institutions.
g. *Development and Standardization of Basic and Functional Literacy Tests I-IV and Refinement of Psycho-social Scales* This study will develop, standardize and administer instruments to a national sample to measure their Basic and Functional Literacy Status, psycho-social characteristics, educational and skills qualifications; categorize the semiliterate, completely literate to functionally literate clientele and the determine the specific level of the population.
h. *Cognitive Consequences of Literacy: case studies of neo-literates from nonformal literacy programs* This case study analyzes the effects of literacy training on the individual. This will also be a significant input into the development of

equivalency tests.

i. *Indigenous Learing Systems*
Preliminary research on indigenous learning knowledge and strategies useful for literacy work in two tribal communities, Sama of Tawi-Tawi and the Cordillera tribal group.

2. Literacy Mapping

The National Statistics Office was commissioned by the Literacy Coordinating Council to identify the non-literates in all the households in the communities identified in the ADB-NFE Project.

The survey sought to find the answers to the following questions;

* Who are these illiterates?
* Why are they illiterate?
* In which level of illiteracy do they belong? (Levels 1, 2 or 3)?
* Where are these illiterates located?
  (Municipality and Barangay)
* What are their problems?
* What can they do about their problems?
* What locally available resources can they harness to solve their problems?

The results of the study was meant to complement the findings of the Ethnographic Study for the development of innovative intervention programs and strategies in literacy skills development.

B. Programs and Projects

1. ADB-NFE Project

To speed up the implementation of functional literacy projects, the Asian Development Bank is funding a five year nonformal education project. The project will be implemented in nine administrative regions, twenty-four provinces, one hundred twenty-three municipalities and one thousand seven hundred forty barangays. Its objectives are:

- reduce the incidence of basic and functional illiteracy in the targeted areas,
- strengthen the system of NFE equivalency testing and accreditation for adults and out-of-school youth
- develop a body of locally-adapted learning materials for literacy and self-learning programs for the poor
- expand the outreach and effectiveness of community-based NFE

through interagency coordination'

- strengthen DECS monitoring, research and evaluation capacity to assess NFE and formulated policies.

2. Regular Basic and Functional Literacy Programs, Such as:

- Eradication of illiteracy in Selected Areas (EISA): Ifugao, Tawi-Tawi and other areas implemented the project with funding assistance from the UNICEF in coordination with local government executives.
- Female Functional Literacy and Parent Education (FFLPE) Ifugao, Negros Occidental, Sulu, Basialan, Tawi-Tawi, Maguindanao, Lanao del Sur, Samar Provinces, Cotabato and others is a community-based project and was especially designed for women and girls in particular and parents in general. The focus is maternal and child health and funded by the UNICEF in coordination with local government executives.
- Project UNLAND- Botolan, Zambales is a literacy project involving Aeta families displaced with the eruption of Mt. Pinatubo. It is a joint effort between and among the DECS, UNICEF, Summer Institute of Linguistics, Mercy Corp and Translator's Association of the Philippines.
- Literacy programs being implemented by the DECS with funding from the government. All regions run this program. The program is mostly school-based because the facilitators are elementary grades teachers.

III. ISSUES

Whereas the Philippines has made great strides in its efforts towards EOI, there are still some problems and issues that this writer feels must be resolved for smoother implementation of functional literacy programs.

A. Utilization of Research Findings

Efforts must be exerted to operationalize the issue. It is felt that project managers will have to train their staff to make full use of research findings for more responsive program designers.

A dissemination and mobilization program may also encourage NGos to use these findings.

B. Structure for Literacy Project Implementation

The UNESCO, through APPEAL and EFA, has proposed the grand alliance between GOs, and NGOs. The GOs are made up of line agencies concerned with social development programs of the government. In reality, this grand alliance has not been fully operationalized.

It is suggested that this structure be reviewed to find out how it can function more efficiently and effectively.

C. Community-based Literacy Programs

Most often, the community members are not the main actors in the program. Therefore they do not develop close kinship with the program.

The community may be made the focal force in problem identification, program development and program implementation, monitoring and evaluation.

D. Role of Local Government Executives (LGE)

A Philippine study showed that the LGEs do not consider literacy as part of their development responsibility. There is in the Philippines a memorandum circular (71) signed by the President making the LGEs responsible for EOI in their area of responsibility but the LGEs are not aware of this.

Close consultation with LGEs may be done to make them aware of their role in EOI. Social mobilization is also suggested.

E. Lack of Full time Literacy Facilitators

As mentioned before, literacy skills development is mostly done by the school system. Whereas there are NGOs doing this, their organization is not as big as that of the DECS.

However, because this is mostly added work, the efforts for literacy skills development still have to be improved.

The Bureau of Nonformal Education was informed that there are some 2,000 items for NFE coordinators being proposed in the CY 1996 budget. If approved, this will be of great help to EOI.

F. Lack of a Functional Monitoring and Evaluation Sub-program

Ideally, each program/ project is expected to have a built-in monitoring program. This enables the project staff and decision-makers to effect changes and modification in program content, strategies and other resource adjustment. This is, however seldom the case.

It would benefit the project to develop this as early as the project development stage.

Evaluation takes its cue from the monitoring results. Monitoring and evaluation are complimentary. Evaluation may be done internally by project staff or externally by a commissioned body. The findings are very useful input to future related projects.

IV. Future Action

A. The LCC is in the process of planning a national congress on literacy where some of the more pressing issues and possible solutions may be proposed.

This will be followed by consultations with local government executive of LGUs where the rate of illiteracy is high. One of the expected outcomes from these consultations is local legislation that will enable LGUs to include EOI in their local development plans.

B. Strengthen the Structure for the Delivery of Literacy Programs

The inter-agency approach to EOI has to be made operational. Clear strategies for interfacing of roles must be done. The IAC must be made to think and work as one instead of clinging to their respective turf.

C. Mid-Term review of EFA Programs and Structures

It is five years before the year 2000. Between its inception in 1990 to date, there have been a number of local and global developments that necessitated the shift of focus in development priorities.

A closer look into these circumstances may provide the chance for program updates or program modification to render EFA responsive to the changing times.

Let us remember that EOI is one of the centerpieces of EFA. A more responsive EFA plan spells a more responsive EOI program.

11

ENGENDERING ADULT LITERACY

David Clarke

The 1995 Human Development Report asserts that the human development paradigm must be engendered to achieve the goal of gender equality. The same report comments that rapid progress has been made in the past two decades but this has been uneven between countries and regions. Overall women's literacy increased in the period 1970-90 from 54% of the male rate to 74%, an increase that was double that of the male rate. Yet the battle is far from won, as a glance at the literacy rates for the countries with Low Human Development ranking reveals, almost invariably, a below 50% adult literacy rate with significant gender disparities. In South Asia alone, there are an estimated 380 million non-literates, the majority of whom are women. Few would deny the importance of tackling illiteracy to reduce poverty, promote gender equity and assist sustainable development, yet the scale of the task is enormous and it is open to question that the problem is being addressed with sufficient commitment in development policies and practice.

While the 1990 World Conference on Education for All (WCEFA) has raised the profile of basic education and 'literacy for all' in development policies and donor assistance, Wagner (1995) reports that observers have noticed 'the considerable reticence of many national, bilateral and international agencies to provide strong fiscal (as contrasted with rhetorical) support or adult literacy efforts.'

This possible neglect of investment in literacy requires further investigation and confirmation, but a cursory examination of development activity in basic education suggests that there is at least a prima facie case for this proposition. A major factor is that governments and donor appear to have taken the long term view in eliminating illiteracy and are in the process of investing in increased access to primary education as the main route to universal literacy. This is what I would term the economists' solution to the problem, since it appears to be the lowest cost approach. But does it fully take into account the problems of primary completion and the ways in which this is gendered? In this regard, are the factors which result in school drop out sufficiently understood and considered-in particular, the effect of non-literate parents/mothers on school-going?

Pursuing the question of gendered literacy, the Delhi Declaration (UNESCO: 1994) adopted by the Education for All Sumit of Nine High-Population Developing Countries identifies gender as the greatest source of disparity in access to basic education. Moreover, where there has been a pattern of boy-girl differences in primary school enrolment and completion, adult literacy rates show a marked gender gap. To address the problem the Delhi Declaration cites the need for a dual approach to achieve basic education for all: (i) expanding primary school enrolment and completion rates, and (ii) providing well-targeted functional literacy programmes to adolescents and adults who have missed out on school. Interestingly, there is no mention of the need for targeting women even though it is acknowledged later on in the document that educated women are more likely to send their children to school and keep them there. Instead the approach advocated entails a focus on providing basic education programmes for adolescents and young adults, especially mothers. The rationale for this is, that given the scarcity of resources, it is better to target the more highly motivated in order to achieve maximum impact. The question of motivation is a dubious one; needs surely should be the priority. It does imply a lack of confidence in adult literacy programmes and this may prove to be an unstated cause for reluctance to invest. The implication of this policy, however, is that access to basic *education for all* will be possible only at primary school.

This approach is understandable as governments usually have a functioning primary education system which can be expanded relatively straightforwardly provided financial resources are available; institutions which deliver adult literacy have seldom been developed on the same scale and perhaps lack the legitimacy of primary schooling. There is the widely held perception that adult literacy programmes do not work efficiently or effectively. For example, adult literacy is characterized as a problem-ridden area by Abadzi (1994). She states that adult literacy programes have yielded disappointing results worldwide, in contrast to children's education. They are subject to high drop-out rates (50% on average), low levels of achievement (about 50% of those who complete the programmes fail to meet terminal performance criteria) and relapse into illiteracy appears to be widespread if there are no opportunities to practice literacy skills in the community. As a result of this ineffectiveness literacy had virtually disappeared from World Bank projects by the end of the 1980s. The 1990 World Conference on Education for All has arguably resulted in a minor resurgence of Bank lending for literacy projects in Ghana, Indonesia and Bangladesh (ibid). Nevertheless, adult literacy remains very much an educational Cinderella.

The development of more effective literacy programmes has been hundred by a lack of investment in research into literacy acquisition; Bown (1990) states that women's literacy is an utterly under researched area. Abadzi (ibid) claims that due to this lack, it is largely unknown what characteristics make adults more amenable to literacy training. Another factor is the poor quality of teaching, lacking effective classroom management, participatory techniques and active learning, and periodic evaluation of learning. This may reflect the relatively low professional status of literacy practitioners and the lack of financial investment in non-formal education. It may also suggest that poor women are accorded a low priority in development policy and practice.

If educators generally have taken relatively little interest in adult literacy, gender specialists have also paid scant regard to the problem of female illiteracy or indeed to female education. Ostergaard (1992) contains little reference to female education let alone literacy, likewise Moser (1993), Kabeer (1994) and Elson (1991). This lack of attention to the consequences of illiteracy for the lives of women represents a lost opportunity to raise the profile of women's literacy programmes and to promote the strategic interests of poor women and their children.

Writing in 1990, Bown, noted that while there had been a considerable amount of rhetoric about women's literacy, there had not been substantial funding from donors. Among her recommendations were that a target be set for a per centage of the UK aid budget to be spent on literacy and that NGOs should include an element of women's literacy in all projects. Setting spending targets for aid programmes is deeply problematic, while integrating literacy in all projects is perhaps rendered more difficult by a shortage of technical expertise in the field, particularly in interdisciplinary frameworks e.g fisheries or agriculture and literacy. In 1995, it is reasonably safe to assert that there has been no significant allocation of donor resources to women's literacy, despite the wealth of evidence attesting to the resultant benefits in terms of economic and social effects (Bown, 1990-Stromquist, 1995).

Is the lack of focus on female literacy yet more evidence of male bias in the development process? I fear that it is. The culture that has created the gender differential in literacy often stands in the way of remediation. At the levels of family and community, female literacy programmes may encounter male resistance, particularly if it threatens the gendered status quo. Governments, which are characteristically male-dominated, may lack the political will to promote the status of women in such a context. If they fail to provide the policy and planning framework for providing female literacy programmes, it then becomes extremely important for donors to assist on a significant scale, for to do otherwise would be to risk a donor-driven approach, which experience has proven to be a certain recipe for failure.

The safest strategy, politically, to increase female literacy is to aim to improve the enrolment and retention of girls at school. This can be done without much overt reference to gender which is invariably a sensitive issue among traditionalists. Whether it is the most efficient and effective approach remains open to question. Given the low level of efficiency to be found in many developing countries primary education systems, there will continue to be female drop outs and low achievers. The Delhi Declaration, in advocating the dual approach argues against investing in primary education only, although I would argue that the document does not go sufficiently far in addressing the educational needs of illiterate women.

What will it take then to increase the resourcing of female literacy programmes?

The following measures are suggested:

- research into the factors that promote female literacy and its use;
- disaggregation of funding by donors for female adult literacy in reporting on aid activities;
- investment in institutional capacity to develop literacy programmes;
- support for innovative approaches to women's literacy programmes which can be shown to be more effective in delivering literacy skills;
- closer co-operation between social development/gender and education/literacy specialists in policy formulation and project planning;
- closer linkage between literacy programmes and primary education.

In conclusion, there appears to be an ongoing need to advocate increased resourcing for women's education. This is likely to be met when there is a genuine commitment on the part of governments to improve the life opportunities of the poor. To achieve this, what is required is long term planning by governments in particular, but also by donors and NGOs to provide an effective policy framework and enabling environment to equip all women with functional literacy skills in the shortest possible time-frame.

Bibliography

Abadzi, Helen. 1994. *What We Know about Acquisition of Adult Literacy. Is There Hope?* Washington. World Bank Discussion Paper No 245.

Bown, Lalage, 1990. *Preparing the Future-Women, Literacy and Development.* London. ACTIONAID Development Report No 4.

Elson, Diane (ed.) 1991. *Male Bias in the Development Process.* Manchester University Press.

Kabeer Naila, 1994. *Reversed Realities; Gender Hierarchies in Development* Thought. London. Verso.

Moser, Caroline. 1993. *Gender Planning and Development. Theory, Practice and Training.* London. Routledge.

Ostergaard, Lise. 1992. *Gender and Development: A Practical Guide.* London. Routledge.

Stromquist, Nelly. "The Theoretical and Practical Bases for Empowerment" in *Women, Education and Empowerment,* Report of International Seminar held at UNESCO Institute for Education, Hamburg, Jan. 27-Feb. 2, 1993.

UNDP.1995. *Human Development Report.* Oxford.

UNESCO. 1994. *Final Report of Education for All Summit of Nine High-Population Countries.* Paris. UNESCO.

Wagner, Daniel A. 1995. "Literacy and Development: Rationales, Myths, Innovations and Future Directions". *International Journal of Educational Development.* Vol. 15, No. 4 pp 341-362. Pergamon.

12

EDUCATIONAL STRATEGIES FOR WOMEN

A CASE STUDY OF MAHILA SAMAKHYA, BANDA

Mahila Samakhya, Banda District, Uttar Pradesh and Nirantar, New Delhi.

This paper is a case study of the Mahila Samakhya programme in Banda District of Uttar Pradesh and documents the different educational interventions and innovative processes that have been carried out in the area of women's education in Banda. It also describes how these initiatives have been sustained, continually renewed and diversified over the past five years.

In retrospect the evolution and growth of the educational work in Banda can be seen in three phases. These are of course not strictly linear in relationship but rather circular, interactive and reflexive. They constitute a process and for the most part proceed together. In the initial phase an environment for education was created and the first few concrete literacy-related interventions were initiated (literacy camps and centers). The second phase consisted of sustaining these initiatives and new innovative experiments, particularly in the area of material production. In the third and current phase a concrete long term strategy and programme is being worked on to incorporate the growing and varied educational needs of the area in the form of a residential educational center for women (Mahila Shikshan Kendra).

The paper is structured as follows. *Section 1* provides a background to the programme and the area. *Section 2* describes the different interventions in the programmes the initial phase. *Section 3* deals with the strategies evolved to sustain and board-base the educational programme. *Section 4* deals with the emerging learning needs and the new initiatives undertaken to meet them.

1. Background of the Mahila Samakhya Programme

Mahila Samakhya (Mahila Samakhya) programme was launched by the Ministry of Human Resource Development (Department of Education) in 1989 as an innovative project in three different states of India—Uttar Pradesh, Gujarat and Kamataka[1]. In the northern Indian state of Uttar Pradesh, the Mahila Samakhya programme is operational in four districts Varanasi, Saharanpur, Tehri Garhwal and Banda.

Drawing on the perspective spelled out in National Policy on Education in 1986, the Mahila Samakhya programme was conceived as an educational programme that would play a positive, interventionist role in the empowerment of women. Briefly, Mahila Samakhya viewed education as an empowering processes that would initiate a process of change in the life situation of poor rural women. Moving away from the dominant mainstream perspective that "literacy equals education', in Mahila Samakhya awareness, building self confidence and a sense of self, collective action, access to information, developing a critical understanding of their life situation were seen as integral to an education programme for women [2].

Banda District: A Brief Profile

In Banda District the programme was initiated in approximately 100 villages spread over two administrative blocks, Tindwari and Manikpur. The programme has since spread to an additional 100 villages. Work has begun in a third block as well.

Banda is one of the more backward districts in India. A significant proportion (23%) of the population is tribal (Kol) and schedule caste. In Manikpur block where the programme is primarily based, the concentration is higher (30%). The dominant caste group of the region are the landed upper caste Thakurs who own and control a large part of the agriculture land[3]. The mainstay of the economy is rain-fed subsistence agriculture. In Manipur there is high level of dependence on the forests and on forests produce for survival. Agricultural labor is an important wage earning activity. As industry or other alternative sources of employment are almost completely absent in the region, migration during the lean agricultural periods is not uncommon.

Social indicators of development reflect a similar scenario. About two-thirds of the population of Banda District is illiterate. The extent of illiteracy is even higher among women and lower castes. The already low female district literacy rate (16%) drops drastically to a mere 8% in Manikpur block. There are many villages in the block where it is difficult to locate even a single literate woman. This clearly has serious implications in terms of initiating and sustaining an educational programme.

Perhaps a revealing indicator of the abysmal status of women in the district is the population's sex ratio of 842 women to 1000 men. Despite the shocking statistic, the figure conceals the horror that the combination of poverty and violence spells for women in Banda. Violence in Banda is constantly manifested in the nexus between highly organized gangs of dacoits, the state apparatus (police, forest, officials, etc.), the upper caste landlords and the political parties. And then there is the equally routine violence against women within the families which in this area often takes grotesque forms-burning, murder etc.

Any intervention, educational or otherwise, must be seen within the context of the situation described above.

2. Educational Interventions: the Initial Phase

From the outset literacy was never a stated objective of the programme. How could it be, given the desperate socio-economic and women's situation in the area. Mahila Samakhya concentrated on building among the women a critical understanding of their life situation. Through collective process of learning and reflection women were encouraged to think, speak and actively seek changes. Village level women's groups were formed to take the process forward.

The decision to steer clear of "padai likhai" (reading-writing) was not out of choice. Education or literacy at that stage was never a priority with the women. In meeting after meeting when informally discussion the need for literacy in women's lives, they would say-"Why should we study? We don't want a job after all" or "what will we get out of studying. We would rather plogh our fields, at least we'll get grain to eat. "Women invariably would rather talk about their "survival" problems—drinking water, ration, minimum wages, tendus leaves, violence or even widow pensions. During the discussions and village meetings illiteracy was never described as a limitation or a cause for shame. Instead conscious steps were taken to erase internalized stereo-typical images of illiterates as ignorant, powerless, lazy hence poor. The simplistic correlation that illiteracy is the cause of the poverty was questioned.

Discussions led to a demand for information at different levels. How do government schemes or the bureaucracy function? Which government department is responsible for handpump repair? What are the minimum wages in the area? Demonstrations, petitions, public, meetings, visits to the various administrative offices, forest department and police became frequent. Sakhis and Sangha Women now confident and informed were capable of taking action. But inevitably when a certain action entailed writing an application, signing a petition or reading a notice they were at a loss again. They had to depend on sahayoginis or the DIU.

However it took some concrete incidents to make irreversible changes in some of the women's attitude to literacy from a complete negation of the value of literacy to actively seeking and demanding educational inputs. An interesting incident which reflects how this shift came about is worth relating. Ram Bai, a Sakhi from Dandi village, took an application for the installation of a new handpump in her village to the block level office. The clerk at the office wrote out a receipt acknowledging the application. Not being able to read Ram bai mistook this for the administration's acceptance of the demand. She conveyed this to the women at the village meeting. The news of the sanction spread. Ram Bai was lauded for her efforts. Finally when the mistake was pointed out it meant a loss of face for her. Ram bai was now convinced that it was not enough to be informed about government schemes and procedures.

If Sakhis were to play an active interventionist role, then they must overcome this hurdle as well. Interactions with structures of power and governance required access to a crucial determinant of power the ability to read and write. This marked a major shift in Mahila Samakhya's educational programme. Some concrete steps were initiated. To create a suitable environment motivational songs and role plays were created by the Sakhis and sahayoginis. These were taken from village to village. Some of Sakhis experiences were reflected in these efforts. The response was not discouraging. International Women's Day celebrations in 1991 became an important forum where both these concerns were put forward by the women.

The demand for specific literacy inputs could not be ignored by the DIU. In response the Banda team began some literacy centers in villages and literacy camps were held for Sakhis.

The Experience of the Literacy Camps for Sakhis

Mahila Samakhya Banda adopted cap strategy to make the Sakhis literate. This innovative strategy had been successfully tried by Nirantar members working in Rajasthan as part of the innovative Women's Development Programme there. Daily pressures of housework, child care and other survival tasks are common obstacles to women reaching out to literacy programmes. The camp method has evolved as an effective strategy for women's literacy as it takes into account women's chronic problem of low and irregular attendance at formal education Centers.

Moreover the literacy camps provide a supportive-threatening atmosphere which is crucial in building the self confidence of women as learners. They are based on collective learning processes where an intense and continuous environment for learning is generated through the use of literacy games, songs, and other creative exercises. A high teacher-learner ratio ensures individual attention and a quick learning pace.

The main tenets of the camps approach and the teaching methodology (word centered approach) was shared with the Mahila Samakhya group at a state level Mahila Samakhya workshop in March 1991. Convinced that was a strategy worth experimenting with, the Banda group went ahead and planned a series of three 10 days residential camps spread over three months i.e. each camp is followed by a month long break. Care is taken to ensure that the camps are organized during the lean agricultural periods so that women can be away from home for such long stretches.

Follow-up

At the end of the three camps the learner acquires basic reading and writing skills. However the literacy levels were extremely fragile and required intensive inputs. This was a particularly challenging situation as many Sakhis were from remote village where there were no literate women. Further the word methodology was something that the village community was completely unfamiliar with. Once the women returned home they would often be the buff of jokes and ridicule in their community for not having learnt the alphabets. However some Sakhis were able to get help from within their families. Follow up efforts were restricted to making informal linkages with the Mahila Samakhya network. Sakhis were encouraged to go the centers in their village or the one closest to their homes. Sahayoginis would take extra time out during their weekly meeting to monitor and help Sakhis with their literacy. Practice exercises were given to them which the sahayoginis would check on. Despite the fact that follow-up was not very high. This was true of the intervening months between camps but once the three phases were over relapse became a serious concern.

Material Creation During the Camps

The camps requires trainers not only to teach but also simultaneously develop reading material for women. Creating wall papers, poems and stories are woven into the day's activities. These are then used as teaching-learning material. From the outset the state produced primers were found to be inappropriate and a new primer was developed during the first camp. Certain key words—namak (salt), anaj (grain), majdoori (wages) etc. were chosen in consultation with the core Sahayogini group. Practice exercises and lessons were woven around the key words. These also proved to be points around which discussions could be generated. This primer was then used in the subsequent camps and the literay centers.

Dissemination of Teaching Methodology

Neany 80 Sakhis in Banda have completed the phases of literacy camps. The learners have included some handpump mechanics as well. What has been remarkable has been the gradual expansion of the trainer group. After the initial external support the responsibility of conducting these camps has been with the sahayoginis and Anudeshikas (teachers). However from the beginning a concerted effort was made to draw in the neo-literate Sakhis of the earlier batches as trainers in subsequent camps. This not only served as a reinforcement of their own fragile literacy skills but also extended the pool of literacy trainers. This was necessary as the camp approach is an intensive process with a high teacher-learner ratio. Monotony, stagnation and high burn out levels of Anudeshikas repeatedly conducting camps necessitated an expansion of the human resource pool. Moreover for neo-literate Sakhis this was an on-the-job initiation to teaching methodology. The growth in the confidence of newly literate Sakhis and their competence at teaching paved the way for a later decision to provide them the opportunity to move onto becoming Anudeshikas themselves.

The Literacy Centers

Almost simultaneously Mahila Samakhya started literacy centers for women. Beginning with a mere four centers the number grew very slowly to seven in the first year. During the initial phase the team was ill-equipped in terms of teaching methodology, teaching-learning material etc. Moreover they had to contend with an additional problem. Being an area with abysmally low literacy levels for women it was nearly impossible finding women instructors for the centers. This problem is particularly relevant in Manikpur where it continues to be a problem. However over the years the demand for literacy centers have grown, particularly in Tindwari block where basic education levels are also higher. Currently there are 40 literacy centers spread over the two blocks.

3. Sustaining the Educational Programme: Making Linkages with the Handpump Project

Once the literacy camps and centers got underway the question of sustaining the efforts became of critical importance The education programme at that juncture received a fillip by making linkages with the recently initiated community handpump maintenance programme. Within this programme women were trained as handpump mechanics, caretakers. Village level water committees were also formed. This initiative led to women learning new skills, increased their self-confidence, and created new roles and identities. It gave the programme and its functionaries a renewed sense of buoyancy and visibility.

What was significant was that throughout the project period steps were taken to build on the educational processes at work within the parameters of a technology transfer programme. Making this link between skill development and education was crucial to the programme. It created new and varied opportunities for the neo-literate women to use their nascent literacy skills. For instance, Sakhis' involvement in water committee training required them to make charts and other educational material. There were new demands for literacy inputs by the handpump mechanics. They had very functional literacy needs-keeping records of their spare parts, inspection visits, depth of handpump bores etc.

Making these linkages triggered off new innovative processes. As the water progrmme evolved the need to communicate and share information across the Mahila Samakhya villages as well as the world beyond Mahila Samakhya grew. In terms of the handpump project the dearth of training and print material, easily accessible to neo-literates was sorely felt.

At this stage Mahila Samakhya sought the support of some current members of Nirantar who were at that point located at the National Institute of Adult Education (NIAE) in New Delhi. The emerging concerns from the literacy effort resonated with the ongoing debate around issues of post-literacy in the wake of the nation-wide launch of the total campaigns. The questions that were central to this debate and Nirantar's interests were:

a) The nature of post-literacy (PL) material;
b) Whether it is possible to produce PL material in a decentralized participatory manner.

The mutuality of these concerns brought Mahila Samakhya and the Nirantar group at NIAE together in exploring the possibility of developing gender sensitive material by involving neo-literate women in defining the content, the actual writing and production of the material. The effort was aimed at integrating the work being done in the area of water and sustaining literacy skills, while simultaneously equipping women with the necessary skills so that material production in general could become a decentralized activity.

The Process of Skills Transfer

A series of three residential workshops (three days each), with a core group of women, were planned over a six month period. The core group was a mixed one in terms of levels of literacy competence and included neo-literate Sakhis and handpump mechanics as well as literate sahayoginis. Facilitators from Nirantar were involved in designing, planning and implementing the three workshops and were part of the creation process of the broadsheet-"Mahila Dakiya" (postwoman).

Broadly the process followed in the workshop was to discuss with the group the important events in their work which they wished to communicate to others. Based on the emerging themes or issues smaller groups would then write and illustrate the items. This was then later share with the larger group after which it went through many rounds of reworking and editing. Attention was paid to the length and simplicity of the sentences and the items. Emphasis was placed on easy readability. Having done this the group then decided on the lay-out of the items. The artwork was then ready for printing.

The Mahila Dakiya (MD) workshops were not just workshops were not just workshops that enabled the transfer of sills in material production to neo-literate women but was also an important point of confluence for the two main streams within the mahila Samakhya programme—the water project and the FE program. Mahila Dakiya was a collective effort where the newly-acquired competence and skills of handpump mechanics and the neo-literate Sakhis blended together to affirm and validate the achievements of both process. Seeing their signatures at the end of the printed Mahila Dakiya gave the neo-literate Sakhis both a sense of achievement and an identity as literate women in the village community. At meetings held to discuss the feedback on the Mahila Dakiya, Sakhis related with pride stories of how people in their village could not believe that they had produced the broadsheet all on their own.

For the hand pump mechanics, the Dakiya became a vehicle for giving voice to their new experience- " When we first started out everyone in the village would taunt us about how we Kol women were only capable of doing mindless kitchen chores. But today they call us to their home, make us sit on the charpai (cot) and even offer us tea". The Mechanics also wrote about what they thought of upper caste people who saw them as ritually impure but could not keep the area around their own handpump clean. The case of Bhaori village was visually depicted in one

Mahila Dakiya and became an issue for discussion in many villages.

By projecting themselves in MD as "bicycle riding women doing a technical job" the mechanics were able to break stereotypical images of women as docile brides or wives in purdah. In Tindwani block for instance where there were no women mechanics. When the Anudeshikas read the Mahila Dakiya at the centers these become images of alternative role models.

Mahila Dakiya did not only become an important document recording the achievements of the programme but also a medium for establishing the identity of the programme in the district itself. The Dakiya also established the most concrete link between work and the use of literacy. The three day workshops saw Sakhis reading and writing enegetically in whatever spare time they could find. Besides the broadsheet has been read and re-read innumerable times by the Sakhis providing them with good practice material to reinforce their newly acquire literacy skills.

After the Mahila Dakiya experiment Nirantar has been working on a regular basis with the Banda Mahila Samakhya group. They have been involved in planning and providing resources inputs in all the subsequent educational initiatives.

Measures were taken to ensure that the skills imparted are not restricted to the core group. Mechanism to ensure a further dissemination of skills were evolved. Similar process of creating a newsletter has been replicated at the village level. This has not only resulted in drawing a larger group of women into the process, but ripples of interest were created at the village level for partaking in educational activities. There has been a further spread of information as 12 independent braodsheets were developed by women (in rotation) in clusters of 10 villages -each with its own name and distinctive features, dealing with issues specific to that village.

Spin-Offs of the Material Production Initiatives

This experiment in interactive material production worked as a catalyst for creating fresh learning needs. One spin-off was that women wanted to be trained in screen printing. The interest was sparked off after a field visit to a printing press during one of the MD workshops. Subsequently a group of about 15 women have been trained in screen printing. This opened up many new possibilities in decentralized material production. The production unit has since then printed a range of material-booklet on tendu leaves, posters for international Women's Day, the second literacy primer and even greeting cards have been produced in house. With this effort a further expansion of the skill based was made.

Upgrading Skills and Knowledge of Anudeshikas

The other significant effort made to sustain the education programme has been in terms of constantly upgrading skills of Anudeshikas and creating new learning opportunities for them. The decision to provide new roles for the neo-literate Sakhis as Anudeshikas has been an important step for the education programme. In an area where finding literate women is such a serious problem, this step was born both out of necessity as well as a well-thought-out strategy to provide rural women the opportunity to seek alternative avenues for employment. Further, within the programme, this provided the functionaries the possibility of growth linked to their own efforts at enhancing their skills.

However, after a point their limited skills (low literacy level) hindered them in carrying forward the teaching-learning process at the center. Specific inputs were needed to upgrade their literacy and numeracy skills, expand their knowledge and information base, and teaching skills. It was seen that while the need was more acutely felt for the newly literate Anudeshikas the problem extended to the Anudeshika group in general. Levels of formal education across the Anudeshika group is not very high. Further the quality of the formal education they have received does not equip them to provide the creative educational inputs that is envisaged within Mahila Samakhya. Moreover, many of the learners having attended the centers for a while had achieved fairly high literacy levels. There was a need now to provide them educational inputs of a different kind.

Linked to this is a larger question—what kind of education do we envisage for the women within Mahila Samakhya? Would simply decoding the written word enable poor tribal women to experience education as a strengthening input in their struggle for survival? At this juncture it was felt that while the Anudeshikas had been teaching for a while they had not received the intensive training inputs that other Mahila Samakhya functionaries had. A workshop on gender issues was thus organized for the Anudeshikas. In the workshop gender issues were discussed by analyzing primers and other standard literacy material.

Initially it was not very easy for the Anudeshikas to be critical as they saw the written word as sacrosanct. Gradually through a process of questioning and critiquing Anudeshikas were able to see that the primers in fact reinforced many stereotypes. For instance, the literate were always portrayed in language of plentitude. They were the repositories of knowledge and wisdom, money and resources. They worked hard, stayed clean and were calm in temperament. In sharp contrast illiterates were always stupid and lazy and were as a result poor, unhealthy and aggressive by nature. Women were virtually invisible. They had access neither to a world of knowledge nor resources. They were also not seen as potential targets for economic betterment. Information regarding schemes and loans were always directed towards men. The lessons in which women featured most prominently related to population control and health. Immunization of children and celebration of festivals, apart from doing household work appeared to be the full time occupation of most rural women. No doubt this turn around was engineered rather than spontaneous but the facilitators felt that it was necessary to emphasize the fact that writing or material production is not just a technical skills but reflective of certain intrinsic principles and prejudices as well.

Developing a Primer Interactively

This analysis formed the basis for developing a new primer. A small group of Anudeshikas and sahayoginis with Nirantar support started working on a primer which would portray women and their world as they experienced it. A number of conceptual issues had to be tackled before actual writing work could begin. Language was one such issue. While it is beyond the scope of this paper to discuss the complexities in detail it is worth a brief mention, as language and the politics surrounding it is central to any educational endeavour. For instance, a question that had to be addressed was -should the language used be the local language (Bundel) or standardized Hindi? It was observed that while the use of the local language was emphasized during oral communication, in the written mode standard Hindi was preferred. The language issue in the written mode proved to be a complex one and came up repeatedly during the primer creation workshops. While Bundle was the language the women were most familiar with, had greatest ease in while expressing themselves, they simultaneously felt that it was "dehalti" and "laath maar bhasha" (rustic and inferior) —a poor alternative to Hindi. This was a reflection of the inferiority they experienced with their caste, class and gender identity. The facilitators, wanting to counter this, argued for the use of the local language. But the women were clear that they sought literacy to be able to negotiate and interact with the mainstream. Hence it was imperative for them to learn Hindi. This and many other complexities were discussed and debated and finally the language that was used in the primers was a mixture of Hindi and Bundle.

During the first workshop different primers were analyzed to understand various technicalities involved in developing primers. For instance, how are key words chosen? What is the procedure for breaking key words into consonants and vowel? In what progression are they introduced?

The second workshop focused on putting together the key words and creating various lessons based on the words. An efforts was made to introduce an element of light heartedness as most primers tend to be restricted to very heavy "survival" issues. The primer was then field tested by the Anudeshikas. Based on the responses changed were made. Then the illustrations and lay-out was worked upon and finally it was screen printed locally. Learners, specially younger women and adolescent girls have found the primer very appealing. Many of the lessons have been the cause for much mirth at the centers.

Regular Inputs to Anudeshikas-Creating New Learning Fora

Besides specific workshops Anudeshikas are given regular inputs every month to upgrade their skills and knowledge base. The monthly Anudeshika meetings have been extended to include day long teaching sessions for the Anudeshikas. An effort is made to make these sessions interesting to create curiosity and a desire to seek more information. Prior preparation is needed for this where Nirantar and the Mahila Samakhya education team sit together and decide what new themes or topics will be taught. Particular problem areas in language and numeracy are also identified. For instance looking at the globe, understanding how the earth, how day and night and seasons are caused. When introducing such topics faciliators try and link to how women understand such phenomena with their knowledge system. Material is collected and practice exercises prepared. Supplementary reading material is also provided where these sessions themselves become a training in teaching methodology. While learning, the Anudehsikas are simultaneously exposed to a variety of new creative exercises, teaching techniques and classroom transactions.

4. Need for a Sustained Education Progrmme

The growth of the education programme described above has led to the emergence of many new learning needs. As the innovations have struck root in Banda the women have had to cope with new situations and questions that came up in the course of their work. Many of these demands cannot be met by present levels of skills available or the structures that are in place. These led to the need for new information, new skills and new structures within the programme. There is a need for specialized inputs for instance in curriculum development, developing teaching-learning materials etc. The areas (which have been touched upon in the earlier as well) where these needs have been felt most critically area:

- *Upgrading skills of neo-literate Anudeshikas*- Sporadic workshops and teaching sessions have been found inadequate in meeting all the needs.

- *Furthering the education process of the younger women and girls who have been attending centers regularly for a while and have attained certain basic literacy levels.* The demand for further education among this group has been so strongly articulated that in the previous year as many as 25 young women and girls demanded special inputs to prepare them to take the class 5 equivalency exams (this demand was articulated by the newly literate Anudeshikas as well). Unprepared, Mahila Samakhya had to hurriedly organize special coaching camps for these women. These women need and are seeking more sustained educational inputs.

- *Demands of the Handpump Mechanics*
Though the mechanics had earlier demanded literacy and some had attended the camps their progress in terms of literacy achievement was low. Unable to initially understand why one later realized that the mechanics at that point were so preoccupied in learning another skill-repair of handpump-that they were not able to concentrate or sustain their interest in literacy. Given their heavy time burden in handpump repair they were finding it difficult to allot time for literacy as well. Moreover their identity as handpump mechanics was so strong that it was a priority for them to sustain learning in this area. Thus attending mechanics' meetings and participating in water committee training etc. took precedence over all else.
Now having consolidated their experience in handpump repair a number of mechanics are once again seeking literacy inputs. Besides they, as well as the group i general have a number of other learning needs. For instance, the mechanics dealing with acute water shortage while repairing handpumps during the summer months, wanted to understand why depth of underground water varies in different area or during different seasons in the year, whether this was a new phenomenon or not. These questions led to a discussion on the falling water table and the broader issue of management of water resources. This had initiated a keen interest in the larger environmental problems in the Banda region. The other broad area of interest had been the interlinkages between water and health. Handpump mechanics increasingly came to realize the correction between quality of drinking water and health.

Planning a Residential Educational Center for Women

Given the nature of the needs articulated, the Mahila Samakhya-Nirantar group feels it is time to plan a more sustained and long term educational strategy. The Mahila Shishan Kendra or residential educational center for women has been conceived of as an educational resource center where these different needs will be catered to. Being a completely new area of work—different to running center or periodic camps—there is a need to develop a common conceptual understanding on a number of issues-curriculum content, the curriculum development methodology, equivalency levels with the formal system (whether one wants it at all or not), reading and writing what other skills and competencies, the teaching methodology etc. At a more functional level issues that one had to deal with are—Who among the different groups are we going to cater to? How is it going to be sustained? How long should the course be? What support material will have to be prepared? Who will teach? How are we dealing with teachers training? What the content of the training will be?

A core group which includes people the DIU, Anudeshikas and Nirantar have been deliberating on these issues. A number of meeting have been held. Other resource persons with experience in curriculum development, planning educational inputs have also been involved. After considerable discussion certain commonalties were arrived at.

- *Who and When*: As a beginning, a six month course has been planned for adolescents and young women, Sakhis and mechanics. These women will already have basic literacy skills. The timings of the course have been planned so as to keep in mind the agricultural lean seasons. Therefore the six month period will be broken up into two sessions. A month long break will be provided for the harvesting seasons. During that month a refresher course will be held for neoliterate Sakhis.
- *Equivalency*: While the MSK will not be based on equivalents with the formal system it was felt that giving the exam might be an expectation of many of the learners. Given the earlier experience this seems like a realistic eventuality. For others the expectation might be in terms of being competent enough to perform an economically viable activity or becoming an anudeshika with the program. Flexibility therefore needs to be woven into the programme. Instead of meeting specific expectations the MSK curriculum will focus on developing skills and competencies of the learners rather than rigid equivalency levels or minimum learning levels.

- *Curriculum*: But the most challenging area of work that the Mahila

Samakhya-Nirantar group has begun working on has been with regard to developing a curriculum. This will be the core around which all aspects of the programme will be woven. The group was quite clear that it wanted to approach curriculum development in a holistic manner rather than the traditional subject wise approach. This is based on the understanding that learning is not liner nor compartmentalized. Central to the curriculum will be certain themes or issues. These issucs based modules will comprise different elements determined by the needs aspirations and relevance to learners.

While an effort will be made to relate knowledge and information to learncrs lived experiences this will not be in exclusion to expanding the information base. Providing information for information's sake will be avoided. What is of importance is the manner in which new information and concepts are introduced. Therefore making linkages with familiar things within their environment will become important. For instance, learning about the structure of governance at the central and state level would seem irrelevant unless it is linked to Panchayati Raj— a system they are familiar with. Thus the curriculum content then assumes great importance. After considerable brainstorming the four major theme areas that have been identified are water, land, tree and forests, and village and society. Different aspects will be interwoven within these broad areas. Gender will be a running theme throughout the curriculum.

As there are certain cognitive sequences in learning, while planning the curriculum content and the different lessons, careful attention will be paid to grading-both in terms of information as well as other competencies.

The curriculum is being developed interactively. An effort is being made to build on the skills acquired earlier while working on Mahila Dakiya and the primer. Work has been initiated at different levels. A small core group of resource persons and Anudeshikas are working on developing the methodology, grading, competency levels etc. Gradually the group will be enlarged. At another level effort will be made to generate material with the Anudeshikas and women at center. There is a constant flow between the field and the core group. Particularly in terms of modification of exercises, cross checking information, discerning comprehension. The curriculum is attempting to steer clear of the lesson and lecture mode of teaching. Instead a variety of teaching modes will be used-structured lessons, creative exercises, experiments, role plays, field trip, etc. The curriculum will also be open ended as far as possible so that teachers will be free to innovate as they go along.

The curriculum being creative and experimental will depend very heavily on how teachers are able to handle classroom situations. The creativity and ability of the teachers will determine to a large extent the success of the curriculum. Thus training of the teachers assumes a great deal of importance. Selection of teachers requires serious thought.

Yet to begin the curriculum development process undertaken so far has already led to certain skill development particularly in terms of a conceptual clarity and other methodological issues related to creation of lesson, curriculum planning, evolving competency levels, etc.

Conclusion

This case study validates the fact that education and empowerment are twin processes for women. For poor rural women whose lives are determined by the realities of their socio-economic context as well as their gender, education acquires a special meaning. It is not simply a transfer of skills but more a question of how these skills help them meet survival needs and negotiates their immediate environment. Innovations in education for women therefore need not merely to be effective, and efficient but must answer the question of how women are going to bring into practice their learning.

1. Need for Responsive and Flexible Structures and Roles

The case study reveals that different educational strategies have been employed at various junctures in the programme. This has been complemented by a movement in roles for functionaries. For any programme to be effective there is a need for structures and roles to be flexible and responsive. For instance Manikpur has a problem in terms of finding literate women to teach at the centers. In response, despite their low literacy levels newly literate Sakhis were allowed to put their skills into practice. As capabilities get enhanced and new roles develop there is a need for new roles develop there is a need for new and flexible structures to support these new abilities. This is synergistic process as new roles and new structures mean the further creation of new skills and abilities. Thus allowing neo literates Sakhis to move into new roles has meant that new inputs must be provided to further enhance their skills. As this could not be met within the present framework there is a need to expand the educational infrastructure. This led to the decision to pursue the Mahila Shikshan Kendra.

2. The Need for Decentralization and Skill Dissemination

To ensure the growth and dynamism of a programme there is a need to decentralize. This leads to a further dissemination of skills and an expansion of the human resource pool. For instance, training neo-literate Sakhis to be trainers at the literacy camps both meant that they have been able to move into new areas of work—some of the Anudeshikas are now moving into the curriculum development process— while simultaneously freeing other functionaries. Similarly transferring skills is an important component that facilitates and strengthens the decentralization process. For instance transferring skills in material production during Mahika Dakiya allowed local initiatives to take root. This was furthered during the primer workshop process. These skills are being built on further during the curriculum development.

3. Enhancing the Conceptual Understanding of the Group

It is not uncommon in educational and development efforts to leave the conceptual (read intellectual) expertise either to select few within the group or to outsiders. In the Banda experience a definite attempt has been made to break these divisions. There at various stages concrete inputs have been provided to enhance the conceptual understanding of the group. For instance, it is not enough to say that locally developed material is preferred. This must be based on a critical understanding of why and in what circumstances. Therefore it was necessary to analyze traditional primers before it was necessary to analyze traditional primers before the group themselves articulated the need to develop their own primer. Group discussions on the issue of language is important if they are to understand the larger issues of politics of language and power dynamics, for instance. Similarly building and understanding on the concepts of curriculum development, is important for the group to grow and lessen their dependence on outside "experts".

1. The programme has been extended to two other states-Andhra Praadesh and Bihar.

2. The organizational structure of the programme in Uttar Pradesh is as follows: at the apex level, the programme is coordinated by the registered society. The State Education Secretary is its ex-officio charperson. The society comprises a general council and and executive committee, which is responsible for providing overall direction to the programme. At the district level, the structure consists of a District Implementation Unit (DIU) with a district coordinator as its head. The DIU plans, implements and coordinates the district level programme. Within the DIU sahayogini are full-time programme func-

tionaries that oversee the work of ten village level animators or Sakhis. The Sakhis are responsible for mobilizing and coordinating the Mahila Sanghas or Village women's groups.

3. The land ownership pattern in Banda District is more skewed than other parts of the country with the upper 5% of the landed peasantry owing more than 22% of the total cultivable land.

13

THE LITERAY PROGRAM OF FRIENDS IN VILLAGE DEVELOPMENT BANGLADESH (FIVDB)

Hasnat Khandakar

Friends In Village Development Bangladesh (FIVDB) is a national non-government development organization established in 1979. Since 1981, FIVDB has been implementing an integrated rural development program in the areas of greater Sylhet, a division that is located in the north-eastern part of the country. The program aims at poverty alleviation through the social and economic empowerment of the rural poor. The activities include formation of rural organizations, non-formal education and functional literacy, child education, training on human and vocational skills, savings, credit and micro enterprise development, promotion of regenerative agriculture through organic horticulture, livestock development and a preventive health care programme.

Feature of the FIVDB Functional Literacy Method

The method combines discussion of rural issues and literacy instructions in each lesson.

- The discussion are based on the life, work and problems of the rural landless poor.
- The discussions involve the participants in finding answers by themselves to their particular problems. Some of these sessions also include information on agriculture, health, nutrition, the formation of people's self-help organization, women's rights, socio-help organization, women's rights, socio-legal issues related to organization, family laws, inheritance, marriage, dowry, divorce, gender equality etc.
- New letters are taught within the context of words and sentences are introduced gradually throughout the series.
- Controlled vocabulary is followed in the sessions. Only a few new

words are taught in each lesson and they are repeated as many times as possible in several lessons in order to build up a sight vocabulary.

- The 60 lessons are divided into three books and are to be completed in 120 session of 2 hours each.
- Learners books are supplemented with charts and flash cards to aid the discussions and retention of literacy skills.
- Guidelines are provided for each day's discussion and literacy instruction.

The basic literacy course is completed in 120 sessions of two hours each spread over about 6 months. Therefore over the six months, the learners on aggregate can have a learning session of 240 hours. In addition, FIVDB has developed a post-literacy follow-up course of three months to further strengthen the literacy, accounting and analytical skills of the participants which follows the basic course.

In order to implement this program, functional literacy materials were developed in 1981 following an extensive field research. Presently FIVDB provides support to 200 development organizations with training and learning materials. It produces and supplies basic learning materials for 300,000 adult learners every year. In 1981 FIVDB assisted development organizations in Bihar, India to adapt its functional literacy materials in Hindi.

FIVDB has also developed a number of reading materials for the neo-literates. A monthly tabloid news paper "Gram Bandhab" (Village Friend) and a bi-monthly journal "Bikash" (Progress) are regularly published to cater the needs of new readers.

FIVDB is continuously involved in the development and publication of reading materials including short stories, case studies, folklore, plays, adoption of classics and information materials in agriculture, health, income generation, women's rights, social-legal rights etc. for new readers. It has also published a poster featuring "Amar Katha Balte Chai, Lekhapara Shikhte Chai" for the neo-readers.

After the completion of the follow -up course. A 'study circle' is formed and a collection of books for neo-readers in the villages are made available through the Village Library Program. Both male and female groups have been carrying out this program since its inception.

On the basis of the frequent visits to these learning sessions, it can be said that the female learners were seen to be relatively more enthusiastic about pursuing such classes. Most of the female learners have been seen taking the classes while holding their six months or one year old children in the arms, while leaving their very important family tasks undone for the time being. These field experience also show that they are very much interested in participating in different curricular activities particularly designing and outlining. Almost all the female study sessions were seen as something that appeared to be very interesting from their part. It is really amazing to see a group of the society's most underprivileged and deprived section taking the education so seriously. All these instances simply imply the emergencc of one truth, that is, these underprivileged women desperately want to learn; want to learn about something they never knew, want to learn about something they never even thought, want to learn about something that they were never told and more importantly want to know about their oppressed lives.

Training on the FIVDB Functional Literacy Method

FIVDB offers two types of training. Training of Trainers (TOT) is designed for literacy trainers and supervisors from different organizations involved in functional literacy programme. The two week long "TOT" is mostly held at its Central Training Center in Khadimnagar, Sylhet. The TOT is organized in Dhaka too. FIVDB offers training of literacy facilitators (Shebok/Shebika) at its Training Center or at the project sites of different parts of the country, depending on the request of user organizations. In these training courses, it has always been observed that the women are participating equally with the men in terms of number and skills.

At FIVDB, each year a few of the functional education graduates become facilitators. For this they certainly need well developed literacy and numeracy skills. Volunteer health workers are also chosen from among the female graduates. They are required to read various booklets and articles on health as well as to keep records of their activities. FIVDB also offers special residential training courses for women on women's specialized social and organizational skills as well as on occupational and vocational skills for economic development. It also supports organized women groups in the village with micro credit and expertise in the village with micro credit and expertise in the small scale enterprises. Organized women groups are also trained to carry out the regenerative and organic agricultural plantation system.

14

MODELS OF LITERACY PROGRAM IN NEPAL

Involvement of different actors has allowed the development of a range of literacy programs in Nepal. The existence of various models is considered an advantage specially in a country like Nepal where languages and culture are different from region to region.

Model 1 involves a twelve month literacy course followed by three month vocational course and community reading center. For the first 6 months the national literacy primers "Naya Goreto" (New Trial) are commonly used and for the next 6 months literacy materials designed by SCUS (Save the Children US) and other organizations, for advance learners are used. At this point implementors have options to select materials they want to use on the basis of priority areas of their program.

The next 3 months in this model has been designed to transfer few practical functional skills to graduates of literacy class. These lessons are concerned with upgrading their existing farming skills as well as business literacy. The Community reading center comes at the end as the Center keeps different types of books used by the graduates. It helps to retain their literacy skills as well as update them on innovations and other development messages.

Model 2 consists of an 18-month literacy course divided into 3 phases. The first part is a nine-month basic course followed by a six-month course and concluded with 3 month additional course.

In the first nine months, emphasis is given to basic literacy while the remaining period focuses on functional skills related with health, family planning, kitchen gardening, child rearing, income generating activities etc. This model especially targets females. The Basic Primary Education Project (BPEP) has developed literacy materials for all the phases.

Model 3 comprises six months and is widely used throughout the country. The national literacy primers "Naya Goreto", are also used in the courses.

The Adult Education Section of the Ministry of Education, Culture and Social Welfare (MOECSW) is using this model as well as a number of NGOs who are being supported to replicate the model by few donor agencies. While the primers have integrated development messages, the 6 month course focuses on the acquisition of basic literacy skills. The key word approach, use of participatory approaches of learning and illustrations of the primers used in the classes have been found to be appealing to learners.

Model 4 involves literacy being linked with women's saving and credit groups where the graduates of literacy class are organized in women's saving and credit groups and initiate different types of income generating activities. The duration of the literacy class is between 9 to 12 months. After completing 6 months basic course of "Naya Goreto", either they go for 6 month advance course or 3 month follow-up course. Literacy materials developed by SCUS, Action Aid, World Education, BPEP and the Adult Education Section of (MOECSW) are available for use in the follow-up or advance literacy courses.

In this model, NGOs primarily manage the program and generate cash contributions from learners in different forms like purchasing of books, registration and tuition fees.

This amount is kept as learners' group fund and later used as capital fund for the credit program among their group members. To increase this limited fund, they have either been linked with financial institutions or given seed money.

Two major issues that have emerged regarding the models are:

* Organizing 6 months literacy course is not enough and even difficult to make women and men literate. Thus, each literacy class needs to be followed up either by 6 month or 3 month additional course.
* The second issue is the need to link the literacy program with income generating activities during or after the advance course.

In the discussion, it was clear that majority of the participants favored model 4 as the appropriate model for Nepal. Reviewing the strategical needs as well as examining how these literacy models can be made more effective, the participants came up with the following points:

1. **Contribution from learners**. As many Non Governmental sectors are raising contributions from learners and have proved effective, the group felt it necessary to replicate the idea. While principally agreeing on this, few participants noted that even at the present situation, where 100% subsidy from Government and few donors have not been able to make effective program, how could one expect that learners would be interested to join if they have to pay? As the government does not have this policy, it might be problematic to introduce this in government-operated literacy programs. However, the group considered that participants could be asked to make cash contribution on registration, tuition, deposit, books, absent fine and others.

2. **Partnership approach**- As international NGOS (INGOs) are equally involved in literacy and other community development activities in Nepal, participants shared their problems as a result of direct program implementation of INGOs. As NGOs are operating comparatively with limited resources, sometimes INGOs' program operating policy and strategies create confusion and competition. One example is the payment of salaries for the facilitators of literacy class where one INGO started to pay almost double salary from the normal. On the other hand, if INGOs work together with NGOs, this increases the chances of program sustainability.

3. **Formation of literacy committee at different levels**- The group realized that it is important to have a literacy committee at different levels (central, district, village development committee and ward level) which would be responsible for coordination. Also, it has been recommended to form literacy class management committee in each class.

4. **Community based participatory approach**-Although participants suggested that programs should be community based, it was not possible to define community based and what makes participatory approach in such a short time. Fund raising, community contribution, partnership with local NGOs and a few other processes mentioned in the next point were considered close to community based and participatory approach.

5. **Designing course according to community probelms**-Some process activities were also presented as necessary to replicate the program

effectively. This include the conducting of a baseline survey, introduction of a village readiness program, group formations before literacy class, selection of facilitator by participants, introduction of social awareness class, functional activities, different kind of training and local and central level supervision.

15

LINKING TOTAL LITERACY TO UNIVERSAL ELEMENTARY EDUCATION

Anita Rampal

I am working with the All India People's Science Network (AIPSN), and especially with an educational NGO called Ekalavya. In the recent past, a separate offshoot of the AIPSN, called The Bharat Gyan Vigyan Samiti (BGVS) or the Indian People's Science Education Forum was formed with a focus on literacy; consequently, we have also been active through that organization. In this presentation, I will combine the experiences of Ekalavya as well as BGVS, because they are both working together. Using Ekalavya's experience in education, especially in science education, we are trying to explore how the Total Literacy Campaign (TLC) and other programmes can link up with elementary education.

Innovating Elementary Education: The Madhya Pradesh Experience

In Madhya Pradesh, we have total freedom to do that we want within the broad framework of the syllabus—something which I don't think any other state has ever allowed. We can work within government system, with government teachers, government schools, and totally overhaul the curriculum as well as teacher training patterns and more importantly, the examination pattern. Even the board exam for class VIII was designed as an open book exam where children could bring their books and answer questions. When children can consult a book to answer a question, the question has to be a creative one. This also made the teachers get into a different mode of thinking—because children were not expected to learn by rote, and the exam is not primarily information—based.

The emphasis was in making learners do various kinds of activities, so that they are fully involved, and not passively sitting and listening to lectures. This involved intensive work, first, in the science programme, and then a programme for social sciences, for middle schools. There is also a package for primary schools—Class I to Class V, in which one departed from the rigid framework of the minimum levels of learning. Rather we try to see who are the children who are coming to us, and what is their pace of learning, what is the method one can use so that they enjoy what they are learning and they start thinking about these concepts and ideas. It is not just basic skills, but also a lot of thinking that goes along with what they are doing. This is a very rich experience and many people from various kinds of institutions and organizations got involved because of the freedom available to do things differently.

Linking TLC with Elementary Education

BGVS was formed to work totally as a literacy mobilization organization, as a support to the National Literacy Mission where it works in districts, setting up separate units in every district and even at the block level. Aside from its mobilization contribution, it is also involved in training. BGVS has been working in may TLCs and in some places it has been effective and successful in trying to ensure that the campaign actually is a people's programme.

In other areas, there have been problems caused by bureaucratic hurdles—the Collector and the Saksharata Samitis (District Literacy Committees) have not really understood how to work in conjuction with NGOs. But in the last few years it has been found that wherever the TLCs were effective, even though there were different spin-offs, diverse programmes evolved as people got mobilized in that area. One remarkable thing was the universal demand for education. We have been discussing how, when women started coming into the Mahila Samakhya programme, there has been a demand for more concrete educational inputs. Similarly here, people who were coming into these centers felt that if I can come, then why can't my child get more meaningful kind of education. For many years we had felt that there is no demand. Now through the efforts of the BGVS there was a concrete demand coming from various sections.

The Joy of Learning Campaign

How do we respond to this? Since there is already enough momentum built, and enough mobilization in districts, as well as a whole network of activists and volunteers working in literacy now, BGVS has decided to work very strongly in the area of elementary education. Their main aim is to link up literacy work with the universalization of elementary education. Towards this, the first step taken this year is the Joy of Learning Campaign.

All of us have been discussing our role in getting children prepared and sending them back to schools—but if the school environment remains oppressive, our efforts are bound to fail. There will be drop-outs, or children may not learn much. By now there have been many studies, government as well as non-government, which show the levels of achievement in schools. Even after class V, children are not able to read, they do not even have the basic skills in numeracy. So the question is, what are we doing? Even if we somehow ensure that children go to schools, what happens in those schools? We really must effect a change there. And secondly, even though people wanted education, there was still this deeply held belief their children could not cope with the culture of a school.

To break that kind of an image, the idea is to make a school like a Mela (fair). BGVs has begun this process in many different states-organizing very varied and structured activities, which are learning activities, for example, origami and painting, along with a math corner, a low cost science experiments corner, a history-walk corner, and science through the kitchen. One has to redefine learning—that history is not just learning and memorizing a lot of names, but something much more interesting. Trained resource persons come and conduct a corner for a couple of hours. About 20 children come to a corner, they will perform those activities, and make it visible to the community. The whole village, parents, teachers, everyone, can see that the child is learning and is enjoying it. So the idea is to make that visibility possible.

We all know that child centered education should be like this, that children should be allowed to ask questions, there should be a democratic atmosphere, but we do not have these models visible to people on a large scale. We might have it in a progressive school or in a few public schools here and there. So the campaign has now been taken up in about 250 districts, making inroads into the block and the Panchayat level committees, to make a dent in their attitudes and promote an alternative form of education. The campaign will continue until next year, in several states, with different schedules. The importance of the campaign lies in the fact that today, when you talk to people about better education, their demand is for things like heavy books, lots of written work, and children learning multiplication tables! This is simply because they think that is what education is. So if you really want people to become critical about the traditional form of schooling, one has to make an alternative visible to them.

The Exchange Visit Programme

A strategy that People's Science Groups have been adopting, and which we have also used successfully, is exchange visits between children of different communities, regions and classes, using the guest-host method of accommodation. Children from different states in India who stayed with 500 Delhi-based children. And even though it is very difficult to organize and arrange such a thing, for many children who had come from villages and interior areas, it was the first time they were staying in someone else's house. This itself breaks many barriers. For example, when a child who knows only Telugu is staying with a child who knows only Hindi, the struggle of living together and communicating with each other for those 5-6 days is an enriching experience. In.fact, teachers have requested a similar exchange programme for themselves. Based on this, wherever we have Bal Melas (children's fair) whether at the District or State Level, we ensure that it is in this kind a guest-host system, where parents also get involved. Parents get curious about what is happening with the children, and they too learn much about other cultures and religions. This learning experience is much more fruitful than reading about it in a book as a chapter or having lessons on national integration. This method also forces the community to get involved and share the costs.

The Challenges Ahead

- **Fostering all-around innovation**—A start has been made with the freedom given to BGVS to launch innovative education inputs in schools in 4 states. Through this process, at least some schools will be reoriented to function more creatively, trying out different packages; the curriculum will be transformed because learning activities will be based on actual experience. Rajasthan had a programme called Shiksha Karmi Project, (Education Worker Project) in which a local youth (a girl who had studied till 4th or 5th, or a boy has studied till class 7 or 8) are trained to run schools in villages lacking a trained teacher, or where regular trained teachers are unlikely to remain, even if posted there. Local youths feel more concerned and their accountability to the community is greater since they too are members of the village. A similar experiment is being tried in Madhya Pradesh, with some modifications. This kind of freedom of innovation should be created in other states too. If such experimentation with different models can come up in different pocket, it could lead to close involvement between the person who is teaching and the community.

- **Motivating teachers**—How do we create an educational model which motivates and excites teachers, gets them involved, and removes the drudgery and frustration they face. And even if we could, would we be ultimately able to change the nature of our schools and the classrooms? If the kind of educational movement described above occurs, then I think teachers will inevitably be transformed by it, and they themselves will begin to develop innovative programmes.

- **Changing curriculum**—Until now the most constraining factor has been the state's rigid control over curriculum. Even if anyone wanted to make a change, it would be subverted by the tight control over curriculum, examination pattern, and teacher training. If the stronghold of curriculum can be loosened, through experiments like the Bihar Education Project in different states, or through the programme of linking TLC with elementary education, and if the space and freedom which has been offered right now in some states is retained and spread, a great deal can be achieved.

- **Creating better teaching/learning materials**— In the TLCs there is one important area of flexibility—that every district can make its own primer. This has been the first time in our history when this decentralized approach has been taken to make teaching materials. Until now it was totally state controlled. So if this kind of freedom is given even in school curricula so that the concerns, culture, and specificity of the area is reflected, this will also create a positive change in the motivation for coming to school.

16

INNOVATIONS IN LITERACY PRACTICE IN NEPAL

One of the major objectives of the workshop was to share innovations in literacy program within the country. The flexibility on NGOs side has allowed the development and testing of different new initiatives in the field of literacy, more often as a response to the problems in the literacy programs.

- **Networking at the Regional Level-** The regional level networking among CARE, Save the Children-Japan, DISVI, SCUS and many other local NGOs in the mid and eastern terai area of Nepal have set an example. It has been proved to be extremely helpful in reducing differences in literacy program implementation, making use of technical support available in the region and development of follow up literacy materials. Networking has served to minimize problems of coordination, low quality training and lack of uniformity.

- **Linkage of Literay with Saving and Credit Programs-** Several NGOs and INGOs and WDD from government sector have linked literacy programs with income generating activities. The graduates of a literacy class are organized for saving and credit programs and then these groups either link with banks or funds are provided by the concerned agencies as seed money for credit programs. Amount of saving, size of loan and interest varies among these agencies.

The linkage with income generating program has been considered as extremely helpful as it provides an answer to what the participants would be doing once they graduate from literacy class and which motivates learners to continue the program.

- **Village Readiness Program-** Introduced a couple of years ago, the program insists on the preparation of the community where the literacy class is expected to happen. The program allows the sharing of each aspect of literacy program with the people in the community people so that they will have a clear understanding. Conducting literacy surveys which involve people from the same community and a program orientation are its key features.

- **Different Versions of Literacy Packages**—While the basic literacy primer consist of one version, many NGOs have come up with different forms for follow-up literacy materials. For example, a basic primer have been developed in Mager language by Action Aid in Nepal.

  Similarly, SCUS has also developed a tarai version of its follow-up literacy materials "Koseli" and widely used in the tarai districts of mid and eastern regions of the country.

- **Learners Generated Materials Development-** The Learners Generated Materials Development (LGM) initiated by SCUS since four years has already become popular through out the country. Today many other agencies like World Education, Annapurna Conservation Area Project (ACAP), Backward Society Education (BASE), CARE and Lutheran World Service have already replicated the idea.

  The LGM advocates learners as writers of reading materials that could be used in literacy classes. Usually LGMs are developed by organizing workshop of literacy participants. The important benefits of the LGM is that it contributes significantly in building confidence among the writers, the materials will represent local issues and thus will be more meaningful and easy to understand and helps in retaining the literacy skill of participants.

- **Language Experience Approach-**The Language Experience Approach (LEA) is an alternative to the "Key Word" method. Participants get the opportunity to create their learning sentences by themselves where they are encouraged to develop a few sentences' stories according to their interest. When they tell the story verbally, the facilitator writes the same story exactly as told. Later the same story is used for introducing letters. In this approach the facilitator uses the selected few sentences to familiarize learners whereas one word is used in the key word approach. As the LEA accepts the flexibility of decoding stories developed by learners in their own language, the approach could be used with the minority groups.

- **Family Literacy-** A comparatively new concept in Nepal, the program involves the use of literacy skills within the family and community. In the family level. Literacy is promoting inter-generation literacy as well as aimed at strengthening literacy skills required to interact with different institutions of the communities e.g. school, health post, post office, bank etc.

Introduction of a "**baby book**" by Save the Children is one of the key activities of the family literacy program in Nepal where it is seen to provide three benefits to its users. *First*, it serves as a resource manual for the mothers of new born babies for child rearing in which they will have to document the first and interesting things in the life of their baby from birth to 2 years of age. *Second*, the book is a good reading material for the new graduates of literacy classes. *Finally*, as the book has provided enough room for documentation about babies, obviously it promotes writing skills of the users. In other words, the book is helpful in retaining and improving reading and writing skills of literacy class graduates.

- **Linking Literacy Program with Parenting and Child to Child Program-** Few participating agencies have been found active in early childhood development programs. Yet parenting education and child to child programs are two major activities linked with literacy program in Nepal. Parenting education has become much popular as almost half of the total participants are mothers. Usually conducted alongwith adult literacy program, parent education classes have made use of primers developed specially for this. On the other hand, child to child program has been linked to out of school children between 8 to 14 years old.

- **Re-producing Authority-**Centralized publication and distribution system have appeared as one of major problems of getting literacy materials in time. As a response, ***Innovative Forum for Community Development***, with the reproducing authority from few agencies is working as clearing house. The Forum collects requests from the users of the literacy publications for which they have been authorized for reprinting and distribution. The reproducing authority has been recognized as one of the effective ways to reduce dependency at one point.

- **Community Literacy-** Community literacy program is the most recent program being initiated by Overseas Development Assistance (ODA) and British Council together with Innovative Forum for Community Development. The project has been trying to promote use of real literacy materials as post literacy in Nepalese communities. Real literacy materials are those printed reading materials used in different forms such as product labels, instructions for the users or buyers, posters, job application forms, bank vouchers etc. The other two categories of literacy materials are especially designed and extension materials. The first one is especially designed or created materials for literacy program and extension material represents materials with development messages.

- **Sarlahi Pilot Program-** The National Non Formal Education Council has been conducting a pilot program to test effective methods of literacy teaching and learning in a community where participants do not use Nepali as their first language and their mother tongue is different. For this purpose the council has selected Sarlahi District.

17

CASE STUDY OF BIHAR MAHILA SAMAKHYA

Sister Sujita

I work with the Bihar Education Project (BEP), which was the first project of its kind in India. Started in 1991, BEP is funded by UNICEF, Government of India, and the state authorities of Bihar.

Presently, the Bihar Education Project has 7 basic components:

1. Primary education;
2. Early childhood education;
3. Teacher training;
4. Women's empowerment (defined and implemented as in Mahila Samakhya);
5. Culture;
6. Communication; and
7. Continuing education.

I am responsible for the Mahila Samakhya part of the BEP and we work in 7 districts at the moment, covering over 1300 villages. Mahila Samakhya alone has a strength of 120 full-time Sahayoginis (activists responsible for approximately 10 villages) and more than 2000 trained Sakhis (village-level women activists/leaders) and more than 20,000 women in village collectives. This does not include those groups which are weak and not meeting regularly.

Within Mahila Samakhya, the pattern of training and working in the field is very much the same as in any other Mahila Samakhya state programme- viz: awareness-building, taking up issues, fighting for minimum wages, protesting violence against women, training activities, and so on. But we have a very interesting component within Mahila Samakhya-

BEP, which we call Jag-Jagi. The origin of this name is very interesting as it comes from the belief that to awaken this world, we must reach that half of humanity (women) who have not been awakened for education. Jag also stands for *jagat* (world) and jagi means awakening. Thus, Jag-Jagi is the educational component of Mahila Samakhya in Bihar.

Components of Jag-Hagi

The school preparedness programme, or **school tayyari karyakram**. Every year in November-December-January, we organise events like **Maa-Beti Melas** (Mother-Daughter Fairs) where women come with their daughters up to the age of 15. They come in big groups, and all day there is singing, talking and hearing about education. This activity is undertaken at this time of year for strategic reasons because school enrolment begins in January, at which point we are right into the next component of Jag-Jagi.

Enrollment and retention of girl children in school. Mahila Samakhya Bihar places as lot of emphasis on primary education of girls. The women's groups in the villages are encouraged to discuss and deal with this as well. In January, all the groups are busy enrolling girl children and by then we have prepared a list of all the girl children in Mahila Samakhya villages. Using the list as a base, women see to it that girl children are enrolled and retained in school. In some villages, Manila Samakhya sangh/samooh (village-level women's collectives) keep watch in the villages to get hold of any girls who are doing other domestic work—like grazing goats—during school hours. They are firmly taken back to school and told to do their chores after 4 o'clock.

School supervision and monitoring by Mahila Samakhya. Initially teachers were very hostile to us. They saw themselves as government servants and resented supervision, especially by illiterate women. So we kept changing strategies. Finally, we taught the Sahayoginis some very good action songs. We asked the teachers to at least allow us into the classroom to teach the students a song. Through the songs, we got inside the schools. Now, the teachers look forward to the Sahayoginis' visit to the school. We have developed a format by which the Sahayoginis keep records of the attendance of school teachers as well as of the children. This enables us to check the total number of children enrolled (especially girl children), how many are present when we visit; if the teacher was absent, where he/she has gone; and if the teacher was late, how late and why, etc., etc., So far, we carry out 6 checks a month for each school. This is too heavy a load, and we intend to cut down this number. I think the teachers have now accepted us, and some districts have responded well to our intervention-for example, in one block where Mahila Samakhya is operative, 95 per cent of teachers are coming to school on time. And, they are afraid of women's groups. Almost 100 per cent of our women are illiterate, but they are monitoring the education of their girls very actively. We have been accepted, I think, because we are part of a wider education program like the BEP. If we were only a women's programme, perhaps they would have thrown us out! Being within BEP gives us acceptance and access to many things.

Kishori Jag-Jagi, for girls over 15 of age, and **Mahila Jag Jagi**, for women both of which are picking up momentum now. The demand for these women's literacy centres came from the people themselves. Our strategy has been to ask any Mahila Samooh which wants a literacy center in their village, to find themselves a person who can teach them so we tell them "We don't know where to go and find a teacher for you". So a frantic search goes on. From our side, there are no restrictions—it could be a man or a woman of any caste, age or community—we don't care whom they choose. But they must choose whom they are confident about, and who is able to read and write and willing to teach. Once the persons identified, we have developed a little test to see whether they can do the teaching. At the moment we are not yet ready with our complete training module. So we use the training developed by BEP for NFE/AE instructors. The jag-jagi teachers are called **sahelis**. After the instructors' training, we give them 3 to 5 days intense training on women's empowement, some inputs on the Mahila Samakhya program and philosophy, and an exposure to different methods of teaching with the women's empowerment concept. Thereafter, the sahelis come together every 2 months for further inputs and reinforcement.

The participation of women is the village education committee (VECs). We lobbied at the state level to get a policy formulated that the sakhis must be members of the village education committee. So sakhis attend the VECs, after which they come to the Mahila Samoohs and share what happened. They then take the problems of the Mahila Samooh back to the VECs. Both groups are strengthened by this participation.

Mahila Shikshan Kendras (MSKs) or condensed courses to enable women who had dropped out of school in childhood to complete their matriculation—6 of them at the moment. We did not wait to set up the

MSKs only after all the materials were ready and everything was in place. We did take a risk and trusted some of the good voluntary groups, or the District Resource Units, to run the MSK in their districts. This component is now 7 months old. We had decided that after 6 to 7 months, we would have a thorough assessment of how things are going, and this evaluation is going on now. But it is absolutely delightful to see some of the groups. The entire student body of one MSK-all 31 of them-were busy practicing Karate! One group is learning electric wiring and another carpentry, along the reading and writing. We try to provide any subject or activity they are interested in. Most of them were illiterate and have now come up to the level of class III. A few were primary school drop outs.

In Bihar we are not thinking of Mahila Shikshan Kendras for matriculation per se. Our goal is more to see that there is at least one literate woman in the distant villages of Bihar. In most of these villages, we still don't have a single literate women. We hope the Mahila Shikshan Kendra will fulfill this need. We have a 14 years old Tharu girl, the youngest in the MSK age group of 18 to 35, who is the first girl to be able to write in that entire area. She has reaches class III level now. I think by the time they are ready to leave, they will definitely come up to class V level. After the evaluation next year we may change our stand and decide to take only primary school drop-outs- we don't know. This whole MSK is an experiment, and we are confident that the *need which emerges* will tell us what to do next.

Methods

As far as methodology is concerned, ours is more or less the same as what others use. In addition, we put up a lot of street plays. All the teams are getting trained in that. Now other groups like the BEP environment building team are asking us to send our women to do street plays for motivation. Initially, we were reluctant, but now we feel it is a recognition of our strength, so why not. We are also participating in many other environment-building activities for education. Another activity we are at the moment busy with is composing songs and poems on the education of women. Hopefully, by the end of the year we will have one or two audio tapes ready. Education is also a very important theme for the Mahila Samooh meetings-what are they doing with regard to enrollment, retention, and so on.

Different groups have their own literacy content based on their needs and priorities. We have several groups in Ranchi now, whose sole activity is centered around protecting the forests. Women's groups guard the forest day and night to prevent logging. Such groups want their education inputs to be linked to forest issues. For every groups, we try to relate learning to their daily life and struggles. Our concern is how to link reading and writing to their realities.

Contrary to what most people think, when poor women become aware of the need for education, there is no limit to what they will invest to fulfill that need. In Bhakarpur, a huge harijan village, neglected by everyone, a Mahila Samooh was formed. The first issue they took up was education for their children. The women themselves-helped by their menfolk-leveled a piece of land and put up a little shed. They asked a couple of literate boys to start teaching their children. The women collect donations from each other and are running the school—and they are very poor harijan women. Today there are 300 children sitting in that little shed there and we are hoping to make that into a model Mahila Samakhya Jag-Jagi school. It seems unbelievable, because we think that poverty is the main barrier—but I think it is lack of motivation.

We have a continuous training process for MSK staff, at three month intervals, when they undergo 5 to 6 days of intesive training in participatory methods, analysis, etc. They have already finished 25 days of training, another 5-day module will be delivered in January. Basically, the teachers bring their experiences to the training where we try and identify their weak areas and provide inputs accordingly. I look at this first year as an experimental period—after this, I think we will really be in a position to give them what is required. We should take some risks, and build them up gradually. In the Jag-Jagi centers we have more than 5,000 women and girls studying, and we are expecting more. The demand is so much that we can not cope up with it now.

In the Jag-Jagi centers, women themselves are the supervisors. They monitor the sahelis the whole month, and at the end of the month, when money is deposited in the savings account of the Samooh by Mahila Samakhya, they pay the Saheli. If a Saheli needs leave she has to ask the Samooh. Two to three sahelis were fired by the Samooh and we felt very bad because money was spent in training them. But the women felt that those sahelis were useless since they were taking too many holidays and not coming regularly. This hiring, firing, supervising, managing, is all done by the samoohs. Yes, they make mistakes sometimes—but has not the government made worse, and far more expensive mistakes?

Problems Faced

Like all other programs, we also have faced a few problems. In some areas, when men came to the centres and saw women practicing yoga, or learning cycling, they got worried by such non-traditional activities. Some of them also suspected the MSKs of various malpractices. In one MSK, some hired bullies (goodas) were sent to harass the women—we got a letter demanding that 4 women be murdered. At first, we waited and then a second threatening letter arrived. The women's reaction was remarkable. They took up bows and arrows, practiced, and guarded the place, saying that they will not close down the MSK. These are ordinary tribal women. This went on for 2 weeks, then again more letters came, and we became a bit frightened, because a man was kidnapped from the same area last year. So we decided to close that MSK for sometime. But they are back at work now and doing very well. The government people who are associated with us feel that we are not helping the women, they are learning nothing but how to fight.

There are lots of problems in Bihar- there is widespread cynicism that nothing positive can happen in Bihar. Even if a good center is running under their nose, people *nothing will change here*". They cannot believe the things which have actually happened.

Sustaining Literacy Efforts

I have been working in this field for nearly 25 years. But the last 3 years have been the most exciting. My only fear is whether we can cope up with the demand for education, knowledge and information, and how are we going to face all these challenges. Women are getting almost restless now, because they want more. To keep up, we are trying to build networks with different groups so that even if Mahila Samakhya stops, the classes and this movement continues. And mainstreaming is also taking place, especially from the Kishori Jag-Jagi groups.

We also have a regular Mela (fair) for Jag-Jagi Kishories and women. This year we are planning to have some camps, but we were not sure whether the literacy camps would be as effective as regular Jag-Jagi centers. We have to discuss this with the women to find out if they are interested in camps. Some groups have said that they have nothing to do, the would like to come to study, but then if there is no center to follow this up, it will not be of much use. The debate goes on. There are so many other things to share, and struggles also, but I am conscious of the time. I see a ray of hope in Mahila Samakhya putting its interest into education. Also, teacher training institutes like DIET, are now requesting Mahila Samakhya to give them at least 2 to 3 house input—and we are taking that up. We have to exert influence from all angles— policy, teacher training, all kinds of things. Our women teachers are no better than men teachers. So we have to really motivate and educate our women teachers.

We do not have total literacy at the moment, but through this we may. We are also trying to see how much effort should we put into skill development in the Jag-Jati centers. So far in Mahila Samakhya, we have not taken up any economic activities in Bihar. Now this question is coming up. Education, empowerment, skill development, how to put it together without minimizing empowerment and education.

Women having taken up the challenge. So we feel that even if Mahila Samakhya pulls out, these will continue. They have got a taste for education now.

18

THE EDUCATION FORUM'S LITERACY-NUMERACY PROGRAM

Cecille Sipin

The Education Forum (EF) was established in 1979 as a taskforce on education of the Association of Major Religious Superiors in the Philippines (AMRSP). Initially, it was organized to be a forum for educators who were the critically examining the state of Philippine education: its philosophy, objectives, curriculum content and instruction. Desiring to take concrete steps to reorient the country's educational system, it evolved to become a service institution which responds to the needs of all those who would share its vision and are engaged in education work—formal schools both public and private, NGOs, community groups, and individuals from various sectors.

EF has established chapters on a nationwide scale coordinated by a national secretariat in Manila. Among its various programs, the major ones are the following:

1. School for the Advancement of Nationalist Education or SANE for seminar-workshops, symposia, and lectures on education issues, theories and approaches, study group for teachers of the same discipline, and exposure-immersion programs. This also provides trainers' training for Basic and Functional Literacy-Numeracy.
2. Alternative Instructional Materials or AIM for development and publication of instructional materials, teaching guides, and sourcebooks for teachers. It also serves as a clearing house for teachers working on some curriculum materials.
3. Teacher Assistance Program or TAP is a monthly (for 10 months, following the school year) publication to update teachers on relevant and contemporary issues in economy, culture and politics.

4. Education Resource Center or ERC provides data on education and makes available resource materials to interested and groups in education.
5. Solidarity Program or SOP conducts lectures, training workshops, exposure-immersion trips and other services for visiting foreign educators and other groups outside the education sector.
6. Education with Production or EWP which pilots projects on education with production in 5 sites in the country.

A. History of Literacy Efforts

Prior to 1986, EF work was mainly with the formal education sector and it did get involved with non-formal education but only in a consulting capacity.

A priest from Nueva Ecija who was doing apostolate work with indigenous Filipinos approached us and appealed that we conduct a trainer's training in literacy-numeracy for the Dumagats along the Ambuklao Dam area who, because of their lack of education, were exposed to manipulation and exploitation by traders from the lowland.

Moved by the plight of the Dumagats, we dared run the training-workshop despite the inadequacy of our experience in non-formal education. We had six trainees from this indigenous group, two of who knew how to read and write and 4 were non-literate. We survived that training. Armed with what we knew then about education, we met them with what they had. From there we developed the module which went through several revisions before having the form which we are using today. That experience was indeed a milestone in our education work. We arrived at an important insight—that non-literates are not simply people who do not know how to read and write. They have concepts. They possess knowledge. For instance, they have the concept of numbers but they do not know the conventional way of presenting it the way which is familiar to the dominant culture.

After that initial involvement, we went deeper into literacy-numeracy work. Our next significant experience was with the Agtas of Sierra Madre who were dubbed as the "poorest of the poor" in the Prelature of Infanta. In partnership with SAKABINSA, an Agta people's organization, and the Tribal Center for Development (TCD), we followed-up the efforts initiated by ECTF (Ecumenical Council for Tribal Filipinos) for in basic education. In February 1988, we facilitated the setting up of a continuing education program which included curriculum development and community teachers' training. We operated on the assumption that the best program in education is that which is evolved by the people themselves upon an assessment of their needs and their capacities through their collective and organized efforts and at their own pace.

Our work with Agta community teachers lasted for several months, even years. We have refined our basic literacy-numeracy module, produced a detailed curricular program which integrates communication arts, math, science and social studies, detailed lessons plans, a detailed evaluation program, a collection of Agta songs, riddles, folk tales, and original stories which became part of materials for the Agta reading program. A newsletter entitled KABINSA was also printed.

By 1989, EF was at the thick of non-formal education. We responded to numerous requests for trainings and assistance for literacy-numeracy programs of the various sectors: urban poor women, rural women, fisherfolks, farmers, formal school outreach programs. Now we have accumulated enough experience and produced materials to adequately respond to the varying needs of our clientele.

We had another breakthrough when a similar education NGO in Italy, the Centro Informazione e Educazione Allo Sviluppo (CIES) agreed to be our partner in "an education with production" project to be piloted in 5 selected sites of the country. To date, the project is on-going in Irosin (Sorsogon), General Nakar (Quezon), Magballo (Negros Occidental), San Miguel (Surigap del Sur) and Freedom Island (Paranaque, Metro Manila). It was a milestone because we were able to pilot test the theoris about education and society which we have long been expanding. One of which, that education cannot be isolated from the lives of the people.

The project, which has been conceived together with the people who are members of the people's organizations in the area is also managed through their organized efforts. It integrates education with production activities. Thus every site has a demonstration farm for sustainable agriculture which includes for instance, vegetables and rice production, livestock, blacksmithing. Each site also has a training center to serve as venue for lessons on the various production phases. Besides the trainings on production there are also sessions on cooperatives, leadership formation and disasters preparedness. Simultaneous with activities in the demo farm and training center is the literacy-numeracy component with centers distributed in several areas in the community either in the houses volunteered by the people themselves, in barangay halls, classrooms in the public school of the area, or in literacy centers built through the people's efforts as their counterpart in the project. Through these trainings in Basic and Functional Lit-Num, we are able to reach a wider group in the community.

From its beginnings in 1990, the project has grown and expanded beyond its original intentions. Various linkages have been established and forms of cooperation have been realized with other NGOs and people's organizations, higher institutions of learning, church groups, government units/organizations and other groups in the community.

B. Salient Characteristics of EF's Literacy-Numeracy Program

- The approach is comprehensive in the sense that it addresses all aspects of community life. It assists the people in their economic needs by providing skills that community life. It assists the people in their economic needs by providing skills that will directly aid them in their income-generating activities as individuals and as groups.

It deepens consciousness and appreciation of the community's history and culture: their prevailing beliefs, norms, values and practices. Fresh meanings are given to certain practices and activities which ensure its transmission to the next generation.

It promotes self-help. It empowers individuals and groups to understand their problems and devise ways of solving them, leading them to form desks and committees within their respective organizations for sustained action. In General Nakar, Irosin and Magballo, the community teachers formed themselves into education desks to start exercising autonomy and generate resources thus preparing for the eventual pull-out of external project funding.

- It utilizes community resources both human and non-human. Trainers are recruited from the community, most of whom are elementary school undergraduates. Community folk through their organizations recruit prospective trainers and trainees. Training venues are provided by the community. The community teachers themselves develop instructional materials needed for the program.
- The program provides for continuing education with graduates of basic literacy-numeracy course proceeding to the functional literacy-numeracy program. Content-wise, the functional literacy-numeracy program is flexible and openeded, as derived is flexible and openeded, as derived from expressed needs and development aspiration of the people.
- The content and methodology, and recruitment of trainers differ from the conventional system:
- There is a drastic reduction in the number of hours spent to teach basic literacy-numeracy. From the usual number of 160-200 hours, our method enables us to teach basic literacy-numeracy within a range of from 25 to 50 hours;
- The content is drawn from community life, proposing practical and feasible solutions to these problems experienced by them, its basic method

utilizes ADIDS (Activity, Discussion, Input, discussion, Synthesis);

- The schedule fits the work schedule of people in the community.
- It uses the national language (Filipino) and other Philippine languages as medium in literacy work.
- It provides a venue for more active participation of women in community life by encouraging them to organize themselves and actively participate in the education program either as trainees or as community teachers.

C. Some Problems Encountered by our Lit-num Workers

In brief, the following problems are common in all literacy sites:

a. difficulty in recruitment because the non-literates are afraid of being exposed, or they see no need of attending classes, they have managed until this far somehow;

b. irregularity in attendance and group meetings.

People are busy for economic survival. They don't immediately see the long term effect benefit of education. In fact some of them view schooling as leisure, a luxury for a person of adequate means.

D. The Women in EF Literacy-Numercy Work

Our long years in education work validate, which observation I am sure you will also share, that education is a major concern of women. Owing perhaps to our biological role at some point of our lives, we respond readily to those matters which have to do with formation. Our spirit of nurturance, a natural tendency for caring, for protecting, developing and sustaining life make us reliable managers of education programs.

In depressed areas where non-literacy is deep, it is the women whom we observe to be taking the lead in education. The various literacy-numeracy programs implemented in our project sites attest to the impressive work of reliable women with valor and tenacity to oversee programs under the most difficult circumstances like militarization and acute economic deprivation. These community teachers who themselves are hungry and burdened with survival problems are zealous teachers and change agents to their people.

With a firm grasp of the situation in the community, they are able to devise relevant curriculum programs. With an understanding of their people's particular culture, they are able to see approaches which stimulate their people to learn. The women's attention to detail, their intutive sense, and predisposition to care for life account for their success as administrators of learning programs.

We started our education program without no particular stress on women whether in addressing their plight or in drawing from their resources. We said it is already included because it is a comprehensive program. This has changed. We realized that the multi-layered program of women requires special attention. We noted, too, that the trend in all sites is for women to take enthusiastically to the program that will improve their lot whether as students or teachers. Where there is a lack of educational service there is a woman ready to take over. They are usually the first ones to respond to organizing efforts and are quick to comprehend the function of education for empowerment. In the next stages of our literacy-numeracy program we have made a commitment to respond to the particular issues of our women and look into the wealth of possibilities in them in providing basic educational services for our people.

19

THE LITERACY CIRCLE

Suddha Sundaraman

The concept of the literacy circle is a genuine brain child of the literacy movement. As the Arivial Iyakkam (Science Movement) project period drew to a close, it was essential to evolve a strategy for the emerging situation. From mobilizing around literacy per se, the activists found that literacy could not be sustained if people did not mobilize around other issues close to their heart.

Hence, continuing education had to make an entry into the village collective. The entry point was the literacy circle, which is a coming together of neo-literates, organizers, resource person and those in the village who wished to join the Arivoli ("the light of knowledge"-viz., literacy) process anew. The circle would meet about once a month where the organizer would have to plan out the basic program along with the resource persons at the center. As the literacy circle aims to draw on the knowledge of the village participants, and involve them in the process, it is important that the program would have to be flexible and open to change.

The literacy circle also aimed at creating a cultural educational nucleus in every village or habitat, which could develop its skills continuously, and become a live transmitter of information that is needed locally. It will consciously cater to sections who have been marginalized by the formal school system hence the literacy circle puts special emphasis on mobilizing women, girl children going out to work, and people belonging to disadvantaged sections, both socially and economically. The circle also hopes to infuse new life into the cultural traditions of these groups—be it singing cradle songs or songs of lament, reciting riddles or folk dance and drama.

As the circle participant sees the books on display, hears their content and is drawn by them, the desire to read becomes greater and transforms itself into a direct reading habit. Once a library becomes functional around this activity, interaction and education would occur simultaneously, and continuing education could become self-sustaining. While the idea of the literacy circle is ambitious, the vision is firmly rooted in the possibilities created by the literacy network on the ground. The implementation envisages the following inputs:

- district level resource persons to produce and collate material for the literacy circle: including bulletins, neo-literate creations, story books, story collections, and information booklets, etc.
- district level organizer, to evolve a monthly plan, sit with block and sub-block organizers, ensure it is put into action and review the feed back. Training needs to be identified as well, and organized accordingly.
- sub block and local organizer-volunteers to be constantly helped to upgrade their capacity in conducting the circle innovatively. Ultimately, the skill of the village level volunteer in maintaining the interest of the participants is the key to making the circles function effectively.

In terms of implementation, the general experience has not been positive as many districts complain of the inability to translate the concept into activity on the ground. But perhaps two examples where it has worked well will encourage practitioners to pursue this strategy.

A. The Literacy Circle Experience in Village K. Mettupatti

The seven of us trudged into the village situated 2 km. away from the nearest bus stop at around 6:30 p.m. It was dark when we arrived, but the children surrounded us immediately and led us to the multipurpose reading room which is the library, the science corner, the focal point of the literacy activity in the area. The occasional street light does little to dispel the darkness. This is Harijan colony area. The organizers (all women) say that drop-outs were much more in the other colony, here the interest to learn is still alive and literacy circles functions well.

We are given tea by the local organizer-cum-resource person-cum-volunteer as and when needed. He has encouraged his wife too, and she is the one who is now going around informing the people that the Arivoli team has arrived. Very soon, under a tube light, some 70 people have congregated. About 40 men, 30 women. And of course, children. They liven up the place with their chatter. But it will interfere with circle activities. One of the organizers draws them away to tell them stories and play games with them.

The circle activity begins with a folk song rendered powerfully by one of the neo-literates, exhorting all to sit down and watch the proceedings (the traditional start to the folk songs), and then a Arivoli song by the organizers. Participants not only had to introduce themselves but had to precede their names with an edible item beginning with the same letter-and what laughter ensued! Laddu-Lakshmi, Payasam-Padmini, etc., are produced amidst the hilarity.

One of the organizers tells the story of a person of unsound mind who wanders into a village and is nurtured by the blacksmith's wife for 10 years. By some chance, his brother discovers him, and comes to claim him. Kirubhu Shanmugham, the mad beggar, is in reality very rich. The whole village moans his leaving and the blacksmith's wife refuses any offer of money. Did the listeners like the story? Yes, who doesn't like stories! Why did you like? Various reasons. An old woman puts it best when she says that the blacksmith's wife, by refusing money for having taken care of Shanmugham for 10 years, shows that in villages people are still willing to help others without expecting money.

This is followed by a math game, where the participants has to find out how many coconuts there were initially. Soon, 27-year-old Mariamma, a neo-literate, has found the answer.

It's time for riddles. The people-especially the older ones-are stock full of riddles. Their minds go off at a tangent we are not able to comprehend-the neo-literate win hands down. Organizers are busy noting down new riddles for the next bulletin, learners and volunteers are thrilled with their victory.

Then an imaginative story line for participants to pay attention and discover the word that has been omitted deliberately during the second round. There is some confusion initially. Once it is clear, there is no hesitation. "What movie did you see last?", asks Malathy (organizer) to Dhanalakshmi who is 16 years old, working in the match industry. After Arivoli, she can read. She has seen Thaimmanasu-Maternal Uncle. Did she like it?. Yes, there were lots of remarks exposing politicians—she liked it. Can she write the name of the movie? That answer was not so forthcoming. Quickly one organizer comes forth, hands around pen and paper. Everyone has to write the names of the last 2 or 3 movies which they liked. Oh-Oh, some of the neo-literates have remembered there is work at home. The local organizer tells them they need not worry, there is no compulsion, the volunteers are there to help if needed. Some write laboriously, some write many names fast, spellings rather weak on the whole. But it's done. Volunteers go around, offering help.

Well, it's 9.30 p.m. We didn't notice the time pass by. If we don't finish now, catching the last bus will a problem. The village organizer insists we should eat and go-arrangements have already been made. We walk back to catch the 1.00 p.m. bus, and before we go to bed, our circle meets, reviews the experience. A very impressive performance indeed!

B. The Sivakashi Literacy Circle

We also visited an area in Sivakashi famous for its fireworks and match industry. There were many young girls in this literacy circle-all working in nearby factories. There was a water-passing game which livened up the session immediately, apart from making the whole place wet and requiring sacks to be brought for sitting down again. Within the same structure, a lot of variety was introduced. The participants were asked to tell a story. A learner came out with a ghost story, a heated discussion on the existence and non-existence of ghosts is initiated. Angamma's brother has seen a ghost. No, she hasn't seen it herself. Murugeswari has the last word. "We know some unnatural incident occurred at that spot, so if anything extraordinary happens, we blame it on ghost", she says. She has quite rightly made it a question of psychology.

In this circle, the organizers have planned a small skit. It's a mime with the central character being a symbol of god as worshipped by Hindus, Muslims and Christians. The same central character's pose is alternately shifted by those belonging to different religions. Ultimately they start fighting amongst themselves. The central character-the symbol of god -lies fallen, uncured for. the participants discuss the theme of how communal disharmony is created by the worshippers, not god. After all, god is one. Why should there be fights? So it goes on. Religious tolerance is a vital presence and we are happy to see people's positive responses on this issue.

The news bulletin is presented. News items are questioned before being accepted. The scandal of the holy man who has raped young girls in his Ashram (religious center) and had videos fitted in the bathroom, is discussed threadbare. Some are aware that AIDWA (a women's organization) has intervened in this issue. They agree that for highlighting and handling issues like this, organizations like this are important.

A small word game is played. Riddles are exchanged. A song. Tea all around. And it is time for reluctant leave taking. The warmth extended to visitors is very inspiring and touching. Here young girls assure us that they will never leave Arivoli, they will continue learning. "There speaks the militant working class spirit' we said, and returned to our center.

Such fascinating experiences are increasingly becoming part of the post literacy movement in district like kamarajar, N. Arcot, Pasumpon and Pudukottai. But they are still sporadic. With wider implementation, the literacy circle is capable of achieving a great deal, and the impetus needs to be sustained.

20

DEVELOPMENT OF METHODS AND INSTRUCTIONAL MATERIALS FOR WOMEN IN BANGLADESH

Rokeya Rahman Kabeer

It is difficult for me to write anything about the development of education materials and its presentation to rural women without saying something about Saptagram Nari Swanirvar Parishad (SNSP) itself. Because the character of this organization itself led to the development of a specialized curriculum.

Saptagram Nari Swanirvar Parished (SNSP) was formed in June, 1976 an organisation for women and by women, working in the rural community of Bangladesh. The women who had launched SNSP have themselves been acutely aware of the subordinate and exploited position women hold in the society in which they live. Though they have come from far more privilege backgrounds, they themselves have been victims of overt discrimination or patriarchal conspiracies, where male privilege has been assured simply by mobilizing the routine institutional procedures. Unlike male run NGOs, SNSP women were understandably more aware of the difficulty they would face in combatting the oppressive status quo which prevails in the social structure.

For development to be equitable as well as successful, poor women have to mount a challenge to existing society in order to achieve their rights. Their current inability to do so it rooted in their socially isolated and materially dependent position in society. Thus SNSP's strategy has been to concentrate on the organisation, conscientisation and mobilization of the women in our target group.

Our original objectives were to work among women of the deprived sections of the rural community in Bangladesh, to make these women conscious of the root causes of their economic, social and legal problems, and try to help them seek solutions, to initiate women's organizations at the village level, to provide credit to women's groups, to encourage them to get involved in cooperative economic activities, thereby giving them an independent source of income, to make them conscious of the health and nutritional needs of themselves and their families, to encourage family planning among the women and last but not least, to provide education to rural adult women and their children.

We have now almost completed two decades of our activities in the field. And it must be made clear here that the objectives which had originally been formulated in the rather remote and stratified atmosphere of the capital, Dhaka, had to be adjusted when face to face interaction took place between our organisation and our constituency. Through the years, adjustment had taken place at a slow but deliberate pace. What had stood the test of time was that women must be organized at the group level, as in unity lay their strength. But what has emerged as being of primary importance is education for our clients i.e. adult women.

Today, instead of the extensive seven objectives, we have come to realize that we can achieve all our objectives through two core programs, which will complement one another, and should play a crucial role in empowering women. First is the Credit program and the other is functional education for adult women, which aims to provide a clear idea of the source of oppression of women, a means of how to combat the situation and a complementary skill which will assist them in managing their economic activities.

Our credit program, after few initial hiccups, which was expected, took off quite well, and within a few years a large number of women's groups got involved in non-traditional income generating activities on a cooperative level. But we faced problems when we tried to introduce education among the Mature women. They showed a complete lack of interest in educating themselves. We understood their resistance to accept our program for adult education, but we persisted with our efforts. It took years before women started coming forward to attend our education classes.

In the early years, we used government primers for our students, but soon we realized that it would take years to provide them with basic knowledge of reading and numeracy. At about this time, we came across functional education materials produced by BRAC. Sometime in 1979 we introduced our adult students to BRAC functional education syllabus but despite all the efforts to expand our education program, progress was far from satisfactory. It was not until 1983 that SNSP's literacy programme received a significant boost. This came about as a result of an incident that drove home the need for education to our target group.

A. The Story of Women in Faridpur Sadar Thana

Under the intensive Rural Works Program funded by SIDA and NORAD and implemented in collaboration with the Bangladesh Government, women were given special consideration and hired in equal proportion to men to build a long road which passed through our project area in Faridpur Sadar Thana. As a result, most women who were hired in the construction work were our group members. According to the contract the laborers were to be paid weekly, and for removing a thousand cubic feet of earth they were to receive Tk. 200. However when time for weekly payment came, all the laborers were short changed since instead of receiving Tk. 200 per thousand cubic feet of soil, they received only Tk. 125.

The laborers also had to give their thumb prints on the master roll. Our colleagues in the field did not waste any time to inform our women members that they had not received the wage they were entitled to, and by putting their finger prints in the master roll, they had legalized the illegal action of the project supervising committee. When the women members were informed of this fraud, angry women laid down their tools and brought out a demonstration against the action of the committee. It was the first time in the history of Faridpur District, our project catchment area, that 500 angry landless women demonstrated. However, when the women reached the District Commissioner of Faridpur they were asked to give in writing their complaint. They had to come back to our colleague to write their representation. By the end of the week the matter was amicably settled, and most importantly, a psychological victory was won by the women.

This incident proved to be the turning point in our education program among the adult women. It gave us the opportunity to recognize that this incident would never have taken place if the women themselves had been able to read, since the correct amount due to them was clearly stated in the master roll. Nor would there be any need for them to come to us for writing down their representation to the relevant authorities. Happily, they found this argument most convincing, and began to spread the word as never before.

Our adult literacy class started expanding fast. But then we came face to face with problems. By this time however, we were dealing with far more socially conscious women. Years of workshops, seminars and group discussions on women's life in our society, had made them conscious of their own position in the environment they were living in.

Furthermore women had learned to protest against exploitation, understood the united strength of women and had become daring enough to challenge the family exploitation, even if that protest was muted.

B. Making Literacy Materials Gender Sensitive

By then these women challenged the BRAC syllabus which we had adopted in our Functional Education classes. All syllabi, whether evolved by NGOs or the Government, had not yet responded to the upsurge of gender awareness in the society. For instance, the BRAC syllabus projects the picture of men in every sphere of social activities, except while portraying the curse of having a big family, where a picture of a women was shown surrounded by a number of malnourished children, and another chapter dealing with the need for cleanliness. In one sat two women picking lice from their hair surrounded by slovenly children playing in the courtyard. The huts looked dark and shaded because of the presence of short trees and shrubs all around it. In another picture, a women is shown busily sweeping the courtyard. This time the courtyard is clean, no children, slovenly or otherwise, no hens, and no ducks. The shrubs shading the hut had been cut down and the hole has been filled. And presto! Just by waving the broom, the woman has cleaned the house.

These pictures clashed with the knowledge women had gained from involvement with SNSP. The objections raised by the learners were both critical and relevant. "Men have been shown in all other charts being boatman, shopkeeper, working in the field etc. except when it comes to family planning. Then it is a woman. Why is it not men's responsibility also to play a role there? Is it the exclusive duty of women to keep the house clean? Should men of the house have some responsibilities to maintain the house neat and clean? Should he not fill up the hole in the courtyard? Should men not cut the unwanted growth around the house? Why do these pictures depict the same old nonsense?"

It was gratifying to hear such pertinent questions, but the fact remained that a more appropriate syllabus had to be found. One that would better reflect the needs of these women. Unfortunately, it was easier said than done, for despite all our searching, not only in Bangladesh, but in the neighboring countries like India and Pakistan, as well as in countries like England, Australia, America and Canada, no suitable books were to be found. Given that fact, there was only one option left, to create such a syllabus ourselves.

It was a mammoth task. As we had no frame of reference, we had to start from scratch, creating a syllabus which would be acceptable to women. A slow and tedious assignment, it involved a considerable amount of research and compiling of facts. The earlier cliches had to be discarded, and a more relevant and factual approach was required. Lessons had to deal with such contemporary issues as marriage and divorce and women's rights. At the same time, this would provide a opportunity to address the whole range of oppression and inequalities that women have to face.

Nor was it just the negative aspects we had to focus on, since it was equally important to highlight those instances where women had managed to achieve a modicum of success. After all, it was this kind of success that would breed confidence and provide the courage to take on further battles.

And thus began the task of compiling a syllabus that would open with the most elementary lessons, and evolve step by step to cover all the topics that are relevant to women. Arithmetic would have a primary place, since it was of vital importance to activities related to income generating. The whole process took five years to collate, as it was based on feedback from the field, but it was finally completed, and today it is proving to be a most effective tools.

C. Preparing Teachers for our Instructional Materials

Saptagram educational material is specialized and gender oriented, so that the teachers have to receive special training in order to present our education material properly to the learners.

- Teachers who are appointed have to initially spend one month moving around with the field workers in order to understand and absorb the philosophy and objectives of Saptagram.
- They are then trained for an additional month at the Saptagram Training Center where they are given lessons on how teach classes.
- Well-trained education supervisors keep them under close scrutiny once they have begun teaching to see how they have presented the materials. It is through relevant words that students first learn the alphabet. They then go on to learn the alphabet. They then go on to learn and appreciate the meaning of the word, and its relevance to their own lives. Each word in the primers has been specially selected to present the different aspects of a woman's life. So learning each word might take a whole day, and sometimes even longer. Depending on the length of the discussions which might ensue.
- There is of course a teacher's guide, which deals exhaustively on the methods of dealing with each word in the primer. With the assistance of the guidebook, the trained teachers can easily present the material to the students in a manner which they can understand as well as capture their attention and interest.
- Once of the most important subjects in the syllabus is numeracy, which starts from simple addition and subtraction and then goes into more complicated accounts-keeping. Therefore, teachers are given special training on keeping simple accounts.

- Finally, for those students who prove to be especially good in accountancy, they are then brought to the center where they receive further training to develop their accountancy skills from trained accountants.

D. Contents of Literacy Booklet

At the primary stage, students follow a booklet which contains thirty-nine words and phrases about health, religious customs, work, social and political rights, and the environment. The aim is to teach women the letters that make up the words in the primer and at the same time, generating discussion about the meaning of the words and their relevance to women's lives. The primer also has a simple numeracy section, introducing women to basic accounts management. This course lasts for six months.

To lead the women through the booklet, teachers use flash cards and a large format seventy-six page primer. The words that are included therein are as follows:

Adhikar	-	Rights
Aday	-	Extract
Akota	-	Unity
Mahajan	-	Moneylender
Union	-	Local Government Administrative Unit
Purdah	-	The Custom of Seclusion of Women
Kabin	-	Marriage Document
Talak	-	Divorce
Balla Bibaho	-	Child Marriage
Tipshoi	-	Fingerprint
Lekhapora	-	Reading and Writing
Ojon	-	Weights and Measures
Thikana	-	Address
Chithi	-	Letter
Joutuk	-	Dowry
Bohu Bibaho	-	Multiple Marriage
Reen	-	Loan
Gorib	-	Poor
Bhaggchashi	-	Sharecroper
Mojuri	-	Daily Wage
Shoshon	-	Oppression
Nirjatan	-	(physical or mental) Mistreatment; Torture; Violence
Jhagra	-	Fight
Julum	-	Torture (similar to Nirjatan)
Shalish	-	Mediation by a Village Council
Fandibaj		Conman
Thana	-	Local Government Administrative Unit
Ghush	-	Bribe
Shongothon	-	Organisation
Bari	-	House

Gachpala	-	Trees and Plants
Diarrhoea	-	Diarrhoea
Khabar	-	Food
Dhilemi	-	Laziness
Dukkho	-	Sorrow
Ashar	-	Certain Month
Short	-	Honest
Vote	-	Vote
Ai	-	Income

All these words portray day to day problems that rural women face, as well as the methods that they can adopt to fight back. Out of all these words, we feel that one of the most important pictures is entitled "address". The picture shows the postman handing a letter to a woman, who is obviously a widow and alone. This, to SNSP, is a very important picture. Women have no identity. You can only write to them care of their husband, father, brother or another male relative. What we are trying to do is to ensure that women get recognition as individuals by society. That women do exist as individual entities.

The second part of the education program develops reading and numeracy skills. Women get a book of five stories written in simple language, with a message aimed at deepening women's understanding of issues, introduced at the primary stage. The illustrated stories touch on subjects like the importance of registering a marriage, family planning, procedures for acquiring land etc. To encourage discussion and thought, students are questioned at the end of each story. It is at the last stage where numeracy and accountancy becomes the main focus, where probelms start. Women tend to lose interest and drop out. We are not sure yet how many will learn to do more advanced accounts, but we do plan to teach at least five members of each group advanced accountancy. If we can manage more, it will be welcome.

We also have two booklets, each of about thirty pages, on health and nutrition. The first focuses on common diseases, cause and symptoms and describes preventive measures. The information is presented in very simple form, and is designed to maintain the women's interest in reading after they have finished the second part of the course.

To provide our learners with follow-up reading materials, we have a plan of setting up libraries at each center, which will have books to stimulate their continued interest in reading. We also published bi-monthly magazines, which contain the writings of the new literates. This is to encourage them to develop their writing skills. They write poetry, prose, stories and so on which are then circulated among all the members.

21

DEVELOPMENT OF LITERACY LEARNING MATERIALS FOR WOMEN

Tran Quang Thong

Women constitute more than 50% of the population, undertake most of the work (two thirds) but only receive one tenth of the total income. Rural women's contribution to rice and cereals production is over 50% but few of them are trained in any kind of agricultural occupation. The working hours of women are longer than that of men, often 12-16 hours per day. In addition to their domestic responsibilities in child care, women have to be responsible for housework, such as fetching firewood, water and cooking and even hard work as ploughing and raking, planting, transplanting and harvesting. Women have to suffer from continuing under nutrition and two thirds of them are anemic. Rural women lack sex education and have poor health due to frequent pregnancies. The illiterate women especially lack knowledge on balanced diet, family planning, house cleaning and other information to improve health and the quality of life. They have lower status and low paid occupations, lower economic positions so they are less-conscious and lack self-confidence. They have a few books and a little time to read so they can not appreciate the benefits of reading and have no motivation for reading.

Therefore, development of literacy learning material is aimed at the following contents:

- To affirm the role of women as a key producer, laborer, continually engaged in economic activities and important contributor to the income of the family.
- To enable women to perform successfully the role of wife and mother, to have needs for sharing the household chores between husband, wife and children, needs for recreation, needs for means of decreasing the hard work for women, and needs for services to help reduce the work-

ing hours for women in housework.

- The role of women in decision making in the family and their attitudes of women towards their main role.
- Enhancement of the equality between men and women, fundamental rights of women, economic status and position of women in family, society and community.

In short, development of literacy learning materials for women with limited reading skills to enhance their role in the family and society, is a very necessary work to enable them easily to find the way to realize their dream and promote their strength.

I. METHODS IN DEVELOPING LITERACY LEARNING MATERIALS (LLMS) FOR WOMEN

To develop LLMs for women the following steps should be followed:

1. Determine the Target Group of the Learning Materials

At present in Vietnam, the main target groups of the LLMS are poor rural women, with little schooling who are owners or main producers in the households and women in remote, mountainous, inaccessible and sea island areas and minority women. They have a low standard of living and have needs for literacy learning so as to gain functional skills which will enable them to raise their potentials, generate income, improve the quality of life and enhance the equalities between men and women.

2. Determine the Needs

When determining the needs, national policies on women and community studies should be taken into consideration. When conducting a survey of the community, the following problems should be paid attention to: the social, economic, cultural and health situation of the community; development needs of the community; resource and available services of the community; status, role and problems related to women development; and problems concerning women education and preliminary information on their reading and writing capacity.

To gather information on the needs of the target group, one of the following approaches can be used (or the combination of these):

- Field visit and observation to identify the needs.
- Interview (a set of questions is used to ask community leaders, each household or each learner).
- Local leaders make reports (about the economic, social, women and

concerned target groups situation).

- Organize meetings, discussion, seminars.

Interviewers' groups should consist of women members so as to enable the women interviewers to easily express their opinions. Groups of interviewers should be accompanied by the elders of the community, heads of mountain village or local leaders who can assist them when necessary.

When assessing the needs it is necessary to answer the following questions:

- To what extent are these needs urgent?
- To what extent are they severe?
- How many women can these needs have effects on?
- The degree of adverse effects which will happen in the future if at present we do not do anything to solve these problems.

To identify the needs to be prioritized, "participatory approach" can be used in training workshops for developing learning materials for women. This entails drawing a map on problems and needs as well as a map on the solutions to these problems and the activities following those solutions. To undertake this activity, the following materials are needed:

> big sheets of paper; small sheets of paper (at least twenty pieces for each one); adhesive tape or glue; a pen to write (at least from 3 colors on); and a pencil or ball-point pen for each person.

Participatory approach involves the following steps:

- All participants involved in the process of developing materials (field study, interviewing, attending training courses.......) are divided into groups of 7-10 persons.
- Each member of the group prepares to make a report on the information of needs and problems of the target group in about 20 minutes. After that each member gives a preliminary presentation to the group.
- Each member of the group writes about the needs and problems into ten (10) small sheets of paper. Each need (or problem) is written into a sheet of paper within 20 minutes. Each need (or problem) should be written as follows:

- Using a simple language and short sentences;
- With a clear and practical content;
- Understandable to everybody.

children, lack of role models and unfriendly classroom environment (Kelly, 1995; Odaga et al 1995; Maimbolwa-Sinyangwe et al, 1995; Mwansa, 1995). The education of the girl child would require simultaneous provision of education to mothers because through mothers some change can be brought about (Sticht et al, 1990).

Literature suggests that literacy and general education for women impact on the health of the family, education for children and on the education of the girl child (see table II). For example educating women reduces child mortality, influences children's propensity to stay at school and is positively related to higher aspirations for participation in education by their daughters.

Table IV: Impact of women's education on family health, children and girl child's education

Impact on the Health of the Family	Impact on the Education of Children	Impact on the Education of Girls
Highly educated parents produce healthier pre--school children	Families with higher levels of literacy have children who learn to read better	Mother's education is positively related to higher aspirations for participation in educa--tion by their daughters
Educating women reduces child mortality	Parents educated in the ways of school spend more time reading story books to the children and have more frequent contact with regard to home work, assignments and other schooling matters	Mother's educational aspiration for their daughter exceeds that of fathers
Educating women reduces fertility		
Mother's education is important in determining how many children will be in the household	Mother's education influences children's propensity of stay at school	
	Mother's education is important for children in later grades of school where more difficult assignments make demands on mother's knowledge for help with home work	
	Mother's education has strong	

	effects on achievements on achievements in academic skills. The effects may persist into adulthood	

Sources: Sticht. T and MacDonald, B.A. (1990). Teaching the Mother and reach the Child. Geneva: International Bureau of Education

Summers, L. (1994). Investing in All the People Educating Women in Developing Countries. Washington: Education Development Institute of the World Bank.

A number of Girl child projects that have been instituted on the continent have also focused on sensitization of the parents. It has been recognised that the education of the girl child is predicated on the eradication of adult illiteracy and change of parental attitudes hence the stress on community sensitization as part of girl child education. The Zambian Declaration on Girl Child Education states thus:

> The high levels of adult illiteracy represent profound personal privations for the large number of people who are not able to read, write or make simple numerical computations. Their state of illiteracy also has a bearing on the education of the next generation.......In particular, mothers who can not read and write, or who are basically non numerate, may not shoe great concern if their daughters do not read and write, or who are basically non numerate, may not shoe great concern if their daughters do not find a place in school and may readily agree their withdrawal once they reach marriageable age (MOE, 1995: 10).

Ultimately what will free the girl child from the shackles of domestic labour and restrictive traditions is provision of education that increases family income and frees women from male domestication, enables women to enhance their productive functions through acquisition of management and marketing skills and credit facilities. Most of the functional literacy programmes have stressed reproduction functions with particular emphasis on productive functions (Lind, 1995). Following the introduction of Structural Adjustment Programme women have increasingly found employment in informal income generating activities for family survival. Functional literacy should aim at promoting women to attain their aspirations in different spheres of human life (social, economic, poltical and cultural). Where literacy has been linked to income generation it has been limited to sewing, knitting, cooking, soap making. Such income generating activities have not produced appreciable incomes instead they have reinforced women's traditional roles. Appreciable incomes have been realised from collective income generating activities such as co-operatives. Thus functional literacy for women girl child education should be regarded as education for conscientization aimed at promoting self esteem, life skills and increasing women's share in division and distribution of power, opportunities and resources.

Methodologies, Models of Success and Innovations

The models of success and failure are discernable in the methodologies adopted for eradication of illiteracy. The methodologies are also related to each nation's political cultural (Bhola, 1988). Three methodologies that have been followed are project, programme and campaign. A Project is provided on the basis of individual motivation and demand, a programme is a large scale incremental educational activity planned for within the national budget with the goal of providing technical knowledge and skills to the "illiterates" and implemented without a sense of urgency and political passion; a campaign is a politically stimulated large scale activity designed to be a vehicle for national reconstruction or integration of masses of the people to participate in issues of development. A campaign is characterised by the spirit of combativeness, passion and a sense of urgency.

Table V: Literacy methodologies in relation to developmental planning, providers, focus of attention and goals

	Methodology		
	Project	**Programme**	**Campaign**
Position in Developmental Planning	Peripheral	Variable	Central
Providers/ Articulators	Individual/Ngos	Government Functionaries	Political Leaders, Mass Organize. Govt. Functionaries
Focus of Attention	Individuals/ Local Communities	Nation/Country	Nation/Country
Goals	Community Mobilization to meet	Modernization/ Provision of Technical Information	Social
	Limited Goals		Mobilization to Meet Broad Goals

Approach I- Project: The underlying principle of this approach is that illiteracy is an individual need and participation is left to those who show interest. The motivation has to come from those affected by illiteracy and providers are those who feel personally concerned. There are no pretensions about popular participation or empowerment of illiterates.

The focus of such an approach is a community-usually small in geographical coverage—and The goals for the projects are defined by agencies with or without the involvement of learners and there are different agendas.

Indications elsewhere are that where governments do not take a purposive attitude to the elimination of illiteracy, NGOS do so with commitment. For example, churches and NGOS have linked literacy to such developmental activities as health, agriculture, home economics, women's issues etc and have expanded their agendas and become strong, powerful articulators of issues related to social justice and equality for the marginal groups. Examples of a projects carried out under the auspices of NGOS are the Girls Attainment in Basic Literacy Education (GABLE) in Malawi and Camfed in Zimbabwe.

The Girls Attainment in Basic Literacy Education (GABLE) of Malawi was initiated in 1991 with funding from USAID. It is implemented by the Creative Associates Inc. Its innovativeness lies in the manner in which it was evolved. Through Social Mobilisation GABLE aimed at developing, testing and implementing strategies that could be used in a national campaign to change attitudes to girls' education by disseminating findings of the research studies on Knowledge, Attitudes and Practices (KAP). Through focus discussion groups, participatory theater and village level discussions the findings of the research were clarified and positive attitudes promoted. A number of interventions were taken that included tuition waiver for non repeating girls, building of class rooms and teachers' houses, input into curriculum review and teacher training. In 1989 the GABLE project increased girls' enrolment from 44.8% to 54% and girls net enrolment in standard one rose to 59% as opposed to 54% for the boys (Burchfield and Kadzamira, 1996; Odaga et al, 1995).

Camfed in Zimbabwe was initiated in 1991 as a partnership between the Government of Zimbabwe and Cambridge Women's Education Trust in London. Its innovativeness lies in its involvement of traditional rulers, parents and teachers in the selection of girls children who should be given support. The project has raised self esteem, and there is a marched improvement in the scholastic performance of the girls.

Unless experiences are replicated the net effect of projects is bound to be slow and benefit only limited numbers of people who can avail themselves of literacy activities. Slow development is not likely to narrow the illiteracy gap because for each male illiterate there are two females made illiterate through failure to enter school, through withdrawal from school and through lack of places or failure to pay for education.

Approach II- Programme: Where governments have recognized illiteracy as an impediment to national development they have made efforts to plan for its eradication within the government budgetary allocations. The main actors have been government functionaries. Government motivation for eradication of illiteracy has come from pressure from such international agencies as UNESCO and UNICEF. The main feature of planning for literacy is centralization relegated to a particular ministry, department or directorate. The program approach lacks the sense of urgency and passion that characterizes campaigns and is constrained by shifting order of developmental priorities. The participation of governments in basic literacy in the 1960s and functional literacy in the 1970s was due to the stimulation from UNESCO. Most government run programmes have been constrained by problems related to the administration and organization of the programmes such as lack of field supervision; lack of interest among some government officers; lack of transport; problems of remunerating teachers; lack of relevant instructional materials; lack of adequate delivery system; lack of linkage between development goals and literacy objectives, etc (Mutava, 1988, Lind, 1995, Mpofu, 1995). Literacy as a government controlled activity shows declining resource support in Kenya and Tanzania (Hall, 1989), Ghana (Mulusa, 1988) and Nigeria (Omulewa, 1988), Zimbabwe (Mpofu, 1995), Zambia (Mwansa, 1995). Literacy programmes have not nurtured the necessary political and national will because they are somewhat detached from the thinking of political leaders and receive attention only on the 8th of September international literacy year celebrations (Mutava, 1988; 340). Thus the programme approach has dissipated energies and the will of government functionaries, and resources allocated to literacy programs have dwindled.

The programme approach holds promise for a sustained literacy program if only problems that have faced it are addressed and it is given a sense of urgency, vision, policy and backed up by political will, national will and resources. Where literacy has made impact and shown appreciable improvement, there has been a cadre of adult educators to advocate for, and translate political will into, educational activities. Without this cadre of adult educators, literacy as a government controlled activity will remain a slow and incremental educational activity, maintaining a cadre of community workers with limited tools and knowledge for making literacy a worthwhile and enjoyed educational activity. Hence the need to produce a cadre of literacy workers through non formal training schemes.

Functional literacy programmes are attended mainly by women because men are shy to learn with women are fear to make mistakes in groups of women. Among the programmes that have provided continuity to women's education are Folk development colleges in Tanzania. The colleges serve a fourfold purpose (political, economic, social and cultural). They provide short courses ranging in length from one day to six months, and long courses ranging from six months, with nine months as the mode. Theoretical teaching is tailored to suit levels reached by learners in both basic and functional literacy and 60% of curriculum content resembles conditions found in the villages, while the other 40% enables students to practical activities. Literacy programmes were also supported by distance education materials produced by the institute for Adult Education and the Correspondence Institute. Overall Tanzania's literacy programmes have reduced female illiteracy from 67% in 1967 to 9.5% in 1986, changed attitudes to innovations, cultivated reading habits and created political awareness among both men and women (Rusimbi, 1992). Even with such record of success the contents of the primers still perpetuate dominant male ideology and do not tackle issues concerning decision making, equality in the division and distribution of resources.

After Jomtien Conference in 1990, governments started working in partnership with NGOS, to initiate projects and programmes aimed at promoting girls education. One such a programme that deserves attention is the PAGE in Zambia.

The Programme for the Promotion of Girl Child Education (PAGE) in Zambia is being implemented with support from UNICEF. PAGE was started in 1996 after carrying out nine research studies. It is being implemented in two districts one rural and the other urban involving twenty five schools. Separately the studies investigated classroom practices, parental and girl child educational aspirations, knowledge and attitudes, school performance, the physical state of schools, and one study surveyed comprehensively enrolments and staffing in all the schools in the two districts. Findings of the studies were discussed with parents, teachers, traditional rulers and members of parliament at provincial level and district levels in order to get the commitment of leaders, teachers and government officials to making a difference to girl's education. The studies were also used as a spring board for formulating a national educational policy. Various interventions have been taken that include provision of books and materials, setting up single sex classes in mathematics and science, teacher education, discussion with parents and teachers, support to girl children not able to meet school costs. Preliminary results indicate that the demand for girls education has gone up and parents have in varying degrees changed their own attitudes.

The girl programmes and projects demonstrate an increasing trend towards partnership between governments and external partners who are supplying financial and at times technical support. For purposes of sustainability and continuity partnership should be encouraged between governments and local NGOS.

Approach III- Campaign: This is the appraoch adopted by governments that espoused socialist ideas when they came to power and include governments which came through the ballot (Tanzania), military take overs (Ethiopia and Somalia) and governments that came through protracted wars of liberation such as the Angolan and Mozambican governments, which were committed to making structural changes that would involve the majority of the people in national development. The aim of this appraoch was to reconstruct or rebuild new societies with new structures based on social democracy. Literacy work was used for mobilization were political parties from the high echelons of political machinery to the grassroots. President Nyerere of Tanzania saw the aim of adult education as to "shake Tanzanians out of a resignation to the kind of life they have lived for centuries past" (Kassam, 1988). President Samora Machel of Mozambique saw the value of education as "creation of a Mozamiquian with a new mentality" (Conchelos, 1990) while the goal of the new revolutionary movement of Ethiopia was to "provide free education, step by step, to the broad masses" and added, "such a program will aim at intensifying the struggle against feudalism, imperialism and bureaucratic capitalism" (Bhola, 1982).

In the campaign approach the political leadership provides the vision within which and other organs of state and the civil society operate. This approach emphasized accountability of experts to the dictates and demands of the party and the people, "the duty of the party is to ensure that leaders and experts implement the plans that have been agreed upon by the people themselves" (Hall, 1978:63).

A campaign is "politically hot" (Bhola, 1982) and is taken up with a sense of urgency. There is a time frame given to it during which everything is put at its beck and call. The more cautious approach of the programme follows after an initial head-on appraoch to the eradication of illiteracy. The campaign approach was used to aid institutional reconstruction to support the envisioned new way of life. The Tanzanian literacy campaign aided the Ujamaa philosophy of villagization. Campaigns have been blamed for raising the profile of illiteracy to high levels and never doing anything beyond them. The campaign approach succeeded where it was linked to other learning designs.

Well managed campaigns, stimulated people's participation in their own learning and opened up possibilities for creating resources within national boundaries without reliance on external support. In Somalia the 25% of the estimated cost for campaign came from the masses (Bhola, 1982: 56). In Tanzania, 10% of the national education budget was spent on literacy (Bhola, 1982:68). Without foresight and plans for continuity a campaign would only have short lived impact.

A campaign requires thoughtful planning and would inevitably necessitate involvement of committees, cadres of people, whether government or from outside, to co-ordinate the campaign. There is a need for devolution of power to organs at provincial, district and grassroots levels. A campaign should be seen as a process of enabling people to take on some power to get involved in matters of their own education.

As far as women and literacy are concerned there no major literacy campaigns going in Africa but a selective campaign aimed at promoting support for Girl Child Education has been spearheaded by FAWE and UNICEF in the ESARO office. The Forum for Women Educationalists in Africa (FAWE) an NGO based in Nairobi with Chapters in over 14 African countries is using meetings, seminars, media and publications to promote girls education in Africa. Complementing this effort is UNICEF's Girl Child Initiative a multimedia campaign promoting a positive image of the African girl through animation films, drama and print media. Both campaigns have been staged at a level higher than what a single is doing. Not only are they able to stimulate commitment they are able to attract financial resources and pool together the intellectual resource that promises to change negative attitudes to girls education in a short time.

Prospects for Each Approach

All the three approaches have a role in the eradication of illiteracy and what a country adopts depends on the level of literacy that has been attained, resources and the commitment to the problem. For countries with high literacy levels selective projects focusing on remaining pockets of illiterate communities and executed either by the state or in collaboration with NGOS would be appropriate. For countries with large numbers of "illiterates" the campaign, as the starting point, would be idea for problematising the issue, stimulating interest with the possibility for generating internal resources. Campaigns would be idea for rural areas where most illiterates are found. Planned development in form of programmes should be each country's moral obligation to the citizenry. The state should find ways of extending functional literacy programmes to its youthful populations now roaming the streets. Some of whom have never been to school while others are push out to whom formal education may not have much value. Functional literacy intergrating basic skills of reading, writing, numeracy with productive skills training can avert erosion of the value of education because of its potential for direct use.

Issues

Issues of literacy are complex and diverse, they are economic, political, educational, linguistic and ethical.

The first issue that is of critical importance is the lack of a meaningful link between literacy and other forms of formal and non formal education. Most literácy projects end with just teaching the three Rs and functional literacy mainly provide skills which some times are not used. Those who see literacy in economic terms only feel it is not worth while investing in it and focus should be on development without literacy (Ng'andwe, 1988:23).

This argument, which sees development only in terms of economic development, is rather narrow. Literacy is communication, literacy is about empowerment. When participants are asked what made them join literacy classes they often say that they wanted to know how to read and write, know the official language of administration and education, be in control of their own affairs, avoid being cheated, be able to deal with banks and hospitals, meet friends etc.

Literacy should enable people to decipher information on their own in order to make final decisions as individuals. Otherwise, the peoples of Africa will remain manipulable by dictators. Any leader who is keeping larger segments of his/her society illiteracy is doing so with a hidden agenda in mind.

The second issue concerns curriculum for literacy. Curriculum should be based on the needs of the people. It has been found that curricula that have imposed from outside have not attracted participants. Literature suggests that curricula that have focused on health, family education including income generation have been attractive to women participants. In the Zambian Literacy programme the government introduced an award of incentives in the form of free fertilizer and seeds to support functional literacy but due to the crippling economic position the incentives were discontinued and attendance dropped. Perhaps what is required is creativity in the design of literacy projects, programmes and campaigns.

The third issue concerns support systems for maintenance of acquired literacy skills. Most literacy programmes and projects lack educational support systems. For example rural libraries. Rural newspapers which were initiated as part of literacy work have deteriorated—there are no proper buildings and new library acquisitions.

Tanzania circumvented the problem of sustaining literacy by introducing district libraries and a newspaper, *Elimu Haina* (UNESCO, 1981: 8). In Mali, literacy education was accompanied by transferring some responsibility to peasants in such fields as health, marketing and keeping of records of birth, death and marriages. Further, the Malian government produced a newspaper, *Kibaru*, for the neoliterates with a circulation of 20,000 copies (UNESCO, 1981:8). These are two examples which constitute an exception to the rule, and have been recognized internationally as imaginative and creative.

Fourth, literature suggests that women willingly take part in income generating activities but may not pursue post literacy education due to discouragement and hospitality from their spouses (Lind, 1995), lack of time, distance from class, increased domestic burden. Thus women require a lot of support in order to participate in post literacy learning activities. The curricula should address issues that prevent women from pursuing further education. The men require education on the benefits accruing to families and communities when women are educated. Male "illiterates" should be attracted to literacy education by initially providing separate learning spaces because they fear to mix with women and are afraid of making mistakes in front of women (Mwansa, 1994).

The fifth issue concerns needs. Whose needs are being met by literacy projects, programmes or campaigns? Most literacy programs in Africa have been designed to serve institutional rather than individual or community needs and male rather women needs. Literacy work should identify different needs and functions that can enhance individual and community growth. Growth of individuals will, in aggregate, contribute to growth of communities and nations.

Literacy that does not identify what the individuals need to get out of the learning experiences is not likely to attract participants and drop out rates are bound to increase. Successful projects and programmes are those that have began with identification of needs by involving the learners. The unsuccessful ones are those that have been instituted without regard to the needs and aspirations of the participants.

Sixth issue concerns literacy and the school system. Literacy work which is predicated on school learning models is not going to satisfy adult learners. A lot of adults in Africa are people who have not been to school or have been to school for short times and have aversive attitudes to school. To keep them interested requires approaches which are flexible and teaching methodologies that accord them respect and recognise who they are. Institutions of adult education should be drawn into the design of such curricular and learning designs. The success story of Tanzania is based on the fact that the nation recognised adult education as a necessary field for the promotion of literacy education.

The seventh issue concerns language for literacy instruction. Most countries of Africa have a multiplicity of indigenous languages enclosed in their geographical boundaries. Apart from indigenous languages, there are colonial languages which have been designated as official languages for education and administration. When literacy is introduced, some countries have been temped to use colonial languages but after some time they have abandoned this choice and have gone to local languages. Sierra Leone tried English, and Mozambique and Angola tried literacy in Portuguese, but all soon went back to indigenous languages. Imposition of a foreign language on people who have their own language has, historically, been resisted (Matshazi, 1987).

A second language can be learned after mastery of reading and writing in the mother tongue. English, French, or Portuguese could be learned as second languages. Literacy in indigenous languages does not require learning a new vocabulary or a new culture which goes with the learning of a new language. Anthropologist Margaret Mead has written that reading skills acquired in a language other than the mother tongue are liable to remain superficial and to have nothing in common with knowledge acquired by people who have learned to read in the language in which their mothers sang lullabies to them.

The last issue concerns instructors. Literacy instruction has engaged different types of instructors, teachers, monitors or animators. They have been involved full time, part time or volunteers and have come from primary and secondary school pupils and teachers, soldiers and extension workers from health and agriculture. The experience has shown that full time instructors may have the commitment but are deterred by low remuneration, volunteer teachers are hard to keep-they can take part when they feel like. Any of these categories can be utilised in literacy instruction but they require training and incentives in order to perform their work. Where women instructors are used participation by women also goes up (Rusimbi, 1992).

Conclusions and Recommendations

A number of conclusions can be drawn from this perspective on literacy in Africa and a few recommendation made which can be looked at in the context of levels of development attained in each country.

Conclusions

First, the problem of illiteracy has in recent years not been treated as priority area though the gap is increasing between male and female illiteracy, rural and urban illiteracy. Literacy programmes and campaigns lanched in the 1970s have not been supported with resources.

Second, the methodologies adopted for eradication of literacy have a bearing on how long it can take to eradicate illiteracy. The project approach can only benefit a few people, the programme appraoch has potential for sustainability but lacks support; the campaign approach can increase awareness of the problem and reach large groups of people in a short time but is criticised for not doing anything beyond its time frame. However, the work of literacy campaigns has been sustained where campaigns have been linked to non formal educational programmes such as the Folk development colleges of Tanzania.

Third, attention has shifted to promotion of girl child education and it is this area that there are innovative projects and campaigns such as GABLE, PAGE and CAMFED, FAWE and GCI and many others that are supported with international funding. Their impact will be limited if the national states do not learn from and replicate such examples.

Fourth, promotion of girl child education without simultaneous attention to the promotion of women's education through functional literacy and non formal education will not achieve much effect because the education of girls is to a large extent predicated on education of the mothers.

Fifth, the major issues affecting literacy programmes and campaigns are lack of meaningful linkage to other forms of learning, limited curriculum content; language of instruction; inadequate attention to learners' needs, training and retention of instructors.

Recommendations

First, countries that still have high levels of illiteracy should stimulate participation in literacy education through selective campaigns focusing on rural areas and women. The campaigns should be followed by well designed programmes and projects;

Second, in collaboration with national governments and institutions for adult and non formal education, UNESCO should support training of cadres who will be able to produce materials, design and implement literacy programmes and projects;

Third, because NGOS are not constrained by bureaucracy NGOS have the potential to penetrate areas where governments may not therefore governments should develop partnership with and give support, in form of grants, to the work of NGOS;

Fourth, in order to complement efforts and avoid fragmentation and duplication NGOS should be encouraged to form literacy institutes, boards or councils to co-ordinate their own work;

Fifth, for the sustainance of functional literacy skills governments should revitalise production of rural newspapers, set up rural libraries and work with financial institutions in finding ways to provide credit facilities to women;

Sixth, the OAU should set up a modest fund aimed at promoting research and shring of experiences among researchers, policy makers and practitioners involved in literacy work.

References

Bhola, H.S. (1982) *The Promise of Literacy, Campaigns. Programmes and Projects.* Baden-Baden: Nomos Verlagsgesellschaft.

———(1988) Adult Literacy for Development in Zimbabwe. *Adult Education and Development.* No. 31, 1988.

Burchfield, S.A. & Kadzamira, E.C. (1996). Malawi GABLE Social Mobilization Campaign Activities: A Review of Research and Report on Findings of KAP Follow-up Study. USAID & Creative Associates International, Inc

Cipolla, C.M. (1969). Literacy and Development in the West. Baltimore: Penguin.

Conchelos, G. (1990). World Literacy Prospects at the Turn of the Century: Is the objective of Literacy for All by the Year 2000 Statistically Plausible? *Comparative Education Review.* 34 (1).

Hall, B.(1989) New Perspectives in Literacy: The Role of Non-Governmental Organizations. Prospects, XIX (4).

Jones, P.W. (1990) UNESCO and the Politics of Global Literacy. Comparative Education Review. 34(1) 1990.

Hall, Budd. (1978). Mtu Ni Afya: Tanzania's Health Campaign. Washington: Clearing House on Development Communication.

Kassam, Y. (1988) Literacy and Development—What is Missing in the Jigsaw Puzzle?" Adult Education and Development. 31

———(1989). Who Benefits from Illiteracy: Literacy and Empowerment. Prospects. XIX (4).

Kelly, M. (1994). Below the Poverty Line: A Situational Analysis of Girl Child Education in Zambia. Lusaka: UNICEF

Lind, A. (1995). Women Literacy with Particular Reference to Southern Africa. Journal of AALAE. 9(1)

Maimbolwa-Sinyangwe, I & Chilangwa, B (1995). Learning from Inside the Classroom. Lusaka: UNICEF

Matshazi, M. (1987). Mother Tongue Literacy: The Importance of Learning to Read and Write in One's Mother Tongue. Convergence. XX (3-4)

Marshall, J. (1984) Links in the Chain Our of Underdevelopment: Report and Reflections on Literacy in the people's Republic of Angola. (Unpublished term paper.) Toronto: OISE

Ministry of Education & UNICEF. (1995). Zambia Declaration on the Education of the Girl Child. Lusaka: Ministry of Education & UNICEF

Mulusa, T. (1988) The International Adult Literacy Inertia. Adult Education and Development. 31.

Mpofu, T.T. (1995). Evaluation of the government Literacy campaign in Zimbabwe. Journal of AALAE, 9(1) 25-34

Mpogolo, Z.J. (1980). Planning and Administration of National Literacy Programmes in the United republic of Tanzania, in International Institute of Educational Planning, Planning and Administration of National Literacy Programmes. Paris: UNESCO

Mutava, D. (1988). Forty Years of Struggle Against Illiteracy: the Zambia Case. Prospects. XVII, (3).

Mwanakatwe, J. (1974). The Growth of Education in Zambia Since Independence. Lusaka: Oxford University Press.

Mwanasa, D.M. (1996) Community Perspectives on Issues of Motivation and Gender in Zambian Literacy programmes. International Journal for Qualitative Research 1996, 9 (2) 181-199

———(1995). Listening to the Girl Child Voices for Change and Redress in Primary Education in Zambia. Lusaka: UNICEF

———(1995) Perspectives on Literacy, Gender and Change: A Case for Zambia. British Journal of Sociology of Education, 1995, 16(4), 495-516

———(1994) Community Perspectives on Gender, Participation and culture in Zambian Literacy Programmes. Gender and Education 1994, 6 (2) 151-168

Nandwe, A.(1988). Literacy for What? The Zambian Case. (Unpublished term paper.) OISE, 1988.

Odaga, A. & Heneveld, W. (1995). Girls and Schools in Sub Saharan Africa. Washington: The World Bank (The World Bank Technical Paper 298)

Omulewa, M. (1988). On the Intractable Question of Literacy Campaigns in Nigeria. *Adult Education and Development* 31

Rusimbi, M. (1992). Women and Literacy Development in East Africa with Particular Reference to Tanzania. In Eve Malmquist (ed.), Women and Literacy Development in the Third World. Linkoping: Linkoping University, Department of Education and Psychology in cooperation with UNESCO and SIDA

Simmons, R. (1990). Alternative Literacy in South Africa: the Experience of Learn and Teach. *Convergence.* XXIII (1).

Sticht. T and MacDonald, B.A (1990). Teaching the Mother and reach the Child. Geneva: International Bureau of Education

Summers, L. (1994). Investing All the People Education Women in Developing Countries. Washington: Economic Development Institute of the World Bank (An EDI Seminar Paper. Number 45)

UNDP. (1995). Human Development Report 1995. New York: Oxford University Press

UNESCO. (1981). *Literacy 81: Eight Hundred Million Illiterates, Eight Hundred Million Starving in the World.* Paris: UNESCO.

Wangoola, P.(1988). The Political Economy of Illiteracy: A Global Analysis of Myth and Reality About Its Eradication. *Adult Education and Development.* No. 31, September 1988.

World Bank, (1980). *World Development Report, 1980.* New York: Oxford University Press.

TRAINING WOMEN AND GIRLS FOR EMPLOYMENT

INTERNATIONAL LABOUR ORGANISATION

I. GENERAL OVERVIEW

The fight agaisnt poverty through the economic empowerment of women and the promotion of existing lasting facilities are an obligation as well as a moral, political and economic respoonsibility of Governments and the international community. The major impediments to access to employment by women with equal chances and opportunities like men stem from many factors, the most common being unequal access to education and training, professional discrimination characterized by employment categorization according to sex, the state of some national legislations, women's ignorance about their rights, uneven access to inputs, poor representation of women in decision-making and social regulation bodies, social cultural stereotypes, and lastly, lack of share of family responsibilities.

Status of Girls and Women in the Education World: Constraints to be Abolished

In most of the regions of the world, several youths have no access to basic education, neither can they read, write nor count. Furthermore, where they can go to school under good conditions it is unfortunately not all children who can do so on an equal basis. The slogan "education for all irrespective of sex" remains an empty slogan for this category of the excluded composed mainly of girls.

Increased inequality between men and women especially in the areas of education and training calls for urgent specific measures in favour of women which reflect their needs and take into account the various obstacles preventing them from enjoying the same rights like men. Today

ers, wives and housewives. Women have their own needs, problems, difficulties and concerns. Therefore, equality does not mean the same in everything or the negation of gender differences.

One of the prerequisites to ensure the success of every adult education programme including literacy programme is that the content should be diversified, rich, flexible and appropriate to the target groups.

Therefore since 1992 the Research Center for Adult Education has conducted a new experimental literacy programme with focus on the gender roles and characteristics of women with the hope that it will be more appropriate and attractive to women especially in the rural areas.

Recently, the inappropriateness of the current literacy programme was recognized by UNESCO/PROAP so we tried to modify the literacy programme of APPEAL (Asia Pacific Programme of Education for All) so as to make it more appropriate to women and their gender characteristics.

I. Description of the process of developing a literacy programme for women.

The objective of designing an experimental literacy programme for women is to diversify the current literacy programme and make it more appropriate to different target groups including women. As any programme designed for any target group, it should ensure and closely follow the national criteria on literacy, literacy and numeracy skills. In this case, the main target audience is rural women because they constitute the majority of the total number of illiterates at present.

The following principles should be observed in the process of developing the literacy programme.

- The principle of appropriateness. The programme should be appropriate both to the objective demands of the socio-economic development of the national and community and needs of women.
- The principle of development. The level of skills of literacy (reading and writing) and numeracy (calculating) should be gradually raised in terms of their complicatedness and difficulties. The functional knowledge should be development and gradually widened through each cycle and level.
- The principle of linkage. The linkage between skills of literacy and lesson levels should be ensured. Among those, the results attained in literacy and numeracy should be seen as the basic result, and functional knowledge is a means to stimulate the learners.
- The principle of participation. According to this principle, the learn-

ers will be the center of the learning process and therefore encourages the initiative and active participation of the women through a system of questions for discussion.

In the planning for a literacy programme, the following steps should be carried out:

1) Conduct survey to know the needs;
2) Study the current literacy programme and current literacy materials for learners;
3) Define goals and objectives of the programme;
4) Identify area of functional contents and topics;
5) Develop curriculum and revision;
6) Modify and readjust.

The objectives of the literacy programme for women are based on the analysis of the needs of women, community and the country. In this case, like the national literacy programme, the literacy programme for women should attain the following objectives:

- To improve the literacy (reading, writing) and numeracy (calculating) skills according to the national criteria; and
- To provide minimum knowledge and skills necessary for women to perform successfully their role in the family and society (as a mother, wife, citizen and productive worker).

In addition, the literacy programme for women also has a special objective to empower women and that means to help them enhance their capacity and consolidate their belief in the role and potentiality of women in general and of themselves in particular, and belief in the ability to take part side by side with men in the development of the community for the improvement of the current living condition.

II. Identification of areas of functional contents and educational topics for women

The functional contents in the literacy programme are minimum knowledge and skills most necessary for women to perform their role and functions in production, family and society. Literacy and numeracy skills are both key objectives and a content of functional knowledge necessary for illiterate women.

However, the functional content is only a means to make the programme realistic and attractive to women and gender characteristic purposeful.

The basis for selecting the contents are:

- Objective needs of the socioeconomic development of the community and nation for women.
- Needs and concerns, condition and circumstances of women.
- National programme.
- Reference of experiences of other countries.

So for example, most of illiterate women (over 80%) according to the data analysis are poor people. Their main and immediate concern is how to have adequate food. If they can receive education they will hope to generate income by means of their literacy skills. Therefore, one of the important functional content is to help women promote production and generate income.

Consequently, the topics of this content area should be supplemented and readjusted to make it relevant to the current needs of rural women and updated problems in agricultural production.

At present, agricultural production, especially household based economy have posed new requirements for women where they should be dynamic, creative, have selfcontrol and have information not only on new technology of production but also knowledge on management, organization, business and market prices. Quite different from the past, the rural women today must be responsible for all the steps of the production process, from means of production, kinds of animals and vegetables, plants, cultivation and breeding techniques, to the problem of harvesting and selling products.

Therefore topics in the area of production and income should be based on the above mentioned requirements.

Furthermore, women have to perform their lofty functions i.e. to be mother and wife in the family. However, the illiterate women due to incomplete schooling, lack of information—meet with many difficulties in bringing up children and taking care of the family. Because they lack information on environmental hygiene, food hygiene and nutrition, women also meet with difficulties in the organization and management of the family.

Therefore, an important and indispensable content area for women (like in the national programme) is the area of family life and health. However, in this area, some topics like common diseases of women, hygiene, diet and recreation of women, should be added.

The functional content for women is important as it must contribute to the empowerment of women. Realities show that the illiterate women are limited in capacity and as a result feel less self-confident.

It is therefore necessary to make them aware of their role, status and contribution in the family and society . And then they can promote their potentiality in every area of the life and actively participate in the development of the community and nation. Hence a new area of functional content needs to be included into a literacy programme which we call "*Women in Development*".

24

THE IMPACT OF LITERACY ON WOMEN IN INDIA

Anita Dighe

A question of great interest and relevance to literacy practitioners, policy makers, planners and researchers relates to **the impact of literacy on women's lives**. In recent years, World Bank has been promoting basic education of women and girls on the basis of research evidence to show that women's education is negatively correlated with fertility rate and with infant and maternal mortality. Public investment in women's education is thus increasingly justified on the grounds that there is substantial evidence from a wide range of countries that increased female education is linked to improved health, lower fertility, and other benefits, and that investment in female education has a high social rate of return.

Researchers, however, have differed in their interpretation of these associations. Thus, it has been suggested that the association with illiteracy is indirect and that there are other factors that are responsible. For example, it has been suggested that lower fertility in countries with high literacy rate is not so much a consequence of literacy as such as it is of wider availability of schooling and hence the tendency for girls to marry later (UNESCO 1993). In any case, as pointed out by Bown (1990), most research cited internationally as proots of a connection between women's education and such phenomena as lower infant mortality rates and small family size are actually based on school statistics rather than literacy data and while such a statistic is useful in the argument for promoting education of girls, the fact remains that very little is known about the outcomes of literacy for adult women. She therefore undertook a study on this almost un-researched subject of the impact of adult women's literacy by studying the outcomes of 43 project case studies and one country case study (Nepal) funded by Action Aid and ODA. On the basis of the analysis of the case studies, she found that certain social, economic and personal changes could be noticed among those women who had become literate.

As the above review has highlighted, **there is an overall paucity of research on women and literacy**. It was in order to begin to understand some of the issues raised above that a research study was undertaken in 1993 in Ambedker Nagar, a resettlement colony in South Delhi where a Total Literacy Campaign (TLC) had been launched by Delhi Saksharta Samiti in 1991-92, with the intention of it being a pilot project for undertaking a literacy campaign on a larger scale in Metropolitan Delhi.

Women's Literacy—What do Women say?

What is presented in the following sections are the highlights from this research study where one hundred women who had supposedly completed the three literacy primers, were selected for the study. While a questionnaire was designed for the purpose, there were a large number of open-ended questions for obtaining qualitative insights on women's views and perceptions on various issues. In addition, more focused and in-depth in terviews were conducted with 5 women respondents.

- The analysis revealed that one-third of the respondents had been to school earlier and had studied up to various levels in the formal system.
- Of the 34 respondents who had been to school earlier, only 4 were still school-going. The rest could be regarded as school drop-outs.
- These women had dropped out of school for various reasons. Some of them had left their studies because their mothers saw no need to educate their daughters. Others had to leave because of household work and responsibilities. Fathers who died caused their daughters to assume greater family burden. Early marriage ensured withdrawal from school for others.
- Almost all of them, however, were keen on continuing with their education. That was probably the reason why they had joined the literacy campaign in the first place.

Motivation for Literacy

Interestingly, most women did not need to be motivated by others to participate in the literacy campaign. Said Asha, a 45 year old woman who was non-literate earlier, "I thought when everybody is studying, even I should start studying and be a part of the literacy campaign". According to Krishna Devi who was also a non-literate earlier, "I thought if I become literate, I'II be able to calculate and thus help my husband in business". Meera, a 35 year old married woman who had studied up to class 5 earlier, joined the campaign because she wanted to improve her reading and writing skills so that she could teach others. Sita Kumari, a 11 year old girl who is studying in class 6, joined the literacy classes because a lot of girls from her area were attending the classes and she felt she would learn "more" through the literacy classes and thereby improve her performance in school.

The reasons for joining the literacy campaign were thus varied. But the expectations were also different. Thus, some wanted to learn just enough literacy to be able to sign their names, or read bus numbers. Others thought if they could "learn a little", it would be to their advantage. Still others felt constrained by their inability to keep accounts. Their expectations were then to acquire appropriate skills that would help them to keep proper accounts. Inability to teach their children and monitor their homework, was yet another reason for some. There were, however, women who felt the need to acquire literacy skills for such private reasons as ability to read and write letters, even books. They were also of the opinion that acquisition of literacy skills would enable them to seek employment.

A related question was the kinds of problems they had earlier faced due to illiteracy. It appeared from their responses that illiteracy had constrained their ability to deal effectively with day to day problems.

These included:

- using the public transport system effectively,
- keeping proper accounts,
- reading and writing letters on their own,
- dealing with written communication in an autonomous manner,
- suffering the indignity of having to put their thumb impression,
- feeling harassed when going out on their own.

Acquisition of literacy skills was therefore perceived to be important in order to enable them to became independent, function autonomously and deal with everyday issues in an efficient manner. Literacy skills were also perceived to be important for seeking employment or even for engaging in petty business. Some were of the opinion that as literate mothers they would be able to teach their children.

Responses to Literacy Classes

All of them wanted to go to the literacy class to study for personal and social reasons. Thus, a large number liked to go to the literacy class because it gave them an opportunity to meet others and study collectively. Besides providing them an opportunity for social interaction, there were others who felt that by coming to the literacy class, they were felt that by coming to the literacy class, they were able to "kill time". But more importantly, women had a personal reason for coming to literacy classes and this was their strong desire for learning.

Despite this high level of motivation, did they have any problems in going literacy classes? Interestingly, the problems were of a personal nature and it is worth considering the reasons given by women for these might well provide a clue as to why women drop out of literacy classes in a large numbers. Thus there were women who complained about headaches and pain in the eyes and others who said they had overall "problems in understanding" as well as problems in deciphering the letters and the "matras". While some of these reasons are a comment on the poor health status of women that has a bearing on their learning abilities, the other reasons are a reflection of the poor self-image most women have and of the manner in which they have internalized their subordination so that they regard their learning disabilities as natural and normal.

Literacy Attainment and Uses of Literacy

A literacy test was designed, based on the norms set down by NLM (Directorate of Adult Education 1992):

From Table 24.1, it is clear that despite the fact that it was reported that all the respondents had completed the three TLC primers, **only 16% of the respondents were able to reach the NLM norm**. The score of more than 50% of the respondents was less than 30. It is possible that the reason for the low scores on the literacy test was due to the fact that the test came at the end of administration of the questionnaire by which time exhaustion may have probably set in for the respondents. A fairly large number evinced lack of interest in taking the test and seemed eager to finish it as quickly as possible. Furthermore, the literacy classes had closed down by October 1992 and the literacy test for the present study was administered about eight months later. It is possible that due to passage of time and lack of sustained post-literacy interventions, a sizable number had already relapsed into illiteracy.

Table 24.1- Literacy Scores of Respondents

Total Scores	Per Cent
0-30	54
31-50	14
51-69	16
70-100	16
All	100

An attempt was also made to ascertain the extent to which literacy skills that had been acquired were put to daily use by the respondents. Simple questions relating to application of reading, writing, and numeracy skills in their everyday life, were asked. The questions varied in their level of complexity. Thus, at one end were simple questions that asked whether they could read names of TV programmes, names of shops, brand names of items purchased, to whether they could read big newspaper, headlines, or letters that were received or children's or any other book. With regard to writing skills, the questions that were asked varied from signing their own names, writing their own addresses, to writing letters, filling money order forms, writing an application, writing a cleque. Likewise for application of numeracy skills, the questions varied from reading time, reading the bus numbers, to reading the ration bill, to working out addition and subtraction on paper, as well as working out rate of interest. Each of the items was given weights on the basis of the level of complexity.

Table 24.2- Score for Application

NUMERACY SKILLS		READING SKILLS		WRITING SKILLS	
<←6	38%	<←5	56%	<←6	89%
7-12	29%	6-10	8%	7-12	10%
13-18	33%	11-15	36%	13-18	1%
All	100%	all	100%	All	100%

It appears from Table 4.2 that **the respondents, by and large, did not use the reading, writing and numeracy skills in their everyday life.** This appears to be so large in the case of application of writing skills. On the whole, it was the numeracy skills that seemed to be used more frequently. It is possible that the questions that were asked of the respondents were not relevant in the case of most women (for example, why would poor women be required to read or fill in money order forms or to fill in a cleque?) But since the NLM has set down norms that are applicable to both men and women, it became incumbent to design a literacy test on the basis of the NLM norms, as well as to ascertain from women about the extent to which they used the literacy skills that were acquired by them in their everyday life.

An attempt was made to correlate the literacy scores with the scores for application of reading, writing and numeracy skills in order to ascertain whether the level of performance of the learners affected their utilization of these skills. For the purpose, the chi-square test was used. This showed that there was a strong association between each of these was a strong association between each of these variables, meaning that **those with higher literacy scores were more likely to apply their reading, writing and numeracy skills in their everyday life as compared to those with low literacy scores.** Likewise, the educational background of the learners also affected their performance level. Thus, those who were non-literate did not perform as well in comparison with those who were school drop-outs and school going.

The women learners in the present study comprised a heterogeneous group in terms of reading and writing skills. Besides their varying educational background, their overall performance levels also varied. Given this diversity, it was felt that rather than ascertaining their performance only on the basis of a literacy test, it would be pertinent to find out if they had experienced any changes or "gains" as a result of their participation in the literacy classes. The relevant questions then were, "Had literacy brought about any changes in their lives?" "Where any changes perceived at the personal level, at the family level"? Interestingly, this question did not evoke a positive response in the case of a large number of women. But when they were probed, it was apparent that some changes were perceptible.

Impact of the Literacy Experience on Women's Lives

Many women felt they had become "knowledgeable, more understanding" through literacy. There were others who had experienced more self-confidence. Said Krisha Devi, a 30 year old married woman with 5 children, "I'm now able to manage our business even if my husband is not around. I am able to help the children with their homework". According to her, a literate woman can manage better because "she is more confident and nobody can cheat her".

Asked about any changes in her relationship with her husband, she had this to say, "Men always try to assert their authority. My husband used to say earlier, 'you don't know anything' but he behaves somewhat respectfully now because I talk back". Her neighbors also confirmed that after joining the literacy campaign, Krishna Devi had become more confident and outspoken.

Wala Devi acknowledged that even though she attended the literacy classes for just one month, she felt she "could understand things better and could communicate better". For her a literate person was one who was more confident, discerning, and one who could manage things on her/his own as opposed to an non-literate person who she felt was often ill-treated.

Meera was a school drop- out and yet her participation in the literacy class had "made her feel good and had enabled her to articulate better". She is fond of reading books during leisure time but due to her participation in the campaign, she now feels confident she will be able to teach others. As a school-going girl, Sita Kumari felt her participation in the campaign had improved her articulation and honed her reading and writing skills.

On the whole, however acquisition of literacy skills did not seem to have altered or improved women's status within the family. For the perception of a majority of them was that there were no visible changes in their relationship with their husbands, children, parents. Some of them, however, did comment that their husbands and children were encouraging and approving of their efforts.

Desire for Post Literacy and Continuing Education

It the desire for basic literacy was strong enough, that for continuing education was no less strong. For a **majority affirmed that they wanted to continue with their education.** There were those who wished they could put their literacy skills to functional use (such as read newspapers, write letters independently, teach children etc.), but there were others who had aspirations to seek employment and those who wanted "to be somebody in life". Of the less than one fourth of the respondents who did not wish to continue, the reasons advanced were lack of time due to household chores, preoccupation with children, lack of interest in future studies and inability to continue due to ill health, advancing age, poor eyesight etc.

Of the majority who wanted to study further, **not all them wanted to pursue their learning for any instrumental goal.** Interestingly about one third wanted to pursue learning as an end in itself. But an equal proportion expressed a hope and a desire to be able to find a job, including a fairly large number who specifically mentioned acquisition of a technical skill (such as tailoring). That the literacy programmes had raised the aspirations of the learners was evident from such statements as "I'd like to be a doctor," "I'd like to be madam", "I'd like to do a course", "I'd like to do business". Participation in the literacy campaign had also kindled the instinct for social service in some who said they would like to teach others.

There was, however, **inadequate articulation about the type of post literacy and continuing education programmes the respondents wanted.** While a need was expressed for tailoring (presumably due to lack of exposure to any other vocational skill women could aspire for), the fact that women were articulating such a wish underscores the importance of planning for providing various types of vocational/technical programmes as part of continuing education. While respondents were of the opinion that opportunities for continuing education should be provided, they were unclear as to what kinds of programmes they would have preferences for.

One of the constituent NGOs that formed the **Delhi Saksharta Samiti**, (Delhi Literacy Committee) ran a library service for children. Under the aegis of this organization, arrangements were made to provide library services in some parts of Ambedkar Nagar.

Even though the books provided were for children, an attempt was made to ascertain if the women knew about the library service and if so, did they use the service. Only three respondents were aware of this service. Only three respondents were aware of this service. The rest were either unaware, or said they had no time or else felt they still lacked adequate reading skills for independent reading. If they borrowed books from anyone, these were mainly children's books or some story books and in case of difficulty in reading, they sought the help of children in the family, or their husbands or relatives, or the literacy volunteers. The analysis showed that the reading habit was still not strongly inculcated among the women and that their reading skills were limited and as a result, they required guidance/ supervision from others.

Interpreting the Findings

The results of this study have corroborated the findings of other studies which have shown that women's motivation for literacy is very high. The fact that women participate in large numbers in the TLCs can be explained by the high motivational levels for the literacy campaign. There is also another reason and this relates to the "social sanction" that is obtained for women's participation due to large-scale mobilization that is attempted by the campaign. There is also another reason and this relates to the "social sanction" that is obtained for women's participation due to large-scale mobilization that is attempted by the campaign. Women are the winners, for various patriarchal considerations that hinder their participation become at least temporarily inoperative as they come out or their homes and take part in the campaign with great enthusiasm. But they also come with varying expectations from the literacy campaign. As this study showed, the reasons for joining the literacy classes varied, so also their expectations. It is worth noting, however, **the importance of contextual factors that determine women's need for literacy**. Living in a congested resettlement colony in a metropolitan city such as Delhi, acquisition of literacy classes becomes important in order to enable them to become independent, and function autonomously. Thus for example, the inability to keep written accounts or write occasional letters and deal with written communication independently, become the very reasons for their joining the literacy classes. Considering the generally low educational attainment of their school-going children and the poor quality of education that is provided by government schools, mothers of school-going children also feel the need to become literate in order to help the children with their studies or at least monitor what is being taught in schools. With deepening economic crisis as well as the realization that very many types of employment are no longer accessible to the non-literates, there is also the expectation that acquisition of literacy skills would enable them to seek employment or at least engage in petty business.

In other words. **The reasons given by women for joining literacy classes are conditioned by the socio-economic milieu in which they live.** In order to understand what are the factors that influence women's decision to join literacy classes, it would be worthwhile undertaking more extensive work in varied situations—most importantly in rural areas. Such studies would be important in order to see whether the type of literacy and post-literacy programmes that are offered at least match some of the expectations for which women join literacy classes.

Besides their high level of motivation, **women also generally liked to attend the literacy classes for personal and social reasons.** Thus a large number liked to go to the literacy classes because it gave them an opportunity to meet others and to study collectively. This social dimension of literacy has been commented upon earlier (Horsman 1988; Dighe 1992). For according to them, literacy classes provide an opportunity to large numbers of women to break the isolation which is socially structured into their lives, giving them a chance to meet other women, and learn collectively-rather than learn singly as individuals. Even the fact that some came to literacy classes to "kill time", is an aspect of social isolation that makes time hang heavily on the hands of some women. What came across unambiguously in this study, however, was women's strong desire for learning.

If women joined literacy classes for personal and social reasons, **it was largely the personal factors that were responsible for their irregular attendance or for their discontinuance**. A comment has been made earlier on the poor health status of women that has a bearing on their learning abilities. It is, however, also a fact that older women in their forties and fifties are constrained due to lack of reading glasses. But more importantly, it is the internalization of their subordination that result in their beginning to feel they are useless and worthless learners—more so because they regard their learning disabilities as natural and normal.

This has implications for the organization of literacy classes for women. For **in order to overcome this attitude which epitomizes the attitude of most poor women towards literacy, the learning process must enable women to be themselves, to be valued the way they are, to experience personhood, to move from a feeling of worthlessness to a feeling of self-worth**. It also indicates that the ambiance of a literacy class must be such that women feel comfortable, relaxed and do not experience anxieties. Since women lack a social space they can call their own, literacy classes must provide them that space. For experience is showing that programmes that provide women the social space to be away from their homes, to be relaxed, to talk to others, to seek help from others, enhance and sustain women's learning.

Experience to date has also shown that **teaching methods play an important role in literacy participation and for sustaining motivation among women** in general. Thus a superior and patronizing teaching attitude discourage interest while a democratic, open and involved relationship—treating women as equal—and creating an atmosphere of confidence, has been found to have a positive influence on attendance and results (Lind 1988). The experience of some of the voluntary organizations have been particularly significant in this regard. For their experience has clearly shown how the attitudes of the volunteers as well as participatory processes of learning that encourage and elicit women's participation, can create the right condition for sustaining women's participation. While research evidence is fragmentary, experience has shown that the process of teaching is very critical insofar as women learners are concerned as approach that elicits learner participation, the use of folk songs and literacy games breaks the monotony and repetitiveness of learning and makes learning more enjoyable and literacy acquisition less daunting.

The present study showed that **the literacy volunteers felt more comfortable in using the formal methods of teaching**. Even discussions on the themes of the literacy primers were minimal. In other words, the main emphasis remained on imparting technical skills of reading, writing, and numeracy skills to the learners. Writing tasks on the blackboard, notebooks and slates were frequently reported. While it was intended that the key word or sentence in the literacy primer would trigger a discussion and thereby gradually raise the awareness of the learners, in reality this did not happen. This was because the translation of a theme (expressed in words/sentence) into sustained dialogue, requires skills that the literacy volunteers did not have. Also, because most of the literacy volunteers were school students, their youth and relative inexperience in life, also militated against the use of such non-traditional methods of teaching. Any participatory, dialogical interactions between the learners and the literacy volunteers would require sustained and on-going training support of a different kind.

The importance of participatory processes of learning becomes evident when an attempt is made to ascertain the impact of literacy on women's lives. The present study showed that for those who participated, the literacy campaign did seem to bring about some changes at the personal level. Thus, some reported more self-confidence, better articulation, better discerning ability, more self-respect, and ability to mange on one's own. On the whole, however, their participation did not seem to have altered or improved their status within the family except for a few women who felt their husbands now treated them with some respect. The gains were limited because the teaching—learning process did not encourage experience-sharing among women—women talking about themselves, their problems, their needs-deciding collectively and taking action to ameliorate their present condition. This process of critical analysis and reflection leading to collective action is so crucial if women have to be empowered at the individual and collective levels. When empowerment indicators were used to assess the impact of literacy on women's lives, it became evident that while literacy *per se* had initiated the process of empowerment at the personal, individual level, and to that extent the direction of change was in the positive direction, this change needed to be sustained and consolidated. Furthermore, attempts would now have to be consciously made to ensure that individual empowerment leads to collective empowerment of women and vice verse.

A significant finding of this study related to the level of literacy reached by women. While the level of literacy reached by women was low by the NLM norms, it is interesting to note that this finding conforms with the African experience (Lind 1992) according to which women take much longer to become functionally literate. Also, women tend to use their literacy skills less frequently (Carron et al 1988). A recent study undertaken by Stromquist (1994) in Sao Paulo in Brazil has shown the variable levels of literacy acquired by women over a three years longitudinal study and has also pointed out that women do read and write in their daily lives but in small and infrequent amounts, patterns that would hardly support the development of literacy habits. This experience has also been corroborated by the present study. For women tend to use their numeracy skills more often and their writing skills less frequently.

These findings have implications insofar as TLC are concerned. **Since TLCs are time-bound and target-oriented, their single-most preoccupation with** literacy attainment would undoubtedly conceal the variable levels of literacy attained by women. According to Brown (1992), **literacy is not a single unified competence nor a fixed measurable achievement. There is hierarchy of literacies and a learner can progress in skillfulness from one level to the next.** While the three IPCL primers might serve such a purpose to some extent, it becomes crucial that in the case of women the literacy skills that are acquired, are consolidated and strengthened so as to prevent their relapse into illiteracy. Maybe women need to be involved in designing their own literacy materials. Experiences are now beginning to show that the stories told by learners become effective learning materials for the learners find these stories interesting when they see their own struggles and experiences reflected. Because language or even the dialect of the learner is used in the stories, women find them easy to read. But it is not enough for women learners to accept such experience stories uncritically. It literacy has to empower women then clearly experience is the crucial point from which to make a beginning. But women must also learn to develop a critical attitude by questioning their experience as well as the rationale behind them.

The different literacy levels reached by women also has implications for developing an appropriate Post-Literacy programme for women. For **rather than perceiving Post-Literacy as a phase that is distinct from the basic literacy phase, in the case of women, it is necessary to consolidate the literacy skills at each of the three levels by developing appropriate literacy materials**, some of which could be along the lines suggested above. Also, given women's lack of confidence in being able to read books on their own (as in library/Jana Shikshan Nilayam), it would be desirable that reading habits are gradually inculcated in say "read aloud" sessions. But more importantly, if the basic literacy phase in the TLCs only focused on imparting literacy skills, it would become incumbent that in the next phase, the focus shifts to group building and group action. In other words, conscious educational interventions would have to be made to empower women. Various skills training programmes would have to be organized in response to their felt need for continuing education.

As the present study has shown, the overall gains of the literacy campaign were modest in terms of the literacy levels reached by women if the NLM norms for a literate person, are used. Likewise, it was found that qualitatively modest gains were made with regard to empowerment indicators. And yet the literacy campaign had kindled the desire in women to become literate and to continue with their education. **Benefits from lit-**

eracy in the form of increased self-esteem and autonomy, however, were considerable. It seems that women find important social spaces in literacy classes.

As in the study mentioned earlier (Stromquist 1994), in this study too, it was found that unintentionally, literacy classes offer women an opportunity to meet a group of women with similar constraints and often, wit similar experiences of poverty and subordination. Literacy classes provide women with a space to which they can get away from home, it is probably the first time that they can see on a collective scale that their personal situations are not unique.

Where do We go from Here?

A the present study was undertaken on the basis of a small sample and to that extent, the findings of the study cannot be generalized. Also, the study was undertaken in one re-settlement colony of Delhi and is not representative of the rural experience at all. And yet, the study is probably one of the first attempts to pay serious attention to women's literacy. The study has attempted to provide answers to questions such as (1) what are women's needs for becoming literate? (2) what are their expectations from literacy? (iii) what are their expectations for continuing education? (iv) what is the impact of literacy on their lives?

While the study has made a modest beginning to answer some of these questions that have policy implications, **it is recommended that systematic and concerted work in this direction is undertaken in future through multi-site action research studies in varying linguistic and socio-economic settings.** The present study attempted to supplement quantitative with qualitative data obtained through open-ended questions and in-depth interviews with a small number of respondents. This experience showed that more emphases on qualitative methods would have provided better and more meaningful insights relating to women's literacy. In future, special attention could be paid to methodological issues, particularly to various qualitative approaches that would enable the researchers to get "inside" the experience of women and hear and capture their voices. For a study of literacy from a gender perspective would need to portray the concrete situation of women in their families and communities, unravel their accumulated experience, knowledge and practices and show how these cumulative and multiple forces interact and influence women's interest in literacy and the uses they give to literacy.

Finally, the overall experience of TLCs to date has shown that women participate as learners and as literacy volunteers in large numbers. Also, it has been commented upon earlier that women receive a "social sanction" to participate in the literacy campaigns. And yet, despite this advantage of securing women's participation, **there is a near total absence of gender issues in TLCs as they are presently conceived and designed.** On the other hand, some of the characteristics of TLCs promote women's participation. Thus, for example, the literacy classes in most cases take place in the immediate neighborhood of women learners; the literacy volunteers largely come from the same milieu as the learners and are in most cases, boys and girls known to the learners; each literacy class sets its own hours depending upon the convenience of the learners; the classes have a low learner-volunteer ratio and there is generally a good relationship between the volunteer and the learners.

According to Stromquist (1994) many of these features are favorable to women's participation which has also been corroborated by the BRAC (Bangladesh Rural Advancement Committee) experience in Bangladesh. Women's participation in the literacy programmes, however, is a complex and multi-faceted phenomenon. In the case of poor women, their poverty and powerlessness (due to problems of class and gender), make the acquisition of sustainable literacy a somewhat impossible dream. **There is presently little awareness among policy makers and planners about how literacy needs fit into the hierarchy of survival needs women have in everyday** life. What needs to be understood are the kind of expectations women have in joining literacy classes, the type of problems they face in attending literacy classes or in literacy acquisition and how they link literacy to their everyday life.

There is a need to raise gender issues in the pre-planning phase of the Total Literacy Campaign, and to incorporate them in the planning and implementation phases. The training programmes and materials prepared for TLCs have to become gender-sensitive. So also, appropriate Post-Literacy strategies for women need to be worked out. But above all else, there is presently little understanding about the importance of 'literacy to empower women. For in order to translate the policy directive of "education of empower women", it is imperative that a broader vision of literacy is taken. Until such a broad vision of literacy is taken, the present attempts will only perpetuate the stereotypical programmes that have domesticated women and have not brought any changes in their status at the individual societal and political levels.

References

Anand A. 1982. "Re-thinking Women and Development: the Case of Feminism," *Convergence*, 15(1), pp. 17-26.

Batiwala, S. 1993. *Empowerment of Women in South Asia: concepts and Practices*, Delhi ASPBAE.

Bhasin, K. 1984. "The Why and How of Literacy for Women: Some Thoughts in the Indian Context", *Convergence*, 17(4), pp. 37-43.

Bhasin, K. 1985. "Illiteracy, Women and Development", *Adult Education and Development*, 24, pp. 94-105.

Bown, L. 1990. Preparing the *Future-Women Literacy and Development*, Action Aid Development Report No. 4.

Carron G., Mwira K. & Right, G. 1988. *Functioning and Effects of the Literacy Programmes in Kenya*. Draft Report, Paris: IIEP (mimeo).

Dighe, A. 1988. "Education for Women's Equality: a pipe dream? A case from India", in *Women and Literacy: Yesterday, Today and Tomorrow*, IIE, Stockholm: Stockholm University.

Dighe, A. 1992. "Women and Literacy Development in India", in Eve Malmquist ed. *Women and Literacy in the Third World*, Linkoping, Linkoping University.

Dighe, A. & Patel I., 1992. "Gender Equity in Literacy in India", *Perspective in Education*, Vol 9:1 1993, pp. 20-14 Directorate of Adult Education 1992.

Modalities of Total Literacy Declaration and Evaluation of Learning Outcomes, Report of the Expert Group, New Delhi, Government of India.

Horsman, J. 1988. "The Dimension of Literacy", *Canadian Women's Studies*, Vol. 9. Nos. 3 & 4.

Johnston, A. 1984. *The Effects of SIDA-Supported Education Programmes in Botswana, Ethiopia, Mozambique and Tanzania on the Status of Women in Society, Stockhlom*: SIDA, (mineo).

Lind, A. 1988. *Adult Literacy Lessons and Promises: Mazambican Literacy Campaigns 1978-1982*. IIE, Stockholm: University of Stockholm.

Lind, A., 1992. "Literacy: a tool for the Empowerment of Women? Women's Participation in Literacy Programmes of the Third World", in *Women and Literacy: Yesterday, Today and Tomorrow*, IIE, Stockholm: Stockholm University.

National Literacy Mission, 1988. Ministry of Human Resource Development, New Delhi, Goverment of India.

Patel, I. 1991. *A Study of the Impact of New Communication Technologies on Literacy in India*, New Delhi, (mimeo).

Patel, I. 1994. *Trends in Adult Education Research in India*, a paper submitted to the UNESCO Institute of Education, Hamburg, for a research study on "Trends in Adult Education Research in the World", (mimeo).

Ramdas, L. 1990. "Women and Literacy: a Quest of Justice", Convergence. 23 (1), pp. 27-40.

Riria, J.V.N. 1983. *Cooperating for Literacy: The Perspective of Women.* Paper presented at DSE Seminar, Berlin, October.

Srivastave K. & Shama H. 1990. *Training Rural Women for Literacy*, Jaipur. Institute of Development Studies (mimeo).

Stromquist, N. 1992. "Challenges to the Attainment of Women's Literacy", in Women and Literacy: *Yesterday, Today and Tomorrow*, IIE, Stockholm: Stockholm University.

Stromquist N. 1994. *Literacy for Citizenship: Gender and Grassroots Dimensions in Sao Paulo*, School of Education, University of Southern California, Los Angeles (mimeo)

Stromquist N. 1995. "The Theoretical and Practical Bases for Empowerment", in *Women Education and Empowerment*, Report of the International Seminar held at UNESCO Institute of Education, Hamburg. Jan. 27-Feb. 2, 1993.

State Education Report, 1993. Paris, UNESCO.

25

THEORY AND PRACTICE OF WOMEN'S LITERACY IN BANGLADESH

PROBLEMS AND ISSUES

Abu Hamid Latif

It is now well established that educating girls is the cheapest and the most reliable way of educating the nation. Explicit recognition of this premise at the policy formulation level in Bangladesh followed by well planned and attainable action programmes would have changed the literacy scenario of the country long ago. Unfortunately, this was not to be done resulting in a very low literacy rate, especially of the women in Bangladesh.

Since the World Conference on Education for All (WCEFA) in Jomtien, Thailand, in 1990, the Government of Bangladesh has taken certain steps to grapple with the Education for All (EFA) issues. One of them is the constitution of a Task Force on Primary and Mass Education in 1992, "to report on the status of basic education in Bangladesh and recommend measures to tackle the enormous problems that beset the literacy scenario for almost a century[1]." The Report of the Task Force and a National Plan of Action are the two documents that provide policy perspectives and programme initiative of the illiteracy within the shortest possible time through universalization of primary education, expanded mass education programme and initiating early childhood care and education programme. The major programme components are as follows[2]:

A: Primary Education (6-10 years)

i) Formal Primary Education

ii) Non-Formal Primary Education (NFPE)

B. Mass Education (6-45 years)

i) Non-Formal Education (6-14 years)

ii) Adult Education (15-45 years)
iii) Continuing Education for all ages

C. Early Childhood Care and Education (4-5 years)

Along with the Government, the NGOs, as partners, are working mainly in the areas of non-formal Pre-Primary, Primary, Adolescent, Adult and Continuing Education Programmes. Although NGOs started work in the literacy field immediately after the liberation war, it was not until 1976 that they made any serious intervention in this field. In 1990 a coalition of mainstream NGOs with major education programmes was formed and called itself the Gono Shakkhorata Ovijan (Campaign for Popular Education or CAMPE). According to a survey conducted in 1992 by CAMPE, there are as many as 326 NGOs involved in literacy programmes of one form or another. It is claimed that over the last two decades, these 326 NGOs have produced some 2.7 million literates including children, adolescents and adults[3]. Yet, in spite of the GO and NGO efforts, the literacy situation in Bangladesh has not changed much since the 1991 census.

Problem Related to Basic Education/ Literacy Programmes

The Government efforts to provide Basic Education by the year 2000 through universal primary education and non-formal basic education programmes are handicapped by many problems and obstacles. One of the highly placed educational experts has recently identified two major obstacles to Primary Education for All in Bangladesh. "First, highly centralized planning and management structure and practices that are inconsistent with local planning, management, monitoring and social mobilization essential for achieving universal primary education, and second, the absence of the institutional capacity for R & D, technical support, evaluation and training for building capacities for planning and managing the largest public enterprise of a national scope which is the primary education system[4]".

Furthermore, in a recent research study on Promoting Female Education in Bangladesh, the researcher summarized the reasons for girls not to go to school:

1. Poverty, early marriage, home-schools distance, lack of congenial environment in school, lack of security, failure in examination, domestic work, non-availability of school dress, expenses for school supplies, gender disparity in curricula and textbooks, lack of encouragement from parents and other members of the family[5].

2. A group of 15 Imams and Madrasha teachers in a group discussion with the researcher of the study referred to above opined that girls can go to school properly dressed and with purdah but they should go to separate schools after primary level. Most of them felt that the girl's role is at home and primarily as mother not outside as leaders in public life. However, the problems of girl's low participation in schools identified by them are: poverty, male teacher's presence, pressure of curricula (for example, three languages at primary levels, e.g., Bangla, English and Arabic)[6].
3. The above source also mentioned that a few funding agencies were of the opinion that the obstacles of girls' education are policy-makers, practitioners and consumers who are not aware of gender issues and as a result, it is difficult for them to draw appropriate programmes and implement these on a priority basis[7].

It is clear that there are certain specific obstacles with regard to women's literacy:

- The traditional male-dominated set up of the society relegated the place of women in the background and they expect them to be in their niche so that the status quo is not disturbed. Women's literacy is suspect in such a situation.
- The religious and societal norms and values have upheld the virtuous wife and affectionate mother image of women in so glorious terms that it is difficult for common illiterate persons to think of their girls growing up in a different way by going to school. Besides, some customs and rituals for girls work as hindrances for regularly going to school and also result to low self-esteem and feeling of inferiority to men. For example, girls are not allowed in certain families, to go out of their homes during menstruation; to take some specific food items during that time; to say prayers; and to touch the holy books.

In another study the gender issues in teaching-learning materials have received closer attention as one can see from the quotations below[8].

a. Representation of women authors compared to their male counterparts, is, as a whole, far less than their actual participation both in teaching and writing. In writing Bengali selections of classes I to V and edition the same from classes I to VIII a total of twenty five persons were involved, of whom only five i.e. one-fifth are women.
b. It is true that Bengali books of each class, which are generally collections of prose writing and poems by established writers, can not be

equally shared by male and female authors. But it is also true that the representation of female authors is still lesser than what actually they deserve. It is a sad reality that of the total ninety one pieces of Bengali selections of classes VI to VIII only eight are written by female authors.

c. We are so biased with a male dominated metal make up that in citing any example even in a gender neutral situation, we readily refer to a man or a boy rather than to a woman or a girl. Most of the plays included in the Bengali selections do not have any female characters, or if there is any, they are portrayed in minor roles. In illustrations or drawings women's projection is far less that of men. Where human virtues or accomplishments are recorded and successes in specific fields are mentioned the people selected, e.g., scientists, social workers, statement, war heroes and such other are men in almost absolute predominance. Stories or poems with female characterization are also very few. Even in cases of articles on folk art and handicrafts where women's participation is traditional and noteworthy, or in articles on cooperatives where women in recent times have proved their worth more than men, they were not mentioned. Where profession of people are described it is men who are cited as example, although in many traditional professions like weaving, pottery and tailoring. Women always shared the work with men.

Issues on the Theory and Practice of Women's Literacy in the Country.

It would have been fitting on the part of a practitioner of women's literacy programme to identify the issues on the theory and practice of women's literacy in the country. As I am not a practitioner, I can only raise the general issues related to literacy programmes in Bangladesh.

- Adult literacy programmes undertaken and implemented by the Government have never been a part of the overall educational policy formulation, as such, there was no regular programme. Adult literacy projects undertaken from time to time were subjected to repeated dislocations with the change of Government. Even after adoption of the EFA National Plan of Action, the situation has not changed.
- Target setting in literacy programmes has, most of the time, been unrealistic. As a result, there has been a wide gap between the expected outcome and actual achievement.
- The Government has not yet been able to put in place an organizational structure for its non-formal educational programmes on a permanent basis. Inadequate institutional capacity for planning, program-

ming, management and execution continues to be a major handicap in achieving the targets set for literacy programmes.

- Literacy programmes suffer from competent leadership and professional expertise as there has been no attempt to create a pool of resource persons for the specific tasks associated with the programmes.
- Social mobilization involving all sections of people at all levels as a strategy for creating a social movement for eradication of illiteracy remains a distant goal.
- Centralized programme planning and center-based and highly structured delivery system of the Government and quite a number of NGO literacy programmes leave little scope for alternative approaches and experimentation.
- Disparity between boys and girls and between urban and rural primary schools exist. Although the recent statistics indicate that the gender disparity in enrollment and subsequent retention can be bridged if concerted efforts are made, the girl child deserves special attention to remove the gender disparity in other forms in primary schools. Similarly the rural schools must be brought at par with urban schools.
- The learning needs of the girls and the functionality of their learning should constitute the core of the curricula, syllabuses, contents and teaching-learning processes.
- The pedagogy should be learner-centered rather than teacher-centered in the training programmes of the literacy workers. In-service or recurring training of literacy trainers is a key determinant for teacher mastery, and teacher mastery is an important factor to understand improved classroom practices. Assistance to literacy workers works best when it is concrete, regular and on-going and linked to practice[9].
- Assessment of learning is one area which has not received due attention in both Government and NGO basic education programs. Minimum learning competencies have to be set for each type of program. Assessing Continuous Learning Achievement is a useful means for improving the quality of education through continuous monitoring of progress. The major focus on this should be to provide a learning package so that the children can find interest in learning and become useful citizens of the country[10].
- Teacher-student ratio is another key factor in the classroom teaching-learning. This is very high in the formal primary schools (1:60) in the country. The nonformal primary schools and other literacy centers run by GO and NGOs are somewhat better in this respect. However it is imperative to keep the teacher-student ratio within a reasonable limit to improve.

- Supervision is another key element in improving the quality of learning in the literacy programs when it is seen as help and it is timely and relevant, related to practice and readily available and practices in an atmosphere of trust.

References

1. Government of Bangladesh, 1993. PMED, *Task Force on Primary and Mass Education*-Report, December, p. (i).

2. Ibid, p. 81.

3. CAMPE, 1993. *The Role of NGOs*, (Paper provided to Task Force on Primary and Mass Education) July.

4. Manzoor Ahmed, 1995. *Two Obstacles to Primary Education for All* article published in the Daily Star, January.

5. Momtaz Jahan, 1993. Summary of the Report on Promoting Female Education in Bangladesh: Potential Roles For the Rockefeller Foundation, p. 2.

6. Ibid, p. 3.

7. Ibid, p. 5.

8. Abul Momen, 1995. Study on Education System of Bangladesh with Special Emphasis on Women Position. Draft Report, Submitted to Bangladesh Nari Progati Sangha, January, P. 15.

9. Abu Hamid Latif, 1994. "Quality of Education: Basic Education" article presented in CAMPE organized workshop, p. 5.

10. Task Force Report, Op. cit., p. 69.

26

WOMEN'S EMPOWERMENT STRATEGIES IN POST-LITERACY CAMPAIGNS SOME EXPERIENCES FROM TAMIL NADU

Sister Sudha

Most literacy activists are familiar with the excitement generated by the tremendous response from women to the Total Literacy Campaigns. All such programmes are replete with inspiring examples of women overcoming antagonistic situations—within or outside the home—and coming together in this effort.

A review of available literature attributes this mass mobilization to the following factors:

1. The high pitch media campaign which obtains temporary social sanction for women to move out of their usual space;
2. The linking-up of literacy objectives with other vital aspects of women's immediate life situation;
3. The flexibility of the teaching model which left the choice of time and place to the learner, thereby accommodating her various commitments; and
4. The extensive use of song and drama which considerably enhanced the cultural appeal of the campaign strategy.

The Samata Kalajatha of March 9th, 1993, was a unique demonstration of the kind of spirit with which women, especially young women, were participating in this movement. The Samata National Convention at Jansi made a conscious attempt to give a direction to this exuberance. It was recognized that the most important task was to sustain the movement. The immediate agenda was to identify and implement strategies which would extend the gains of the literacy campaigns. The participants agreed that a larger, more in-depth gender content should be introduced. They were also categorical that strategies would not be centrally formulated and passed down to the states. Instead, it was suggested that states should interact with local activists and design strategies that would cater to their diverse needs. Common features that were to be kept in mind were:

- There were three categories of activists who had to be addressed at the field level the organizer, the volunteer and the neo literate.
- A conscious effort to draw on the creative energies of the young girls-jatha artists, volunteers and motivated learners-was to be made.

The complexity of requirements was indeed a formidable challenge. The great variety of strategies emerging from states have been little documented and even less analyzed. Often this failure to document is misunderstood as "nothing much is happening in post-literacy". This is not true. This presentation attempts to report on some of the initiatives being pursued in Tamil Nadu. How have the strategies been conceptualized? Are they gender sensitive? How effective are they proving to be on the ground?

The Case of Panchayat (or Leadership) Training for Women

In the wake of the 73rd-74th Constitutional Amendments, and the provision of reserving one-third of all membership in these bodies for women, this was identified as one of the important areas of intervention. If women could be properly trained, given the existing network and the implications of the reservation for women, panchayats were seen as a tremendous opportunity for women to enter into decision-making that could shape their lives. These 4-day residential training camps for women had fairly ambitious objectives, as well as a rigorous, meticulously planned schedule.

The core objectives of this training for about 30-50 women are:

- Provide the knowledge, skills for women to participate in decision making (for development at the local level).
- Extend support to panchayat level functionaries or themselves become capable panchayat level functionaries.

The methodology adopted was a mix of 2 kinds of sessions. Type 1 sessions covered information inputs on a range of topics. To the extent possible, the information was provided in writing, so that they could be re-read, studied and referred to when necessary by the participants. The content was simple and direct, and made use of the BGVS mode of stress on a motivated transfer of information.

The Information Content included topics on:

a) Panchayat Laws;

b) Politics of Panchayats;
c) Panchayats new agenda;
d) Gender issues;
e) Larger socio economic background in which panchayats function.

The type 2 session comprised Mahila Samakhya gender-sensitive participatory sessions which were altered according to local needs. Their main objective was to develop personality and skills. Participants were encouraged to overcome their inhibitions, gain confidence in themselves, apply their mind critically to what others said, think for themselves and acquire certain minimum skills in communication and organization. The challenge was to draw up a schedule of the right mix of both type 1 and 2 sessions so that the programme was participatory, and informative without becoming too heavy. Sessions were interspersed with games of different kinds, as well as songs. At the end of the 4 days, when the objective and a subjective evaluation was done, the feedback in all 6 caps was extremely positive.

The Generation of skills included.

1) conducting a group meeting and/or a discussion;
2) sustaining routine activities and programmes in a group;
3) giving a speech;
4) writing and presenting a report;
5) developing self confidence and overcoming inhibitions;
6) listening to and critically analyzing what others say; and
7) reading a newspaper critically.

An attempt was made to ensure that a section of the participants were neo-literates. Except for 2 districts (our of the total 6 where such camps have been held), other districts did not pay sufficient attention to this aspect. It must also be mentioned that the extreme poverty of the neo-literates and the consequent need to secure income, made it very difficult for them to attend 4 days of training at a stretch.

There were too many sessions to attempt a total discrete analysis for presentation here. However, experiences regarding a few of the sessions are placed here to indicate the scope of this training camp as a continuing education strategy.

I. Drawings- Participants were asked to draw an object which, to them, embodied a prominent quality of women. There was a lot of stereotyping-many flowers and trees were sketched. These were later brought into discussion—are these true? what effect do these images have on women? etc. There were also different images coming through—some drew stars, flags and other such symbols reflecting changing aspirations. Introspection was not too deep—the main aim was to get participants to objectify and draw—some women later said this was the first time they had drawn anything outside of a kolam. In one district, acclaim went to a young girl who had drawn a computer—yes, the modern women was beginning to peep through (or was this too a new stereotype?).

II. The theme of **myths** regarding women as the basis for soul-searching group discussions. Topics chosen were controversial and complex, e.g. a woman's place is in the home; women are naturally inferior to men; a woman is a burden to her family; woman is her own worst enemy etc. It was sobering, indeed, almost frightening to see how deeply embedded these myths were among majority of the women. Through a process of dialogue, questions and examples, it was possible to derive the alternative to the first 3 arguments. However, the woman as her own worst enemy was a topic which entailed maximum discussion. The inability to see beyond the actions and consequences of the mother-in-law's behaviours; the strong temptation to absolve the male and blame the woman were difficult concepts to contend with. The task of getting the literacy activists to extend their questioning attitudes to this dominant ideology still remains before us.

a) These 'myth' sessions proved to be eye openers all around. An incident which was presented as a drama by a particular group was as follows: A young girl grew up doing the housework, taking care of children, going out to fetch water and fuel. When the time comes for marriage, the brother curses her for being a burden. The mother comes forward in defense of her child, enumerating the ways she had supported and worked for the family. The brother becomes ashamed and resolves never to insinuate such a thing again. Happy ending!

b) However, in many groups, participants found it difficult to evolve and dramatize the alternative, positive image of the woman. Much more inputs are required on this ideological front.

III. Question Time: A particularly invigorating session was 'question time'. An activity familiar to all participants was selected-"making tea" or "cooking rice". The idea was to make women think of innovative questions around this small everyday activity. Initially, there would be some starting trouble—a groping around for questions. Early questions would generally be knowledge—based, for instance: "*How does rice* *grow?*" "*What vitamins are present in rice?*", "*How much water is necessary for rice to get cooked*" and so on. But, with a little pushing, the questions would become more ambitious, more starting—"*Why can't rice be cooked in kerosene?*", "*Why isn't rice blue in color?*". And then came wider questions like. "*Who fixes the price of rice-the farmer or the trader?*". "*Why is rice not properly available in rations shops?*"- and then, ultimately "*Who cooks the rice in the house?*". The progression in the format of questions also indicates a progression in the participants' minds relative to the whole business of cooking rice. This simple technique served as a starting point to go into why we need to ask questions regarding things around us, and what are the different kind of questions that need to be asked. Participants enjoyed this session in great deal. They had never realized how much could be done, armed with a simple question mark!

IV. Dream Session: Another favorite panchayat-related participatory session was the dream hour. Women were to dream that the panchayat was theirs—to do with as they pleased. They could effect any changes they wished. Women were amazed to discover, during the review, how eminently realizable their dreams were—bus facilities, toilets (with water-what luxury!); nurses present in the hospital which was open 24 hours and never ran out of medicines; a night without mosquitoes—and many more such visions.

a) There were the few who had bigger visions, who dreamt that all castes would intermingle and live together, and there would be no separate colonies in villages; those who wanted to ban arrack and reclaim their husbands; some who dreamt of marriages for all rights without dowry, one who dreamt that all people would be equally rich (or equally poor), another who dreamt of bigamy disappearing in practice.....and so on.
b) The motive was to create dreams, to capture them. It was to show how it was possible and necessary to dream, to capture them. It was to show how it was possible and necessary to dream, to have various kinds of dreams. Secondly, the achievability of dreams relating to local facilities-in the context of a functioning panchayat was highlighted. It was important for women to see that their intervention in panchayats could bring their own dreams closer to reality.

V. Rural Development Survey: The presentation on the issues before rural women (including development directions) was followed by a field trip to a nearby area. A questionnaire on conditions of rural women would be taken along and a survey done. This was followed by a cultural programme organized by the participants themselves.

a) This composite activity session achieved many things at the same time. The personalized interview session with individuals brought to light a number of problems—which differed in nature from area to area. Women participants found this experience very moving. The skills that formed part of the survey were:

- Recording the experiences of individuals.
- Putting this together and making generalizations
- Presenting the analysis in the form of a report
- Discussion ways of addressing problems.

b) The cultural programme, we found, really brought out the organizing abilities of the participants. Preparations were left entirely to participants. Apart from the performance (which was anyway usually well received), the review assessed whether the programme had been well planned; were all members involved in some way or the other, was there a proper seating and stage arrangements, how was the audience mobilized? Who conducted the programme—was this decided before hand, did she do her role effectively, etc., etc......

The review made in the aftermath of a successful communication with lay people helped the participants to understand organization of functions in villages much better. In some cases, we were surprised by the efficiency with which a particular participant stage managed the whole show. The discovery of such natural leaders was one of the long term gains of the training camps. At the same time, others also saw the need to start preparing themselves to hold such events.

An exhaustive account of each and every session being out of question, these few instances are a sample to show how a serious effort was made to upgrade the level of literacy activists and empower them to think and function independently in their areas.

In some districts, the activists have taken the initiative to hold block and village level camps. The long-term impact of these camps is more difficult to gauge. Unfortunately, though most districts wanted to hold many such camps at block and village level, there were hardly any funds available for this, and only about 2 or 3 were held at the block level. However, what is important is that subsequent to the camp, a group of women with leadership abilities who could provide leadership at the district level emerged. Today, in all 6 districts where these camps were held, there is a district galvanized positively into action. The camps have proved to be a good strategy to sensitize women in literacy campaigns to the possibilities for intervention at the gram panchayat and to effectively coordinate panchayat intervention with post-literacy work.

27

SITUATIONER OF WOMEN'S LITERACY IN INDIA

Anita Dighe

Longitudinal literacy statistics show considerable improvement in the educational scenario in the country where overall, the literacy rate increased from 28% in 1996 to 52% per cent in 1991. However, these figures obscure disparities in literacy in terms of gender, regions and minority groups. Women constitute the largest group among the adult non-literate population in India. Though the female literacy rate (age group 7 years and above) has gone up from 9% in 1951 to 39% in 1991, India still has a vast non-literate female population. The magnitude of the problem of illiteracy can be gauged if one looks at the absolute number of non-literate women where in 1991, there were 329 million non-literates of which women numbered 200 million. A comparison with Census data two decades earlier shows that the absolute numbers of non-literate women have increased considerably over time.

Despite recognition by policy planners that the problem of illiteracy is grave amongst women, women's literacy has never received the priority attention it deserves. For gender disparities in literacy have continued to exist, with male literacy rate being consistently ahead of female literacy rate. While gender disparities have continued in most states, there are, however, certain regional variations. The disparities are far wider in the four northern states of Bihar, Madhya Pradesh, Rajasthan and Uttar Pradesh. There are also intra-district differences. In fact, the largest number of districts with high gender disparities between rural males and females are concentrated in the four states mentioned above.

Besides the urban/rural and regional disparities, there are certain sections of the population, such as scheduled castes and scheduled tribes that also have low levels of female literacy. The educational status of women in certain minority groups such as Muslims, is also dismal.

The problem of women's illiteracy has been exacerbated due to low enrollment and high drop-out rates among girls who enter the formal schools. While the enrollment of girls has shown a steady increase, it is still not commensurate with the enrolment rate of boys. The drop-out rate among girls, particularly those who live in rural areas, continues to be very high. Once again, it is the four states mentioned above that have overall low enrolment and high drop-our rates among girls.

Until the late seventies, literacy programmes, both for men and women, tended to be adhoc, shor-term, and limited in scope. It was only in 1979 that a nation-wide Programme (NAEP) - was launched. While NAEP acknowledged the severity of the problem of illiteracy among women, no specific programmatic interventions were designed for them. With the launching of the National Policy on Education in 1986 and its subsequent revision in 1992, the problem of gender inequalities in education received concrete attention for the first time in India. Thus the policy document has unequivocally stated that education should play 'a positive interventionist role in the empowerment of women'.

The recognition of inequalities in education led to the formulation of Mahila Samakhya Programme that is now in operation on a limited scale in five states of the country. Mahila Samakhya is an innovative approach aimed at raising women's consciousness on their marginalization and deprivation in the family and in society at large. Experience has shown that as women have become empowered at the personal and collective levels, they have experienced the need for literacy. In contrast, the Total literacy Campaigns (TLCs) have now become operational in more than 250 districts in the country. While the Mahila Samakhya appraoch is slow, process-oriented and allows women to seek literacy as and when they feel need for it, the TLC strategy is to deal exclusively with imparting skills of reading, writing and numeracy to the non-literates, most of whom are women. By and large, TLCs have paid little attention to specific issues relating to women's literacy. The TLCs are implemented in a campaign mode, and gender issues so far have not been consciously built either in the planning or in the implementation phases.

28

LITERACY POLICIES AND PROGRAMS FOR WOMEN IN THE PHILIPPINES

The Philippine Development Plan for Women for the period 1989-1992 manifests the Philippine Government's commitment to bring into mainstream the concerns of women in the development process. It operationalized the development policies of government into gender-specific policy statements, programs and projects aimed at addressing the equality and developmental issues of women in the different sectors and within their social concerns. Here literacy is viewed as the key to the improvement of Filipino women.

On the other hand, the EFA Philippine Plan of Action for 1990-1999 focuses its policies and strategies on specific groups, including women. It expects to bring basic education to women through non-traditional methods and mechanisms. The primary goal of basic education is to meet basic learning needs or the knowledge, skills, attitudes and values necessary for people to survive, to improve the quality of their lives, and to continue learning.

Programmatically, the Functional Literacy component of the nonformal education of DECS is being widely conducted in the country. Its target clientele includes out-of-school youth and adults (male and female) with different literacy levels. It utilizes the literacy materials based on the needs, interests and competencies of women, including adolescent girls.

Focusing on women's literacy is viewed as an investment of an unquantifiable value. The returns of this investment can be the most effective use of the country's limited resources, a more balanced growth in the labor force, security for Filipino families, and the possibility for better health, education, nutrition and personal development not only for women but for all people.

Making women functionally literate will help them gain courage and confidence in themselves, so that they would understand the causes of injustice and find the strength to change their way of life.

The Female Functional Literacy and Parent Education Project, an inter-agency endeavor which commenced under the Third Country Program for Children and is being expanded under the Fourth Country Program for Children, targets women and girls in areas with very low literacy rate. It seeks to address the problems of child survival and development through strengthening nonformal education to promote effective parenting and more effective utilization of health, including prevention and early detection and childhood disabilities. These are integrated into the curriculum, training design and educational materials of existing major NFE functional literacy programs.

Certain measures in favor of women are being observed by DECS and its partners in literacy promotion. These include:

(i) development of instructional materials dealing with subjects of interest to female learners;

(ii) encouraging female participation in community affairs;

(iii) providing a forum for parent education, values clarification, moral recovery and effective leadership of women; and

(iv) providing materials and financial assistance to livelihood development of women and their families.

29

TWO VIEWS ON LITERACY STRATEGIES IN INDIA

Manisha Priyam, Suddha Sundaraman

Strategies for imparting literacy in Mahila Samakhya range from the absolutely impromptu, to the camp-based and center-based approach. The selection of teachers was done by the Sanghas but since it was not always possible to find trained women in most cases it worked out that whoever was a literate woman in a village turned out to be the instructor at the village level. Training inputs were given later on.

Evaluation methods were also quite varied. Wherever there was a link with TLC, they adopted TLC evaluation methods. In some areas, certain other adhoc methods have been developed and successfully used. In Bidar a method of assessment which I would call the post card method involves giving every learner 30 postcards for them to keep writing letters to the Mahila Samakhya office with those postcards. These postcards turned out to be a huge volume of written data on every learner. The letters were examined and used as a basis for the continuous assessment of every learner. And the areas that needed to be emphasized on every learner, for example, someone's spelling was weak, and so on, would be followed up.

As women gained knowledge in letters, they often found the material that was given to them-either from the TLC or through Mahila Samakhya/ NGOs-very uninteresting. Sometimes, women have been complained that the materials given to them are "gender-bombarded", and not appealing enough to sustain their interest. There was great demand for material that was interesting in itself, and which could sustain their enthusiasm for learning.

It was also realized that there is a greater demand for systematic resource inputs that are educational in nature. These are demands for systematic teacher training as opposed to gender training where literacy teachers would like to go through a training which equips them to manage the classroom situation. There are also requests for inputs on innovative learning. Finally institutionalization is also one direction for literacy workers as seen in the case of Mahila Samakhya workers who are demanding that educational institutions for women with an integrated empowerment framework be set up.

The total literacy campaigns (TLC) represent a significantly new appraoch to the mobilization and empowerment of women. Its essence is a joint, massive campaign by all governmental and non-governmental forces acting unitedly, in a spirit of voluntarism.

Unfortunately in many districts of the country today, the programme has become bureaucratized with the voluntary sector having little or no role. One obvious consequence of this is that the aspect of women's empowerment is never followed up. Conscious of this danger, Bharat Gyan Vigyan Samithi initiated a women's movement called Samata (Equality). Samata was to ensure that the literacy campaign remains linked to women's issues and that the mobilization of women that occurs in the literacy phase is developed into a full-fledged movement for women's empowerment in the post-literacy and continuing education phase.

While there have been different strategies to integrate the concerns of the women's movement with literacy efforts, we are also conscious of how limited such attempts have been. The limitations flow from three major obstacles.

One barrier is that such strategies require a very sensitive, trained, committed district and block level leadership. Whereas literacy work can be carried out relatively easier by a large number of persons, the higher levels of awareness and commitment needed for gender equity campaigns cannot be produced overnight.

Though there is no absolute scarcity of funds, in practice at the district level funds are a major constraint. For example in all the six districts where panchayat leadership training camps have been held, women have requested funds for holding 30 to 40 more such camps at the block and gram panchayat level. This has not been made available. Urgent intervention is needed to ensure that the NGOs involved— in this case Samata / BGVs are able to access to district level funds for this work.

Consensus on gender equity in literacy work has not been arrived at. Very often junior district officials or even literacy activists object to or do not prioritize this work. As a result, this has not become a major campaign for women's empowerment as such.

30

NON-FORMAL EDUCATION FOR WOMEN IN THAILAND

Wileka Leesuwan

There are a lot of organizations who run education programs on women an development. Their activities include education in school and non-formal education, vocational training, information services, community library, village reading places and radios. The targets of these programs range from community women leaders, housewives, rural women to women workers.

In the practice of non-formal education, there are five key principles.

1. Use of life-long education leads to development in women, families, community and society.
2. Life-long education emphasizes not on individual women but groups in order to have power in development.
3. Learning is a process based on situations and women problems.
4. Learning process does not stress on learning from text books but instead encourages women to think, analyze, discuss, plan and practice what they want to do and what they believe can solve their problems. This will lead to the real development.
5. The learning process focuses on localism and resources from the communities accompanied by modern technology. Moreover, focusing on life-long learning means linking government organizations with public and private organization, academicians, and community women leaders.

A. Content

Given that non-formal education should be learner-centered, problem-oriented and action based, the content of programs are planned according to the following:

• Consistent with existing situations and problems in the community which have different contexts. Hence some may focus on environment, AIDS, drug addiction and others on migration. In the northern region, they focus on child prostitutes while for central region, it is women laborers. The Muslim women and their status are the thrust for the south.

• It should encourage women in a variety of skills from planning, project writing, marketing, accounting, facilitating meeting, delivering public speech, technology for communication and development, monitoring and evaluating and raising their awareness on laws affecting women.

• It should recognize women's needs and problems according to their backgrounds and professions. This also means including development areas such as natural resource conservation, integrated agriculture, long-life development, human-rights, community participation and democracy.

B. Learning and Teaching Approach

The programs rely on the following methods:

• Discussion and exchange of ideas, active planning to solve problems.

• Group study and self-studying are encouraged by using learning kits and teaching-aids.

• Focus on learning by doing.

• Continuous development of curriculum, teaching aids, learning kits as well as methods on how to effectively evaluate teacher manuals and teacher training which are consistent with the new concept of women life-long education.

C. The National Literacy Campaign Project

This campaign was conducted from 1983 to 1987 resulting in literates being increased to more than 500,000 among the 14-50 year old population. In this project, anybody could be a volunteer teacher to help teach the illiterates who are his/her fellow citizen. The learning/teaching method depends on their dexterity, such as each one teach one, and integrated methods. The place and time for learning is based on the readiness of the learning and teacher.

The learner need not pay for any expenses and the learners will even receive tests free of charge from the National Literacy Campaign. The Provincial Non-Formal Education Center administers the tests and those passing will receive a literacy certified document. This document can be transformed into accumulated marks to be used for continuing study in non-formal education of primary level.

31

GTZ- BEFARe
FEMALE LITERACY

Waheeda Farouk Adam

In the rehabilitation of war- torn Afghanistan, there is a greater need for literate people and it is in this context that GTZ-BEFARe (German Government Organization for Technical Cooperation/Basic Education for Afghan Refugees) launched its female literacy programme. Catering to (a) Afghan women who are unable to attend formal schooling but want to become semi-literate and to (b) girls who are unable to go to the formal system because of unavailability of schools or for cultural reasons, the main objective of the literacy programme is to enable the graduates of literacy course to read, write, calculate and understand the simple texts of daily life.

While GTZ-BEFZRe is aware that its literacy programme is not a substitute for formal education, they consider it crucial to make these Afghan women semi-literate so that they are able to contribute in the development and rebuilding of Afghanistan in a positive and productive way.

Hence before the start of a course, meetings are held with the heads of the tribes and elders of the camp to convince them to approve the programme. Women are keen to attend but without the consent of the males, they are unable to participate in the courses. It is therefore critical that the communities are involved to gain the male's approval. The courses are mainly conducted in the private residences offered by the community of the camp which in one way, guarantees that the programme is not imposed but is needed by the target group.

Lasting for a period of six months, the programme has two terms, one starting on the first of January and the other, in the first of July. While classes are held at times which are suitable to the women so that they do not affect their normal daily, the course runs for five days a week for one and a half to two hours daily.

The course has three levels starting with the Primer, then the Reader and, finally the Mathematics. In the Primer level, women have to undergo a series of tests meant to evaluate what they have learned before being invited to the next level. In the Reader phase, the participants improve their newly acquired literacy skills with a series of exercises and work assignments. In the last phase, the participants are taught numerals, simple calculations and tables taken from their daily lives. Maximum number for the Primer level is 20, which slowly declines through the levels due to various reasons from failures in tests, repatriation, or some family problems.

Each level has a complete set of books designed and developed for that phase. Using the GTZ-BEFZRe materials with the help of guides, charts, cards and teaching materials, instructors lead the learning process.

For its female literacy program, dedicated women instructors are identified using the following criteria:

a) resident of the camp where the course will be conducted:
b) at least 25 years old;
c) graduated at least from 8th grade;
d) mother tongue should be Pashto;
e) she and her family must be highly regarded and accepted by the community;
f) must present a list of 20 illiterate women who have shown their willingness to attend her literacy class; and
g) must have organized an acceptable place where she can conduct literacy course for 6 months.

Upon selection after the interviews, the women are either called to the office or are given training in their own camp/residential area, which lasts 10 days for every level. During this period, the women are exposed to extensive instruction on the teaching methodologies of the different levels as well as given guidance on the preparation of the courses and how to solve the learning problems of the participants. Final selection of instructors is made according to the performance of the women during training. To upgrade their skills, they have refresher seminars every 3 months.

Meanwhile, there are field officers who supervise instructors as well as monitor weekly attendance of instructors and participants. They are responsible for sending regular reports as well as giving periodical achievement tests to the learners. They also have teaching responsibilities as they take over classes when instructors are absent and provide on the job training to the instructors if and when required.

32

COMPLEXITY OF LITERACY PRACTICES

When women READ the world, it can be one of the most powerful experiences. For indeed, literacy is a tool that can help women and men understand themselves, their communities and society at large. Literacy involves change because it offers possibilities of new ways of looking and doing things. Finally and perhaps more importantly, literacy is about power. It involves the power to definc and label others as 'illiterate' which stigmatizes and consequently marginalizes. At the same time, it can also mean power for the women to name their experiences as well as read about other women's lives and realize that theirs is not an isolated situation. The elements of literacy program can be described through the following questions:

1. WHO will be Involved?

- The individuals (in this case, women) who attend the classes
- The family members who have to be convinced of the importance of literacy classes for women (this could be the father or the husband)
- The leaders of the community who are key to the mobilization of other members
- The community members who support the program, for example, through building the classroom
- The teacher of the literacy classes
- The government and NGO worker involved in the literacy program
- The external agency (government, NGO, foreign organization) providing support (financial and human resources)

2. WHERE are the Opportunities for Learning?

- classrooms
- literacy centers
- camps
- library
- community centers

3. WHERE are the Opportunities for Learning?

- weekends
- evenings
- after harvesting, work
- every day or every other day for three months or six months

4. WHAT can be Learned?

- basic reading and writing
- functional and integrated skills that would cover health, income-generating, savings and credit
- critical awareness of political issues like gender inequality

5. HOW will these Learning Opportunities be Organized?

- strategies and approaches
- materials to be used (basic and post-literacy)
- language to be used
- partnerships necessary for such programs

In every element, there were key issues that have emerged and as a way of organizing the issues, the key word LIFE is used.

L-earning Environment
I- ntegrated nature of Literacy
F-emale Literacy as a critical concern
E- mpowering literacy practices

Learning Environment

■ **Motivation**

"......the importance of motivating women for literacy given the various psychological, physical, economic and social obstacles which make literacy an unattainable or unnecessary goal for women."

■ **Socio-cultural Environment for Learning**

"As part of the learning environment, we need to address socio-cultural factors affecting women's literacy like language, religion and patriarchal ideology which views women as instruments in the family, community and national."

- **Training of Teachers**

  "How do we institutionalize staff development and training of teachers?"

  "How do we resolve the problem of lack of qualified female teachers or having very young volunteers to tackle adult women?"

  "Neo-literates are often used as teachers which gives them confidence and sustains their literacy level. In some places, the women are now capable to run their own literacy centers with minimum supervision. But their capabilities have to be developed and strengthened."

- **Sustaining and Replicability for Literacy Programs**

  "This is an important issue since the success of a particular project is not a guarantee that it will be successful if replicated in a larger scale. Attendant problem to this are: confronting the problem of large figures, motivation, and language."

  "Can there be one model of literacy? In many of our discussions we have said no and the mere fact that we can have as many literacy programs as we have presented here. Related to this is the very issue of replicability. Once we know there is a success story we want to try and see if it can be replicated in other situations. But it is not easy to replicate models because of difference of social context."

- **Role of External Agencies**

  "The role of the NGOs or people from the outside should not be undermined because they are the catalysts who bring possibilities in a community who may not be aware of these because of individual and structural constraints."

Integrated Nature of Literacy

- **Literacy is not simply reading and writing but encompasses other areas of life.**

  "It was also found that most of successful programs are those which have an integrated/holistic approach to literacy. Example of these are literacy combined with the provision of basic services, literacy combined with income generation and basic services, and literacy combined with infrastructure"

- Literacy does not only involve the pedagogical process but should include other support areas like research.

"To what extent are we going to pour our efforts in research when we develop our curriculum and instructional materials."

"There is a need for research in the following areas:

1. Theories and concepts of empowerment especially with reference to women;
2. Elements/ strategies of empowering education;
3. Content analysis of literacy primers;
4. Study of training methodologies;
5. Evaluation methods/impact assessment;
6. Methodology for material development including pre-testing methods and visuals; and
7. Survey of literature/ annotated bibliographies of existing research studies."

- **What are the linkages made in the formal and non-formal system?**
  "One is the question of equivalencies. If you have a certain curriculum, how is that going to be translated into the formal system? So this is very much related to the relationship of formal and nonformal education. How can our non-formal activities be legitimized in the formal setting."

  "The need to link micro efforts to mainstream realities was stressed, and other experiences with assimilating students with non-formal education to the mainstream education system were shared. Mainstreaming is essential to give students an identity with others as well as to get a certificate to prove their education level. The efforts get foiled when the mainstream is not prepared to support them by being flexible in enrolment rules or in the curriculum."

Female Literacy

"...women need to be prodded to attend literacy programs especially those who have small children. The lack of enthusiasm can be traced to women's multiple burden and participation in economic activities."

"In some curricula, they have managed to incorporate a WID component. But this is subject to discussion of what we mean when we say women in development. This is a whole area of debate especially now when everybody says that women should be integrated in development. Women are asking, can't women just be better mothers and wives, in their traditional roles?".

"What can we do if this alternative literacy programs are gender blind? Here comes the importance of the women's movement in trying to incorporate a gender perspective in the curriculum and instructional materials."

"It was clear that the most successful strategies were those which linked literacy to a broader process of empowerment in the minds of women—i.e. which enables women to see illiteracy as one of the factors which perpetuates their powerlessness and marginalization within the family, community and society at large."

Empowering Literacy Practices

- Developing Curriculum and Materials

  "We have all been saying that it is important for our curriculum and materials to be learner centered. And that means we should use generative themes for our curriculum as well as our textbooks. It also includes learner generates materials."

  "...development of instructional materials and curriculum should be collaborative with government, NGOs and academe, working together."

  "in developing curriculum and materials, one is faced with the issue of flexibility. While we are supposed to be developing curriculum and instructional materials that we want to disseminate as widely as possible, we also know that there are different communities with different conditions. So how can we be flexible? Related to this, is the use of pilot programs or projects in the hope that after the pilot program, we will be able to use lessons here to disseminate. But then you get caught in the question of, "Are you really able to replicate?"

- Language

  "It is not only what language to use, whether the dominant language or the ethnic languages, but how are we representing women, the sentiment of the language".

- Teaching Methods

  "There is great variation and uneven quality in this area because of the decision of the groups involved to be flexible and participatory, and more responsive to the needs of the community."

- On People's Participation

  "There demand for literacy must come from the grassroots. It should start with participatory planning to weave the needs of the community. The point of view of the learners must count first and foremost. The positive experience of tapping community teachers should be continued. For a literacy program to be successful, it has to satisfy the basic needs. If not interwoven with the life and aspirations of the community, literacy program work would be meaningless."

- On Evaluation

  "Learning from experience should be the main goal of evaluation. Towards this end, the focus should be on documentation, analysis, culling out key principles, and evolving state-of-the art methodologies which balance qualitative and quantitative indicators. There must be a balance between external and internal evaluations."

33

THE CHALLENGES AHEAD

Lalita Ramdas

If I am painting a grim scenario there is good reason for this—the situation is nothing short of alarming. So **What can be done**?

I am especially happy that this group here represents a mixture of those working in education and with a focus on women. Clearly there are synergies that need to be harnessed and put to further creative action in the future. In this section I would like to list out a number of concrete steps which I believe we need to take collectively in order to turn the tide.

- **Mass mobilization of all sectors in society for quality primary education for all-with a special focus on the Girl Child**. This is the best insurance against illiteracy and it should be put as top priority on the Agenda of every NGO, Government department, Panchayat, Corporate Body. As women interested in enabling and empowering women to gain direct access to information, knowledge and therefore creating decision-making capacity, it is my increasing conviction that true interest and fluency in, reading and writing really develops at the school level. And **all our efforts must be mobilized to enabling at least the next generation to be genuinely literate, unlike at present.**

- Leading from the above—give a call for **a ten year mass campaign for primary education**—like a new freedom struggle—with emphasis on quality teaching, relevant content, learning that is creative and fun, and building up a generation that is a learning, thinking and questioning citizenry.

- **Launch a National Platform or Network for Education—involv-**

ing a wide cross-section of people from several sectors. This is particularly critical in view of the current trends: liberalization, Structural Adjustment Programmes, and the increasing investment by foreign agencies in Education in the so-called BIMARU States - i.e. Bihar, Madhya Pradesh, Rajasthan, Uttar Pradesh.

- **Mobilize a wider cross-section of citizens in support of the struggle for women to become literate**— using the issues significant in the day to day lives of women- i.e. rising prices, water, health and education for children, the job market and employment.

Issues like public health, sanitation, garbage clearance, local environment need to be taken up in local communities by NGOs who have also been so busy with the "larger" issues, that we have often tended to neglect the more "mundane" things like those listed above.

For instance if we can mobilize communities to improve the atmosphere and environment of every classroom for the child in primary school. The world view of the future citizen in the country is shaped in those millions of dreary classrooms. In their present condition can they ever provide an inspiration to perform, to aspire to excellence, to create any form of aesthetic sensibility?

- **Develop a broad framework of issues, around the basic understanding of citizenship building and ensure that all our institutions from the school level up include a more proactive and creative way in which citizenship education can be propagated.**

- **Work with all available partners regardless of political and other ideological barriers to achieve universal learning**— perhaps the one non-controversial objective. It is essential that we rethink our positions on partners building—and I am specifically talking of some of the following:

- **Trade and Industry**— the emerging dominant force in the new 'global' economic order.

- **Government sector-social welfare, education etc. at local levels- we need to reharness their considerable infrastructure.**

- **Traditional women's organizations**— the Mahila Mandals, satsangs, Bhajan groups— these need to be contacted, reached out to, "infiltrated" so to speak.

- **Trade Unions**
- **All Community Based Organizations**

- **Understand, refine, develop and propagate the concept of a Life-long Learning Society as part of Post-Literacy** in its widest connotation. This also calls for an understanding that as presently structured, the life of an average girl/women in Indian society does not provide her with either the leisure or the environment that encourage her to continue to study, read or write. The need to create a "learning environment" has been much talked about, but continues to remain an ideal only.

- Perhaps we need to **set targets whereby groups of NGOs, corporate sector and citizens can together create community libraries/ reading rooms and ensure the provision and supply of relevant materials.** In places like Thailand, local organizations like the temples, the monks, Association of Librarians etc. were mobilized to set-up and run libraries etc. Perhaps we need to explore the local resources available to channel them in this direction.

- **A well developed supplementary programme for women needs to be developed wherein their role as citizens, members of the Panchayat, can be encouraged and supported.** This involves working with existing local administration and officials to orient and educate them to be more receptive to such ideas. A recent article by an IAS officer from Maharastra published by MANUSHI eloquently portrays that more often than not, the present 30% reservation for women in Panchayats, can easily become a complete farce and a mere token. The need to intervene at the level of the Panchayat is all the more critical given the increasing role envisaged for local self-government in almost every sector of developmental activities. Empowering women for greater political participation can only be facilitated by the right kind of education that prepares her for that role from very early in her socialization.

- **Formulate a creative new vision on the use of media for literacy and education.** The power and potential of the present day electronic media has not been harnessed by us. Can we hire a transponder exclusively for beaming "alternate" programmes?! Perhaps some of these ideas sound wild—but it is perhaps time to think boldly!

- Finally, I would urge that women's groups work much more closely with men and women in achieving several of the goals identified above. The entire strategy for Empowerment of women has to be brought onto the agendas—both political, and personal, of the men in our society.

34

SKILLS-BASED LITERACY PROGRAMME FOR WOMEN

Namtip Aksornkool

Introduction

Qi Yiling comes from a village in Xuan Wei Country, hidden amongst the steep rocks and hills of the mountain province of Yunnan in China. Life here is not easy for anyone, particularly for women. The day is one long cycle of cooking, cleaning and washing, not to mention the hard work in the fields. There is never a moment to rest, never a moment to complain. This is a woman's life in the province of Yunnan.

Like most women in her village, Qi Yiling is completely illiterate. Recently, she had to collect her daughter from hospital. She got off the bus in the main market square but in her panic forgot-to mark the tyres of the bus to take her home. Later when she returned with her sick daughter strapped to her back, she went round and round the bus station incapable of reading the signs or finding her bus. She didn't know where to go. She went left and right, too humiliated to ask anyone.

At home, in her village, Qi Yiling faces similar problems and doesn't do much better. She is constantly battling with the family, trying to keep everything going. Her husband doesn't understand or appreciate her feelings. When things go wrong, it is always her fault. Qi Yiling sometimes asks herself whether all this is worth it, why she does't just lie down and die. But Qi Yiling and thousands of other women like her, living in the remote mountain villages of Yunnan, need not feel as isolated as before. The All China Women's Federation, the Yunnan Education Commission, UNESCO, UNDP and the Ford Foundation have joined forces to improve life for the women of the region by forming a project called the Xuan Wei Skills based Literacy Programme for Women. It teaches literacy but also encourages women to take control of their lives and income. Qi Yiling, for example, received intensive training in tree grafting skills, something she never even dreamed possible as the villagers believed that trees grafted by women never gave fruit. Last year's bumper harvest did much to dispel the myth that women bring bad luck.

There are many other women like Qi Yiling who have been able to increase their income and self-reliance. Shen Yidan, for instance, has managed to raise pigs. Through the project she learnt how to select healthy piglets, nurture them and give them the right feed. Women like Qi Yiling and Shen Yidan now lead a different and more fulfilling life. Their confidence in their strength and intelligence has increased. This important improvement in both living standards and self-reliance could not have come about without special measures and local will. The balance of power between men and women is slowly changing.

Women's Status in China: Beginnings of the Programme

In the former days of China, most women had no formal names before marriage. They adopted their husband's names after they were wed. Children used their father's name.

(The situation of Chinese women, all China women's federation, ACWF, 1994)

According to the recent **Study on Portrayal of Men and Women in Chinese School Textbooks and Children's Literature** carried out by the Ministry of Culture of the People's Republic of China and UNESCO, China's past feudal system has weighed heavily on women's conditions and status. Even as early as 1925, Chairman Mao Zedong noted the secondary status of Chinese women when he wrote in his **Report on the Investigation of the Peasant Movement in China**, that a Chinese man is dominated by three systems of authority, the State, the clan system and the supernatural. Chinese women, however, Mao said, are strangled by a fourth '*thick rope*'-men.

Common saying and superstitions denigrating women abound throughout the world. The province of Yunnan has its own which go a long way in explaining the battle women have had to lead to assert their rights and gain access to education. The Dai community in southern Yunnan, for example, compares women to crabmeat, inferior even to mutton. If a Dai fisherman accidently touches a woman's sarong (skirt), he is, according to popular belief, haunted by witches and demons. The Sani people bar women from building houses as they believe a house built by a woman will collapse. The Han even have an old saying that ,woman and inferior men (slaves) are hard to get along with.

As women's emancipation was intimately related to the national liberation movement and the socialist revolution, it is considered an inseparable part of the ethics of New China. The law stipulates that women enjoy equal rights with men in all spheres of political, economic, cultural, social and family life and by comparison to their sisters in other countries, Chinese women have made great strides. Thanks to political will and the relentless efforts of the All China Women's Federation, Chinese women are no longer, in general, household servants.

Great achievements, in terms of education, have been made and the momentum is being kept up. According to statistics, since 1987, women's illiteracy rate has dropped to thirty-eight per cent and since 1986, 150 million people have attended training sessions in various practical technical skills, and half of these trainees were women. As a result, women's technical qualities and skills have been remarkably enhanced. Education has enabled farmers to be aware of the strength of women's work. Traditional models of division of labour with the man in charge have changed. A great number of women have started up businesses or became industrial workers and rural women are now important contributors to family income. Women now hold leading positions. There are women members in the Standing Committee of the National People's Congress and Chairwomen of the Chinese People's Political Consultative Conference. There are women ministers and women at governor and municipal level.

Although such remarkable achievements have been made in women's education in China, a number of problems and difficulties remain, particularly in remote and rural regions. There has been an inadequate balance in the spread of women's education and although education has been carried to most provincial prefectures, in many rural areas women's education is out of date and women's status, in both family and society, still apparently, lower than men's. Old traditional values have impeded progress. In rural areas, the ideology of *"respect men, look down on women"* can still dominate. For instance many poor farmers keep their daughters at home to manage the housework and the enrolment rate for girls is four per cent lower than that of boys. Of those children who do not enrol in school, eighty-three per cent are girls and they also make up seventy per cent of all the drop-outs from primary school.

Education personnel, funds, and materials resources are, at times, inadequate and rural schools for adult education cannot cope with the scale of the task. There are not enough country, township or village technical schools for farmers. Less than ten per cent of adults in rural areas participate in cultural and technical education. In addition, a lot of schools are short of the necessary teaching instruments and equipment for modern teaching and literacy programmes for women. Furthermore, there is a need for systematically trained personnel to be in charge of both management and teaching. (The Report of the Regional Planning Meeting for the Skills-based Literacy Programme for Women, UNESCO/PROAP 1990).

Many experts in women's rights and adult educators believe that once women's earning capacity is strengthened, their status in society will automatically increase. Wang Rangxue, the project director for the Skills-based Literacy Programme for Women in Xuan Wei, gives the example of a woman from the Dali prefecture who started raising quails. Her status and standing began to rise with her income. It was not just a case of having greater earnings but the fact that she had the power to decide, the power to spend her money. In the past men dictated how the money was to be spent. According to the All China Women's Federation (ACWF), many couples now share in the decision-making process when it comes to money and other important family matters such as children's schooling.

This change is essential to the concept of empowerment that is central to the All China Women's Federation and the UNESCO-UNDP *"Skills-based Literacy Programme for Women.* Both stress the idea of the *"four selves"* which are the four fundamental prerequisites for progress. These are self-reliance, self-esteem, self-confidence and self-improvement.

Across Asia

The Xuan Wei project is part of a larger regional project: RAS/8/013 Skills-based Literacy Programme for Women. Initiated in 1989 and implemented in 1990 with seed money of some one million U.S. Dollars from the United Nations Development Programme (UNDP), this regional project was designed to strengthen national capacity in preparing learning programmes which would equip women, of all ages, with knowledge, skills and attitudes to participate fully and meaningfully in national development. It was launched in seven countries in Asia and the Pacific-Bangladesh, Bhutan, China, the Lao People's Democratic Republic, Papua New Guinea, Union of Myanmar and Viet Nam. Within the vast framework of the project each participating country prepared an action plan for its respective select sites. In China, work began with a seminar hosted by the Yunnan Education Commission and the Chinese National Commission for UNESCO.

After the first regional training workshop and seminar, each country conducted five workshops of their own. The training programme concentrated on the theme of promoting women's status in society through enhancing knowledge, skills and attitudes. Methods of changing mentalities to lighten domestic burdens and demonstrate women's importance in production were set out and some twenty-nine booklets were developed as reading material. The units were written in accordance with the needs of the identified target group of women. Relevance to the lives of the learners was considered to be one of the most important elements.

All the training followed certain guidelines and a curriculum, which have come to be known as the *"Educate to empower"*. approach. Indeed the culmination of all the preparatory work and the regional and national training was the publication of a manual entitled *"educate to Empower"*. In many ways this text retraces the steps of the Skills-based Literacy Programme for Women. It spells out the whole basis of the programme and has been essential in disseminating the programme which is now being replicated in the South Asia region (the ESCAP project on functional literacy for female youth is carrying the project to Malaysia and Pakistan). So far, *"Educate to Empower"* has been translated into eleven languages including Dzongka (Bhutan), Bahasa Melayu (Malaysia), Bangla (Bangladesh), Burmese, Chinese, Lao, Tok Pisin and Motu (Papua New Guinea), Thai, Urdu and Vietnamese. The manuals in each respective language were used to guide further in-country training. As a result subsequent workshop were able to concentrate on how to provide supplementary reading materials and curricular units. Some 700 pieces of learning material were then developed in the various languages of the participating countries.

The UNESCO Principal Regional Office for Asia and the pacific (PROAP) was responsible for regional project execution and for facilitating inter-country co-operation. It also served as an advisory body and provided technical support for the countries when necessary. A team was then set up in each country for carrying out the various activities outlined in the individual country plan.

National Problems, Local Solutions

The economy of our country will approach the level of developed countries by its 100th anniversary. One of the reasons we say so is that we possess the power to develop education, to increase the scientific and technological manpower at all levels in time before the 2040's. Our country, its power and the potential of economic development depend increasingly on the quality of labour and the quantity and quality of the intellectuals. "(Deng-Xiaoping, 1985).

This promise of progress by Deng Xiaoping has since modelled and structured the Chinese approach to both education and production. Education, as is obvious from the Xuan Wei experience, has to be led towards greater productivity and needs to meet the demands of the economy.

The Skills-based Literacy Programme for Women is, in fact, a unique mirroring of the country's needs and its educational goals. For many years, as Xu, Zheng, Little and Lewin note in "*Educational Innovation in China rural school graduates*"....lacked knowledge of production and were unable to adapt themselves to the needs of the market economy. They had passed the examination of chemistry and physics but did not know the nature and uses of pesticides and agricultural machinery. "When the skills-based literacy Programme for Women was established in Xuan Wei county, it was precisely to remedy this kind of situation and to focus on the problems of rural women with little or no education.

Deng Xiaoping's 1985 introduction of the Responsibility System had also brought about dramatic shifts in agricultural practices and changes in the system of ownership. More and more farmers owned little plots of land yet the demand was for greater productivity and a great deal of farmland was being "eaten up" by industrialization. Small plots of land have to produce great quantities of food, so education and training are the only means to help establish agro-technology and help Xuan Wei maintain its self-reliance in food.

Xuan Wei county is a border area in the Yunnan Province of south-west China. The land is rugged and communication difficult, great distances separate one village from another. The province has some twenty-five minority groups and the existence of so many different ethnic groups over the centuries has led to a rich local culture where the acceptance of others features strongly. Only ten per cent of the land in Yunnan is arable and it requires a great amount of work but since ancient times terraced fields have been built into the mountains. The fields mould into the mountain landscape perfectly and are a typical example of humankind's adaptation to the demands of the land. Xuan Wei County is known throughout China for it ham production and the growing of maize and potatoes.

Here women are generally burdened with fourteen to eighteen hours work a day. This overwork and the multiplicity of tasks can lead to sickness and chronic health conditions. Women's opportunities are much more limited than men's, particularly in education and technical agriculture training. Young women may suffer from the ill effects of early marriage and not have the chance to develop their potential. An initial survey in the area noted that women played a very small role in decision-making and family business. The Skills-based Literacy Programme for Women was seen as instrumental in raising awareness. Women and girls seemed quite aware of the power they could hold if they were to become active income earners. The benefits they could draw from literacy and training had, up till then, appeared almost irrelevant. This was particularly the case amongst women who lacked basic production skills and who had no chance of improving them—most of these women were illiterate. They didn't know how to make money with their products although they spent their days hard at work. Their economic status was as low as their belief in themselves.

Xuan Wei County became the seat of the project because it is a country that is typical of the Yunnan Province. It was felt that if the project was successful in this particular region it could be replicated elsewhere. Furthermore, the area had already served for various other ventures: the "Spark" Project, the Project for "Enough to Eat and Wear", an FAO project and a Population Education Project. These projects had proved successful and had paved the way for a wider, more comprehensive project such as the Skills-based Literacy Programme for Women.

The Xuan Wei County authority, under the Skills-based Literacy Programme for Women, runs some seventy-five skills training classes. Women can choose the courses they want and are advised on those which best suit their situation. They also include other skills necessary for the improvement of living standards such as pre-and post natal care, health care, family planning, and various income-generating skills. The women of Xuan Wei have very few moments in the day to stop and rest. Their life is a continuous cycle of labour and fatigue. As education and training had been seen as a privilege often exclusive to men, the women too had to be convinced that they could learn and that they would not be wasting their time. Moreover, they could choose what to learn. What they learnt would be useful to their work and actually boost the productivity on their farms and, hence, their economic self-reliance.

By purposely linking literacy to actual production and other vital aspects of daily life, the project was able to create a demand for learning. This valuing and relevance of education means more and more women want their children to get a good education. Before it would have been the man who would have gone to the programme or made the decisions about the children or the farm, now it is the women who go to classes and it is difficult to imagine how the trend can be reversed. It is hard to comprehend the enormous benefits experienced by these illiterates-turned-readers. As those responsible for the Skills-based Literacy Programme for Women say these women now feel that "*they can do anything*".

Reading and Writing

Sixty-six per cent of illiterates in Xuan Wei County are women. Literacy classes take place in the early evening around seven to nine o'clock. The women sit by hurricane lamps and learn to read and write the basic

1,500 Chinese characters following standard textbooks. The material covers a wide range of topics from classics like Aesop's fables and Chinese war stories to practical skills, such as pig raising, duck, chicken or quail raising and dofu making or family issues. There is also teaching of arithmetic, simple accounting and abacus use. The activities in the classroom vary but generally, it is a facilitator-centred appraoch. There are songs about the virtues of literacy which learners enjoy singing among themselves or to their friends.

Once learners acquire a basic level of literacy, they can carry onto more interesting post-literacy books printed with the assistance of the project. To support these literacy activities, the project produces supplementary reading materials in practical Chinese, mathematics, post-literacy and continuing education. According to Wang Rongxue, the project director, it is difficult for these women to relapse into illiteracy because, even in far-flung villages, new literates are exposed to written words such as posters and wall newspapers. Newsletters are now being sent out to villages.

Due to the lack of learning texts for the teaching of productive skills, the various townships in the country produce their own materials on technical subjects such as pig raising, bee keeping, mushroom cultivation, fruit tree planting, sewing, embroidery, grain production techniques, township and village enterprises. Since functional contents are also covered in the standard literacy text and classes, learners are taken to observe and try out actual practices of new technology at an experimental farm connected to a secondary vocational school. Women can also observe professional embroidery work.

In cases where learners choose to learn skills for future employment in factories, their newly acquired skills are tried out during a two-month probation period. During this period it is established whether the learner has reached the standard required for employment or whether further training is needed.

At the same time, videotapes, slides, posters and supplementary learning materials are exposed to the learners. As the literacy workers also teach primary school classes, methods used with primary school learners are often used on women learners. The teachers stand at the front of rows of desks and benches. The learners read along with the teacher, read individually and then in unison. The learners, for example, match synonyms or fill in the blanks. They also learn to use the Roman alphabet to read Chinese characters they can't pronounce. The approach to literacy training is continually strengthened by the successful integration of topics adjusted to women's needs. For example, one former textbook showed a man writing letters to another man. The present textbook now shown a woman writing to another woman.

By closely co-operating with the community, the Skills-based Literacy Programme for Women has succeeded in creating a conducive climate which has lent support to community development and raised public concern for the need to educate women. Committees have been established and sub-projects founded to generate interest in the general thrust towards development and literacy. To make sure women attended classes regularly was no easy feat. The project organizers and the All China Women's Federation (ACWF) had to carry out door to door campaigns. Teams were organized to ensure women did come to classes and men were encouraged to look after the home in their absence. The teams talked to reticent parents and husbands, persuaded them that women should be allowed to come to school. As women should be allowed to come to school. As women often have to walk long distances to classes in the evening, the community ensures their safety by electing members to serve as security guards for learners. These "guards" show up at the end of each evening class and escort the learners home. The local media disseminated information on women's education to the county population. Some twenty-three articles were published altogether. Blackboards and wall news-papers were put up in the villages and written materials were spread around to mobilize the greatest number of literates to help in the drive for literacy. It is an inherent part of the programme to work with the media for the promotion of women's status, to develop publicity materials and to link project activities to other ventures.

To encourage the women to come to classes and learn literacy skills, the programme designed an original strategy for easing women's household burdens. Recognizing the unjust balance of power between men and women, the project urged men to take on their share of the housework. Men are shown that they can play a significant role in the education of their children and the family has a chance to better itself by sharing responsibilities. Household chores are no longer to be seen as burdens but rather a chance for husband and wife to come together with their children.

Initially the project met with local resistance and camp up against the remnants of feudal concept of male superiority. As Wang Rongxue says the programme is trying to break traditions and mentalities. Many men objected to their wives or daughters attending lessons when there was so much work at home.

Women who participate in the project vary in age and educational background. Young girls of sixteen learn alongside forty year old mothers. Some are still illiterates, others have been to school and dropped out. Some were fortunate enough to stay until the end of primary school. A few were even luckier-they finished junior secondary school. All had finally accepted their inferior status-they themselves didn't consider they should be educated. The multiple background of learners has proved to be an asset as more educated learners can help others whilst everyone learns at their own pace. The heterogenous background and age of the participants added to the challenge facings the project. It affects the content selection and, to a certain extent, the training methods. But despite their differences, these women now share a common purpose.

Teachers and Facilitators

In the 1980's China began a new drive for education reform. One important move was that primary schools should be run and financed by the communities themselves. The Skills-based Literacy Programme for Women encourages each school to assume a two-pronged function—as a primary school during the day and as an adult learning centre in the evening. This means, each facilitator (teacher) has to teach two classes, one for children and one for adults. In return for this extra-work, they receive a subsidy of then per cent of their salary. The township shoulders the responsibility of covering the facilitator's subsidy which in Xuan Wei county is rather low.

For the production training, the organizers of the project call upon health workers or agricultural officers to give lectures and demonstrate new farming techniques. Specialists from organizations like the Agricultural or Livestock departments and experts on local crafts regularly run training which can last between half a day to two weeks.

Fifty-eight project administrative personnel were trained by the provincial government and thirty other personnel were trained by the Country Government. A hundred and sixty-one facilitators were trained, and altogether ninety-six teaching material compilers were trained by the State, Provincial and District Governments and UNESCO.

Top level project administrators such as the director and managers were trained at regional level alongside their counterparts from other participating countries. They joined study visits such as those to central and northern Thailand to observe non-formal education programmes for women.

They also attended the three regional training workshops for curricular material development in India and Thailand in 1990 and 1992. The training, or orientation, was in project management and monitoring, programme planning and curricular and material development. At the regional workshops, they underwent participatory training where they had hands-on experience in preparing gender-sensitive curricular units which were later published in Chinese for use in the project.

Those who received wider regional training, in turn, trained programme co-ordinators at county, township and village level. Again, training workshops were aimed at preparing post-literacy material. For practical purposes, the training materials were derived from the manual "Educate to Empower", produced by the project and available in Chinese. Training also covered gender sensitivity in women's education as well as how to use reading materials among villagers.

Designing Relevance: Material Development

In recent years, questions have been raised as to whether traditional contents and materials in nonformal education designed for women actually contribute to learners' progress and overall development. Analysis of sample material across the world points to the fact that conventional material has often been irrelevant to women's real needs and ignores their actual conditions.

Most conventional materials for women learners are related to only one of women's multiple functions—that of mother and wife. There has been an unbalanced concentration on improving domestic work, childcare and nutrition and sanitation. While these are important they are not the only work women have to do. Advocates of alternative approaches have argued that non-conventional material designed with sensitivity could contribute to women's development as well as to the development of their society and nation.

Wang Rangxue, programme director, is convinced that his programme cannot be successful without being relevant to women's actual problems and conditions. We give them what they ask for and not what we have to offer and since they are farmers looking for ways to improve production, we show them how to improve production. This is one of the most important lessons learnt from the programme.

Women's productivity as earners and farmers is rarely reflected in the texts or illustrations of conventional material. In so doing, according to K. Chlebowska in *Literacy for Rural Women in the Third World*, authors are sending a message to learner that women "don't contribute to productivity or that their contribution doesn't count." Women learners are deprived of realistic and positive role models. When women's work is covered, it is often as if their activities are no more than an extension of their domestic roles. Educational specialists have explained this in terms of society's belief that women's paid work is secondary and contingent since they are, anyway, considered financially dependent on their husbands.

Relevance was, therefore, seen to be the key to the acceptance of the programme. For the materials in Xuan Wei care was taken to follow the three main principles in preparing material for women, namely: recognition of women's double responsibility (as housekeepers and economic producers), the need to acknowledge and strengthen women's productive contribution, activities and potential and the realization that when women's productive roles are strengthened, the balance of power between men and women will become more equitable and women's domestic tasks lightened facilitated.

The material produced within the regional context of the Skills-based Literacy Programme for Women shows how women's economic self-reliance, self-confidence, self-respect, self-improvement and status within society can be enhanced if the following conditions are met.

Condition I:

Presentation of women's actual condition and double responsibilities.

The needs assessment conducted in the target areas was long and thorough. It became clear during the survey that women's work was being taken for granted. Prejudices remained. Women worked long hours, society didn't recognize their contribution, they had limited access to education and training. The material, therefore, was adapted to translate this situation into words so that learners could see a realistic portrayal of their lives.

In one book, *Cashing in on Cornleaves,* women are portrayed labouring in domestic chores. Danfen in the text *Chicken Care* is seeking new ways to make much-needed cash. In *Beautiful and Productive Courtyard, Qiaozhen, a young married woman,* works alongside her husband and in-laws to make the most of their land. Xi Mei, a young mountain girl, with her baby sister strapped to her back watches longingly as her brothers go to school. Xi Mei is shown as conditioned into accepting that she, as a female, has to accept her status and more than her fair share of the household burden.

Condition II:

Enhancing economic productivity

The most basic prerequisite for empowerment is economic self-reliance. Everywhere in rural Xuan Wei, women following literacy and agro-technology classes say they are doing so to become rich. All material reflects this desire for lucrative activities: Xi Mei is fish farming, Dongfeng is using modern techniques in chicken care, Fuji has become successful in the craft business and A Xiang is using new farming skills. These are a few examples of the skills women can master and want to learn. By proving women can be successful with these materials, the message is clear-women, like men have the potential to master science and technology.

The material is effective because it provides knowledge and skills that relate directly to local conditions. The project appreciates the women's social, cultural and educational background and their potential as well as the limitations that exist in the Province of Yunnan (weather, water and soil conditions). For example, mushroom growing is particularly appropriate in Yunnan where more than 200 varieties of mushroom thrive. Similarly, taken Xuan Wei County's fame for ham, production and pig-raising could be enhanced. The material is clearly based on scientific knowledge. Material developers and agricultural officials work together to prepare adapted learning material that is technically accurate and, at the same time, reflects the learners's environment. It is easy to understand for learners with limited reading skills and experience. Co-operation between farmers, workers and material developers carries on with training sessions. During these sessions, the agricultural experts demonstrate, in actual conditions, how to improve crops or livestock. Follow-up sessions are vital if the learners, in turn, are to become competent and able to teach others. Lastly the skills taught go well beyond simple production skills. They also cover management skills, including accounting, decision making, problem solving, managing people and allocating resources.

Condition III:

Promoting women's status in society.

Portraying actual conditions is only a part of the success of the material. This does not mean these conditions are accepted unconditionally. On the contrary, the texts condemn overburdening housework and the way young girls are deprived of education. In the Changing of a Girl's Life, Xi Mei's persistent desire to learn leads to heated discussions between the teacher and her parents on whether girls should be educated. The teacher wins the argument and takes Xi Mei in. The text then shows Xi Mei's progress until she becomes a model farmer and receives the title of sister of a thousand yuan.

Qiaozhen, in Beautiful and Productive Courtyard, is an active learner at the night school where she learns new farming techniques. With her growing confidence, she convinces her husband to start an integrated farming project on their plot of land. She ends up teaching other village women how to turn their courtyards into orchards. When the villagers congratulate the husband on his success, he points to her and proudly says it was "Qiaozhen's idea".

Condition IV:

Lightening women's domestic work

From the needs assessment, it was clear that women in Xuan Wei were continually busy and occupied—both inside and outside the home. The literacy and training material reflects the emerging trend in China, where men accept more and more of their share of the housework and childcare. In *Murderer in your house*, for example, Jinfeng is seen enjoying her hard-earned income whilst her husband reads funny stories to the children. Qioazhen in *Beautiful and Productive Courtyard* is shown by candle light as her husband talks to their small daughter. When Qiaozhen works her daughter work too. They laugh a great deal and what was previously a chore is turned into a co-operative effort.

So for many years the mistaken traditional idea that women's work was housework has determined the contents of literacy materials and restricted their themes. The so-called female skills, like tailoring, embroidery and handicraft arts have usually made up the educational materials for women but it makes no sense to teach them how to paint little flowers when their concern is how to produce a solid and healthy pig. Furthermore, vocational skills will continue to have little effect unless they are linked to management or entrepreneurial abilities. This is the strength of the Skills-based Literacy Programme for Women which answers specific needs in a particular area. It is prepared to first fill the technology gap by educating women in modern agro-technology and afterwards prepare them to cope with China's shift towards a market economy. The pupils need not go through examinations, or sit through endless classes on irrelevant material. Their test lies in the application of what they have learnt in their farming techniques and production. So much so that their family's well-being is at stake, if they fail. A great challenge and reward for them also lies in the immediate use of their new knowledge and skills without having to wait for graduation. Successful experiments in farming can be replicated to hundreds of farmers rapidly. This innovation is vital to the success of the programme and ensures that a woman is rewarded with the satisfaction that her technique is helping other women in the same situation. It encourages the women to come up with new methods but also gives them a strong sense of duty and citizenship. The farming system of the programme is at the heart of its success.

Management and Co-ordination with Other Ongoing Projects

The Skills-based Literacy Programme for Women is closely co-ordinated to agricultural agencies as well as to other activities involving women such as the "Spark project" conducted by the Science and Technology Commission to develop township and village enterprises. The programme also worked with a project run by the Agricultural Department, "Project for Enough to Eat and Wear" and the project "Activities of Study and Competition in Both Aspects". The Skills-based Literacy Programme for Women is, moreover, also directly linked to programmes supported by the UN Food and Agriculture Organization (FAO) and the United Nations Fund for Population Activities (UNFPA).

As these projects were already operational in Xuan Wei Countt, they greatly eased the introduction of the Skills-based Literacy Programme for Women. And since they were all under government sponsorship, they shared the same directive. It seemed only wise to maximise chances of success by pooling human, material and funding resources together to support the overall activities.

Monitoring and Evaluation

One of the project's major strengths is regular and systematic monitoring. Monitoring was done at three levels—county, province and regional. In China, project managers, led by the county adult education chief, visited the villages on the project site at six month intervals. Formal reports were also submitted to the provincial and prefecture authorities. The provincial focal point for project implementation in Kunming also paid a yearly visit to the Xuan Wei project site, where discussions on project progress and obstacles were carried out. There are also informal visits allowing for close observation of project activities as well as interaction with learners, their families, community leaders, facilitators and co-ordinators. As this is a wider regional project, arrangements were made for progress sharing at all three regional training workshops. In addition, two tripartite reviews were organized in 1992 and 1994. At the tripartite reviews, obstacles in project implementation were discussed among country representatives, UNDP and UNESCO. The tripartite review discussions were based on the papers each country prepared prior to attending the review, and based on common guidelines.

Consultants were also sent from UNESCO PROAP to assess the strengths and weaknesses of the project and to discuss ways and means of expanding the project into other areas in Yunnan. In assessing progress and identifying areas for improvement, care was also taken to qualitatively review material produced as well as to verify that those who had undergone training in the project were applying the knowledge and skills they acquired in their everyday work. Informal communication with individuals at all levels added a degree of authenticity to official reporting. Anecdotal details on the impact of the project on learners' lives are recorded in all fields although systematic individual follow-up of learners is not available to date. For future project monitoring this gap might have to be bridged.

The earning capacity of participants of the Skills-based Literacy Programme has risen considerably. New skills double or even triple income. The example of Shu Ling from Lai Ping Township is revealing. Before the Xuan Wei programme she earnt well below the average per capita rate for the province which is of some Y 600/year (40 US dollars). She had to depend on government subsidies for fertilizer, food and medicine. After a couple of months of machine embroidery training, Shu Ling became the best learner and was able to earn enough to live without subsidies. This newly-found self-reliance gave her confidence in her capacities and she is currently saving up to buy herself an embroidery machine. Another woman Lhuo Lu Lin, aged forty followed the advice of those teaching her on the farming programme of the Skills-based Literacy Programme and began to grow fruit trees on her strip of land. She soon had to hire two workers and get her brother and sister-in-law involved. Her present income stands at Y 10,000 a year (900 US dollars). She is using the money to buy household goods, rice cookers and children's clothes.

Achievements have been reported throughout Xuan Wei county: 36,000 illiterate women have become literate and the illiteracy rate among young girls has dropped twenty nine per cent to below the average for the whole province. Some 313 classes were held for technical training, these were attended by 275,000 women between the ages of thirty and fifty. Out of these women some 7,215 were then able to play a major role in carrying out new production and management teachniques. There were over seventy five training courses, mainly techniques for growing vegetables or animal breeding, which cover subjects such as health care, ecological matters and other production and living skills. The social and economic benefits of the training courses which were attended by many people were considerable and specific technical advances greatly contributed to the well-being of the villagers. For example, energy-saving kitchen stoves were built which managed to conserve forty-two per cent more heat and limit pollution within the home. The maize harvest was increased through the simple technique of close planting of seeds and the latest pig-breeding techniques meant an average thirty one per cent rise in earnings and greater sanitation.

It is not enough, though, to measure the achievements of the programme in terms of economics and material well-being. By becoming literate the women open up a whole wealth of possibilities. By joining literacy classes, one woman Chu Yun Song, managed to turn part of her house into a small mushroom growing concern. It's not that she just learnt about mushrooms but as she says "I learnt to read brand names of goods in the market, I learnt to read about methods of mushroom farming". She now manipulates glasstubes, chemicals and special lamps with great skill. This transformation after the literacy programme is compared to a kind of revelation by many of the women. One young villager remembers how she used to get lost in the streets of Kunming as she couldn't read the signs. This same woman now has a small shop and sells clothes. She feels capable of doing much more and is aware of the possibilities ahead. Du, a young mother, remembers how when she was young there was no possibility of schooling. Girls didn't go to school. She herself was illiterate only three years ago but now conducts embroidery classes. These changes have transformed the balance of power that used to dominate the lives of many of these women.

Political will and local structures were such that they helped the programme reach out to the widest group of people possible. Those co-ordinating the project did all they could to ensure the sustainability of the programme by monitoring and listening to feedback. They did not hesitate in front of corrective measures and made sure that participants and facilitators were well-suited to the programme.

Furthermore, the various skills of the participants and facilitators were deliberately focussed on those which seemed the best adapted to the project's targets.

Funding sources were purposely diversified to avoid the programme becoming dependent on one source. The implementation of the Skills-based Literacy Programme for Women has reached a wide range of poor women from the farming communities of one of the poorest areas of China, but has cost the country not more than 810,000 Yuan (54,000 US dollars) of this 200,000 Yuan (18,000 US dollars) were provided by the Yunnan Province; 130,000 Yuan (10,000 US dollars) by the districts and 430,000 Yuan (31,000 US dollars) by the county, UNESCO contributed 33,000 US dollars worth of seed money which was used for:

— organization of training of managers and teachers
— printing of nine booklets of 20,000 copies
— gender-sensitive materail development
— equipment such as camera and computer

— regional training and field visits

By comparison with other non-formal education programmes, the cost per head of this project is amazingly low. This, as well as the drastic increase in the learners' income means that the programme has been remarkably cost-effective.

In brief the project's strengths can be stated as the following:

— a centralized planning combined with a well established management structure from the provincial level down to the village level.
— involvement of the local Women's Federation to provide external support to the project, e.g. mobilizing learners, intervention when learner's family prohibit participation and launching a campaign to promote the lightening of women's domestic workload,
— serious focus on women's income-earning capacity combined with health and civic awareness,
— effective co-ordination between various relevant ministries: education, agriculture, health, environment,
— pooling of resources from donor agencies, eg UNDP, UNESCO, WFP,
— overall, the matching of socio-economic goals of the nation with individual needs and aspirations has been the major hallmark of this project. It has meant a particularly pragmatic version of 'functional relevance' which has led the project to success, despite its relatively traditional educational base.

As the Skills-based Literacy Programme for Women will continue its fight to improve the condition and education of women in Xuan Wei County, improvement will be needed in the following fields:

— continued upgrading of personnel involved in the project, notably as concerns gender-sensitivity,
— future project activities need to involve and educate husbands and children to a greater degree;
— the empowerment aspect of the programme could be strengthened.

Finally, if the full impact of the project is to be measured, the improvement in income, the effect on children's education and changes in family patterns need to be monitored in a simultaneous fashion.

CONCLUSION

It is obvious from the Chinese experiment of the Skills-based Literacy Programme for Women that literacy and production projects for women need to tackle the issues which lie at the heart of the learner's aspirations and feelings. Effective literacy materials alone do not guarantee and improvement in women's productive roles. The successful programmes run in Xuan Wei county show that education for development must also reinforce a woman's self-esteem. The Xuan Wei programme is already a success in terms of its outreach, sustainability and measurable economic improvement. It shows that non-formal education can be used to enhance national economic development and that women have a vital role to play in the process.

This success of the Skills-based Literacy Programme for Women in Xuan Wei can be explained in many ways. Firstly the Chinese Central Government's policy to strengthen economic progress in the remote rural areas formed a solid basis for the programme and non-formal education was seen as the most effective way of delivering science and technology to a population previously deprived of education of any kind. Secondly the Government's goals were swiftly translated into definitive directives and disseminated to people who were able to identify with them.

Ingenious methods of assessing the economic potential of the region and then combining this with the needs of the population were turned into a pragmatic and realistic project appraoch. Furthermore, once the project authorities were convinced of the merit of their appraoch, the project was integrated into the existing practice of non-formal education in Yunnan and found a way to sustain itself and even expand into other areas. The fact that the programme responds closely to women's needs and that participatns' achievements are tangible and visible created further credibility in the community around.

In shor, the project and the scale of its success have been made possible because of a convergence of the government's economic goals, the villager's actual needs, the integration of gender issues into learning material and a pragmatic appraoch perhaps unique to China. The single greatest conclusion to come out of the Yunnan Programme is that quite apart from literacy, basic education for women, whether it be formal or nonformal, is the best investment China can make for its future.

35

SAPTAGRAM: A WOMEN'S SELF-RELIANCE AND EDUCATION MOVEMENT

Cynthia Guttman

Introduction

A decade ago, 300 angry women workers on a road-building project in Bangladesh, most of them illiterate, surrounded their district's Martial Law Office after realizing they had 'signed up' with their fingerprints for a smaller wage than they had been promised. It caused a political upset and convinced the women of the need for education, so as to secure their basic rights.

In a traditional Muslim society like Bangladesh, women are not often seen working on roads—admittedly a low status employment—or staging demonstrations. But most of these women belonged to Saptagram Nari Swanirvar Parishad—the Seven Villages Women's Self-Reliance Movement-a grassroots organization founded in 1976 by history professor Rokeya Rahman Kabeer. Today, the movement, to help deprived, landless women understand the causes of their oppression, take charge of their lives and work on income-generating projects, has spread to over 900 villages, reaching 22,000 members.

One of Saptagram's most original features, introduced in the mid-1980s, is a gender-oriented syllabus that has attracted the interest of other non-governmental organizations (NGOs) in Bangladesh. This year, to relieve the shortage of female teachers in the expanding education programme, Saptagram has begun hiring its own graduates as future instructors, giving women an additional source of income and enhanced status in a country where only one in five primary school teachers is a woman and female illiteracy, at 77 per cent, is one of the highest in the world. The women-centred curriculum is especially relevant, since the government has promised to aim at Education for All, of which non-formal basic education is a key part.

What makes Saptagram different from the several hundred NGOs working in this country of 114 million inhabitants, one of the five poorest in the world and regularly devastated by natural disasters? From the start, Saptagram has seen its struggle as a challenge to keeping women inferior and separate from men. "We have been told all our lives by our mothers, aunts and grandmothers that our place is at the feet of our husband", says Lily Begum, a Saptagram member. Girls are often married at 10, payment of exorbitant dowries can ruin families, and women are supposed to be invisible and isolated, in accordance with the old idea of female seclusion, or *purdah*.

Rather than taking a welfare-biased or short-term appraoch to development, Saptagram concentrates on empowerment of its members, starting with the assertion that strength lies in unity and group solidarity. Its aims are:

1) To work among women in poor rural areas ;
2) To make them aware of the causes of their social and economic deprivation and give them the means to gain more control over their lives;
3) To initiate non-traditional income-generating activities on a cooperative basis and give women some control over resources;
4) To provide education to groups, with emphasis on book-keeping. The gender-oriented syllabus also reinforces women's knowledge of their rights. The education programme grew from the women's demand for classes, as they came to realize the links between education, employment opportunities and basic human rights; and
5) To provide knowledge of health and nutrition.

The presence of women at all levels of the organization, from senior management to the field, is unique in rural development work in Bangladesh, and kills the myth that women need male protection if they are to work in the countryside.

For the past fifteen years, Saptagram has received funding from OXFAM, the Swedish International Development Agency (SIDA) and the Norwegian Agency for Development Cooperation (NORAD), and one-off grants from other sources for special projects. To speed up the time-consuming process of applying for funds, Saptagram has drawn up an integrated rural development programme for 1993-1996. Based on the recommendations of an evaluation report and a 1992 management review, it aims to consolidate Saptagram's activities, and is being funded by a consortium.

Tackling Gender Disparities in Bangladesh

When Rokeya Kabeer returned to Bangladesh in 1976, five years after it emerged from a nightmarish civil war, she resigned from her position at a government college. An upper-class woman from Calcutta, she set off for the village of Komarpur, where her in-laws lived, in Faridpur district, one of the country's most backward regions.

Saptagram began in the early days of the United Nations Decade for Women. Aid donors in Bangladesh (where foreign loans and grants were 7.2 per cent of GDP in 1990) gave more for women's programmes, emphasizing women as producers, not only child-bearers. At state level, General Zia-ur Rahman, who came to power in 1975, zealously took up the cause of Women and Development, creating a Ministry of Women's Affairs and increasing to 30 the number of parliamentary seats reserved for women.

In those days, the notion of 'women development' helped to challenge the age-old preconception of women at all levels of Bangladesh society. It also opened up new possibilities for women to organize and struggle for their common interests. Women's organizations started campaigning against dowry and opened shelters for women who had been victims of violence. As a result, the government passed new laws on these issues.

However, "in their quest for internal constituency and external legitimacy, successive military regimes have sought to reconcile apparently contradictory political programmes", writes Naila Kabeer, a scholar at Sussex University's Institute of Development Studies. "The contradictions are most apparent in the sphere of women's rights, since state policy has, on the one hand, championed 'women in development' values and the emancipation of women, and on the other, set in motion a 'creeping' Islamisation process, thereby encouraging those who would snatch back the gains that women have made."

At state level, promises of emancipation and participation in development have not been followed up. Public sector funding for women's programmes only got 0.06 per cent of the budget under the first five year plan and around 0.20 for the second and third.

Today, some 99.4 million people live below the poverty line, a disproportionate number of them women. In 1989-90, the nutritional intake of women was 88 per cent that of males and they earned 40 per cent less than men. While 8 per cent of male-led households were classed as very poor, the corresponding figure for female-headed households is 33 per cent. Only 23 per cent of the female population is literate, compared to 44 per cent of men.

In 1993, compulsory primary education was extended to the whole country, and as part of a pledge to narrow the gender gap in education, free education for girls in rural areas has been extended from Grade 5 to Grade 8. Secondary education, from the age of 10, lasts for up to seven years. 22 per cent of the country's 17.6 million primary school-age children never attend school. Of the 13.7 million who do enroll (67 per cent boys, 57 per cent girls), 60 per cent drop out before completing the five-year cycle with most dropping out in the first three grades. Enrolment ratio at the secondary level was equivalent to 18 per cent (24 per cent of boys, 11 per cent of girls).

Growing landlessness is slowly deteriorating the social fabric of Bangladesh, where 80 per cent of the population is rural. Nine per cent of Bangladeshis own 80 per cent of the land, and some 60 million people are functionally landless. Studies predict that by 1995 three quarters of the rural population will be in this category, partly because of inheritance rules which divide property equally between all sons. (Muslim law allows daughters to inherit land, but in practice, social factors and family politics prevent women claiming these formal rights).

Many NGOs are working—and often competing—throughout the country. Most have integrated the 'women and development' component into their strategies. But many put women into labour-intensive, low-profit sectors, such as handicrafts or poultry rearing, using very simple technology. One study found 70 per cent of training curricula in women's programmes (government, private and international), were mostly embroidery, sewing and knitting. On the other hand, country-wide initiatives such as the Bangladesh Rural Advancement Committee (BRAC) and the Grameen Bank have encouraged women to start up small businesses and other productive activities outside the home. Over the past two decades, BRAC has promoted income generating projects among the rural poor and created a network of over 12,000 primary schools.

Despite their involvement at grassroots level, Kabeer argues that none of these programmes are completely geared towards women, partly because they are not run by women. "If you want to work with women, you must have women to understand what the problem is. But that is not done by male NGOs", she told a seminar at Reading University in 1992. "They are now desperately trying to get women on staff because there is pressure from the funders to have competent women in their organization."

SAPTAGRAM:Confronting Problems Together

Saptagram is based on the belief that women, once united, can work for their own development. The movement's target groups have not altered since it was founded in 1976: women from poor peasant families (0.5-1.5 acres of land holdings, a half-acre of land being worth approximately Tk 25,000/$665); rural households depending on wage labour or non-agricultural incomes, and women who have been deserted, divorced or widowed. Women who have drifted into towns alone or with their families, often after being cast out of rural society, are of growing concern to Saptagram, which, since the early 1980s, has included a few male groups. These were formed at the insistence of women group members who felt that working with poor, landless men could help improve their own lives. The ratio of women to men's groups is 4:1. About 40 per cent of Saptagram's members are under 25,40 per cent between 26 and 40,12 per cent between 41 and 55 and the rest over 56.

Saptagram's appraoch towards forming groups of women, usually of 25-30 members, has changed little since the organization's beginnings. Trained field staff approach women in villages on foot, talking to them, listening to their concerns, and winning their confidence. Although today groups of women often approach field staff to ask for advice and help to form a new group, the task was a more dangerous one when Saptagram planted its first seeds.

Kabeer was the first to run afoul of the pivotal role played by class and kinship in the village. Kerosene was poured over one of the project's centres and Kabeer got death threats. "The main problem was from the rich", says Kabeer. "I was told I would be killed. They wanted me to leave the place in fear, and if I did leave, I knew I would never return. So I just stuck it out."

Saptagram tries to keep its distance from village leaders. "When we set up new groups, we don't contact the village leaders because we're a government-registered NGO" says a senior member of Saptagram. "But if any problem arises, then we contact the village leaders." She explains that religious political parties like the Jamaat-i-Islam often propagate the notion that women should respect purdah by remaining secluded at home. "We try to overcome this propaganda through discussion."

Credit is one of the main motivations for forming groups, and is given at group level. The importance of capital formation is stressed from the very first loan. To get a loan, a group must save money: groups decide how much each member much save, from Tk 5 to Tk 10 ($0.15 to $0.25) per month. For the most destitute women, a traditional method of setting aside one handful of rice per day from the daily family allotment is encouraged. As a guide, one kilo of the lowest quality rice costs about Tk 10, while a kilo of mutto would be worth Tk 100. It usually takes about a year for women to save the fixed amount. As savings grow, women gain a sense of security and confidence, as well as a feeling of group unity. As of December 1992, total group savings were Tk 5.86 million ($0.15 million).

Demystifying the Lives of Women

As group build up savings, field workers visit them about once a week to discuss their plans for a cooperative economic venture. Since women's first choice is to opt for home-based programmes, discussions turn into a broader debate on taboos governing their lives, from sexual division of labour that keeps women in low-income activities, to social issues, such as early marriage, household violence, rape, and land and wage rights. Saptagram's staff refers to this as the 'nursing period', or a time of 'consciousness-raising', during which a strong relationship develops between group members.

Groups are advised and guided, rather than led, forcing them to take more responsibility for action. These months are a time of 'demystification', aimed at examining the contradictions inherent in the tradition of *purdah.* "Women in torn sarees working behind the dilapidated walls of their huts are hardly secluded from the view of outsiders", says Kabeer. When asked about their oppression, they will tend to say passively that it's their *Kismet*, or God's will. Field staff will mildly challenge this, gradually giving them a greater awareness of their condition, and a sense of initiative.

Collective action, or *andalon*, is urged to resolve legal and economic repression. This generally involves marching on the local union council's office to report abuses (theft of money, extortion of dowry, threats of divorce, rape) and demand for action. In 1992, the groups were involved in 84 such cases and solved their problems in 70 of them.

With each case, women gain a moral victory and a sense of power, though sometimes at great cost. When SIDA's first secretary for development cooperation visited a Saptagram group in the mid-1980s, she recalls that the men would't allow women to come together. "They were so daring. They said 'We don't care. We are coming outside to meet, to talk about what is happening in our lives and our families'. Women often used to be beaten by men when they went home. But they had the strength of the group behind them."

Taking out Loans: A Collective Decision

In 1992, Tk 2.1 million ($56,000) was disbursed in loans, an average of Tk 13,000 ($346) per group. Saptagram loans up to half the total cost of the project, with the remainder met by group savings. The organization says it has an almost 100 per cent recovery rate. Groups may share out profits or add them to their savings to increase investment potential. As loans are repaid-according to a schedule decided by the group-new, larger loans may be requested on the basis of greater experience and savings. Under pressure from funders, Saptagram started charging five per cent interest on loans in 1990, which increased to 10 per cent in July 1993 to cover inflation, identified as the main reason for leakage in the revolving loan fund.

"We want to make women aware they can do everything men can", says Kabeer, explaining Saptagram's approach to rural credit. Groups are involved in a range of economic activities.

Breaking the tradition of only participating in post-harvest activities, women are now leasing arable land as well as tilling land themselves. Landowners seeking mortgages against their land frequently approach the local women's group which charges less interest than money-lenders. Mortgages are given for two years or more, during which the group works the land, enjoying full benefit of the crops produced on it.

This greater interest in agriculture has led women to produce processed rice and sell produce at the weekly or bi-weekly village market, the hat, a sphere traditionally reserved for men. "At first, women said we can't go to the market", recalls Kabeer. "We went with one of the oldest women—she was 45. Nobody jeered. The women then said they could continue alone. It's a giant leap forward for Muslim women to sit in the market and sell their goods."

With training and technical assistance from the Mennonite Central Committee (MCC), groups have also re-excavated ponds for fish breeding—a source of seasonal income—and horticulture, which includes home vegetable gardening. New seed varieties and food-crops have been introduced, such as soya dal, which provides an extra source of nutrition for families.

Saptagram is also proud of giving women access to modern technology. At the time of the 1992 evaluation, six power tillers and three shallow pump machines had been bought with Saptagram loans. In the village of Ghonghosail, a men's and women's group joined in managing a successful power tiller business. It took them two and a half years to save enough to buy a power tiller. One woman and one man were trained to drive it. During the season, a group can make Tk 1,200 a day ($32). Part of their earnings are invested in petty trade for greater economic security. Besides breaking the taboo of women ploughing land, the experience also shows that men's and women's groups can work together, and that the latter are perfectly able to participate in a technology project.

About a third of Saptagram loans are for petty trade and stock business, which involves opening small grocery shops, and the buying and reselling of goods. Other activities are more traditional, including poultry and livestock rearing, and poultry vaccination.

One Saptagram member sums up her feelings: "Before, we did not come out for work, except to work in the houses of rich people. We are now doing earth work, selling our products in the village market, even selling things from house to house. This could not have happened before. We would have faced punishment. Village elders could even have turned us out of the village." Today, as Saptagram becomes more established, the vitriolic reactions it drew in its early days have given way to tolerance, even acceptance. Men's support groups have sprung up, leading their voice in social actions.

This year, Saptagram plans to give its first individual loans to women actively involved in the organization for at least five years. Women can apply for an individual loans if they have shown leadership and management skills in social actions and income-generating projects. They must also be graduates of the adult literacy course and have sound accounting skills.

Sericulture: Women at All Stages of Production

Sericulture-the raising and care of silkworms to produce raw silk—was seen as a sector which could provide employment to women at all stages of production, and so has been one of Saptagram's most comprehensive income-generating projects. The current programme has group members involved in mulberry plantation, cultivation of sapling nurseries and cocoon rearing. Nine staff members specialized in sericulture work closely with field staff and group members.

The programme's success led to setting up of a silk production centre in 1986 at Rajbari, Faridpur, with a grant from the Swiss Development Cooperation. By putting in reeling machines for yarn production, Saptagram has become a buyer of cocons in a fiercely competitive market. The factory indirectly benefits about 800 mulberry-tree farmers. A total of 183 women are employed at the centre, and have gained experience in reeling, spinning, weaving, dyeing and twisting. Saptagram also runs literacy classes for women at the centre. A feasibility study commissioned by Saptagram in 1990 led to the project receiving additional funding totalling Tk. 20 million ($0.5 million) from the Danish Development Agency (DANIDA), and Bread for the World. The project includes building a factory and installing new equipment. In 1992, the centre produced nearly 5,000 meters of silk cloth and had sales of Tk 830,000 ($22,100), 26 per cent more than in 1991. Saptagram is aiming for Tk 4.8 million

($126,000) in sales in 1993-1994 with a more aggressive marketing strategy and the hiring of a marketing advisor.

The bangladesh Sericulture Board has supported the centre by giving technical training to workers, displaying Saptagram silk products in its showrooms and inviting staff to seminars and workshop to promote the industry.

Learing: About Health

According to a 1993 report by the Bangladesh Institute of Development Studies, "the most distressing statistic is the position of the government system as a source of rural health care. Only 10 per cent of rural illnesses are treated through government health care, which represents a slight decline from 1990." Group members needing medical attention are often accompanied to government health centres to ensure that they receive proper treatment. Saptagram's work focuses on preventive health. Field staff include health, nutrition, hygiene and family planning in village seminars and literacy programmes. Group members are taught to prepare saline solutions to fight dehydration in diarrhoeal diseases. Children are treated against worms. In addition, after pressure from the field, Saptagram devised a 'Pure Water to the People' programme and a sanitation programme.

In the first of these, group members are encouraged to use tubewell water for drinking. Impure water causes almost 60 per cent of disease in rural Bangladesh. Saptagram provides tubewells to the groups, which pay for boring and a concrete ground at the base. Some of the groups have been trained to install and maintain tubewells. In the sanitation programme-access to sanitary latrines. Both programmes have introduced group members to alternative sources of employment.

Saptagram sells a low dose birth control pill to members, informs women of family planning measures but goes no further than providing them with a referral service.

Education: A Course Designed for Women

"One of the first things I did when I started Saptagram was to introduce education among women", recalls Kabeer. "It completely failed because adult women were not interested in education. They asked us to teach their children." It was only after women started getting more involved in income-generating activities—and were cheated of their full wages—that they began to realize the need for education in order to keep their accounts. "We could have tied our credit programme to education, making it a rule that only those who attended education classes could get credit. Instead, we waited for the women to appreciate the importance of education themselves. The women came to us for education", says Kabeer proudly.

Saptagram used government and then BRAC-designed literacy materials before concluding that both projected a 'male-oriented' view of development. Women themselves questioned the pictures in the books that portrayed men earning money and ploughing the fields, and women looking after the house, fetching water and looking after chickens. The pictures clashed with the knowledge women had gained from their involvement with Saptagram.

From its experience in working with deprived, rural women, Saptagram developed its own syllabus with the help of a specialist in adult education. The materials were reviewed after input from field workers, and have won government prizes two years in a row. Within Bangladesh, other organizations, including Save the Children-USA, Polly Sree and the Social Development Society, have introduced the materials into their adult literacy classes and have asked Saptagram for teacher training. Saptagram sells each set of primary level education materials for Tk 500 ($13).

The first stage of the literacy programme lasts about six months, with an average of six classes a week. Students follow a booklet containing 39 words and phrases about health, religious customs, work, social and political rights, and the environment. The aim is to teach women the letters that make up the words, at the same time generating discussion of the word's meaning and relevance to women's lives. The primer also has a simple numeracy section, introducing women to basic operations. To lead the women through the booklet, teachers use flash cards and a large-format 76-page primer. Each meaningful word is illustrated. In one drawing entitled 'Seclusion', a veiled woman is walking with her husband and boy. In another, entitled 'Dowry', scales are shown with a woman on one side, weighed against a bicycle, a radio, a clock and other goods. Early marriage, repression, corruption, violence and divorce are also portrayed. Offering women a different vision of their lives, illustrations show the power gained from unity, the importance of education, and women working in non-traditional activities and attending meetings to defend their rights. On the pages opposite, the syllabic structure and letters forming the word are shown. The teacher helps students to make up other words with the letters just learnt.

In Kabeer's eyes, one of the most important pictures is entitled 'Address'. A postman is handing a letter to a woman. "This is a tremendous achievement", says Kabeer. "Women have no identity. You can only write to them care of their husband, their father, brother or another male relative. We managed to get recognition by society, government and police that these women do exist." In another lesson, a woman is writing a letter, one of the assignments in Saptagram classes.

The second part of the education programme develops reading and numeracy skills. Women get a book of 15 stories, written in simple language, each with a message aimed at deepening women's understanding of issues introduced at the primary stage. The illustrated stories touch on subjects like the importance of registering a marriage (a contract spelling out marriage payments), family planning and procedures for acquiring land. To encourage discussion and thought, students are questioned at the end of each story. During the six-month course, numeracy gets special attention so as to help women with book-keeping. "At this stage, we introduce more advanced mathematics, not merely numeracy, because we want group members to be able to maintain their accountbooks properly and independently", says Saptagram's senior education officer. It is a testing time for both teachers and students: "We're not sure yet how many will learn to do more advanced accounts", says Kabeer. "If we manage to teach five members from each group, we will be satisfied, even if we hope to do better than that."

Saptagram also publishes a 60-page booklet on health and nutrition entitled 'How we can get rid to diseases.' It focuses on common contagious diseases, their causes and symptoms, and describes preventive measures. The information is presented in very simple form, and is designed to maintain women's interest in reading after they have finished the second part of the course. A similar booklet is being prepared on legal aid. Saptagram also plans to publish a newsletter to encourage women to continue reading and keep them breast of events affecting their lives.

About 40 per cent of Saptagram 1,120 groups participate in the adult education programmes, which are also open to non-members. Assessing its adult literacy programme, Saptagram cites an 8 per cent drop-out rate and praises women's regular attendance that partly results from letting them determine class hours. In addition, realizing the importance of learning, women have started coming to classes with their daughters when the latter can't attend regular schools. One of the most rewarding results of the programme is to see women keeping their own accounts, taking down minutes in group meetings or helping their children with school homework. Knowing how to keep accounts can also increase their influence in the household: "Now my husband talks to me and asks my advice", says one group member.

The Teachers:Keeping up with Demand

"We can't keep up with the demand for education amongst women, it has suddenly taken off", says Kabeer. In 1992, Saptagram had 167 teachers, who taught 296 classes involving, 3,485 students. Most teachers give two classes a day to different groups and receive Tk 800 a month ($21).

Saptagram advertises for teachers in the local press and hires after an interview and a written test. Until now, teachers have come from different social backgrounds and have usually finished secondary school. But joining Saptagram's teaching staff also means understanding the organization's goals. "We sometimes have difficulties in making them understand that they are not merely teachers but are helping to develop society", says Saptagram's senior education officer. "It also takes time for them to understand the cause of exploitation and oppression in society, as well as the status of women in the development process." It is why new recruits spend four weeks in the field to witness the 'consciousness-raising' process at work. The second part of the training is an intensive seven day session in a classroom situation. It deals with social awareness, legal literacy, gender relations and Development, and practical demonstrations of the lessons, with emphasis on participation. After six months in the field, teachers return to the training centre in Swastipur for a three-day refresher course. A maximum of 20 teachers are trained at a time.

Teachers have several guides to help them through the course. All emphasize the need to make each class relevant to women's lives and to encourage participation.

Due to the difficulty of recruiting female instructors, Saptagram has decided to train some of its graduates to become teachers. In July 1993, it chose 50 students from its group members for a six-week training course before being assigned to the field. Besides providing a respectable employment option to rural women, Saptagram believes its own learners may be best at educating rural women. Over the next three years, Saptagram aims to increase its teachers to 300, in order to reach 7,200 students.

Saptagram's Management: Women at All Levels

The presence of women at all levels of the organization, from the field to the executive board, has been one of Saptagram's earliest hallmarks.

The project area, now covering a fifth of the country, has two zones, the Faridpur district, and the Jessore and Kushtia districts. Each is run by a zonal coordinator, with four centres under her authority. Each centre has its own director. These centres, located in the villages, are catalysts for change. First, they attract attention, since eight to ten field staff, generally female, live there together, which is very unusual in rural Bangladesh. Second, they are places where group members can come for information or to attend workshops. Every week, field staff meet with their centre directors to discuss programme activities, and their experiences and difficulties.

Every two months, the zonal coordinators meet with the four centre directors of their region and at least two field staff members, chosen on a rotation basis, to discuss progress in implementing programmes.

The Dhaka head office, with 19 people, acts as a coordinating agency. The organization's main policy-making body is the 13-member central committee of the centre heads, the zonal coordinators, the sericulture coordinator, and representatives of field staff and management. Policies are decided at this level, after hearing feedback from the field. All central committee members are required to make regular visits to the villages to keep in close touch with field staff and group members.

The present set-up dates from the mid-1980s, when Saptagram restructured itself, improved staff training and decentralized decision-making. This was in response to an evaluation by OXFAM as well as to the sudden swelling of its ranks by staff and target groups from Nijera Kori, a women's organization that had recently split. Another turning point was the appointment of a project director, Tahera Yasmin, to succeed Professor Kabeer. "My arrival sent a message to Saptagram and to the NGO community that there had to be changes in the leadership and that an organization can carry on with people other than its founders", said Yasmin, noting the importance of a change in leadership for organizational growth. As a report by SIDA noted, "it requires a certain confidence in one's ability to take over from the founder of an organization, especially one who has managed every facet of its development to date." During her tenure (Yasmin resigned in 1993), she worked towards the institutionalization of Saptagram. "Like most NGOs in Bangladesh", she says, "Saptagram was run like a voluntary organization and there was a need for a move towards professionalism." This resulted in strengthening training and commissioning a management review. Its recommendations, currently being implemented through a technical assistance plan, include installing a computer-operated system to better analyze and systematize field reports, and improved monitoring of programmes.

The Field Staff: Key Agents of Change

Saptagram's first efforts were hampered by the choice of upper-class women, often daughters of influential figures in the community such as the landed gentry, to work with the deprived in their own villages. "These girls were not only required to work among the poorest section of the community but also to act as the vanguard of a movement to bring about social change, starting from their village", explains a Saptagram report. "This approach failed because the barriers between the workers and their target groups proved to be impregnable."

This forced Saptagram to scrutinize the social and economic background of staff. Today, most are from the lower middle class, and have completed secondary education. They are chosen by application to the regional offices. After interviews and a one-week orientation, they are placed with an experienced field worker for a one-month trial. The new recruits observe how groups are formed, learn to conduct meetings and workshops, write reports, keep minutes at the meetings and prepare monthly field visit schedules. To avoid conflicts of interest, they never work in their own villages. After this month-long session in the field, recruits return to the Swastipur Training Centre for a two-week course on theoretical and practical issues.

The field worker plays a key role in nurturing groups, through dedication, listening and regular visits to the village: "The skills of the field staff worker is vital to the formation, development and longevity of the target groups", writes Inez Gibbons in an evaluation done for SIDA in 1990. "Her ability to motivate, inform, counsel and encourage the members is essential to the group's cohesion, financial success and often community relations. A well-qualified field staff worker will bring a group along quickly while one with poor skills can destroy a group that is not strong from within."

Saptagram has 55 field workers, 80 per cent of them married and 60 per cent with children. Each is responsible for supervising 20 to 25 groups. About half the field staff live at the Saptagram centre in their district, with their children. A field worker's average salary is between Tk 2,000 and Tk 2,500 ($53 to $66) a month. Every year, all staff attend a three-day field animators' workshop at the Swastipur Training Centre, set up in 1986 to provide gender-sensitive training in group management, legal literacy, health and sanitation, accounting, project planning and budget, and social development. Taking into account the evaluation report's recommendations, Saptagram plans to increase its field staff over the next three years to maintain a ratio of 1 staff to 15 groups.

Moving Towards: Self-sufficiency

Saptagram field staff members act as advisors to groups, helping them in the aim of giving women greater control over their lives. Saptagram's ideal is for women to gain enough knowledge, skills and strength to do without the organization, and continue its work on their own.

"The women who have chosen to be part of a Saptagram group have shown persistence, courage and determination by maintaining their membership and resisting the oppression of their families and the community", writes Inez Gibbons. "They have demanded changes in their economic conditions." But the 1992 evaluation warned that insufficient attention had been given to group dynamics. Different levels of commitment from group to group, and among women of the same group, highlighted the difficulty of maintaining homogeneity. Difficulties with savings and loans are one of the commonest causes of a group's break-up. Sometimes the loan does not equally benefit all members. In one extreme case cited in the evaluation, male relatives forced their wives or daughters to take loans which they used for their own consumption. A lack of expertise in maintaining accounts, fluctuating market prices and the absence of proper staff supervision can combine to break up a group. While Saptagram hopes the extension of literacy classes will help women keep better accounts, it also plans to reinforce credit supervision over the next three years by improved staff training.

A group's solidarity is enhanced by workshops at the centres and regional offices. The themes of these workshops which range from legal literacy, preventive health care, leadership and management, specialized technical training are usually the outcome of discussions in the villages Once a month, group members send a representative, on a rotational basis, to one of these seminars at the Saptagram centre. These meetings bring women from different villages together, often for the first time. Discussions, sometimes with overtones of 'group therapy', make women aware that they face similar problems and can jointly seek how to overcome them. The staff serve as facilitators. In 1992, a total of 155 seminars and workshops involved 6,715 members.

Some group members emerge as leaders and take over many of the field staff's functions. Saptagram estimates it takes about five years for a group to function independently. Rather than wait for field staff to come to the village, they will go to their closest centre for information and advice. Cooperation between these mature groups—ones that have undertaken a successful economic venture, participated in social actions and followed the literacy classes—has started in a number of villages with formation of village or *gram* committees. Members of these are 'graduated' group members with leadership qualities. Saptagram given them training in group management, microenterprise, and education. There are 27 *gram* committees with the participation of 178 groups and 50 villages. They are the base of a federation with an apex, rising from the village to the union and district community levels. This federation building is meant to further women's self-reliance. With the help of functional literacy and economic programmes, Saptagram believe the groups will ultimately be strong and sufficiently knowledgeable to control their future....without Saptagram.

Saptagram's Impact: The Value of Time

"Can you really fight the whole society, Chachiamma? I somehow do not think you will win. This social order has been there for thousands of years, like an old banyan tree which has stretched its roots deep into the earth. Storms will not be able to uproot it. The only way is to cut the tree down. Can you do that?"

These are the words of a group member, Lily Begum, included in a book of forthcoming case studies collected by Rokeya Kabeer over 15 years. They reflect the enormous task Saptagram has set itself. Such an organization could not have overcome the huge obstacles of rural tradition without the vision and commitment of a leader who has put all her influence and energy into building Saptagram. "No one else could have done it", stresses Eva Joelsdotter Berg from SIDA.

To measure Saptagram's impact in facts and figures is hard, if not impossible, due to the lack of comprehensive studies. A study by the Bangladesh Institute of Development Studies (BIDS) estimates that target group households get at most 20 per cent of their income from involvement with Saptagram. According to Saptagram's 1992 annual report, "most of the group members confess that while previously they would sometimes have to go without food for days, they now at least have two square meals a day."

There is, however, another dimension to change that demands more intimate knowledge of the country, and of the great ambivalence of relationships in rural society. One report talks about 'an air of confidence' projected by women who are firmly committed to Saptagram. Working within the parameters of a strict Muslim society, some of Saptagram's boldest inroads can be summarized as follows:

Gaining Initiative

Many NGOs working in Bangladesh are struggling to deal with a 'dependency mentality' on the part of recipients. Saptagram has been prone to lose members who have moved to other NGOs offering individual loans, quicker access to credit or free food rations. It is where Saptagram goes beyond a poverty alleviation project towards perceiving its mission as a much vaster project to make women agents of change. For this to happen over the long term, Saptagram believes that a 'consciousness-raising' process is essential. This takes time, requiring patience and extensive discussion that are not necessarily poverty's most obvious allies.

Breaking Out of Isolation

Coming out of the home to meet with their group and travelling to centres for seminars and workshops is revolutionary in a country where the ideal is female seclusion. This has favoured development of a network among women, the cornerstone of a broader women's organization. "Women have learnt what it means to be members of a network. They can support each other within their families", says Ms. Joelsdotter Berg of SIDA. "This mobilization factor is the major strong point."

Becoming a Visible Financial Provider

Women have started to earn respect by playing a role on stages that were once *terra non grata*, such as selling goods in the market, leasing and cultivating land, and in some cases using modern technology. Trying to give women some control over resources and turning them into decision-makers avoids succumbing to welfare biases often contained in programmes working with women. The more experienced groups are planning micro-enterprises to provide jobs and produce goods from local materials. This partly stems from the emphasis on capital formation from the moment of the first loan.

Letting Women Decide

Saptagram has been able to back down when its assumptions proved wrong. Education is the most telling example. Initially shrugging at the need for education, women eventually demanded classes. Faced with an injustice, women realized that literacy and numeracy were crucial tools that could be used to defend their rights and improve living standards. When they found that the curriculum portrayed them in traditional situations, running against the grain of group discussions, they once again confronted Saptagram with the need to develop a 'gender-oriented' syllabus.

Linking Education to Economic Betterment

Part of the adult education programme's success comes from women's perception that it can improve their living standards. This underlines the importance of tying education to broader rural development, specifically income-generating projects.

Uniting for Change

Women have understood the strength to be gained from unity through their success in confronting injustices. "When women become conscious, they become political", says Kabeer. Group savings and cooperative loans have also strengthened ties between women, increasing their sense of initiative and ultimately giving them greater control over their lives.

The ripple effect of discussions: Through 'awareness-building', women have jointly stood up to injustice and started to see the future in another light. "In the beginning, we would have married off our daughters when they were very young, now we don't", says one group member, reflecting the benefits of 'awareness-building' discussions. Similar reactions crop up with regard to work outside the house, family planning and education, especially of girls.

Field Staff Dedication and Creation of Role Models

Strong bonds are sealed in Saptagram, which has not been spared the clashes inherent in a relatively small and dynamic organization with a political vision and a charismatic person at the top. Yet, there is very low staff turnover. "We have worked in the project for so many years", says one field worker, "that it has become part of us. We would manage somehow, even if Saptagram didn't pay. We are completely involved with the women's lives, their joys and sorrow. We truly want to make them independent. We will never agree to work else where. We are like a family."

Challenges and Perspectives for the Future

The next three years are vital for Saptagram. Born of the vision of one woman, Saptagram is fine-tuning its programmes by investing in better management at senior level and increased supervision of credit at field level. Rather than expand to other parts of the country, the organization has chosen to consolidate its experience in the regions it knows best: "It takes too long to fight power back in the village", reflects Kabeer. "It would also be impossible to maintain the intimate relationship amongst groups and staff if we worked at the national level."

This notion of time is central to Saptagram's movement, for which change can only come from awareness. It is also a difficult notion to espouse in one of the world's poorest countries, where daily survival takes precedence over a longer-term vision.

A report by the Bangladesh Institute of Development Studies on poverty notes that increases in the income of poor households are constantly affected by extreme vulnerability to crisis (natural disaster, illness, etc.). In its aim to make women self-reliant, Saptagram has to remain attuned to the needs of the most deprived while ensuring more mature groups act as agents of change in their community.

Saptagram must continue to build on its expertise and strength as a women's organization to become a reference point in Bangladesh's competitive NGO world. This is beginning to happen: women leaders of Save the Children/USA's women's savings groups are participating in leadership and management training organized by Saptagram. This is a first for both organizations. "We hope to continue working together, sharing ideas and encouraging exchange visits", says Elke Krause, a Save the Children representative.

Similarly, the education programme is of great interest to other NGOs seeking to better integrate adult literacy into their women's programmes, since its impact can be important: "The education programme also forms an excellent basis for other development activities, including employment, health and wider political participation", says OXFAM's Mark Golding. At national level, adult education programmes will become more important. The government has prepared a $4.7 billion 'National Plan of Action for Education for All' that includes a three-year mass education project. Functional literacy and continuing education programmes for adults, particularly for women, are to be established. Existing programmes will be evaluated and literacy centres created in each village by 1995. Saptagram could have input into this drive to reduce illiteracy, especially among women. One of the organization's most valuable insights is that literacy programmes work when women ask for them. It is harder to create and maintain motivation when such programmes are not integrated into a larger development project (income-generating activities, for example).

Economic changes are also pushing more and more women towards towns, a new terrain of work for Saptagram. "If women do not have a basic knowledge of how they will be exploited when they get out of the house, they will be in an inferior position. They need to network", says Eva Joelsdotter Berg of SIDA, stressing the need for adult education. "This is where Saptagram can do wonders." Part of Saptagram's future strength lies in its capacity to identify and open up new job opportunities for women, in which they will earn a reasonable income. The Silk Production Centre is a good example of this capability.

"Our programme is a survival kit, says Kabeer." Women must be organized to defend themselves against exploitation. Saptagram's ongoing challenge is to maintain Professor Kabeer's fundamental and courageous vision of leading the poorest women forward while remaining alert to changing needs, demands and trends in the course of this transformation.

36

THE ROLE OF LITERACY IN THE PROMOTION OF GENDER EQUITY

Dr. Mrs R.H. Daude & Prof. F.S. Idachata

Introduction

The women is a central figure of the family; the position that a woman occupies in the society is so vital that educating a woman benefits the family in particular and the society in general. Magaret Safa (1993) reaffirms this, when she said, "when a woman learns every one benefits." There is therefore a link between women's education and national development through the reduction of fertility rates, the improvement of natural resources management, increased public investments, enhancement of developmental processess, through increased productivity levels and the developing of permanent postive impact on the economy. "The empowerment of a woman is not only an important goal in and of itself, it is also essential to the achievement of sustainable human development" UNDP (1994). That is to say, a woman who is literate is able to expand her learning capabilities through expanded reading, exchange of ideas, and active participation in transformation programmes geared towards the enhancement of the larger society. It is therefore important to state that any society that toys with the education of her women folk toys with the prospect of its National Development.

Nigeria has had its share of neglect of the education of the girl child. This has primarily been due to societal values that place the male child at an advantage when compared to his female counterpart in all aspects of social training especially in the area of formal education, worst of all when society has to make a choice.

One major reason has contributed tremendously to the lopsidedness in the educational structure of the Nigerian society vis-a-vis girls and boys, that is the man made belief that the female is seen as mainly a supporter of the male and accepted as caretaker of the household and nothing more Ijere (1991). She is not considered in any other aspect of societal development even on issues that concern her overall well-being. For example, she is not consulted on health issues that concern her, she is restricted in taking leadership roles, she is discriminated against by financial institutions and governmental agencies and often harrased on the political arena by the larger society.

The problem of lack of genderequity in the Nigerian Society is so real that except individuals and governmental bodies address the issue with all honesty and dedication, the problem will remain within the system for a long time.

Universalization Policies on the Education of Women

There is no doubt that all over the world at one time or another, educational opportunities for both sexes have been biased in favour of the male child (Igbtzu & Ruth (1980), UNESCO (1993), Fafunwa (1994)}. However, the degree of lopsidedness in favour of the male child, differs from country to country. For example, Britain, America, Russia and Germany have given recognition to the need for equity in education for all much earlier than the developing countries, especially Africa where the wind of change manifested late. This development has placed the female child/mother at a disadvantage and has retarded the wheel of progress in some countries of the world. Egunjobi (1990) agreed with the above statement, when she said that "women constitute 70% of the labour force world wide." Regretabily though, "women have less access to education, than men". The United Nations Population Fund (UNFPA) reported that, "Two-thirds of the world's estimated 960 million children denied access to primary schooling, 790 million are girls". Despite these negative observations on the education of girls within the last decade there has been a pressing need the world over to know what women are doing, what they are saying and what people are saying about them. This development ignited the need to re-examing the educational status of women/girls with a view to concretizing and strengthening what obtains in order to achieve the desired equity in educational opportunities for all. This is desirable because education is the bedrock of all forms of development and there is no doubt that gender equity can only be achieved through equal educational opportunities. The crusade for gender equity has been spearheaded by the United Nations, since 1945 to date. The United Nations has organized the following seminars, workshops and conferences for women and for the enhancement of women all over the world.

1945: The UN Charter declares the principles of equal rights for all, without distinction as to race, sex, language or religion.

1946: The Commission on the Status of Women (CSW) established by the UN Economic and Social Council.

1952: The Convention on Political Rights of Women.

1957: The Convention on the Nationality of Married Women.

1962: The Convention on the Consent of Marriage.

1967: The General Assembly adapts the Conventions on the Elimination of all forms of Discrimiation against Women.

1975: The UN observes Inaternational Women's Year. First Women Conference, held in Mexico city.

The Un General Assembly declares 1976-1985 United Nations Decade for Women.

1979: The General Assembly adopts the Convention on the Elimination of all forms of Discrimination against Women.

1980: Second World Conference on Women (Copenhagen, Denmark) adopts a programme of Action for the Second half of the UN Decade for Women.

1981: The Convention on the Elimination of All forms of Discrimination against women comes into force.

1982: The Committee on the Elimination of Discrimination against Women (CEDAW) begins its work.

1985: The Third World Conference on Women (Nairobi, Kenya) adopts the Forward-looking strategies for the Advancement of women to the year 2000.

1990: CSW begins work on reviewing progress towards implementation of the Nairobi forward looking strategies.

1993: World conference on Human Rights (Vienna Austria); recognises Women's rights as human rights and recommends appointment of a special Rapporteur on violence against women. Declaration on the Elimination of violence against women is adopted by the General Assembly.

1994: Regional preparatory process for the Fourth World Conference on Women; regional meetings are held in Indonesia, Argentina, Austria, Jordan and Senegal. International Conference on Population and Development. (Cairo, Egypt); underscores the empowerment and autonomy of Women as the basis for development.

1995: World summit for Social Development (Copenhagen, Denmark) calls attention to the pivotal role of women in addressing the problems of poverty, unemployment and social integration. Fourth World Conference on women (Beijing China).

(Source: Sunday Times, August, 20, 1995.)

Globally, there has been positive response to enhance the empowerment of women through education. It is believed that education will ensure the relaxation of discriminatory policies both in Government and in the Private Sector and a strengthening of societies' awareness to the plight of women.

Education in Nigeria: literacy and the Nigerian Women

Before the Europeans came to Nigeria, all the ethnic groups in Nigeria had their own distinctive cultures, traditions, languages and their indigenous systems of education. Although they all had common educational aims and objectives; methods differed from place to place as dictated by social, economic and geogarphical circumstances {Fafunwa (1971)}. Education at this time was for functionalism, therefore the education of women was geared towards achieving the objective of making them good wives and mothers. The societal orientation militated against the enhancement of women education; for example, where there was always a choice between a boy and a girl, for school enrolment, the boy was given preference. From Table 1 there is a clear disparity on the enrolment of boys and girls in primary schools in Nigeria.

Table 1: Primary Enrolment by Sex, by Region, Nigeria, 1937-1972.

	North				South			
	Girls		Boys		Girls		Boys	
Year	No.	%	No.	%	No.	%	No.	%
1937	18,810	81.8	4,180	18.2	216,979.	84.3	40,55	15.7
1955	129,523	76.8	38,998	23.2	1,024,031	68.7	465,644	31.3
1961	230,500	72.8	85,764	27.2	1,509,868	60.7	977,704	39.3
1966	367,776	70.8	151,088	29.2	1,477,591	58.9	1,029,526	41.1
1972	602,229	70.4	252,237	29.6	2,072,637	58.6	1,464,094	41.4

Source: Colony and Protectorate of Nigeria (1938), Federal of Nigeria (1959), Education in Northern Nigeria, Federation Nigeria, New Nigerian Newspaper (1968,1976b).

Primary education enrolment had increased by five times from 1960 to 1980, while secondary education had increased four times what it was in'1960. The most remarkable increase has been in University enrolment from 1, 395 in 1960 to 53,000 in 1980 representing 53%. In other words these figures suggest hightened awareness of the value of education within society resulting in greater enrolment in schools over time although the drop in figure for 1966 was due to massive movement of Igbos from the North to the South due to the Civil War.

Table 2: Education Enrolments, Nigeria, 1960-80

Year	Primary	Secondary Garmmar	Sec. Tech. & Vocational	Teacher Training	Universities
1960	2,912,618	135,364	5,037	27,908	1,395
1964	2,849,486	205,002	7,702	31,054	6,719
1971	3,894,559	343,313	15,590	38,095	14,371
1973	4,746,808	448,904	22,588	46,951	23,173
1980	11,521,500	1,555,180	177,686	234,680	53,000

Source: Federal Republic of Nigeria 1975, Education in Northern Nigeria, Vol. Tables 16.1-16.5

Table 2 Shows the rapid expansion in school enrolment due to increased awareness of the value of education.

Table 3: Expansion of Primary Education in Northern Nigeria, 1960-1966.

Year	Boys	Girls	Total
1960	206,443	76,405	282,284
1661	230,500	85,764	316,264
1962	262,083	97,851	359,934
1963	295,644	115,062	410,706
1964	323,399	128,920	452,319
1965	381,900	152,300	534,200
1966	366,550	148,860	515,410

Source:C.O. Taiwo (1980 p. 133)

The achievement of the goals of education continued to be vigorously pursued by various state government. However, disparity in enrolment numbers for male and females continued to widen. This laudable task of heightened enrolment in schools got a boost in 1974 on January, 24th when General Gowon said that his government intended to launch UPE (Universal Primary Education) on the 1st of April, the following year (Daily Times, 30th January, 1994).

Government Policies on Education in Nigeria

In trying to highlight the problems that bedeviled the education of women/girls in Nigeria, the contributions of the government in power is vital, especially their educational policies, the implementation processes and the attitude of the Minister of Education at each given time to the education of the female child. This is important because educational policies in Nigeria have been formulated and implemented by the Federal and Status Ministries of Education. The Ministry is financed by the Federal Government and its activities are directed by the Minister and his Director General. Here, the individual preferences of each Minister influence the implementation of any government policy. In other words, policies are formulated, but implementation of these policies depends on the Minister who selects which policies he wishes to pursue to a logical end, In most cases, government functionaries have consistently paid lipservice to educational issues affecting girls/women. Hilda Adefarisin (1992) speaking in her capacity as the President of the National Council for Women Societies stated that, "Government is yet to realise and harness the potential of the Nigerian women". She said policy makers who have mostly been men, and who have benefited from education did not address the issue in question. Table 4 presents ministerial appointments for the educational portfolio from 1970 to 1995. During this period, only two women served as ministers of state, in the ministry of education. It is important to note that the decision in the Federal Ministry of Education are normally taken by the senior minister who has always been a man, and who has not been seriously inclined to pursuing programmes that enhance gender equity in education.

Table 4: Federal Ministers of Education in Nigeria 1970-1995

Regimes	Date	Name of Minister
Gowon	1976	Col. A.A. Ali (He was pioneer Director, NYSC before he became Federal Minister of Education).
Obadanjo	1976	Y.A. Eke
Shagari	1979	Mrs. Ivase (Minister of state for Education)
Buhari	1984	Alhaji A. Ibrahim, SAN
Babangida	1986	Prof. Jibrin Aminu
"	1990	Prof. B. Fafunwa
"	1992	Prof. Nwabueze
Shonekan	1993	Prof. Abraham Imogie
Abacha	1994	Dr. Iyorchia Ayua
"	1995	Dr. M. I. Liman
"	1995	Mrs. Iyabo Anisilowo (Minister for States)

Nevertheless, some regions took the initiative to address gender equity in education in Nigeria, foremost amongst them are the military regimes as indicated in tables 5 and 6 that went a step further to encourage girls/women to develop their capabilities for the benefit of all. A comparison between the Shagari regime, a civilian regime and Babangida's regime a military regime clearly shows the military regime as having played a prominent role in enhancing the upliftment of Nigerian women educationally.

Table 5: Shehu Shagari's Regim: 1979-1983

1. Appointed Mrs. Adenike Oyagbola as Federal Minister for National Planning and Mrs. Ivase Minister for State for Education.
2. Encouraged state government to appoint at least one woman commissioner in their cabinet. During this period 12 state governments appointed women commissioners: Bauchi, Anambra, Sokoto, Bornu, Kano, Niger, Oyo, Lagos, Ogun, Bendel, Gongola and Kaduna. These states are predominantly (NPN) and they had alot of followership in the ruling party, the National Party of Nigeria.
3. More schools were established in the states thus giving room for more enrolment of pupils and an increase in the number of girls that went to school.
4. More adult education programmes for women introduced.
5. Lowering entry grade into Universities for female.

Major Appointments in Favour of Women and Policies for Education of Girls in the Babangida's Administration, 1985-1993

In the Babangida's administration, women were given "token positions in the cabinet of state governments" most state government appointed one women commissioner in their cabinet, Adeferasin (1988). The Babangida administration contributed tremendously to the enhancement of female education in the country. During this regime the following government moves favoured women:

1. Three female permanent secretaries in the Federal Civil Service appointed.
2. The important role the former first lady Mrs. Maryam Babangida played led to the launching of the Better life programme. Mrs. Babangida believes in the enhancement of the status of women.
3. Appointment of one woman commissioner in some states of federation.
4. Appointment of the first female vice-chancellor in the person of prof. Alele-Williams of the University of Benin.
5. Definite educational programmes for girls intensified in Borno, and Sokoto States.
6. More government support for Enhanced Programme in Immunization (EPI), health programmes for the direct benefit of women.
7. Establishment of Peoples' Bank, and the appointment, Mrs. Maria Sokenu as Managing Director, (Peoples' Bank readily gave loans to women and women groups).
8. Appointments of six women to the boards of some Banks.
9. Formation of more women cooperative societies.

10. Access to loan acquisition for small scale businesses from Community Banks all over the federation, from which women benefittes (e.g. gari processing, tailoring, hairdressing and other vocational skills, related business).
11. More women were appointed into some state cabinets for example, Sokoto state appointed four women commissioners (New Nigeria 2nd February, 1995); more women were appointed as Chairman Caretaker Committees for Local Government Areas. Benue State for example appointed three women Caretaker Committee Chairmen for Makurdi, Guma and Gwer Local Government Areas respectively.
12. Review of the JAMB Admission grades for girls and the establishement of more unit schools.
13. Some Northern States such as Bauchi, Kano, Adamawa, Jigawa and Yobe made the education of girls free at all levels.
14. In 1992 three women were appointed into the National Universities Commission.
15. The Babangida Administration established the National Commission for Women at Federal and State levels and the Abacha regime created the Ministry of Women Affiars in1995 and appointed a female Minister to head it.

Positive Effect of Education on the Nigerian Woman

In order to discuss the positive effect of education on the Nigerian women adequately, this paper looks at the Nigerian woman in three categories.

Category One:	The Educated Nigerian Woman
Category Two:	The School Drop-out: Mostly young girls below twenty years of age.
Category Three:	The Rural Women; mostly uneducated with a few having received some form of adult education.

Category One

The educated Nigerian woman is one that has acquired primary, secondary and tertiary education and in some cases tertiary education at the university level. She may be a holder of a Diploma, National Certificate or a holder of several degree certificates, such as Master and (Ph.D) Doctorate of Philospphy in one or more subject areas. She is a professional in her own field. In this case the overall university enrolment for females in Nigerian universities is significant. Out of a total of 10,381 students that applied for B.A. administration in all the universities 2,045 were females (20 percent of applicants). An appreciable number of female students also applied for science based courses. Out of the total number of 27,338 that applied for science, for 1988/89 academic year, 7,411 were females, representing about 25 percent of the total population. All applications for Law indicates that of the total of 7,597 in 1988/89 session, 2,353 were female, a quite remarkable performance. Although JAMB admission each year indicates low intakes for female against male.

However, an appreciable progress on the career line has emerged for Nigerian women. Virtually every job in the private and government sector has an appreciable number of women. For example, the Federal and State Civil Service has a large percentage of women administrators, accountants, secretaries, typists, clearners etc.

On the educational sector there are women lecturers in the universities and colleges of education and many female teachers in primary and secondary schools. For example that in 22 universities in Nigeria, with a total number of 1,526 Professors, Associate Professors and Readers, 65 are females, this figure represents 3.6% of the total number. That is a remarkable achievement, because to become a Professor is the greatest achievement of an academician and every academic, looks forward to becoming a Professor one day. It is therefore a great achievement to observe that, 61 Nigerian women have already achieved this academic height.

Other sectors (public or private) of the economy such as health, the military and police, have been all success stories for the Nigerian women. No matter the number, the presence of women in these organizations serves as evidence of some representation.

Educated Nigerian women realize the importace of having a common front to fight their course. They have therefore formed various organizations to push forward their case. Some of such organizations are as listed below:

A List of Some Women Organizations in Nigeria

1. National Council of Women's Societies (NCWS)
2. National Commission for Women (NCW)
3. National Association of Women Journalists (NAWOJ)
4. Women in Nigeria (WIN)
5. Association of Professional Women Engineers (APWEN)
6. International Federation of Women Lawyers (FIDA)
7. Medical Women Association of Nigeria (MWAN)
8. Professional Insurance Ladies Association (PILA)
9. Society of Women Accountants of Nigeria (SWAN)
10. Association of Lady Pharmacists (ALPs)

11. Nigerian Army Officers' Wives Association (NAOWA)
12. Naval Officers' Wives Association (NOWA)
13. Nigerian Market Women Association (NMWA)
14. Police Officers' Wives Association (POWA)
15. Nigerian Air force Officers' Wives Association (NAFOWA)
16. National Association of Women in Bussines (NAWB)
17. Women Health Research Network in Nigeria (WHERNIN)
18. National Association of Media Women (NAMW)

There are a host of other smaller organizations within the Nigerian Society that are not registered but functional. The political awareness of the Nigerian woman is also tremendous. The Nigerian woman has of recent presented a vibrant front on the political arena that the political scene is going to become alive with more women vieing for elective post in the fourth republic.

Category Two

The school drop-out: Mostly young girls, below twenty years of age.

The Ouagadongou Declaration (1993) recognised that, "There are 26 million African girls out of school and most of them in the rural areas and that this figure is estimated to reach 36 million by the year 2000 and that, women illiteracy rates are over 60%".

The Nigerian young girl is not left out of this predicament. Many girls every year drop out of school. The reason for this could be due to either the parents inability to pay their school fees, or as a result of unwanted pregnancies, or in order to get married. Fatinobi (1990) stated that half of the nummber of girls that graduate from primary school and enroll into secondary each year, end up as drop-outs. This is alarming because, these girls come back to the larger society and society pays for it. Most of them end up as house wives and became permanent liabilities to their spouses. A few of them enrol in local professional training such as hairdressing and tailoring, while a large number end up as farm hands in the villages. This generation of productive female Nigerians are wasted by the larger society. Discussions and interviews conducted indicated that even those who engage in a few years professional trainings, end up not setting up their own business premises because of lack of funds. Government has not addressed the problems of this group and no programme is drawn up to cater for them by government.

Category Three

The Rural Woman: Mostly Uneducted.

"Plant a seed and it shall grow" Mafo (1992); the Nigerian rural woman has been in the forefront in the struggle for better living conditions for her family in particular and the society at large. She constitutes 50% of all the work force in agriculture and animal husandry, as well as engaging in agro-based industries. But like her counterparts in Africa and other parts of the developing country, she is denied almost everything; she doesn't receive formal education, no adequate health care, no conducive shelter, no access to farm impliments that will lighten her labour and she is even denied the opportunity to enjoy the proceeds of her labour. The atmosphere is clumsy for the average Nigerian rural woman with the very little offered by government tagged, "Adult education", until, the launching of the, Better Life for Rural Dwellers' a programme by the former Nigerian first lady Mrs. Maryam Babangida. The target audience was the Nigerian rural woman.

The Better Life for Rural Dwellers

The Better Life for Rural Dwellers (BLRD) sought to improve women's social, economic and political status. The programme has achieved dramatic results since it's inception in 1987. To date the programmes has achieved the following:

7,635	Cooperatives
997	Cottage industries
1,751	New farms and gardens
487	New shops and markets
419	Women's centres
613	Social welfare programmes.

Source: Journal of African Farmer, Number 8, March, 1993 p. 29-34.

Nigerian Women under Mrs. Babangida's leadership were empowerment to improve their own lives through various programmes in Adult education, primary health care, agriculture, trade, craft and food processing. The Nigerian rural women are currently moving towards self-sufficiency and in some cases are in the vangaurd of agricultural production in their areas, increasing food production and reducing post harvest waste.

CONCLUSION

Forward Looking Strategy for Nigeria

There is no problem without solution options therefore, the problems enumerated in this paper as they affect Nigerian women have solutions. But solutions in themeselves can became major problems if appropriate implementation modalities of suggested solutions are abused. Gender problems in Nigeria can be eliminated completely if the society is sensitized to see and accept gender problems as problems that *AFFECT NOT ONLY WOMEN BUT ALSO MEN*. One basic step in achieving gender equity in Nigeria is the elimination of lipservice by individuals and governments when addressing gender issues.

Poverty, unemployment, under-employment, employment in low paying jobs, high fertility, non participation in training activities, non-awareness of basic legal rights and human rights, low representation in decision making processes at all levels and low level of educational attainments for women can be minimized and finally eradicated if the following suggestions are carried out with sincerity of purpose.

Poverty: Government and NGo's should give women financial assistance, expose women to technical know how allow women access to information, allow women full participation in the planning stage and give women fair share of the proceeds of their labour. This can be achieved through dealing directly with women.

Unemployment: Expose women to training programmes, encourage women to participate in public enterprise and give women adequate representation in civil service jobs. A percentage of the civil service employment should be researved for women.

Employment in low paying jobs. Abolish written and unwritten policies that assign certain professions to women and give women the freedom to develop their capabilities fully in areas that interest them. For example, women should be encouraged to take-up training in the operation of farm impliments such as tractors operation, director maintainance, motor mechanics services carpenters, masons building engineers, and a host of other professions that had in the past been dominated by men.

On high fertility rate of women, government should also direct family planning campaigns at the men, who usually dictate the number of children a woman should have for him (the man). High fertility rates among Nigerian women will continue except government encourages men not to have more than four children, regardless of the number of wives. Such campaigns should be mounted in all native languages for easy assimilation by the general public.

On low or no participation in training; traditional restriction, curtailing movement of women should be abolished and a law or decree promulgated to deal with anybody that tempers with the rights of another human being. Government and NGO's should mount public enlightenment programmes on television and radio to educate the public on the importance of harnessing the potentials of women.

Non awareness of legal rights and human rights is a major problem that not only affects Nigerian women but also the men. Most Nigerian are not adequately informed on when and how to expercise their legal rights. Justice Oputa (1995) stated that, "at least 50% of Nigerians hardly exercise their legal rights". He stated further, "everything has a corresponding duty which must be stressed along with rights, said he, the legal status of the Nigerian women leaves much to be desired and our customary laws worsen the situation by practicing dehumanizing practices which cannot be eradicated with clubs and swords nor by public outcry but by higher methods such as education". To crease an appreciable legal awareness amongst Nigerian women, our institutions of higher learning should as a matter of urgency admit all qualified females who apply to study Law each year. Female lawyers should take it upon themselves to enlighten their rural sisters who are suppressed by societal traditions that can be challenged in the court of law. The federal government through the Nigerian Bar Association in collaboration with NGO's should appoint legal firms who will offer free legal services to women. This will go along way in creating legal awareness and encouraging women to seek redress in courts of law when need be.

The low level of educational attainment amongst women has been with us for along time, efforts made so far to uplift that, through free education for girls, adult education, better life and family support programmes have only exposed the gravity of the problem rather than solving them. The situation is so bad that, Mrs. Abacha at Beijing (1995) stated that, "the path to follow is humaning our Societies" in other words if society is humane towards everybody, equal opportunities for all will prevail.

Massive enlightenment on the importance of educating the girl child should be mounted in daily papers, television and of radio by Government. NGO's should also sponsor programmes that cater for the girl child in all states of the federation at subsidised rates. Women bodies should educate, their rural sisters on the need to send their daughters to school instead of getting them into early marriages.

Finally suggestions for projects that will address probelms of target groups in Nigeria are made below.

If carefully implemented, target groups within Nigeria will benefit from these suggested projects resulting in the upliftment of the standard of life of the average Nigerian family, there is no doubt that Nigerians can make things happen, idachaba (1992) identified the source of strength of the Better Life Programme, "which has its major source of success in the power that it commands at the highest level of political authority in the states". In other words every programme can be a success if supported genuinely by political authority.

These suggested programmes can go along way in promoting gender equity in Nigeria if they are given adequate political backing both in nigeria and abroad.

Suggested Projects that will Address Problems of Target Groups in Nigeria if Adequately Implimented

1. Pre-school Children

Government should promulgate a decree banning child abuse and exploitation. Children found hawking instead of being in school should be arrested and their parents or guardians prosecuted. Each guardian should by law send his ward to school, at least primary school. A monitoring team should be set up by government. Financial commitments: Government should set up an agency to monitor child abuse. About N500,000.00 will adequately train, equip and keep afloat members of the task force.

2. Girls and Women in Romote Rural Areas

Provide access to educate girls/women by building at least one girls school in each locality and one adult education centre for rural women. Design and provide training facilities for handicraft, how to use farm impliments, food processing and storage marketing strategies and create awareness for active participation in community meetings. N200,000.00 from each Local Government with additional support of N200,000.00 from the Federal Government and half a million from NGO's will adequately create reasonable impact in rural area in Nigeria.

3. Drop outs from the Educational System, Pregnant Teenagers, Girl Mothers and Abused Women and Girls

Set up professional training centres in each local Government Area for these category: Tailoring, hairdressing, poultry farming, poultry feed production, etc. Small scale farming, trading (buying and selling) and create opportunities for eventual return to school if so desired. Financial implications: Each state of the federation should have one training centre and should contribute half of the required amount of N 500,000.00 for purchase of equipment and payment of salaries of staff. Each state of the federation will be required to provide a suitable building as part of its contribution to this laudible cause.

4. Girls who because of Traditional Customs and Practices are

Prevented from going to or continuing school after the age of Puberty.

Suggested solution is as in No. (1) above.

5. Illiterate Girls/Women who Never had the Chance of Schooling and Remain Unaware of the need to Learn.

A massive public awareness campaign in native languages on the need and advantages of schooling:

Items for campaigns for each local government.

Translators: (Human Resources), Radio Broadcast: Radios to be distributed to each locality. Town public meetings at least once a month with the major objective of enlightenment campaigns. Implementation Team:

Costing: N100,000.00 for purchase of Transistor Radio, 30 vehicles from NGO's for the imlementation team one for each state of the federation.

6. *Girls/Women with Little Schooling Bogged down by Traditional Roles and Excessive Work Load in the Homes and the Farms*

Suggested remedy as in (2) above.

7. Traditional Leaders (Religious, Cultural and Community)

Suggested remedy: Massive public awareness in form of commercial jingles on television, television soaps operas, radio broadcast, posters, film shows handbills on the impediments created by rigid traditional values and the appeal for traditional leaders to eradicate such traditions through the acceptance of change in societal cultures and tradition. The federal government should set up a handsome reward of N100,000.00 for each traditional leader who relaxes effectively discriminating traditional values that hamper the empowerment of girls/women of all categories.

Finally, the world will be a better place for all if both men and women Collectively address the issue of gender equity, with all honesty and the serousness it deserves.

References

Africa who's who (1991) p.p. 266, 267 & 6468

Anietie U. (1990) "Women in Nigeria", Newswatch Magazine pp. 22-42

Aneittoe S.A.T. & Jaja S.O. (1991) "Margaret Ekpoilioness in Nigerian Political",

African Leadership form, pp. 127-162.

Babs Fafunwa (1974) History of Education in Nigeria, George Allen & Unwin Limited London, pp. 3-18.

Bolanle Awe (1992) "Nigerian Women in Historical Perspective", Polygraphic Ventures Limited, Ibadan, pp. 15-45.

Champion Woman (1995) "Obstacles to women Empowerment", Daily chmpion, August, 3rd, pp 17.

Champion Woman (1955) "Women fight sexual Unequality", Daily Champion, September, 21st pp 15.

Egunjobi (1990) "The contribution of Women in Addressing the Food Question" A paper presented at a National Seminar on the food question held at the university of Agriculture, Makurdi.

Idachaba F.S. (1992) "Agriculture and Rural Development Under the Babangida Administration". (1990) Convocation Address

Igliezin & Ross (1980) "Women in the World, A comparative Study- Studies in Comparative Politics", Clio Books, Oxford, pp. 1-105.

Ijere M. O. (1991) "Women in Nigerian Economy". Acena Publishers, Enugu, pp. 1-122.

Joint Admission and Matriculation Boare (1985), "Annual Report and Accounts" pp 63-78.

Mafo R.C. (1992) "Two African Women Share 1991 Africa Prize", Journal of African Farmer, Vol. 3,pp 15-17

"Women Seek Control of the Land they Farm", Journal of African Farmer, Vol. 3 pp. 2a-34.

"Women Work: African's Precious Resource", Journal of African Farmer, Vol. 5 pp. 23-30.

Marie C. (1993) "When Women Learn, Every one Benefits", Journal of African Farmer, No. 8 March 1993, pp. 15.

Maryam Abacha (1995) "The part to follow is, humanising our societies", Daily Times, September 19th, pp. 19

National Universities Commission (1992) "Annual Report", pp. 2-4.

National Universities Commission (1993) "Statistical digest on Nigerian Universities 1988-1992", Abuja, Nigeria.

Oputa C. (1995) "Legal Status of Women in Nigeria" VANGUARD, 19th July, pp.7,
Osande E. (1995) "Gender Gains at Beijing" Daily Times, 16th September, pp. 20

Taiwo C. O. (1980) "Education in Nigeria" Nigerian Press pp. 132.

Tamuno & Atanda (1989) "Nigeria Since Independence, the first 25 years", pp. 1-35, 220-245.

Tijjani A. & David Williams (1981) "Shehu Shagari: My Vision of Nigeria", pp 20-51

United Nations (1995) "640 million Women are illiterate", Daily Champion 11th July, pp. 1.

VBO Internatioanl Limited: "Giant Strides" (1987) Vol. 3, pp. 11-74, 79 and 84.

37

FUNCTIONAL LITERACY: A PATH FOR EMPOWERING WOMEN AND GIRLS

Dickson Mwansa

Introduction

The problem of illiteracy in Africa requires concerted action for its eradication because of the high levels and big numbers that unequally affect rural areas and women. The World Conference on Education All held at Jomtien Conference recommended a provision of basic education to adults, youth and children. In the actual implementation of EFA adult literacy has not received much attention and the focus has shifted to basic education because of the assumption that through formal education illiteracy can be wiped out. Provision of more schools and teachers is no guarantee that illiteracy would be eradicated because illiteracy is interrelated to many other factors that are attitudinal, social, cultural, economic and political.

This paper:

a. Examines African literacy in global context
b. Highlights some of problems inherited over time
c. Analyses the problem as it affects the continent
d. Provides an outlook on functional literacy projects and programmes
b. Highlights some innovations in terms of successes and failures
d. Discusses some issues that affect the provision of literacy education

This paper relied heavily on available literature on literacy education and the experience emanating from some of the research done in my own country Zambia (Mwansa, 1994; 1995 and 1996).

Literacy in Africa: The Global Context

Africa has the second largest number of illiterates after Asia. In absolute terms in 1970 there were 540 million illiterates in Asia, 139 million in Africa and 63 million in the rest of the world (Table 1). In 1990 the figures increased to 654 million for Asia, 168 million for Africa and dropped to 62 million for the rest of the world.

Table1: Number of Illiterates Aged 15 and Over in Asia, Africa and the Rest of the World 1970, 1980, 1990 (Estimates)[1]

	1970	1980	1990
Asia	540	599	654
Africa	139	156	168
Rest of the World	63	59	62

Source: UNESCO. Literacy 81: Eight Hundred Million Illiterate Eight Hundred Million Starying in the World. Paris UNESCO, 1981.

In terms of per centage change, Africa's level of illiteracy shows a decline from 71.1% in 1970 to 47.4% in 1990, and by the end of the century it is bound to decrease to 35.2% (Table II). The decline can be attributed to increasing provision of primary education. However, female levels of illiteracy are still higher than male levels and by the end of the century there will be almost twice as many female illiterates as male on the continent and rural illiteracy is higher than urban illiteracy and the enrolment gap between boys and girls remains at 20%. By the year 2000 the gap between male and female literates will be reduced to a point where the ratio will be almost one to one (see Table II).

Table II: Illiteracy in Africa. Age 15 + 1970-2000[2]

	1970	1980	1985	1990	2000
Population					
Male/Female	196.6	259.1	299.9	348.0	478.5
Male	96.1	127.3	147.4	171.5	236.4
Female	100.5	131.8	152.2	176.5	242.1
Literates					
Male/Female	56.9	102.9	137.7	183.1	310.1
Male	37.4	64.3	83.7	107.7	173.3
Female	19.4	38.5	54.1	75.7	136.8
Illiterates					
Male/Female	139.7	156.2	161.9	164.9	168.4
Male	58.6	62.9	63.8	63.7	63.0
Female	81.1	93.3	98.1	101.2	105.4

Illiteracy Rate(%)					
Male/ Female	71.1	60.0	54.0	47.4	35.2
Male	61.0	49.5	43.3	37.2	26.7
Female	80.7	70.8	64.5	57.3	43.5

Source: UNESCO. Office of statistics. A Summary Statistical Review of Education in the World. 1960-1982, Paris: UNESCO, 1984.

The key areas requiring urgent attention are female illiteracy and rural illiteracy. The decisions concerning illiteracy which leaders of the continent have to make will be influenced by a set of complex political, economic and linguistic issues. The map of illiteracy for the continent overlap with many variables. According to the UNDP report of 1995, Sub Saharan Africa had the highest infant mortality rate (97 per 1,000), lowest life expectancy (51.3 years) and the second lowest enrollment (36%) after South East Asia (UNDP, 1995: 214). Further, areas which have the highest levels of illiteracy have experienced frequent military coups and inter-ethic clashes. These are places where, in the absence of a literate and articulate citizenry, power changes hands between military and civilian elites with little or no regard for what citizens can do.

Inherited Problems

In the 1960s, 1970s and the 1980s when African countries gained independence they inherited large populations of "illiterates" because literacy education was never widely spread to the larger populations. The colonial powers tended to accentuate discrimination in many ways (Lind, 1995). For example Mozambique, Angola and Guinea Bissau emerged with illiteracy levels between 85% and 90% among indigenous populations (Marshall, 1984 : 36) while Tanzania and Zambia had illiteracy levels of 75% and 61% respectively (Mpogolo, 1980; Mwanakatwe, 1968).

Though the failure to eradicate illiteracy can not be squarely blamed on the colonial past, the fact that colonialists did not do as much in spreading education or literacy to a larger segment of the population left a heavy burden to be shouldered by the new leaders of the continent.

Second, when the new governments came into power, priority was given to child education and the development of much needed human power, and adult illiteracy did not receive much attention. The 1960 Addis Ababa conference for African Ministers of Education put emphasis on increasing the educational infrastructure and school enrolments.

Literacy began to receive more attention after the 1965 UNESCO's Teheran Ministers of Education Conference. UNESCO's World Experimental Literacy programme carried out between 1966 and 1974 in which a number of African countries (Algeria, Ethiopia, Guinea, Madagascar,

Mali, Sudan, Tanzania) took part (Jones, 1990: 56) gave literacy education an added visibility.

In the 1970s when education for young people began to face problems and some countries began educational reforms, adult education started to receive attention. The world bank supported alot of programmes which focused on provision of basic needs. Countries like Tanzania saw the value of adult education and instituted campaigns that were multimedia and multi sectoral in content.

In the 1990s. educational efforts have eschewed literacy education and the problem remains intractable. In 1995 (See Table III) fourteen countries had less than 40% level of literacy-seven of which are found in Sahelian region. The highest concentrations of illiteracy were in Ivory Coast, Benin, Guinea, Liberia, Gambia to Mauritania, Ethiopia, Mozambique and Burundi.

Five countries had literacy levels between 40-50%, four of them are former French and Portuguese colonies. The majority of the countries (13) had literacy levels falling between 60% and 83%. Highest levels of literacy are found Zimbabwe (83), Madagascar (81.4) Mauritius (81.1%).

Countries with literacy levels between 60% and 83% should be considered literate. History shows that at the time of Industries development the industrialized countries of the world had reduced illiteracy to levels below 40% (Cipolla, 1969).

The response of the leadership and governments of Africa to the eradication of illiteracy has varied and depends on the model of social economic development that was followed particularly in the 1970's. The reality is that the rhetoric given to literacy education does not match the practical support that is accorded to literacy education.

Functional Literacy and its Relationship to Girl Child Education

According to UNESCO a person is functionally literate "when he has acquired the essential knowledge and skills which enable him or her (personal emphasis) to engage in all those activities in which literacy is required for effective functioning of his/her group or community" (UNESCO, 1971). The inability of women to function effectively is due to the marginalization they have suffered through socialised and institutionalised discrimination.

Equally the problems affecting the girl child are attributable to discrimination and unfair treatment in the home, at school and in the larger society. In recent years problems affecting the girl child have been identified as early marriage, pregnancy, cultural attitudes, poverty on the part of the parents, preference for boys' education, harassment from the boys

Table III: Distribution of Literacy (%) By country 1995

20-30%		30-40%		40-50%		50-60%		over 60%	
Niger	12.4	Senegal	30.5	Namibia	40.0	Guinea Bissua	51.7	Tanzania	64.1
Burkina Faso	17.4	Ethiopia	32.7	Angola	42.5	Nigeria	52.5	Congo	70.7
Mali	27.2	Burundi	32.9	Sudan	42.7	Central Af. Re	53.9	Swaziland	74.0
Sierra Leone	28.2	Benin	32.9	Djibouti	43.2	Malawi	53.9	Zaire	74.1
		Guinea	33.0	Chad	44.9	Rwanda	56.0	Kenya	74.5
		Liberia	35.4			Uganda	58.6	Zambia	75.2
		Gambia	35.6			Gobon	58.9	Eq. Guin	75.3
		Mauritania	36.2			Cameroon	59.6	Sychelles	77.0
		Ivory Coast	36.6			Ghana	60.0	S. Africa	80.6
		Mozambique	36.9					Mauritius	81.1
								Madaga.	81.4
								Zimbabwe	83.0

Source: UNDP. (1995). Human Development Report 1995. New York: Oxford Univerity Press.

- After writing, each member reads aloud what he/she wrote before other member of the groups. The others listen to him/her to classify according to the content area. All the members of the groups classify the small sheets of paper (made by each member) and stick them on bigger sheet of paper.

- Each area is arranged like a fan (or a circle) and all the contents written in small sheets of papers are combined to come up with a brief summary. The number of the sheets of paper for each are will be an indicator for reference in the determination of the needs (or problems) to be prioritized.

- The first map on needs (or problems) is completed. After that, use the same procedure to form a second map on the solutions for these priority needs or problems. Based on the map of solutions and national goals, a curriculum or a learning material for the target group is developed.

3. Section of Themes or Topics

When selecting topics, developers must use priority needs and give these topics attractive titles so as to draw the attention of the learners and urge them to look at and read.

The topics can belong to any of the three following groups:

- The various roles of women;
- Techniques for generating income, management, services;
- Agricultural techniques, child caring methods.

4. Determine Specific Objectives

After selecting topics the objectives should be determined before writing the materials. The objectives should be based on the circumstances and needs of the target groups. Specific objectives will be the basis for the selection of contents and the ways of presenting contents and writing materials. The objectives should be selective and specific as too many objectives will make the focus of the contents diluted.

5. Selection of Contents

Selection of contents should be based on and consistent with the objectives. Therefore the clearer the objectives defined the easier the selection of contents. Moreover, careful selection of contents will facilitate the writing of materials in the following stage.

To evaluate the relevance of the contents to be selected, the following questions can be used:

- Is sex stereo-typing avoided in the content?
- Is there a content of shared responsibilities between men and women?
- Are women described positively and with adequate number?
- Is the status of women enhanced?
- Are the rights of women affirmed?
- Are women stimulated to raise questions?

6. Selection of Type and Format

Format to be selected should be compatible with the objectives and contents and based on the actual situation of the target audiences, their concerns and their literacy level and skills.

Type and format of materials used to reflect the content can take the forms of booklets, leaflets, picture. Slogans, cassette tape, video tapes, slide films, plastic films, game, and puppet shows. For each type, one of the following forms can be used: stories with various illustrations, questions and answers, folksongs, long poems, pictorial funny stories, poems, simple plays or the combination of these.

7. Developing Outline and the First Draft

When writing the first draft, it is necessary to determine the size of reading material, number of pages, the length of the text, the number of words, size of word, size and type of illustration picture, language to be used, the balance between words, illustration pictures and the space in each page, relevance and attractiveness to learners.

When the objective are clearly defined, contents and format are selected, outline and the first draft are developed, the problem of writing the text is not a difficult one.

However, it is necessary to pay attention to the presentation of stories so as to make it reasonable and realistic, its evolution and characters should be natural, the dialogue in the stories should conform to the surroundings of the users. After writing, the authors should use the above-mentioned criteria to evaluate whether the contents are appropriate to women's issues and problems.

8. Illustrations

Illustration preparation is a very necessary step in developing the learning materials for women with limited reading skills. Illustration makes the materials more attractive and it can draw the attention of the learners. It also helps to communicate an intended message to the user and makes the materials more understandable.

Therefore illustrations should be carefully prepared and conform to the surrounding of the target audience to ensure the attractiveness. They should not contradict the text and should supplement to the text.

9. Field Testing

Field testing is a necessary step to revise and finalize the draft. When testing, the following questions can be used.

- Are the themes or topics related to the needs identified?
- Do the objectives selected satisfy the needs?
- Is the objective of enhancing the status of women attained?
- Do the contents cover all the objectives?

For illustrations, the following questions can be asked:

- Are they clear?
- Do they help the text?
- Are they appropriate to the literacy level of the learners?
- Do they supplement the texts?
- Are they attractive?

10. Finalize the Draft

This is the last step before printing the materials and distributing them to the users.

II. SOME PRINCIPLES IN DEVELOPING THE LITERACY LEARNING MATERIALS FOR WOMEN

When developing literacy learning materials, the following principles should be paid attention to:

a. The Principle of Consistency

Objectives, contents and style of presentation should be consistent with each other.

Example 1: If the objective is to give information on a certain topic, then the content should consist of all necessary and relevant information concerning that topic. The presentation should take the form of a simple story so as to enable the learners to easily understand that information. The presentation should also be systematic.

Example 2: AIf the objective is the permeation of a certain attitude toward a special practice then the content should bring out the positive aspects of that practice or the negative effects if that practice is not realized. The content should be presented in a way that will not impose on the learners but should be indirect subtle and persuasive. The presentation should arouse emotion but not intellect. The content should be presented through a play or a plight of characters rather than an insipid story.

b. The Principle of Attractiveness

Style of presentation should be attractive, interesting and arousing. The contents should be presented in a way that will draw the attention of the target audiences. They look at the material, take it up, turn over the next page then begin to pay attention, read and continue to read to the last page.

c. The Principle of Appropriateness

The contents and style of presentation should be appropriate to the life style of the target audiences in terms of physical, economic, social, political aspects, cultural environment, level of skills, benefits and needs. The more the materials are appropriate to the learners the more they attract the learners.

d. The Principle of Promoting Ability

This principle is aimed at helping this target group enhance their ability (that does not mean to promote and encourage women to take up arms or find ways to dominate men). Promoting and encouraging the learners to analyze their status and circumstances, raise questions and find out answers, think over and decide, actively promote their ability, have self-confidence to change and be the master of their life. Without ability women are less hopeful to improve their status and circumstances in society.

The objectives, contents and style of presentation should focus on the ability of women (illustrations of women should be best presented). Women should be described in a positive aspect, in their numerous roles. They should be described as those who dare to make decision and have authority. It is necessary to avoid sexism and sex stereotyping.

CONCLUSION

Developing learning materials for women with limited reading skills is a significant work. Because whatever we write affects the knowledge, skills, viewpoint, system of values, awareness and behavior of the target group. These, in their turn, affect the family life, community of women and the whole society. Therefore, if we are not careful in writing (for example: if we only describe women in passive, inherent, stereotyped role as the wife, house wife and mother), we will consolidate the cultural and social system that held back women in a low status. We should always be clear about the concept women in development and always keep in mind the following questions: Why do we write? (objective), What do we write? (content), and How do we write? (style of presentation).

22

ANALYSIS OF TOTAL LITERACY CAMPAIGN PRIMERS

Ila Patel

Curriculum research in adult education is a neglected area of inquiry among researchers in India and elsewhere. Unlike the extensive curriculum of formal education, the curriculum of adult literacy programs is very limited and fragmentary. Nevertheless, adult education is an integral part of the larger system of education in society and is conditioned by the existing context of society. Furthermore, curriculum of adult education is characterized by selectivity, involving choices of what to teach. This selective tradition of knowledge in turn highlights the ideological nature of adult literacy curriculum.

While research evidence on gender issues in adult literacy in India is incomplete, existing literature highlights how literacy primers reinforce patriarchal roles of women as wives and mothers, and ignores women's active participation in the economy. An analysis of seven literacy primers used by the government agencies and non-government organizations in North India by Bhasin (1984) showed that the content focused primarily on housework, child care and family planning. Patel (1986) in a detailed study of Gujarati literacy primers for women reveals the similar trend. She argued the despite lip service to "integrating" women in the development process, the primers ignored women's role as productive workers and active citizens, and focused exclusively on the domestic and reproductive spheres of women's lives.

Against the background of paucity of research on adult literacy curriculum from the feminist perspective, this paper focuses on the study of how gender ideology is articulated in literacy primers that are used in the government-sponsored Total Literacy Campaigns (TLC) in Gujarat. Discussion in this section is divided into three sections. The first section highlights the context of curriculum development for the Total Literacy Campaigns in Gujarat. General characterization of male and female characters is discussed in the second section. The third section examines the nature of gender ideology through a detailed analysis of the content of literacy primers and shows how the text marginalizes women's productive role and reinforces their domestic and reproductive roles.

The Context of Curriculum Development

How is the adult curriculum designed in the Total Literacy Campaigns in Gujarat? Who actually participates in the process of curriculum development? Before examining the content of adult literacy curriculum, it is important first to understand the context of curriculum development at the national and state levels.

In India, the central government defines the adult education policy and to a large extent, finances large-scale programs of adult education. It maintains hegemonic control over knowledge-production in adult education by financing State Resource Centres (SRCs) that produce literacy primers and other materials for illiterates and ensures that materials produced at the regional level is approved at the national level. The central government also articulates the general conceptual approach that stipulates the process of curriculum development, and national goals and values as espoused by the educational policy. By doing so, it maintains its control over the content of adult literacy curriculum.

Nevertheless literacy curriculum and materials are designed by local curriculum designers at the state-level on the basis of general guidelines and parameters set by the government at the national level. Development of teaching and learning materials at the state-level also enables local curriculum designers and the state to incorporate their world views. Thus, literacy primers contain explicitly ideology of the nation-state but at the same time also constitute ideological orientations of local curriculum designers that often contradict the former.

The adult literacy curriculum of the TLCs has been shaped by the broader context of the program. It was the National Educational Policy (1986) that first emphasized promotion of adult literacy as an important area of national concern in order to prepare the literate labor force for the modernizing economy. The National Literacy Mission imparted a new sense of urgency in tackling the problem of eradication of illiteracy and provided impetus to the mass approach to literacy by mobilizing and harnessing all sections of society (Directorate of Education 1988). Apart from promotion literacy, the NLM also stressed linking adult education with national goals and inculcating the values of national integration, conservation of environment, observation of small family norms and promotion of women's equality.

Furthermore, to promote rapid learning of basic literacy skills, the NLM articulated the technocratic approach to literacy learning, known as the Improved Pace and Content of Learning (IPCL) and prepared a detailed guideline for designing literacy curriculum and materials in the TLCs (Directorate of Adult Education 1993). The major thrust of the technocratic approach to literacy learning remains on rote learning than acquisition of critical thinking and analysis. Hence, the programmatic focus of the NLM has remained on imparting cognitive literacy skills despite including functionality and awareness in the definition of adult education.

Sample Literacy Primers

In Gujrat, three literacy primers—Janchetana Vachanmara (1,2 and 3) were prepared by the State Resource Center at Gujarat Vidyapeeth in standard Gujrati on the basis of the IPCL approach stipulated by the NLM. To develop locally relevant literacy primers, the Total Literacy Campaign gives some flexibility in developing the district-specific literacy primers in collaboration with local curriculum designers, women's groups and non-government organizations. However in Gujarat no locally-designed primers have been used in the TLCs. To continue the control of SRC over knowledge-production in literacy campaigns, the State Literacy Mission Authority of Gujarat stipulated the use of only SRC primers in TLCs. The SRC primers have been designed primarily by curriculum designers affiliated with Gujarat Vidyapeeth and other Gandhian non-government organizations in the process of curriculum development in Gujarat was minimum.

Each primer consists of several lessons and four literacy tests where each lesson can be broadly divided into three parts: visuals the main text, and exercises. The primary material for analysis consists of visuals in the beginning of each lesson, the main text of a lesson and an exercise for ending and writing comprehension towards the end of a lesson. The analysis in this section is based on 44 visuals, the main text of 35 lessons and 29 exercises.

In general, the content of literacy primers in Gujarat can be broadly divided into four areas, namely development, social issues, national integration, and equality (see Table 22.1). The major thrust of the literacy primers for total campaigns in Gujarat is on imparting development-oriented messages. Nearly three-fourths of lessons (26 of 35 lessons) are on development and though equality and national integration are stated as core values in the curriculum, each one of them are conveyed explicitly in only two and three lessons respectively. The content area of social issues has very limited coverage through four lessons only.

As the primers are designed for both, men and women, it is assumed that all the lessons in the primers address to both sexes. Although women are identified as an important target group in the Total Literacy Campaign and women's equality is stressed as one of the core values by the National Literacy Mission, women's issues are assigned low priority in the literacy primers. Only 6 out of 35 lessons (17%) specifically deal with women's issues, such as equal wages, girl's education, dowry and age at marriage.

Profile of Characters

Representation of male and female characters in the primers appears somewhat equal. Among the characters in the primers, there are 151 males compared to 154 females while the text depicts more girls than boys.

Appearance of characters in the visuals and the text indicate that on the whole primers have portrayed rural characters where among 308 characters, 216 (70 per cent) appear to be rural. Most often, neither visual portrayal of characters nor their characterization in the text gives us enough clues to assess their social class. Social class of only 101 characters can be identified mostly on the basis of landholdings, social status and occupational background described in the text and occasionally from appearance and dwellings in the visuals. Nevertheless, more characters appear to be "prosperous" (21 per cent) than "poor" (12 per cent). There is no significant difference in representation of the social class of male and female characters.

Similarly, limited cues are given in the primers to interpret cultural and religious background of characters. Although an attempt is made in visuals and the text of a few lessons to depict multi-religious comminity, Hindu characters dominate the primers. About 80 per cent of characters in the primer can be identified as Hindus. Among non-Hindu characters, more male characters and more Muslim characters are shown. Except in one lesson (Lesson 1 in Primer 2) that depicts a tribal family, no attempt is made in the primers to portray ethnic minority groups other than religous minorities. If we define the ethnic style of dressing prevalent in rural areas and among specific cultural or religous groups as "traditional", then most characters in the visuals (86 per cent) appears to be in "traditional" dress.

In general, educational background and marital status of most characters cannot be inferred. Among educated characters (14 in the visual and 20 in the text), there is slightly more females than males. On the other hand, the text have shown more married women characters than men.

In summary, general representation of demographic and socio-economic background of characters does not indicate a strong gender bias in characterization. However, further examination of the portrayal of principal characters in the primers reveal gender stereotypes.

Portrayal of Principal Characters

Principal characters are the protagonists through whom main messages are conveyed in each lesson. They can be identified from the visuals and the text of 32 lessons of the primers. In Gujarati literacy primers, women are not invisible as protagonists as the primer has at least made an attempt for positive portrayal of women through principal characters, who are shown as conveying information on 13 themes in the content areas of development, social issues and equality. While the visuals and the text give us limited information about the demographic and socio-economic background of protagonists, a cursory look at the main concerns and activities reveals gender stereotypes in the characterization.

The content area of development has received highest attention in Gujarati primers. Development-related themes are conveyed predominantly by male characters, who are depicted as knowledgeable, progressive and modern. Specifically, agriculture, cooperation and environment are exclusively the domain of male protagonists. Invisibility of women characters in these key development sectors gives us the impression that women are ignorant, traditional and lack new knowledge to play a role of a protagonists in these areas. Even when women are portrayed as protagonists in the development sector, conveying information on 9 sub-themes, their roles are restricted to conveying messages on "women-centered" topics, mostly in the areas of health and hygiene and girl's education. Thus, women protagonists are perceived as knowledgeable only in areas that deal with their traditional role of caring and nurturing the family. Even in the content area of social issues, women protagonist discuss the topics, such as dowry and alcoholism, that relate to their marital and family life. On the other hand, role of men as protagonists is not restricted to production-oriented development sector. men in the family (as a father or a son) are more frequently shown as informing and advising family members about issues such as marriage, sanitation, smokeless chulcha and dowry, than the other way around.

Further analysis of interaction patterns of male and female protagonists in the public and private spheres reveal subtle gender differences. Men protagonists advise and inform the community, involving both the sexes. In contrast, women protagonists mostly address a group of women (for example, mahila mandal, neoliterates in a literacy class, village women, etc.) in the public places.

Thus while the primers have a least made an attempt for positive portrayal of women through principal characters, they are however confined primarily to the areas, such as population control, health and hygiene and education, which are perceived predominantly the domain of women. Invisibility of women protagonists in productive sphere and in the larger community makes their role limiting. Although women protagonists are shown as interacting with men in public spaces and in the family, their role is restricted mostly to advising and informing women on the women-centered topics. Such characterizations of male and female protagonists reinforces the existing stereotypes that women are knowledgeable only in a limited range of subjects relating to women's lives and can only influence women.

Marginalizing Women's Productive Role

The primers used in the Total Literacy Campaigns show women characters as engaged in several economic activities. What is striking is not the invisibility of women's work, but overall marginality of their productive role where women's economic activities are often depicted as supplementary or secondary.

Despite women's active participation in agriculture in Gujarat, marginality of women is very striking in the lessons on agriculture. These lessons reinforce existing sexual division of work while making women's participation in farming secondary. Furthermore, visual representation of activities of men and women in the fields reflect prevalent sexual division of agricultural work. In general, men are shown as engaged in primary farming activities, such as ploughing, digging, spraying pesticides, driving a tractor, etc. while women are engaged in secondary agricultural activities, like picking vegetables and assisting in unloading the manure from the cart. On the other hand, except two lessons on agricultural labor that portray women as engaging in work and demanding wages, women's participation in agriculture is almost invisible in the text of these lessons. Not a single lesson on agriculture makes a reference to women as farmers or show them as participants in decision-making pertaining to agriculture. Exchange of agricultural information is primarily between male farmers. Thus, women as productive workers in agriculture remains more or less invisible in the primers.

In addition to agriculture, women are shown as engaged in income-generation activities in the lessons on cooperatives, labor, etc. Specifically, two lessons on the themes of self-employment (Lessons 2 and 11 in the Primer 2) reveal gender-bias in economic activities of male and female characters. For example, *ambar charakha* is proposed as a home-based economic activity, specifically for women to supplement family income. It is assumed that as women are home-bound they would use ambar charakha more frequently than men who mostly work outside the home. Advocacy of home-based income-generation for women also implies that activities of the domestic sphere are not disturbed. Such income-generation is not proposed for women as a full-time vocation, but as a leisure time activity for supplementing the family income. Thus economic role of women is perceived to be a secondary to their domestic roles in the family. On the other hand, self employment through running a camel cart is proposed as an occupation for men only. The wife of the self-employed is not expected to independently take up employment, but play as supportive role in her husband's occupation.

In summary, despite lip service to integrate women in the development process and women's equality, the primers reinforce the existing gender division of labor in the economy and presents women's economic participation as marginal and secondary. Marginality of women's role as productive workers is further accentuated in the primers by emphasizing women's primary role as caretakers in the patriarchal family.

Dominance of Domestic and Reproductive Roles of Women

Invisibility of women's productive work represents only one side of the story. What is noticeable is the overall tendency in the primers to emphasize domestic and reproductive roles of women, while depicting them as passive recipients of information. Further analysis of the portrayal of men and women in the home environment and the content of lessons on health and hygiene, population and social issues shows how women's primary role as caretakers in the family emerges.

General representation of male and female characters in the home environment gives us an impression that there is no sex segregation within the household. While both men and women sit together and interact with each other, there is subtle role differentiation in their activities within the household. An analysis of 16 visuals in 11 lessons reveals sex stereotypes about gender roles.

Men are portrayed as decision makers in the home environment, advising female family members about age at marriage, benefits of ambar charakha for home-based income generation, benefits of a smokeless chulha, etc. Women's advisory role in the household, however, is restricted mostly to women characters in the areas of health and girls' education.

On the other hand, domestic work appears to be exclusively women's domain. Men are not at all shown as engaged in any domestic work at home. It is the women characters who are shown as performing household work, such as watering a plant, sweeping the floor, tiding the bed, and decorating the house.

In the eight lessons dealing with health-related topics, such as personal hygiene and cleanliness, village sanitation, material and child care, home remedies, and smokeless chulha, women's role as a caretaker in the family is highlighted.

While the major thrust of these lessons is on increasing health awareness among learners, a closer look reveals how health and hygiene is defined primarily as the concern of women. For example, three lessons on personal hygiene and sanitation attempt to create general awareness about health and hygiene while emphasizing women's domestic role in household cleanliness.

Though one lesson mentions about the participation of young men in the community action for village sanitation, maintaining household cleanliness is advocated essentially as a woman's responsibility. On the other hand, two lessons deal directly with the topics of immunization and prenatal care. The text of both the lessons is centered around female characters, particularly mothers. It is assumed that mothers are ignorant about the benefits of child care and prenatal care. No serious efforts are made in the text of these lessons to show a father/husband actively participating in child care or prenatal care. Thus, child care and prenatal care emerges as the responsibilities of a mother only.

On the other hand, gender-bias is not explicit in the four lessons on population. Messages on population control are conveyed through both male and female protagonists. The text of two lessons in family planning emphasizes equal treatment of children from both sexes. Nevertheless, an active role of a wife in decision-making about family planning is not stressed.

Furthermore four lessons on social issues also center around the domestic sphere of women's life. While discussing child marriage, dowry and alcoholism as social evils, these lessons implicitly underscore significance of marriage. Although the treatment of the topic and characterization of women differ in each lesson, in general, male characters are depicted as progressive social reformers, opposing the social practices of dowry and child marriage. Meanwhile women are portrayed as obedient, submissive and passive in their roles as daughters, wives and mothers. Even when an attempt is made in two lessons to show women as active and strong characters mobilizing women to protest against the social custom of dowry, there is no critical questioning of patriarchal norms and values that subordinate women in society. For example, dowry is simply perceived as a social evil that increases economic burden to a daughter's parents. Although women are shown as active protagonists spearheading the anti-dowry movements no effort is made to link the dowry problem with the broader structural reality of women's oppression. Similarly, the lesson on alcoholism depicts an alcoholic Hiras wife as a typical tolerant and self-sacrificing Hindu woman who suffers, but nurtures her family.

Thus, the primers focus on women's domestic life and their roles as caretakers in the family-caring, nurturing and nursing as a wife and a mother. In contrast men are depicted as decision makers in the family but are seldom shown as actively participating in domestic work or child care. Such stereotyped representation of gendered roles again reinforces patriarchal norms and values.

CONCLUSIONS

What is apparent from the foregoing analysis of literacy primers in Gujarat is that there has not been any significant change in the portrayal of gendered roles in society. Although the literacy primers are designed on the basis of guidelines provided by the national bureaucracy, the content of the primers hardly reflects serious concern about the core values of the National Literacy Mission, such as national integration, population control, environment, equality, etc. Concern for women's a equality is neither addressed adequately nor reflected in the text all throughout the primers.

On the whole, the primers do not display overtly sexist bias in characterization of men and women characters as there has been some attempt to show positive images of women as protagonists. However, by and large their role as protagonists is confined to their caring and nurturing tasks in the family while men are protagonists primarily for the themes related to various production-oriented development sectors, such as agriculture, income-generation, cooperative, self-employment, etc. In other words, concerns of women and men protagonists reflect stereotyped gendered roles in society.

Occasionally, women are shown as engaged in economic activities, but their economic participation is presented a supplementary or secondary. Neither are they shown as breadwinners nor are their economic roles emphasized. In general, the primers reinforce existing gender stereotypes about economic roles while superficially advocating gender equality. In fact, marginality of women's productive role is further justified by the idealization of their domestic and reproductive role as wives and mothers. Women's roles and responsibilities revolve primarily around their role as caretakers in the family, while men continue their authority as decision-makers within the family. Such stereotyped depiction of women and men in literacy primers perpetuates patriarchal ideology and prevents them from developing critical understanding of gender issues.

Table 22.1- Content of TLC Literacy Primers in Gujarat

Content Area and Themes	Primer Level			Total No. of lessons
	I	II	III	
A. Development	**9**	**10**	**7**	**26**
Agruculture	5	1	1	7
Health	1	5	2	8
Population	1	1	2	4
Education	1	1	1	3
Income Generation	-	2	-	2
Cooperation	-	-	1	1
Environment	1	-	-	1
B. Social Issues	**2**	**-**	**2**	**4**
Dowry	1	-	1	2
Age at Marriage	1	-	-	1
Alcoholism	-	-	1	1
C. National Integration	**-**	**2**	**1**	**3**
Equality of all Religions	-	1	-	1
Equality of all citizens	-	-	1	1
Voting	-	1	-	1
D. Equality	**2**	**-**	**-**	**2**
Equal Wages a	1	-	-	1
Social Equality	1	-	-	1
Total	**13**	**12**	**10**	**35**

23

THE CONTENT OF FUNCTIONAL KNOWLEDGE IN LITERACY PROGRAMS FOR WOMEN IN VIETNAM

Thai Xuan Dao, Bui Van Thu

It is the right time to discuss and agree upon a literacy programme and contents for women alone because of a number of reasons.

Women constituted and are constituting the majority (70%) of the current total number of illiterate people in the whole country and most of them live in the rural, mountainous and remote areas (89%). Due to many difficulties and constraints in terms of psychological and socio-economic aspects the proportion of women in literacy classes is still low. The mobilization of women to go to literacy classes is not only propaganda, or providing of material incentives such as books, pens, money, and rice. For us, the education branch should improve the content of curriculum so as to make it appropriate to the target group which means diversificaton of literacy programme. Functional knowledge must be presented in a rich and attractive content and form. Gender roles, needs and circumstances of women should especially be paid attention to. Because, in the last analysis, illiteracy eradication at present is in fact a problem of, illiteracy eradication for women and girl children.

The current literacy programme is designed for all target groups in every area of the whole country. To a certain extent, it has provided women with necessary skills and knowledge to enable them to perform their traditional roles and functions in the family and society. However, many problems concerning women, and the new problems of peasant women in the renovated economy of the rural areas at present, especially in the context of "Women and development" have not been dealt with or clearly reflected.

Today women are equal to men in socioeconomic and cultural activities but, women are still and will be women for ever. They are the moth-

one woman out of three can neither read nor write.

Education is a key factor in the development and well being of societies. Consequently, priority should be given to education of girls and women on account of the discrimination and marginalization they have suffered in the past. Education is also a powerful tool for social, economic and political integration of women.

As well as the crucial problem of access to education, the problem relating to the type of training offered women constitutes another impediment to their access to productive employment. Women generally choose subjects considered as "feminine" subjects rather than scientific and highly technical subjects with job opportunities and considerable chances of promotion.

Professional segregation manifested by employment categorization according to sex is badly understood for want of adequate statistical indicators. The following paragraphs will highlight what ILO hasa done and what it proposes as measures to increase employment and training of women and girls.

II. ILO'S POSITION WITH REGARD TO TRAINING AND EMPLOYMENT OF WOMEN

By virtue of its mandate, ILO's action in favour of women has always been guided by two major concerns: The first is to guarantee equality of chances and treatment with regard to access to education, training, employment, organization and decision-making and to secure equal conditions in terms of salaries and employment-related social services. The second is to protect female workers. During the past decade ILO's action aimed at ensuring better access of women to employment should be viewed within the context of the Nairobi Forward Looking Strategies.

Promotion of Education and Employment of Women: A long Way towards Equality of Chances and Treatment: Conventions Nos. 100, 111,156.

Since its inception in 1991, ILO's action in favour of better access by women to employment centered around International Labour Norms and legal instruments focusing on the principle of equality of chances and treatment for men and women in the area of employment both in terms of acees and career prospects. As before stated, the major obstacles to acces toemployment by women with equal chances and opportunities like men are due to many factors, the most common being unequal access to education and training.

According to UNICEF, in 1995 40% of girls reached primary 5 in

Sub-Saharan Africa, compared to 48% of boys. During the 1992/1993 biennium ILO implemented an inter-departmental project on equality. The objective was to help ILO mandators to reduce discriminatory practices and to create favourable conditions for the promotion of equality in employment. Employoment in general and women employment in particular constitutes one of the universal priorities and at the same time one of the most difficult problems to resolve. Employment creation is indeed one of the most effective ways of controlling the growing poverty and social exclusion. In this connection, education and training allow for the attainment of this objective. They make it possible to break the poverty chain by providing women and girls with the necessary skills and by opening up for them prospects on the labour market.

The major norms for the promotion of equlity are Convention No. 100 on equal pay, Convention No. 111 on Discrimination in Employment and Profession and Convention 156 on Workers with family responsibility. These Conventions were ratified respectively by 36, 34 and 2 African States out of a total number of 52. Apart from the fact that these ratifications are sharply inadequate, they have still not been translated into reality through national legislations and, where they are, many workers are ignorant about them.

The conclusion that can so far be drawn is that despite the major meetings held, the situation of girls and women has not changed much. This is the reason why ILO through active partnership is helping Member States to review legislations and their education practices in force in order to provide in educational institutions vocational orientation programmes which are non-discriminatory and not based on sex, and which are likely to encourage girls to choose technical subjects in order to widen the range of professions they can exercise.

Science and Technology: Two Key Areas for Equality

Improvement of the situation of women is also dependent on the type of training selected, for it is no longer enough to have basic education. What is also necessary is to choose scientific and technical subjects "reserved" for men.

Experience has shown that young girls generally get training described as feminine, which unfortuantely does not offer many job opportunities. ILO therefore addressed the problem of education known as "formal" education where only few girls received scientific education and it was realized that this category of women could benefit from another type of education geared towards employment. The acquisition of new skills would enhance their chances on the labour market.

ILO strategy in this regard is based on the right of every child to go to school and to receive education. If for one reason or another this is not possible, the UN system in general and ILO in particular proposes the system whereby the child can catch-up by learning a trade.

ILO also believes that female technicians, engineers and scientiest should be trained in a way as to conduct researches on the improvement of educational policies and programmes on the basis of full equality. Women in this profession should have the same salaries and responsibilities like their male counterparts. The RIO Coference recalled, and rightly so, the need to provide scientific and technical training to women, which is not only a social justice but also, and more importantly, the protection of the human species.

Shortage in Terms of Scope and Nature of Statistical Data on Education, Training and Employment of Women

Even though all African States are unanimous in acknowledging that the point of departure of any programme aimed at promoting women access to employment consists in mapping out appropriate strategies, the issue of the choice and formulation of these strategies remains a difficult task to be accomplished. This is due to the fact that realistic and effective strategies presuppose a clear knowledge of the contours and nature of the problem to be resolved. Now, in Africa the statistical and conceptual tools capable of gauging the scope of the unequalities women are subjected to on the labour market and determining the causes thereof are virtually inexistent.

Raising the Level of Qualification of Girls and Women and Drawing up Continued Training Programmes for Female Salaried Workers

The last decade has witnessed very significant changes relating to the rapid development of new technologies particularly in the areas of communication. It is clearly established that it is mainly in the area of manufacturing industry and services that computer and communication technologies have had a visible impact on employment of women. The introduction of certain techniques aimed at freeing women of their chores has somewhat led to the transfer of employment, economic management and potential revenue of female workers into the hands of men. The typical example cited in west Africa is the masculinization of the work of a miller once a mill has been installed, whereas this work, when done manually, is the responsibility of women who are still entrusted with the most difficult manual tasks.

Such transfers in the division of labour between sexes raise the serious question of access of women to new technologies, which has been made difficult through training in order to ensure optimal utilization. In order to give equal chance to women faced with technological innovations, it is necessary to provide them with training to up-grade their skills. For those of them who are laready salaried workers, a continued training programme should be instituted to enable them adapt to change in their sector of activity.

Women in the Informal Sector: Training that can make the Difference

Experience shows that women occupy the largest place in the informal sector in the world in general and in Africa in particular. Sectoral policies including the stimulation of the informal sector and the subsistence farming sector play a considerable role in job creation. Furthermore, women need to be trained on how to increase their revenues in the respective sectors of activities. This type of training may relate of activities. This type of training may relate to management, development of skills, access to credit etc......

III PROSPECTS AND RECOMMENDATIONS

The strategic objectives mentioned above to ensure equal access of girls to education and full employment can really be attained only if states, International Organizations and all people of good will pool their efforts for the same fight, namely, the eradication of poverty of women.

National Strategies

All the studies conducted on uneven access of women in all professions the world over, more specifically in the areas of science and technology, have underscored the fact that no solution is possible without a strong political will. Consequently, before undertaking any action aimed at promoting the advancement of women it is necessary to reflect on a long term strategy from which will emerge a national vision of the relationships that should exist between men and women. This means developing strategies that will help master the future.

The progress made in the area of education and training of girls also stems from the commitment and active participation of parents and communities. However, traditions remain a serious handicap as far as education of girls is concerned.

States have the primary responsibility to enact laws, regulate and implement education and employment promotion programmes. In this connection, they should reflect on a long term strategy with regard to women employment, multiply large-scale information and training sensitization activities in order to change mentalities and systematize group strategy, increase women access to employment through gender planning, review laws and regulations that have an impact on women access to employment with a view to identifying the discriminatory provisions therein and abrogate them; multiply statistical data collection in order to understand the obstacles to a better access of girls to school, training and employment; ratify Conventions nos. 100, 111 and 156 and reflect them in their national legislations, mount sensitization campaign on the content of these Conventions.

Workers Organizations

Should multiply their sensitization activities on the obstacles to women access to employment and initiate actions aimed at projecting them as discrimination problems that constitute an impediment to the development of the national economy. They should also multiply actions in the direction of women in the informal and rural sectors so that they organize themselves and form as many pressure groups are possible to reject discriminatory practices and provide alternative solutions; work for the equality of all workers through training aimed at popularizing the rights of female workers and acquainting them with the legal procedures to follow in case of violation.

Employers Organizations

Should draw up information and training programmes aimed at removing prejudices against women and making a better use of their productivity and creative abilities. They should also increase the number of female employers through management training, improve the working conditions of women through the promotion of International Labour Norms, particularly those pertaining to hygiene and security at work place, encourage the practice of apprenticeship in enterprises for girls and women without qualification.

National and International Organizations

Should increase their technical assistance according to the needs expressed and encourage exchange of experience at continental level. They should systematize gender appraoch in project implementation, encourage activities in the rural areas and those that take the interest of handicapped female workers into account, encourage researches on subjects dealing with women employment, increase their efforts in order to provide greater assistance to the education sector as well as to scientific and technical training in favour of girls and women.

IV. CONCLUSION

For the majority of women and girls, employment training still remains an objective to be attained, more so as the changes that are taking place in the continent have frustrated an evolution which, though slow, was yielding positive results especially in the areas of education, training and sensitization in general. However, much remains to be done to guarantee women equal chances and treatment in terms of education and employment. In order to overcome these obstacles, it is necessary to put in place effective education and training systems, particularly a basic education system of good quality available to each and everyone irrespective of sex.

Access to basic education and training should be broadbased and should cover all sectors including the rural and urban informal sectors in order to reduce inequality in income distribution. There is no doubt that many African countries will have to restructures their education and training systems in order to take up the employment challenge. Special emphasis should be placed on the development of skills that will improve productivity. The restructuring of the education and training systems should aim at putting a stop to the reproduction of "trained unemployed people" by ensuring a better relationship between the demand and supply of qualified manpower on the labour market. The high rate of unemployement or underemployment of women calls for the integration of the question of sex in the entire planning process. Strategies based on sex will remove the specific obstacles to women's entry on the employment market and guarantee for women equality on the employment market, access to credit and training opportunities.

It is necessary, more than ever before, to implement the Beijing recommendations and ILO is ready to lend its assistance to the realization of the objective of combating poverty of women in Africa through equal access to education, training and employment.

39

ALTERNATIVE APPROACHES TO EDUCATION

Catherine A. Odora Hoppers

1. EDUCATION: THE PROCESS AND SYSTEM

1.1 Women and Education: Beijing, Amman and After

In the recently concluded Mid-Decade Review of progress towards Education for All held in Amman Jordan, the rationale behind expanding educational provision was started as follows:

> ......*Education is empowerment. It is the key to establishing and reinforcing democracy and development which is both sustainable and humane, and to peace founded upon mutual respect and social justice. Indeed, in a world in which creativity and knowledge play an ever greater role, the right to education is nothing less than the right to participate in the life of the modern world (The Amman Affirmation June 1996).*

It was in recognition of this tremendous power of education that action at both local and international level has, through the past decades been mustered to attempt to meet the basic learning needs of every individual. Several world conferences have repeatedly endorsed the central role especially of basic education in preserving the environment, managing population growth, combating poverty, promoting social development and equating equality between the sexes.

By the time Beijing came around exactly 20 years after the declaration of the Women's Decade by the United Nations General Assembly in 1975, a number of issues had already sunk in as being critical in the area of girls' and womens' education. Not only had significant empirical and analytical knowledge and information been generated about the status of women and the conditions in which they live, but a growing recognition had emerged that unless action is taken to enhance female education, the ambitious goals set for education and development particularly in Africa will remain out of reach. Accordingly, the Ouagadougou Declaration and Framework for Action reaffirmed what can be understood to be the fundamental rationale for providing education of girls as seen by the African ministers there gathered. I quote:

> *.....That girl's education contributes to improved quality of life and enhances national development through increased economic production rates; improved hygiene and nutritional practices; reduced child and maternal mortality rate; and reduced fertility rate....) Ouagadougou Declaration, p: 5)*

Research has also generated data. Most of these data, information and knowledge have been laid at the doorstep of the policy makers, decision makers and various related practitioners. If quantity and quality are anything to go by, then certainly the intervening years since 1975 have produced an ample and robust amount of valuable material in this area. Agencies, research institutions and governments have commissioned numerous studies covering the status of female education, socio-economic and socio-cultural factors influencing female participation, factors related to school environment, and political and institutional factors. Seminars, workshops and training sessions have also been organized to sensitize practitioners and policy makers on issues related to gender.

Despite all the research, awareness raising and advocacy especially at the national and international level however, the Beijing Declaration and Platform for Action concedes that although progress has been recorded in some areas, equality between men and women has not been achieved and under representation of women in strategic nodes of power and decision making continues even within the United Nations. The Ouagadougou Declaration not only notes the quantitative magnitude of the problem (26 million African girls out of school), but also that Africa is lagging behind other regions of the world in female enrolment ratios and female illiteracy.

A 1995 review on Girls and Schools in Sub-Saharan Africa conducted by the World Bank still list the same factors constraining girl's education in 1995 as has always been the case: poor returns to female education in the labor marker; persistent apprehension and ambivalence on the part of parents, children, teachers and society at large regarding female education and the value of keeping girls in school; the quality of teaching and the endemic issue of learning environment; sexual harassment; high levels of wastage; and the issue of self esteem among girls regarding their status in society. The review however, calls for a fundamental change in attitudes about girls education, and increase in political will, the promotion of dialogue among various stakeholders/partners, and better utilization of research findings (Odaga & Heneveld 1995).

1.2 Questioning the Egalitarian Expectations of Schooling

1.2.1 Schooling the Girl-Child

These kinds of findings and conclusions are not new. What one finds so striking in the advocacy for education in Africa, whether it is "Education for All" or that for girls, are the patterns of articulations and silences that characterize both the research agenda and the perspectives adopted in the advocacy. A typical treatise on education in Africa is prefixed by a preamble that pays tribute to the arrival on the continent of a 'non-indigenous' education that was introduced in the context of the colonial conquest of the continent. Fleeting references are then made to the otherwise crucial fact that this education in largely 'irrelevant', 'de-linking and pacifying' in character, 'incapable of arousing in its consumers sensitivity to local realities', and in general extremely problematical even before the routines of funding, attitudes by gender and such dimensions are brought in. Gender analysts and feminist advocates for women's education for their part also point to the 'domesticating' and 'dependency generating' nature of that education. Adhiambo Odaga, an African scholar at the World Bank had the courage to admit in the above mentioned study that:

> *......In the process (of consuming that type of education), the notion of the African woman as a dependent housekeeper and housekeeper wife and mother confined to the home and economically dependent on a husband, the breadwinner, was introduced into African culture. This western patriarchal view ignored the central value of African women in the public and economic spheres of society.......A new tradition was established for transmitting values of humility, low ambition, systematic underestimation of girl's and womens' ability in cognitive achievement, social attainment and capacity to work in the public sphere.....The cost of this externally imposed tradition in conjunction with the local tradition was heavy for African woman (Odaga & Heneveld 1995: 6-7).*[1]

Yet by some curious twist of conception in our every dream connected

*[1] See also Odora C.A. 1995. *Women and Education: Beijing and After. An African Perspective*. In Kehitys, Paper prepared for the Finnish Ministry of Foreign Affairs.

with egalitarian ideals, this 'de-linking' education is the reliable agency to infuse empowerment, bring development, equalize the imbalance between men and women, reinforce democracy and usher ideals of sustainable development.

The advocacy for the education of the African girl child side-steps the crucial mention of the fact that as a tool faithful to its objective, educational systems reflect the values and practices of the 'larger society'. What, ask, are the contours of this larger society?

1.2.2 Schooling and the "Wider Society'

This 'wider society' is one which consists of two parts. The first is the neo-colonial one that bespeaks the intensity with which Africa and the Third World has been subjected to the violence of colonialism as Gramsci wrote:

> ....*During the war (of colonialism), the colonies were exploited in an unheard of measure, with an inhuman and inflexible method which can only be conceived of in a period of admirable civilization like the capitalist one. The natives of the colonies haven't even been left their eyes for crying......Everything has been plundered, with that shrewdness, and that ruthless efficiency which belongs to the bourgeois world.....(Gramsci 1970: 119).*

Colonialism, it is known, is not satisfied merely with holding a people in its grip, and emptying the native's brain of all forms and content. By a kind of perverted logic, it turns to the past of the oppressed people, and distorts, disfigures and destroys it (Fanon 1980, Chung & Ngara 1985). Today, in attempting to name that 'wider society' whose image is reflected in the education system, we are able to go beyond the understanding of dependency which signifies the *continuity* of the impact of western institutions, political power, languages and culture on the Third World; to a grappling with neo-colonialism. This latter, Altbach states, differs from dependency in that it is a *deliberate policy of the industrialized nations to maintain their influence in the Third World.* Neocolonialism represents a productive process by which those patterns established in the colonial past are *sustained promoted, and extolled as essential and universal* for all mankind (Altbach 1982). The contours of this 'wider society' quickly becomes obvious to any African government which tries to act on economic and other matters in the interest of national development for the betterment of the masses as former Tanzanian President Julius Nyerere captures:

> *...for such a government soon discovers that it inherited the powers to make laws and to treat with foreign governments and so on, but that it did not inherit effective power over economic development of its own country. Instead, there exists in its land, various economic activities which are owned by people outside its jurisdiction, which are run in the interest of those economic powers. Neo-colonialism is very real....and imposes a very severe limitation on national sovereignty (Nyerere 1967, quoted in Nabudere 1989).*

As African governments are cornered into this forced romance[2], a second image of the 'wider society' emerges. It is one whose basic metabolism is being destroyed. Ki-Zerbo has argued that in its normal rendering, education should contain in its mandate, the element of social reproduction and renewal that is essential for the progress of any society. When this element is abolished, there occurs a deep reduction in the basic metabolism of that society. For Africa South of the Sahara it has been argued, instead of giving rise to a higher level, the educational system has helped to dismantle these elements of social reproduction in traditional African society from an assumed high moral ground that all that is contained in such a traditional society is primitivity and backwardness. The base of the African indigenous educational system which was open, and not closed between four walls, was dealt a severe blow quantitatively and qualitatively, first by the slave trade, then by colonialism working hard with Christianity to replace the existing system not just with one that is closed, hierarchical and constrained, but also one that is unique indeed in its ideological and operational design to facilitate the subjugation of the continent to European needs. At that point, for African societies Ki-Zerbo states, education lost its functional role. Schools were no longer natural organs connected in vital ways to African society. Instead they became artificial accretions from elsewhere aimed at gaining instrumental control over African resources. When the colonial system retreated from the continent Ki-Zerbo states, it left behind its school system to operate as a kind of *time bomb*. As we struggle today to adapt and retool this *time*

[2] The notion of 'romance' in this paper is applied as a derivative from Professor Nelly Stromquist's usage in her seminal Presidential Address to the Comparative and International Education Society entitled '*Romancing the State: Gender and Power in Education*' in which she articulates the phenomenon of gender activists 'dealing with the State, the tensions involved in having to do so being at times, a 'contradiction-in-terms'. In this paper, it is meant to underscore the factor of constrained space for the exercise of will power in the post-independence period, and thus to continue in the context of neo-colonialism, to 'eat with short spoons' with the jackals.

bomb to make it serve as a missile propelling African society into a fresh new world, and to call this convicts ball our very own, Africa's endogenous system has been left fallow, ownerless and uncultivated.

We may also dare to acknowledge the process of atomization of child-parent relationship in Africa especially as education, tailored as if every African family is a model urban Western industrial society, does not consider establishing a system of parent-teacher associations capable of looking after parents' rights and maintaining their bargaining capacity in the school system viz-a-viz the African indigenous educational system. The school system has not only remained impossible to merge with the environing society, but has also persisted in its imperviousness to any really profound inputs from that society; thus standing forever the *square* construct amidst *round* huts.

1.2.3 The School System is Limited, Hierarchical, and Colonial for All African Children

If the education system prevalent in Africa is essentially colonial, then indeed we are chasing our tails tinkering with a system that is not only entrenched, supported and defended by powerful theories of 'development' but also by the entire coalition of actors and agencies responsible for funding learning and human development world wide. What we are talking about is a system that is acutely pyradidal, basically narrow, very limited and very limiting. It is one whose very creed it is, not just to restrict and ration both quantity and quality, but also it is one that at its core supports patriarchy, elitism, westernization while maintaining an underlying disdain for any positive reference to African values and traditions. It is the imperative of the socialization component of this system to transmit, constantly and judiciously those patriarchal values, role models, accepted gender biases, and promote western values and orientation (Odora 1993).

In advocating the need for more 'forceful and concerted action' as it is in admitting shortfalls, educators are aware that this late in this fourth development decade, education has yet to stand up to the occasion, defy in its genetic makeup, and deliver the 'goodies' expected of it. Yet, pet to academic research and policy attention remain an all too familiar list of *problems*: 'lack of resources', 'poor planning', 'inefficient use and management of resources' or 'lack of capacity'.

If the advocacy for more and more education is not urgently accompanied by a profound reconsideration and a very transparent debate as to the fundamentals of this system, what we are doing to the girl-child and the women of the future is essentially that we are trading the African traditional practices and norms for the *new patriarchy* of the Western variety. In fact shrewd observers have already noted that the convergence between the capitalist logic of production and patriarchy produces an acute hybrid of oppressive gender relations sustained by a subtle patriarchal ideology of which the school is the official carrier. The costly fiction that the school is the site and location for democratizing society by making itself available to all members of society (UPE) and subsequently letting merit emerge as the main basis for the distribution of rewards and privilege is debunked by the lucid analyses by feminist scholars who point out that the schools, as the agent of the state operates at two levels: *manifest*—advocating liberalism and formalistic equality, and *latent*-endorsing patriarchy (Stromquist 1987).

As education is only fulfilling a task assigned to it by the on-going socio-economic arrangements, making education per-se the villain of the piece by dwelling on symptoms evidenced within it, and strategies aimed merely at ameliorating these while congratulating the parent system represents a tinkering with the notion of change that is not only pretentious but also a clear reflection of schizophrenic thinking. This would be like returning to the days when 'development' was understood only in terms of practical rather than the *strategic gender needs*; an approach that obsessed itself with getting rural women to weave baskets all day because their 'work' in the framework of rural agriculture was not an 'income related activity', and hence, not work.

Finally we also have to remember that education reproduces gender and oppressive relations not just for girls, but also boys. The crisis created by schooling affects ALL children, although it is more so, for the girl-child. Moumouni (1968) has argued that by trying to effect a veritable 'depersonalization' of Africans using every possible means to imbue students with an inferiority complex and the idea of the congenital incapacity of the black person, colonial education sowed a seed pregnant with consequences. It not only corrupted the thinking and sensibilities of the African and filled him/her with abnormal complexes, but set out to train an intelligentsia that was not a national intelligentsia. The African product of the colonial educational system through the culture he/she was taught in those schools, the political content and orientation, the methods utilized as well as the social, educational, political context in which he studied, matured into an entity that was in itself, *a contradiction to his just being*. His learning and social position tended to push him towards to colonizer, but this tendency was quickly squashed by the internal logic of the colonial (and neocolonial) system in which the native had 'to know his/her place' (Moumouni 1968). The challenge for all educators is therefore to deconstruct both femininity and masculinity in the process of working out the lost identity of ALL the children being entrusted to this system.

1.2.4 Yet all these seems 'beside the point'.......................

That with all the complexities in its genetic makeup, education and learning modes is so easily collapsed into 'schooling' is evident in discourses that allude to the issue of human capacity and resource development. Coming home in the context of Education for All for instance, not only is this socio-psychological consequences of education totally missing with all attention given to 'access', 'quality', but of the 6 bullet points on the Jomtien Declaration, it is only the one that refers to schooling that contains the word *universal*. All others apply words like 'expansion of provisions' (pre-school and basic skills), 'increased acquisition' (of life skills via media), or 'reduction' (of the illiteracy rate) prompting commentators to note quite understandably that:

> *....only school education merited the idea of Education for All. In a real and literal sense.....EFA at the Jomtien was only about Schooling for All (SFA) and not about Skills for All, or Literacy for All.....Like the primary school suggested target, the adult literacy target also aimed at the millenium....But the scale of what was suggested was fundamentally different.....There is not even a hint of universal literacy but (rather) an illustrative indication of what a nation might undertake. (Norrag News, 1996).*

This continuing unevenness in the treatment of the two streams of education, itself, reflecting the differential weighting of the targets by the sponsors of Jomtien, have had implications among other things, for the development and support to the broader notion of 'basic education', in effect helping only to reinforce the image of the non-school forms and types of learning including adult learning as the 'poor relative' of the primary school system, and others such as African indigenous education, as most certainly 'irrelevant to their use' (Odora 1995, Foucault 1980, Norrag News 1996).

2. THE CONSTRAINED SPACE FOR POLICY ACTION: EDUCATION IN THE CONTEXT OF AUSTERITY

2.1 Austerity and Disinvestment in Human Resource Development[3]

Turning from the system to contemporary economic arrangements under the Economic Structural Adjustment, for many countries the recent years have been harsh indeed. As they wrestled with seemingly intractable economic problems, the Economic Structural Adjustment Programmes were adopted, frequently on the pressure and 'advice' of external organizations. As they sought to cut spending as recommended and reallocate resources, many countries realize that they have effectively weakened the social services they hoped to provide, including education and training. Even where governments have maintained their commitment to education and training and endeavored to protect them from severe budget reductions, austerity measures have, in practice compromised either access or quality or equity, often *all three*.

The consequences of this slow motion disinvestment in the skills and knowledge of the future citizens are yet to be contemplated. Suffice it to say however, that the countries' recovery and longterm development prospects may be permanently demented. As government programmes are eliminated and demand-reduction measures are adopted, industrial restructuring requires layoffs and real wages decline. In actual fact Samoff writes, the term 'adjustment' in the compound term 'structural adjustment' is itself misleading since to adjust (to make small incremental changes) 'is what people do to the radio volume when they find it too loud' The misnomer that it is, Structural Adjustment is actually meant, and intended to produce fundamental reorganization rather than incremental modification (Samoff 1994). The emerging scenario is one in which governments have had to cope with the ripple effects of the adjustment programmes by making rapid policy adjustments in other sectors as well. The common guiding adages used in the whole development assistance stage are '*restructure* the......sector', '*increase efficiency* of resource use', and '*mobilize new sources of income*.' It is generally acknowledged that the dialogue between funding agencies and governments as well as national involvement in policy reform are basically insufficient, limiting both policy and project sustainability. Moreover, the forced rapid adoption of the adjustment policy reform measures totally skips the crucial importance of letting a country first develop over the long term, a capacity to implement reform. All in all, allocations to educations fell, both in relative and absolute terms.

[3] This and the next sub-section draws upon the findings of a project of the UNESCO-ILO Task Force on Austerity, Adjustment and Human Resources entitled Coping with Crists: Austerity, Adjustment and Human Resources edited by Professor Joel Samoff. The project was initiated to examine, on the basic of a number of case studies, the responses of education and training systems to the pressures of economic adjustment programmes. The countries examined were Brazil, Costa Rica, Hungary, Senegal and Tanzania.

2.2 The manifestations

First of all, crisis and adjustment have effected *education and training finance* especially in the way unrelenting pressure has been exerted to reduce the wage bill which, in practice has meant efforts to reduce the size or income of the instructional staff (or both), increase its workload, replace higher paid with lower paid personal. Despite this pressure however, Many countries have found ways to try and protect teacher's salaries. Secondly, the *quality of education and training* have also been affected. In part because of the declining resources but also because of incessant efforts to reduce teacher's effective salaries or at least restrain their increase, morale has declined among educators.

Thirdly, crisis and adjustment have affected not only what happens within schools and other programmes, but also the *relationship between education and training and the larger society*. The privatization drive have gone hand in with increases in fees paid directly by students and their families. In most countries, inequality in access to education, and to promotion within the education system seem to have increased, with more affluent families either purchasing the higher quality private education, or organizing politically to protect the level or type of education which serves them, thereby permitting the rest of the education system to deteriorate. In Brazil and Tanzania, privatization has accelerated and intensified regional differentiation, to the disadvantage of the poorest areas of the country. The explosive growth of local non-governmental organizations unleashing diverse energies quickly translated into community based schools can be celebrated as the beginning of a dawn of creativity and grassroots innovation. But in the context of austerity, cost deflection, and diminishing role of the state, such jubilation should be viewed with caution. Constant crisis distracts attention from broader issues and more distant time horizons.

Fourthly, crisis and adjustment have also affected the actual *education and training agenda* that broad set of goals, objectives and priorities that inform and guide specific programmes (see also Hoppers & Komba 1995:28). Particularly acute is the fact that the fixation on finance *has eclipsed the broader goals of education*: national integration, citizenship, self-reliance, self-confidence, equality, equity and even learning.

Fifthly, crisis and adjustment have affected *how education and training policies are made*. Since ESAP, several new actors have entered or become prominent in the policy making process, including external assistance agencies, international and national non-governmental organizations, local communities and enterprises. As the providers of critically needed funds, the foreign aid agencies have, in several countries acquired the most influential voice, both directly and indirectly. Planning and decision making have become so oriented towards the agencies' view that the agenda setting process has, in the view of many observers been "hijacked'. Research that under normal circumstances should provide the basic for policy formation and formulation, is used increasingly to justify and legitimize policies already made elsewhere. That the external agencies provide funds and commission research has affected the kinds of research that are undertaken, controlled the nature of findings. And how the results are used (Samoff et. al. 1994)

2.3 *Austerity and the Snake in the Baggage*

Finally, crisis and adjustment has revitalized the modernization paradigm. In its naked rendering, this paradigm has been responsible for the making the link between education and the formation of 'modern attitudes' that become synonymous with the acquisition of 'western attitudes'. The meta project is that in which a system of forced cultural convergence is established with formal schooling as the fulcrum and site for the pruning of the cultural values and norms of those numerous 'Others' into a new cultural order that is compatible with the western (Ekins 1992, Fagerlind & Saha 1989).

Today in the context of austerity, the significance of this is seen in the convergence and interconnection between research, external funding, and education and training programmes on the one hand; and the understanding and definition of development and the role of education and training in such a development on the other. The failure of the economies of the Eastern European countries tainted anything even vaguely associated with socialism. To continue to insist on redistribution and allocation to (what by now are being called) the 'non-productive' social services is to evoke the wrath of the neo-liberals and be accused of wanting to 'perpetuate poverty'. In no time at all, the sources and causes of problems of the poor countries was located once more *within those countries* (Samoff, ibid). Contemporary poverty can then be explained insultingly as of old, in terms of a *distant past* (a legacy of rudimentary technology and primitive small scale societies), or the *climate* (abundant tropical bounty stimulates neither hard work not invention), or *missing factors of production* (lack of appropriate skills and technology), or even *socialization, attitudinal orientation and psychological mind set* (stoic passivity, fatalistic submissiveness, low need for achievement) (Mama 1991, Pawar 1992).

More than this deletion of the global and structural factors from thought and practice in education and development however, the modernization approach views policy as a purely technical administrative process. In this frame of reference, development has to do with applying knowledge and manipulating inputs which, for the most part are regarded as technical and administrative tasks to be managed by a modernizing middle class. Only that class, imbued through its education with the requisite skill, and socialized to value individual economic and social mobility, can be entrusted with national reform. Peasant political mobilizers, trade union militants, radical critics of imperialism and neo-colonialism (like politics in general) are all regarded as obstacles to progress. Empowerment, democratic participation and collective liberation are considered inimical to modernizations' agenda; and are mostly heard of either in acutely deradicalized/domesticated versions in conservative settings, or when empowerment is meant to target private enterprise in the context of the neo-liberal framework much as ESAP.

That the ideology of modernization has to a significant extent been internalized by both the elite in the Third World and the populace at large is nowhere more clearly seen than in the case of education. Popular demands for expanded access to education are often conservative, and is less and less linked with fundamental social or economic transformation. By and large, parents' vision of the new society is to be achieved by improved access to the old order. Admission to post primary schools is valued not because it portends fundamental societal transformation, but rather because it holds the promise of increased income, job security and an improved standard of living. Parents become defenders of their own exclusion from educational policy making: 'the experts should take such decisions'. The head teacher know better' comment the members of the school committee as they agree that the major elements of school policy need not be brought to their attention. By a strange twist of circumstances, those very people who are serve least well by this ideology are also its purveyors (for further analysis and country case illustration, see also Samoff 1991, 1992, & 1994).

3. WHAT ABOUT ALTERNATIVES THEN?

3.1 System change and innovation

Discovery and the desire for change, according to Kuhn, commences with the awareness of an anomaly. This is followed with a more or less extended exploration of the area of anomaly. At times, novel ideas emerge only after a pronounced failure in the normal problem solving activity. However, fundamental changes in systems or perspectives require the reconstruction of the same field from new fundamentals, and is a process that changes some of the field's most elementary theoretical generalizations as well as its methods and applications (Kuhn 1962).

In their optimistic analysis of innovations and change, Havelock and Huberman state that human beings are not only remarkable, but are also capable of innumerable creative acts, self-reflexion, self enhancement and manipulation of many other physical and biological systems to enhance his/her sense of well-being. It is in pursuit of such enhancement that humanity is ever organizing and re-organizing itself into social systems and sub-systems. Systems, it is stated, are constantly moving either towards completeness, or away from completeness. Following from this, system change is any event which alters the level of completeness or equilibrium, while system development refers to a transformation from a status which is, by some definition, considered to be less satisfactory. As an innovation is a system within a system, it is characterized by an intensity that is at once fragile, and it is the fragility of the innovation process that makes the knowledge of how it works in different settings so important (Havelock and Huberman 1977).

3.2 The Non-Formal Approach: a Supplement or an Alternative?

The *supplementary function* in the non formal approach to primary schooling takes as its starting point the bad situation as it is. Millions of children are not enrolled in school, and those who get enrolled *either drop out* attrited by the rituals within the school system, are *repelled* by the internal culture of the school, *pulled out* by parents who recognize that the school is not about to recognize the life world of the family and the child, or are simply phased out over time as the top of the pyramid affirms its narrowness. The formal system maintains its rigidity even in the face of massive dropouts; as it maintains systemic indifference to the issue of time space and time use viz-a-viz survival needs on the home and family front. Non-formal approaches have therefore had as their target children and young people who are not enrolled in school; early school leavers who have not completed the primary education cycle; and special population groups identified by their particular situation and environment (e.g. girls, disadvantaged groups, indigenous groups, nomads e.t.c.).

The *alternative approach* in the systemic sense of the word is best exemplified by the '*popular education* movement in Latin America. This is not some obscure, poverty induced nimblings at the hems of the colonial education system. Popular education proceeds from the assertion that:

> *.........traditional (formal) education approaches are characterized by the application of powerful central control by the dominant*

culture over the curriculum, the methodology, evaluation, and the patterns of school organization and school-community relations. It is held that this transmits the dominant culture and thereby contributes to the process of sorting the population into a social hierarchy....In contrast, alternative approaches are those which attempt to undermine the power of those in control who are promoting the dominant culture (emphasis mine, Zuniga Escobar 1989:137).

Alternative approaches would permit the main 'actors' of the educational process to select and organize the curriculum. The pedagogical process is designed to suit the interests, pace, and time, cycle of the learners. The process and criteria for evaluation is determined to a great extent by the learners, teachers and parents. The pattern of organization of the learning center and the social relationships are established by the learners, teachers and supervisors. The community participates in the instructional process as well as in the social organization of the learning center, which also becomes a social and cultural center of the community. The life world of the learner is a living, a real, and important one, and is central in determining the way the educational process is organized.

The approach, especially in its articulation of the structural factor, sits in quite well with broader concerns with the 'improvement of the quality of life' of people; the 'achievement of better life' for both individuals and collectives through education; the move towards 'democratization of educational opportunities' and the recognized of education as a basic human right; the belief in education as a means of emancipating people from the ill effects of colonialism, poverty and exploitation; the aspirations embedded in the idea of 'life-long education'; and finally the key objectives of Education For All in which attempts are being made on a global scale to promote access to education, eradicate illiteracy and provide basic education to all (Ranaweera 1989).

The third approach, which is found in most of the cases seen in Africa, begins from the recognition that the system is inadequate, has created residues; but that system in itself is *left intact* (see appendices 1 & 2). In this middle way, the target groups are those residual groups, already marginalized or disadvantaged. The meta strategy is to find ways by which these can either survive, or cope, or find their way at some point back to the parent system (integration). Ideas such as life-long education and methods embedded in self learning, interlearning or self directed learning is applied in order to get these residual group to survive as best as is possible, and to make the best use of their disadvantaged situation. The curriculum content attempt to be more flexible and 'need-based'. But the personnel system is ad hoc, relying on volunteers, community personal. The resources base is weak and is often left to fate except in the cases in which a strong life line is made with some external funding source.

In the case of the Community Schools in Zambia for example, the existence of those schools represents both attempts to express existence of demand for education, as well to resolve the residual problems on the supply side of the equation. One type of these schools begins through community initiatives and aspires to become a full government primary school. This aspiration may be optimistic especially as government may not have clear guidelines to regulate the absorption of these initiatives. The second type of community schools exist almost wholly outside the government system. These types have greater flexibility in responding to the needs of different children. In such cases, suggestions have been that government takes these initiatives constructively and uses them as *pilots* in new and alternative approaches in terms of school organization, time use, relationship between school and community, and assists where possible with materials. Community schools remain difficult to replicate. The contributions of parents and guardians in terms of time, labour and materials is often great, and many parents, already in poor socio-economic situations find themselves stretched to the limit. Moreover, the Ministry of Community Development and Social services in Zambia which is officially responsible for youth, recognizes the importance of community schools and the problems of schooling in general, but it sees a role for itself in raising awareness of the importance of education but not is present form. (Durston 1996).

4 GENDER: THE CRITICAL BATTLE A BIG WAR

4.1 The Linkage

To create a linkage between the Non-Formal Approach and the agenda of empowerment, and its potentials for transformation, it may be appropriate to visit the world as seen from women's perspective, and to enlive the challenge that this perspective posits for those to whom responsibility is given for the nurturing of the young children, the adults of tomorrow towards a future that is not only fair, but also just. The privilege of recognizing the structures as unveiled by this perspective is especially valuable for African and Third World scholars and policy makers who, by their very existence, are what Professor Wamba Dia Wamba once called 'radical' and empirical witnesses to the nature and consequences of living in an oppressive and subjugating global relations. Women have been through this, often in silence, but not anymore, for a silent cause, Torild Skard once said, is a lost cause......and like other just struggles, this too shall be overcome.

4.2 The Feminist Lens, Patriarchy and the Challenge of Emancipation

Feminist[4] philosophy and theory is that part of scholarship that implicitly or explicitly presents a generalized, wide-ranging system of ideas about social life and human experience as can be understood from a woman-centered perspective. It is woman-centered in three ways: *firstly*, its major object for investigation, and the starting point for all its investigation is the situation and experiences of women in society. *Secondly*, it treats women as central subjects in the investigation process and seeks to see the world from a distinctive viewpoint of women in society. *Thirdly*, feminist theory is critical and activist on behalf of women, seeking to produce a better world for women, and through that, for humankind.

As to patriarchy, the most significant rendering of the concept is posited by socialist feminist theory which defines patriarchy in the first instance as a form of social organization founded on a force based ranking of the male half of humanity over the female half, in which the men of different social classes are united in their relationship of dominance over women. Researchers looking at the convergence between patriarchal system of relations and recurring situations of gross abuse of institutional and personal power, extended this definition of patriarchy to embrace a '*power over*' other people, mostly the power of some men over other men, women, children and nature (French 1986; Brock-Utne 1989). More recently, African scholars in their struggle to make sense of the persistence of structural violence that characterizes global relations in which Africa's positions is itself severely eschewed, have taken this second definition one step further. Applying an African indigenous perspective they put the definition of patriarchy against the backdrop of Africa's history and identified in colonialism and neo-colonial relations, a form of global patriarchy operationalized through western capitalism. This perspective

[4] By 'feminist' is meant that family of scientists focusing on the study of gender and power relations and applying this framework in their analytical and research work. This theoretical framework and the subsequent development it has undergone has evolved such profound tools of analysis of power relations and the relations of ruling as to warrant it a status of 'the epistemology of the century'. The insights from this theory has generic conceptual significance in particular for those wanting to interpret and transform oppressive relations; understand the constructed tension between the 'private' and the public', the 'personal' and the 'political', and make sense of the politics of knowledge, its production, definition, its use, and its abuse in a context of unequal relations.

extends the definition of patriarchal subjugation from a gender and class issue to a comprehensive cultural and knowledge control. It (patriarchy) becomes a relation in which *some men, some women and capital* rule over *millions of other men, women, children, nature, culture, and knowledge*........(Odora, 1993; Odora 1996 forthcoming).

It can be said that over the past decades, feminist activists and scholarship has addressed a number of issues revolving around women and societal, and economic development. They have drawn attention to the issue of women's invisibility from strategic arenas of power and policy despite the fact that they number half the firmament.

They continue to speak out in instances in which women's efforts to enter those domains are being deliberately blocked, and continue to fight against the violence of the patriarchal relations which engenders and routinizes human subjugation. Thus over time, the struggle for feminist enlightenment has evolved into a universal struggle against victimization that arises from being different in the first instance; against marginalization that comes from being unequally located in the scheme of things in the second instance; but most of all, it is a mobilization towards a total rejection of any system of relations in which any portion of humankind is *systematically restrained, subordinated, oppressed, used, and abused* (Odora 1993).

Women sought to liberate themselves and society from the male and societal biases found in attitudes, mentality, feelings and practices both private and public. They sought to liberate themselves and society at large from the male bias in all human knowledge which had resulted in the denigration of the female experience and of the female perspective (Bernard 1987). In scholarship, women recognized that the tension that permeate women's lives simultaneously creates the potential for both *alienation and liberation.* They gave critical attention to content, methods, and purpose of knowledge about women as defined by the social sciences. Warning against the very strong likelihood of 'women' becoming the latest 'academic fad', feminist scholars attacked the proliferating market trade in 'women's studies':

> *.....As object of knowledge, women have become marketable commodities measured by increasing profits for publishers and expanding enrollments in women's studies courses......In this respect, we have much to learn from the academic social science exploitation of the poor, especially Blacks, in the sixties. In the name of academic liberal concern and compensation, the black ghetto was measured, analyzed, processed and dissected-in short, reduced to manipulable data that advanced the career interests of the inves-*

> *tigators, but did little to improve the plight of the investigated...... Women are an attractive subject to exploit so long as we hold that the purpose of social knowledge is simply getting more information. In social science's unrestrained pursuit of information, any new object of study that can generate mounds of data is of interest so long as it is a prolific source...... When the data are no longer new, the object of study loses its primacy....(Weskott, 1979).*

In the area of development, it became evident that planners and administrators began with their own conceptions of what was suitable for men and women as they knew it from colonialism or from the United States, namely, that agriculture was what was suitable for males, and running households was for females. Thus in places where men were not farmers, men were given training in agriculture while women who were, in fact the farmers, were not.

> *.....By ignoring this world of women, so basically involved in human productivity of every kind, development planners were not only perpetrating an injustice on the women themselves by failing to help them improve their conditions of working and living, but they were also sabotaging their own development strategies. How was it possible to make such a mistake? How is it possible to continue making it right up to the present?.....Development planners have predominantly been Western men or Western trained men, imbued with the western myth that a woman's chief place is in the home....This myth has been so persistent that Western development experts have been able to go into the Third World countries to give development aid without ever noticing the female world at all....(Boulding 1980:5).*

In the area of democratization, feminist analysts observed that the study of politics tends to emphasize people's engagement in formal politics, reducing the notion of 'citizenship' to the legal rights that individuals hold against the state. Political behavior has then remained hung up at the level of participation in electoral politics, running for office, lobbying. Dominant versions of democracy, it is argued, constantly refer to the existence of competitive political parties, the exercise of free elections and the making of decisions that receive majority approval.

For women however, it was soon noticed that this conception of democracy has been limited because it bypasses critical terrains of social behavior in which democratic practices may not exist such as in *homes* and in *schools*, and assumes that stable and legitimate institutions are necessarily democratic in their provision of social services:

> *...For many women especially in the Third world, whose demanding existence does not allow them to use their citizen's rights or for whom social norms about femininity are very constraining, the concentration on formal political institutions focusses on a segmented and rather peripheral aspect of their lives (Stromquist 1992: 1-2).*

Notions of democracy therefore need to change to incorporate both micro forms of democracy and women's lived experiences. This alternative approach to politics focuses on the exercise of power in interpersonal relations; it shifts attention from the means by which the powerful *maintain ideological control* to the forms by which the powerless *produce a new culture*. In education, Stromquist outlines how a definition of democracy that drawn attention to micro levels or interpersonal relations has substantial consequences for education in the following ways:

1. It would bring to the fore a much greater need to transform *hidden curriculum* of schools, not only to focus, (as is perennially the case), to the overt content.
2. It would help expose the nature and techniques that engender and sustain the sex stereotyping that leads to *preferential treatment and higher expectations of boys*, as well as exposing the *authoritarianism in the teaching modes* so routinized in the schools.
3. It would also be easier to unmask and render open to both research and reform, those administrative structures that present hierarchical distinctions with the dichotomous representations by which *male authority* (administrators and principals), and *female obedience* (teachers) are created.
4. Transparency could also be rendered on the issue of sexually, the language of sexual abuse, physical harassment, and the male use of space in schools that shape girl's negotiations of not just segregated labor markets but also the marriage field.
5. Since authoritarian patterns at home develop in part through physical coercion by men, a focus on micro-democracies would provide space for introducing to schools knowledge about violence and its limiting consequences for women; moreover,
6. It is easier to infuse a polity with democratic ideas from below than from above.

According to Stromquist, everyday practices involve personal interactions which occur in micro settings such as the family, classroom, and the workplace. It is in these settings that most authoritarian practices are produced.

> *....a setting of critical importance is the home because it is there that the undisputed father authority, the practice of domestic violence, the hard to avoid submission, and the arbitrary sexual division of labor create the seeds of authoritarian norms later transferred to other spheres of social (and political) life (Stromquist ibid: 21)*

These settings must therefore be targeted as spaces for the creation and maintenance of democratic norms. Moreover, the fundamental antithesis to democracy may not be dictatorship or oligarchy but *authoritarianism*. It is authoritarianism that goes beyond the 'right' and 'left' of the political spectrum in that it touches the *interpersonal interactions* in the multiple settings of everyday life (Stromquist ibid). It is against this awareness of the big picture that right here in Africa, we have to begin the debate about change in the social, economic and political systems.

4.3 Educating the African Girl Child: a Relay Between Patriarchies

What we are witnessing today in the education system, is a slow-motion relay ritual as the traditional African patriarchal order passes the girls child to the 'gentle care' of the Western patriarchal form, somewhat akin to what athletes do on the running track. Evidence of this confronts any reader who picks up and flips through a document or analysis expressing concern about the education of the 'girl child'. The list of 'constraints' to girls education today documented even by constituencies most uninterested in fundamental transformation of societal relations can be recited with the eyes closed:

- negative traditional attitudes and social practices;
- competing demands on the girls' time;
- lack of places and appropriate facilities;
- lack of security both in and outside of school;
- gender stereotyping in curriculum;
- irrelevant and rigid curriculum;
- gender unfriendly classroom culture;
- hostile policies or lack of it;

- limited prospects in the labor market (e.g.Hyde 1996; Namuddu 1992; Lalonde 1996; Odaga & Heneveld 1993; Mbilinyi et.al 1991; Ougadougou 1993).

Although the uniformity in listing is quite striking, one observation can certainly be made. And this has to do with the naked way the traditional and the western patriarchal coalition crystallize, reproduce and enact the violent propensity of their nature especially on the girl-child in the context of the school. The corollary to this is also to bear witness as to how this violence in the boy-child! In spite of the negative, painful and contradictory experiences, the African girl child is fights her way, surviving against the odds at times to achieve the highest excellence in the system. More often however, in the tension and power struggle between these two pervasive forms of domination she is to fall in between the stools, branded and stigmatized.

In the context of the family, the traditional patriarchy pits her against her brother in a bizarre twist of commoditization precept in which she less in the contest for access to school education because after a dowry is extracted of her in the marital process, she is not considered of direct value to the blood family. In the case that she enters the school, she faces a teaching style, school culture, teaching aids that are all pitted against her, or constantly drumming home her evidently low, subordinate, and subservient role and value in school and in society. If she is wise, she would do well to hold fast to training that can enable her to fulfil her future roles equally meekly as a well trained person equipped to handle the home efficiently without destabilizing the status quo.

If she would squeeze through this gorge and proceed to secondary and tertiary levels, ah! well, then there appears the 'labor market' and its vetting procedures. What she has learnt, she discovers pretty soon, has next to no value in terms of the 'modern economy' whose entry codes were all denied her throughout her academic studies during which she had passed with 'flying colors'. What appeared in the beginning as the sympathetic and knowing guidance of the primary and secondary school teachers that made the boys get support in studying maths, sciences and economics while she was edged into sewing and cookery now reveals itself as part of a wider strategy to keep the likes of her permanently from certain domains which control and direct the 'modern sector'. Even those women who may have pushed through as doctors, or economists and lecturers would soon realize that something embedded in the sexual differentiation and gender construction will ensure that her pay cheque will always be lower than that of the male counterpart. Once it reaches this stage, as if by some unseen signal, all national systems seem to be devoid of policies that prevent or at least anticipate this outcome.

A typical empirical statistical cartography of this narrative of the survival path of the girl child as she navigates the cataracts of the education system looks like this: she enrolled......she passed her exams......she disappeared...as the following tables from Zimbabwe well illustrates (note that Zimbabwe is cited merely as an illustrative of a very typical scenario). In 1980 following its independence, Zimbabwe announced free primary schooling for all, with the result that enrolments soared from 819, 586 in 1979 to 2,456,843 in 1994 representing a trebling in total enrolment so....At Zimbabwe Junior Certificate (ZJC) level, all students are required to write core subjects offered and usually, the results of the ZJC examinations will determine the subjects the students will pursue for O'level. There is an overall low achievement rates with boys performing only slightly better than girls in most subjects. Yet as Table 2 and 3 show, by the time the children write O'levels, the acute differentiation in numerical terms is very evident. Only half the number of candidates who took sciences were girls.

Table 1. She enrolled.......

Year	Primary Schools	Enrolment Total	Male Enrolment	Female Enrolment	%Female
1984	4161	2132304	1101899	1030405	48.3
1985	4234	2216878	1142480	1074398	48.5
1986	4297	2265053	1160166	1104887	48.7
1987	4439	2251319	1146361	1104958	49.0
1988	4471	2212103	1122662	1089441	49.2
1989	4504	2233340	1126992	1106348	49.5
1990	4530	2119865	1073452	1011545	47.7
1991	4559	2294934	1168450	1126484	49.0
1992	4569	2305765	1162565	1143200	49.6
1993	4578	2436671	1258465	1178206	48.3
1994	4588	2456843	1251058	1205785	49.0

Primary School enrolments by Gender 1984-1994

***Source**: MoEducation 1995. Zimbabwe Basic Fact Sheet on Education p.1 (quoted in Dorsey 1996:9).*

Table 2. She Passed the Junior Leaving Certificate......

Subject	Boys	Girls
English	39.37	38.75
Mathematics	25.00	24.75
General Science	39.75	39.37
Shona	50.50	49.00
History	36.63	36.00
Ndebele	46.75	41.25
Agriculture	39.36	37.63
Commerce	29.50	29.90
Accounts	43.62	44.00

National Average Per centages-ZJC Examination Results-1993
Source: *Central Computing Services 1994*

Table 3. The Streaming Starts to Show.....

Subject	Boys	Girls
Science (Chemistry, Biology)	429	278
Science (Physics. Chemistry)	3376	1784
Biology	4343	2774
Physics	500	223
Chemistry	409	244

(Number of Boys and Girls who Wrote O'Level Science Subjects in 1993.
Source: *Central Computing Services*

Table 4. The Streaming and Marginalization Becomes More Evident.....

Faculty	Gender		
	% Males	% Females	Total (N)
Agriculture	74.6	25.3	208
Arts	63.7	36.3	1138
Commerce	65.6	34.4	599
Education	69.4	30.5	399
Engineering	94.9	5.1	608
law	67.7	32.2	245
Medicine	65.2	34.8	846
Science	70.5	29.5	766
Social Studies	65.5	34.5	1031
Veterinary Science	80.2	19.8	121
Total	69.8 (N=4211)	30.2 (N=1822)	6033

Undergraduates Student Enrolment by Faculty and Gender 1995 (Full Time)
Source: *University of Zimbabwe, Students Statistics 1995 (AC/220/95) (in Dorsey ibid. p:18)*

Table 5. The Same Pattern in All Technical Colleges......

Subject Area	Gender			
	Male	Female	Total	% Female
Automotive Engineering	1367	56	1423	3.9
Business Studies	3059	1114	4173	26.6
Computer Science	239	154	393	39.2
Construction Civil Engineering (1)	353	29	382	7.6
Electrical Engineering	916	77	993	7.7
Hotel Keeping/Catering	107	77	184	41.8
Instructor Training (FETC)	200	38	238	15.9
Library and Information	71	35	106	33.0
Mass Communication	65	50	115	43.5
Mechanical Engineering	1507	49	1556	3.1
Printing & Graphic Arts	149	49	195	23.5
Plastic Technology	20	3	23	13.0
Rubber technology	21	3	24	12.5
Science Technology	368	83	451	18.4
Secretarial Studies	259	1252	1511	82.8
Textile Technology	6	43	49	87.7
Wood Technology	86	0	86	0.0
Total	8793	3109	11902	26.1

Enrolment in All Technical Colleges by Subject Area and Gender
Source: *Min of Higher Education Annual Report 1995 (in Dorsey ibid: 23)*

Taking the gender gap as a fundamental yardstick for judging the *quality* of education in Africa, it is clear that whatever those imperatives at are that so persistently pervert and subvert the possibility of the learners to acquire not only technical knowledge but also a strong and consistent sense of social justice, are also education's enemy Number One. When violence, marginalization, oppression and suppression permeate the ethos, content and organization of all teaching, it is unlikely that the same educational system can be one to be entrusted with changing the behaviours of people and to enlighten them to take decisions that support the intellectual and social integrity of the people under its care and to whom it is accountable. It would be an educational system that cannot move beyond the narrow and mechanical role of passing on technical knowledge and skills, and even then, it is passing on knowledge and skills to those chosen groups and categories of people already well identified. Writes Namuddu:

> *.....Evidence that education has not become a political tool and project to enlighten all those who come under its influence, is provided by the continued gender gap itself, manifested in the*

> *underutilization of the intellectual, social economic potential of half the human resources in Africa....In the case of the traditional curriculum, education is so totally inefficient and ineffective, that it perpetually defeats two of the cardinal foundations of education. namely: its effect as a multiplier of intellectual and social capital; and its ability to spiral the economies of scale from one school cohort to another and from one generation to the next (emphasis mine, Namuddu 1992:26).*

Ignorance and violence compete for clout in the mind space of those in charge of curriculum at nearly all levels. At tertiary levels, it is even more acute because it is there that the curriculum is most silent about the issues of social justice. Instead of taking leadership positions on key issues confronting the developing societies of Africa and the structural limitations to real progress, these institutions housing African academicians and manufacturing senior policy makers, are fossilized in the identity ascribed them in and by the colonial era. Trapped both in time and space they lament the rarified glories of the past 'like nobles marooned in their crumbling castles as feudalism declined in Europe' (Cannon Doyle, in Namuddu ibid:30). Instead of organizing courses on gender for both males and females and making these imperative, the male academics subject any female who attempts to introduce the subject of gender to a continuum of responses ranging from outright resistance to direct insults and harassment to diversion tactics such as changing the topic away from that concerning gender.

> *....Females, particularly those who have benefitted from higher education are agitated by society's disregard of their potential, their knowledge and skills which lie dormant, even after surmounting such difficult odds. Many professional and long serving females watch helplessly in their gatekeeping roles as male with less qualification and experience move up the ladder to become 'those in command'. Females in teaching and administrative positions at the university are disheartened by the economic crisis which has brought them below poverty line.....Combining their dual role as professionals and housewives does not afford them the time and opportunity to hold a 'third job' at a time when holding a 'second job' is something which has become more or less normal for their male colleagues....Women. educated or not, remain overburdened with work, live on marginal incomes, participate peripherally, if at all, in important national decisions, and rarely have the peace of mind about their future and that of their*

children....(Namuddu ibid: 44).

5. Alternative Approaches to girls education: Some cases

5.1 Girls' Education in the Context of Educational Reform: Benefits by Default

It must be stated from the very beginning that in none of the cases studied has the notion of 'alternative' or 'educational transformation' been used in the context of gender. Even where girls education has gained points, these have been within the framework of a general reform of the system. *Secondly*, that the aspect of reform that is most celebrated whether for all children or by women activists on behalf of the girl child is the quantitative yardstick. The sheer chorus of jubilation round this indicator continues to obfuscate further understanding, analysis or even investigation of the education system as a whole.

Thirdly, in those instances that countries in Africa have clearly attempted to break with the colonial past, the neo-colonial coalition comprising the countries of the former metropole have not been at all amused. In fact, such reforms or efforts at transformation of the system have been at best treated as fundamentally inimical to 'progress', at worst undermined with the ruthless efficiency[5]. *Fourthly*, in the context of the 'new poverty' and the ensuing dependency, the scope for fundamental reform cannot escape the cold, clinical and watchful gaze of the giver of aid. In a recent review of over 120 cases of Education Agency Sector Studies, it is evident that the common denominator as to what they are interested in is precisely the de-politicization of educational policy and compelling it to be reduced to a technical administrative activity[6]. By delimiting the bound-

[5]For an insight as to frightening and bloody efficiency with which this was done in the case of Mozambique see for instance Hanlon J. 1991 *Mozambique: Who Calls the Shots?*

[6]Professor Samoffs analysis entitled *Defining What Is, And What Is Not An Issue* provides a telling empire evidence in this case. All the agencies are formally charged to assist educational development in Africa. But all of them, in all the countries in Africa they operate, have a common starting point as to what constitutes a problem. These are a concern with *impact, effectiveness and 'quality' of education; access, educational sector institutional network; educational finance, the increased role for the private sector*; (the near adulation of) *the non-governmental organizations; the vocational content of education; the* (perceived) *developmental benefits of education; and a preoccupation with the amelioration of the Adjustment Programmes*. These, to the agencies, constitute what is 'wrong' with the educational system, and how it should be rectified. All the goals set by African governments such as: the expectation that education will implant and nurture an *inquiring and critical orientation*; or that 'education will promote *national unity and especially national integration of diverse ethnic, cultural, religious, racial and regional communities*; or that education should engender *collective competence, self reliance and self confidence; reduce elitist orientations*; and finally, schools as a site for *political education* receive little or no attention.

Collated from: P. Obanya 1994: Patterns of Educational Reform in Africa

Reform Approach	Country	Objectives
Redical-Revolution. Approaches	People's Rev. Rep of *Guinea & Ethiopia*; People's Rep. of *Congo & Benin* Rev Movements: *Cape Verde, Guinea Bissau, Angola, & Mozambique* Republic of *Tanzania*	* Break with col. past, and build a 'people's republic'; * universal access; *educ. Policy stressed and reflected 'self reliance', the building of a new nation; *radical reforms of curriculum incl. introd. of indig. language. a closer rel between education and production, re-emphasis on exam-propelled curricula; *creation of a 'learning society' (adult literacy & adult education); * close involvement of local communities in the dev. of educ, and the promotion of civic/political educ;
Realistic Revolution. Approaches	Zimbabwe, Nigeria, Zambia, Botswana Kenya, Ghana, Sierra Leone, the Gambia, Namibia	*improved access e.g. incl. through NFE, innov approaches to science educ, expansion of teaching force, * national consultations or needs analysis often prefixed by some mention of 'the inherited colonial system' emphasizing its inadequacies; * restructuring meaning reorganization of the educ. cycle 8-4-4 or 6-3-3-4 etc. * no mention of interntion to break completely with col past; * times establishment of structures for national curriculum development; * very popular with international audience

Collated from: P. Obanya 1994: Patterns of Educational Reform in Africa *{cont.}*

Ad Hoc Approaches	(variously) Nigeria, Kenya, Ghana, Sierra Leone, the Gambia Cote d I'voire, Uganda, Cameroun	* addresses just one issue at a time; * reform by decree e.g on 'modern mathematics in the 1960s & 70s, cycle restructuring, use of indigenous languages; *usually influenced by the culture of pilots e.g. educ. tv project (Cote d'Ivoire), Banumbu (Sierra leone), the Namutamba (Uganda), the IPAR (Cameroun); * little or no articulation of people's expectations of education
Evolutionary Approaches	Almost all French-speaking countries (esp. in reforms of higher educ.);	*inappropriateness of the 'inherited col educ system is acknowledged, but; * no efforts to engineer change in any radical or systematic manner; * direct link with reform procesees in metropolitan countries; * curriculum 'enrichment' programmes in lukewarm areas such as enironment, population studies (often on urges from international community; * Syllabuses are revised in respect of specific subjects on the school curriculum.

aries of what constitutes 'legitimate policy discourse' to technical downstream activities, and heavily funding those areas they have delineated to be 'important', it is the agencies who are, in effect, the new gatekeepers of policy direction and dreams.

This is a challenge to African integrity that cannot be left for chance or posterity. The reform initiatives here sampled have variously led to overall improvement of enrolment, but with mixed rationales, and implications for transformation. Girls enrolment especially at the primary level is vastly improved particularly in those countries that adopted the radical revolutionary and realistic revolutionary approaches to reform. During the consultations leading to the Amman Mid-Decade Review conference, a study of the state of education in the Eastern and Souther African countries states that the challenge for these countries today is how to sustain the gains made by the earlier policies (Hyde 1996).

New directions and achievements of reforms processes have been: the continued questioning of the relevance of education in Africa, emerging forms of national consultations on education (often as part of the democratization process); renewed attention on African indigenous languages (though with very mixed application), institutionalization of educational planning & management in African countries (sometimes at the acute expense of political or ideological engagement on education); curriculum enrichment through integration of new perspectives on African history, social studies and science (Segou Perspectives 1995; Obanya 1994). The 'Segou Perspectives' in particular seeks to demonstrate the will of African to mobilize themselves for the 'reconstruction of the education systems' in Africa from three critical premises:

1. The reconstruction and the development of the cultural identity of the learner.
2. The link between school and the 'life-world' through a pedagogy and educational content that would assure the learner a mastery of the environment;
3. Involvement of all the actors (parents, pupils, teachers, communities and development partners) in the management of the school (Segou Perspectives 1995: 13-14.

The Ougadougou Declaration itself urges governments to give priority to quality and equity in the education of girls, and to draw upon positive aspects of historical, cultural and religious heritage as a means of improving education and equity. Questions relating to the mission of higher education have yet to be responded to. Similarly, larger cohorts are attending school but questions remain as to the direction of schooling as a whole. From these efforts at reform, the following 'intervention strategies' in favor of girls can be gleaned.

5.2 Intervention Strategies by Governments in Favor of Girls

In this section, the attempt is to give pointers as to what strategies countries that have scored well on quantitative indicators did to reach this goal (some strategies have a specifically qualitative dimension). Note that the noble notion of '*alternatives*' in the context of government quickly collapses into '*intervention strategies*'. These summaries are merely to provide pointers as to type and scope of interventions as it is impossible to cover all countries in Africa individually. No judgement or comments are passed at this point.

5.2.1 Zimbabwe

Zimbabwe has nearly achieved universal access to primary education. Gender rations are also favorable with less that 2 per cent fewer girls than boys in school. However, between 20-30 per cent of primary school pupils drop out before completing Grade 7, this figure being 10 per cent higher for girls especially from the rural areas. Enrolments is considered to have stabilized and government does not anticipate continued expansion except to cater for population growth. The issue now is 'quality' improvement for all especially rural children, and for girls. Accordingly the following strategies can be said to be specifically targeted to girls education.

1. Ten years before Jomtien, the government adopted a policy of education for all. School fees at the primary level was abolished. This abolition of fees at the primary level *reduced the cost of education to households* even though there is still the cost of school uniforms. This accounts for the quantitative gains and successes of Zimbabwe's educational system in the part 15 years.
2. When school fees were reintroduced in 1994, it was restricted to the urban areas *but not in the rural areas where the gender gap is larger.*
3. At the A-level, the government has introduced an *affirmative action policy* with regard to entry selection in order to increase the number of girls who qualify. This has contributed to reducing the gender gap especially the proportion of boys to girls.
4. Assisted by donor agencies, government is working to improve facilities and amenities in rural schools in order to attract more trained teachers and improve the quality of education for both boys and girls. This is a systemic improvement.
5. Meanwhile government encouragement of donor agencies has been

critical in mobilizing resources necessary in addressing gender issues in education, it is not clear whether this is a manifestation of internal resistance within the system to specific budgetary allocations being made in this area and thus leaving it to 'posterity' and the generosity of foreigners.

6. An affirmative action policy and strategy in is operation at the university level in the selection of students into the undergraduate degree programmes by lowering the entrance requirements for girls by two points. In just one year, the per centage of girls has gone up from 26 per cent to 30. One aim is to continue with this policy until the rate is at least 40:60.
7. Government tolerance and token recognition of single sex schools for girls. Despite the contestations to this model from a socialization point of view, achievement levels bear out the advantage of this system in which the detrimental stress factors associated with having to deal with the discriminatory practices so bent in favor of boys is at least postponed till the girls have gone through critical stages of the schooling system (Colclough & Lewin 1993; Hyde 1996; Dorsey 1996).

5.2.2 Malawi

Women constitute 52 per cent of Malawi's population of 8.2 million. Approximately 70 per cent of full time farmers in the country are women. 30 per cent of rural households are headed by women. The average family size is 7.7 children. Women's access to non-agricultural formal and informal sector employment is constrained by the yoke of double patriarchal relations operating in both the traditional sphere and in the modern sector. The educational system is typically pyramidal with only 50 per cent of primary school age children in school. Despite near parity in enrollment and a very serious malaise of dropout for all school children, the dropout rate for girls are higher. The ripple effects upstream are familiar. Until the late 1980s, Malawi had the lowest enrolment rates in Southern Africa except for the war torn countries of Angola and Mozambique. Accordingly the following can be listed as specific government strategies to address the issue of girls education.

1. An affirmative action programme established by region for the entry of girls into secondary and higher education.
2. Strategies aimed at addressing *retention* through bursaries and fee waivers in primary and secondary levels were given to encourage girls who drop out through an inability to pay fees to continue their education. (This project in Girl's attainment in Basic Literacy and Education -GABLE-is support by USAID).

3. The present government came to power with free primary education as an important part of its manifesto. Primary education became free in 1994. The increase in enrolment was an astounding 68 per cent.
4. To keep costs down, government declared uniforms to be optional.
5. Policies which discouraged girls' re-enrolment in school has been reviewed and the following were the results:
   a. Readmission of girls who became pregnant while in school after delivery and guaranteed child care.
   b. Increase of the quota of girls selected into secondary school from 33 to 50 per cent.
   c. Review of curriculum to make it gender appropriate. (This is on to of other dimension of curricular reform which seeks to make it more functional and train pupils in general in skills needed for life outside of school).
6. Government plans to expand the number of secondary schools by 250 anticipating an increased enrolment from the expanded primary school system.
7. Half of these schools will be single sex schools for girls.
8. A campaign of social mobilization aimed at promoting the importance of girl's education among pupils, teachers, parents and communities utilizes a theater group from the University of Malawi to produce a series of 'gender-sensitive morality plays'.

In 1992-93, for the first time, girls net enrolment outnumbered boys by 3 per cent. The number of girls who did not drop out but who persisted to standard 8 increased from 30 per cent in 1988/89 to 38 per cent in 1992/93. The GABLE project made provisions of school fee waivers for non-repeating girls form standard 2 though to 8. During the 1992/93 school year, over 400,000 girls benefitted from these waivers. The following year, the number went up to 600,000.

Gender streaming at secondary level has produced positive results with pass rates for girls at the Junior Certificate Examinations jumping from 20 per cent in 1988 to over 80 per cent between 1988 and 1991. Male pass rates also went up from approximately 70 per cent to 100 per cent (see also Hyde 1996; Dorsey 1996).

5.2.3 Burkina Faso[7]

Burkina Faso's educational system comprises formal, non-formal and informal systems. The formal education sub-system comprises preschool education, primary education, secondary education and tertiary educa-

[7] The following country summaries is derived from a Universalia study entitled Female Education in Africa and the Role of NGOs. Vol II; Country Reports.

tion. The non-formal system comprises literacy training, training for young farmers, and education specially designed for girls. Informal education covers includes education via radio, TV, movies, theater, libraries e.t.c. An obvious discrepancy exists between objectives and content of formal education on the one hand, and the *needs* of communities and their social and economic realities on the other. Teacher training does not acknowledge special issues related to educating girls, while the education is bedeviled with its rigid schedules. The present strategies towards improving girls' situation undertaken by government include:

1. Implementation of the Project d'Egalite d'Acces des Femmes Jeunes Filles a l'Education (1968-78) with the support of UNESCO;
2. Creation of public girls schools (primary, secondary, and female technical institutions);
3. Publication of a decree *changing* the policy of dismissal of pregnant female students (1974);
4. Creation of a department promoting the education of girls (SPSF) affiliated with the Institute Pedagogique du Burkina (IPB);
5. Creation of female literacy centres from 1990.
6. Creation of a seven facetted plan of action for the education of girls with a time frame to equalizing participation by the year 2000.
7. Establishment of satellite schools which have mandates to shorten the school cycle, bring schools closer to the children and especially to facilitate girls' access and participation.

5.2.4 Guinea

The primary cycle in Guinea lasts six years followed by a lower secondary education from seventh to tenth grade. Upper secondary 11th and 12th Grade ends with a high school leaving diploma. The primary and secondary Muslim sector comprises *mederas* (theological instruction), and French Arab upper secondary schools (classical and religious instruction). The primary and secondary religious Catholic sector was substantial until the beginning of the 1960s when it was nationalized. Following Sekou Toure's death in 1984, the government has advocated liberalism. Despite measures and political will, the per centage of girls registering in school only rose by 6 per cent from 1989, 25 per cent between 1990 and 1994. In this grim situation, below listed are the measures adopted to address the gross gender inequality.

1. A political will evolved in which the education of girls became a priority of both the ministry of education and the government as a whole.
2. Following a 1993 directive pregnant girls are automatically entitled to maternity leave until after childbirth after which they are allowed to

continue their studies.

3. An interministerial committee on equality was set up.
4. Inclusion of statistics on girls participation and achievement in the Ministry of Education's annual statistics.
5. Setting up of a multi sector/ multi disciplinary consulting body on basic education.
6. Appointment of women to positions of power (ministerial, directors, United Nations e.t.c.).

5.2.5 Kenya

To its credit the education sector in Kenya has grown rapidly enabling the Kenyan government to provide educational services to the majority of its school aged population. Female students have benefitted in terms of access and participation from this provision By 1992 for instance, the per centage of girls enrolled in secondary education had increased by 500 per cent, decreasing the male female ratio at that level from 2.6 to 1 in 1970, to 1,32 to 1 in 1992. However, disparity by other indicators such as regional, achievement, retention and at tertiary levels still persist. The following are pointers as to what the government has put in place to address this issue:

1. Setting up of a national target of universal access to *quality* and ***relevant*** education by the year 2000.
2. The creation of a gender unit in the Ministry of Education mandated with the task to mainstream gender at all levels of education. A task force to support, monitor and evaluate the educational progress of the Kenyan girls is said to be in the making.
3. Encouraged the intervention of donor agencies and NGOs in this area.

Like many other countries, the Kenyan government, educators and researchers recognize that 'socio-cultural, economic and institutional obstacles exist' to constrain the effectuating of these goals. Accordingly, calls are becoming ever louder that a more holistic approach and analysis of female education in general and the quality of education in particular should be adopted, and even greater support should be given to building up more model institutions such as the 'Alliance Girls' in Kenya, the 'Women's University' in Ethiopia.

5.2.6 Senegal

In Senegal participation rates in the formal education sector in 1990 was 37 per cent for males and 25 per cent for females. The already lower rate for females increase further up the ladder. A high female failure rate at the end of primary and secondary cycles creates a bulge in enrolment in private schools at this level as most of the girls who do not make it to the formal national structure get integrated into the private system where entrance requirements are less stringent. The government's effort to address this problem includes systems wide strategies, and those specific for girls:

1. Introduction of multi grade classes and double session school days.
2. Promoting the integration of formal with non-formal education for greater coordination and coherence.
3. Setting up of national targets for girls' participation in schooling from 42 per cent to 65 per cent by the year 2000.
4. Decentralizing school management to regional and departmental levels to increases efficiency and effectiveness.
5. Development of a national plan of action for Girls Child Education to be operationalized through an accord with UNICEF and Canadian CIDA. The action plan utilizes a four prong strategy among which are:
   * *social mobilization* to sensitize parents in rural areas to enroll their daughter in school;
   * *action research* to study underlying causes for low levels of girl child education as well as experimentation with new models;
   * *training* of school inspectors on monitoring the progress of the girl child education;

The social mobilization has been well under way since May 1995 and preliminary results show an increase in the enrolment rate of girls in primary education of 3 per cent from 41 per cent to 44 per cent for the year 1995/96 alone However, it is noted that despite considerable interest and support for girl child education on the part of the Senegalese government, both policy and action in this area are fairly recent. A more comprehensive, if not holistic approach to comprehending the problem is still needed.

5.2.7 Tanzania

From a situation in which the policy of Universal Primary Education in Tanzania had led to a near parity in enrolment rates between boys and girls especially at the primary level, the economic factors appears to have exacted their toll. The government of Tanzania which was traditionally the sole provider of education services, is now unable to fulfil this role. The mixed bag of liberalization policies have resulted in the mushrooming of private initiatives of as yet unclear quality-into which girls tend to flock owing to the rigorous examination system in the formal system. The government has taken a look at the situation and adopted the following measures among many:

1. Legislated laws to *force* parents to send all children to school, and where parents are taken to court for keeping children at home; laws to prosecute those who make school girls pregnant; and laws to bring about change in customary practices of early marriages.
2. Increased the number of girl's boarding schools;
3. Providing scholarships to those girls who come from poor households.
4. Encouraging NGO and bilateral agency intervention in improving girl's education.

5.3 Educational Reform, NGOs and the New Partnerships

In the 6 countries reviewed; Burkina Faso, Guinea, Kenya, Senegal, Tanzania, and Zimbabwe (see cartography in appendix 2), all are experiencing significant deterioration in the quality, accessibility and *relevance* of public education. All of them are involved in some form of reform, and the imperatives of decentralization and democratization are compelling the fostering and mushrooming of new models and the involvement of new partnerships involving networking with NGOs and bringing them closer to government agenda. These are evident in Senegal, Tanzania, Burkina Faso, Zimbabwe and Guinea. The aim is to increase democratization and involve local communities in greater decision making, and naturally, *cost sharing* for social service delivery. Echoing the Jomtien declaration itself, the new Tanzanian Education and Training Policy states that the government shall no longer be the sole provider of primary education but shall provide incentives to individuals, communities and NGOs to establish and develop primary education institutions. In Zimbabwe, the Education Act of 1990 stipulates that every primary school must have a School Development Committee to manage and finance the school beyond teachers salaries and the grants per pupil given by government.

Synergy between formal and non-formal systems are being promoted at the primary/basic education level. In Senegal and Burkina Faso alternative models for basic education are being developed that shadow the content of formal school but make it *more relevant* (through inclusion of production skills, language training); *more efficient* (self-sustaining through community contributions, income generating activities, shorter time frames); *more accessible* for girls (linked to girl's needs, closer to home, supervised by the community). Guinea has established community-based Nafa centres for under-educated and uneducated adolescents in an attempt to reintegrate them into the formal system of provide them with economic production skills. But the question of constraints to equal access to educational benefits remains a looming problem.

Also quite clear is the fact that NGOs appear to lack strategic coordination among themselves and with government, thereby diminishing their potential effectiveness in supporting female education. Non the less, even as they lack the crucial 'bird's eye view' of the whole nation, they represent society's way to rise up to the challenge of survival, governance, and democratic participation. NGOs have introduced innovative programmes in the educational system such as the *Umati* in Tanzania (serving girls who have left school due to pregnancy); *Undugu Society* in Kenya (for street children); and the *Camfed Programme* in Zimbabwe (to assist girls from families who cannot afford fees). Community groups have provided their services, time and attention to both initiation and maintenance of the school system.

6. LOOKING FORWARD

6.1 Turning Schooling Around: Changing the Mind set

(1)......Basic Education for All is a profound political choice and current difficulties can do nothing to shake our determination to achieve this goal.....(M. Samassekou, Hon Minister of Education-Mali); (2).....Girls are the main victims of the formal school system (EFA-Making it Work. (3)......the school is the vehicle for the attainment of UPE (various......)

It is precisely the contradictory messages in the above quotes that forms the crux of the dilemma for educators today. There is a strong determination to achieve the goal of basic education for all. But the achievement of this goal is to be realized within or with the leadership of the formal schooling. At the same time, schools are premised upon, contain and sustain some of the most pervasive forms of structural violence that is inflicted on the children who pass through it. The numbers are not few. World Education Report states that Sub-Saharan Africa alone registered a entrusted a total of 57,700,000 children to the primary level of this system in 1985 (of which 25,800,000) were girls). During the year 1995, a total of 68,900,000 children were enrolled at that level (of which 31,300,000 were girls) and the question on the lips of educators continue to be 'how can we give more?'

It is proposed here that in reflecting about alternative approaches to education, we cannot any longer avoid confronting the education system with the epiphany of its internal culture which not only alienates, but also constructs and reinforces gender stereotyping with well documented consequences for the future woman, mother, and citizen. Most of the non-formal approaches skirt around this problem by attempting to create 'own projects'. Most of these are poised to deal with the *effects* of schooling in terms of either its restricted absorption capacity (unenrolled), or in terms of its attrition characteristic which expunges a huge number of children at particular points in the system (drop-push outs), or in terms of the morally castigated (pregnant girls). We should be happy for those who have shown compassion and courage to create systems that can take in these various categories of 'rejects'. Non the less, this is simply NOT ENOUGH.

The formal primary school sits pedestalized and highly regarded at all levels. It is a privileged form of learning among the supporters of education efforts (most of whom in any case despise anything else but school education), and is accredited with an entire ministry (sometimes ministries) and a network of schools and trained support staff. Citizens pay taxes to uphold this system even in a context of heavy debt repayments. This system must stand up to the occasion and demonstrate its capability, if it exists, to engender *empowerment, reinforce democracy, human development and promote peace*; because as it stands now with the evidence that girls participation in the system unravels, the formal educational system STANDS INDICTED on counts of connivance and engendering *disempowerment, thriving in inequalities*, reinforcing authoritarianism, and laying a basis for relations of *dominance*.

It is clear that what we need is an urgent exercise in transformation of the school culture in the African context. For this to take root, it is important to move from parroting the litany of the historical, cultural and economic deeterminants and constraints to fuller learning and education of the African child, to *a vision of the school* as an arena in which *contestation, resistance and creation* can be enacted. If it is so that in the site of the school, two major streams of patriarchy come home to roost and stunt the participation of girls, then it is also precisely there that change has to begin. This would enable actors in education to reconstruct and supplant traditional notions associated with schools, teaching, and education as a whole. The project would permit the investment in the *human agency and will* of the public and teachers as starting points for change. In this way, teachers cease being seen as part of some mechanism, and whose lives are 'pre-ordained' to act the way they do. This framework enables teachers to retain their ability to be conscious, and to analyze and act within the socially defined site (the school). In this way, they are intellectuals and act as intellectuals to critique school, its culture, and attempt to transform the social world they inhabit.

Transformation is taught through both process and content. The constraints to girls education well listed by researchers constitute and are constituted in the living world within which the school is located. These should become key items in the syllabi and curricula, for group work in schools, for community discussions, and sensitization campaigns at all levels. They should become items for debate in parliaments and topics for research until the issues are recognized enough to be considered fit for resolution. It is only by confronting the schooling system itself with the epiphany of *its being* that this site for reproduction of oppressive relations can liberate itself and in that process also liberate the children entrusted to its care. It is only schools constituted in this way that can recognize the multiple subjectivities of the African girl-child, and the ways in which different forms of oppression may overlap or come into conflict in the classrooms:

> *.......A critical pedagogy....would focus on the study of the curriculum not merely as a matter of self-cultivation or the mimicry of specific forms of learning and knowledge. On the contrary, it would stress forms of learning and knowledge aimed at providing a critical understanding of how social reality works, it would focus on how certain dimensions of such a reality are sustained, it would focus on the nature of its formative processes, and it would also focus on how those aspects of it that are related to the logic of domination can be changed (Aronowitz & Giroux 1985:217).*

For the students, a reconstituted school would enable them to analyze the forces acting on their lives. At the same time, activists and progressive educators must at all times remember:

> *.......the power that social forces exert on themselves and on the students and that they always recognize the limits of what it is possible to accomplish.......But by recognizing the limits of what is possible. (all of us) should recognize the value of doing what is possible (Weiler 1988: 153).*

6.2 Equity is Not Enough!

Meanwhile it is acknowledged that the quantitative yardstick maybe the most 'measurable' way to assess progress in the path of securing a more just social order, it must not become a fixation, an end in itself. To the extent that this is a useful indicator, it can be said to have become *so useful* as to have eschewed understanding of the root issues connected with the education of the girl-child in Africa.

We know that discrimination and violence persists in the education system. We know that we are functioning within a framework of the *education for adaptation;* one whose success is measured by the scaling down of expectations, and a meek adaptation to the 'world of work' whether as waged labor or as improved farmer. It is one that retrenches women into the status quo in the *modern sector* rather than one which will show them the codes of emancipation. In their analysis of Education in Tanzania with a Gender Perspective', Mbilinyi (et.al) state that the principles of a liberating or transformative education aims to raise peoples expectations and consciousness, their ability to engage in critical and creative thought, and their ability to directly control the economy, government and all other institutions. For women as well as other oppressed groups, such transformative or liberating education *is a tool for empowerment* (Mbilinyi et. al 1991). The failure to bring about a transformative education has affected women in particular in that gender discrimination (as separate from "parity in enrollment") and differentiation has persisted at all levels of the formal education system. These are not matters that numerical expansion alone can address.

Moreover, the whole sphere of governance is permeated with ESAP-induced flag-carriers such as 'liberalization', 'democratization', 'decentralization': a project of deconstruction of these concepts and principles must begin, and investigations as to what they portend for women must be exposed *in good time*, preferably before other strategic action have been taken by government already. Reform processes must be scrutinized for their transformative potentials for all children, but especially for the girl-child and women.

6.3 Policy Makers: Reclaim Your Space and Mandate!

Perhaps it is the debt crisis, perhaps it is poverty. That we might never absolutely know. But it is clear that in the context of the continuity of neo-colonial relations (Altbach), the consequence of outranking the winner has been that the defeated one *not only loses his life space, but also his word.* That is why, we experience that the communication that takes place in the horizon and in search of a true universal that expresses itself in the diversity of existence forms, has turned out to be a *struggle for truth.* It also becomes part of a process of deliberate scrutiny of seemingly innocent emancipatory western discourse in the area of education that:

> *....serves to uphold and knowledge upon dominated societies by monopolizing the parameters for interpretation, by marginalizing*

> *whatever has not been determined by western conquest, and by domesticating other subject positions as historically obsolete and self-defeating otherness-pre-colonial, pre-capitalist, ir-rational, pre-modern, non-modern, non-literate, un-democratic e.t.c. (Dias 1993:230).*

No bilateral or multilateral agency is going to give us this sense of 'truth', or the 'space' just like that, because their truth is what is being effected through the global trade policies, through the Economic Structural Adjustment Programme, and through the powerful theories of human development they have themselves put in place. Youare being invited to facilitate change. You are being challenged to initiate change. The children in schools are in anguish about the system into which they must entrust their whole lives. The parents are at a loss about what to do. TAKE IT ON, and use this mandate to reclaim your lost spaces. No Non-Governmental Organization is about to acquire the profoundness of national sovereignty that it takes to run a government and state system. Help those who have ideas and creative methods, approaches and perspectives and learn from them. But the challenge is yours. In looking aside while the education system crumbles along with the dreams of the children, you are witnessing your own gradual demise. In looking aside as the girl child is abused, harassed and excruciated by structures and practices that you control, you are endorsing that culture and effectively partaking of it; for silence is also policy (see also below).

6.4 Researchers: Deal Boldly with Research Questions

This is not easy, given the existence of what Professor Samoff called the *financial intellectual complex*. Most research commissioned by agencies today are made to justify some policy decision *already made*. Thus when agencies are about to alter their course of support to some education or development sector, watch how research agenda gets oriented, and the type of questions that get asked. The rationale there is to gain a high 'impeachable moral ground' by citing that *research has shown...* Policy critiques that do not cite supporting research are then ignored and brushed aside. The result? Only those agenda points that are 'supported by research findings', in other words, only those that in the first place could win favour with the funding agencies as dealing with 'important issues', are those that get researched. This has killed innovative policy formation in Africa. It is a sick cycle in which to acquire the visa to 'cross funding's frontiers' as Samoff states, a researcher must demonstrate that he/she shares common understandings about the conception of development and therefore the strategies for achieving it; that he/she share a sense of the nature of the obstacles to the changes that are deemed desirable and therefore tactics for addressing them; and usually a vision of the role of the western framework itself in guiding development.

Moreover, there is the infrastructure conditioning methodology that has derailed research into a domain 'deeply immersed in uninformed and uncoordinated empiricism' with the consequence that research has become the gathering of facts, facts, unconnected facts that cannot be compared or added together (Datta 1990). This can stop. The proposal here is for African researchers to look for unconventional donors and file petitions with African business groups such as the African Business Roundtable and perhaps several other new constituencies that may not have as warped a conception of the role of research as has been the case with traditional funders.

Research can be made to focus on the process of growing up in the educational system, the crisis of identity, the reasons for parental reluctance or at times resistance to schooling that is not merely one more of the socio-Darwinist argumentation that it is due to 'ignorance' and 'backwardness'. Why would parents rather face jail sentences and floggings at police station (Tanzania) than acquiesce to sending children to school? Because the prevailing development paradigm modeled on the modernization frame insists on pressing the distinction between the developed and underdeveloped societies into a distinction between *good* and *bad*, the underdeveloped societies of Africa are treated as though they have neither validity nor integrity and may be violated at will. Their validity relies on their repudiating what they are in order to be reconstituted into something new and 'better':

> *......the task for development is no longer how a people might move forward on its own terms given all that it has, but how it might be transformed by other people in their own image of what they consider it ought to be. From this perspective, development becomes an exercise in self alienation and humiliation (emphasis mine, Ake 1988: 19-20).*

Finally, for African researchers, the issue of gender invokes a powerful urge to regurgitate 'established findings'. The ahistorical category of 'tradition' has become the repository of all the forces contributing to women's oppression. The role of schooling and the development it serves is not invoked. By escaping into words like 'alternatives', we are endorsing the existence of the central definition that should remain intact. Words like 'alternative', 'human scale', 'another' are forced by the nakedness of circumstance onto innovators precisely because the original monolith is trademarked and not to be disturbed. The master/mainstream terminology remains all the time eerily exempt from the need to explain or defend itself. By participating in an alternative discourse, we are endorsing our implicit internalized acknowledgment of a presumed uncontestable *appellation controlee* as Raff Carmen calls it, in precisely the same breath that we confess to the second rate nature of the initiative we are embarking on (Carmen 1994).

African educational alternatives for societal development in Africa cannot avoid confronting the issue of 'which education' for 'what kind of development' in Africa to the C21 st. Such a confrontation must be clear from the outset whether it is aiming to butler the dominant definition, or to transform that dominant definition and indeed make it qualitatively, ethically, and morally more fit for the tasks expected of it. Researchers and policy makers in Africa must make up their mind!

6.5 For Activists and Agents of Change: Strengthen the Strategies for Policy Dialogue

The Forum for African Women Educationalists have led the way. It can be strengthened, it can be even better. Policy dialogue as an exercise in *strategic communication* (Odora 1995) does not dichotomize the participation into the Orwellian 'two legs good, four legs bad' formation, but:

1. attempts to get the parties to the conflictual, or unresolved issue to recognize that they are confronting an *issue*, or a *system of relations* of which the parties may be unwitting carriers, but which is acting to constrain constructive action in specific areas. The idea is to get the parties to become familiar with the problem area, and how they can *act together* to alter or change the named relationship.
2. The investment is in constant improvement of the *communication* strategies and methodologies that are applicable to different constituencies.
3. Investing in positive identification of new constituencies who can be targets of intervention strategies.
4. Keeping a sharp eye for on going-reform initiatives and programmes in which gender can not just be integrated, but in which the expertise in gender training can be incorporated further upstream so that a gender perspective or less in infused from the beginning, not just grafted onto it.

Activists and change agents in the area of gender should not avoid the fact that any struggle against oppression gains power by *drawing people's heritage and experience of liberation into dialogue with other interpretations* (Saphiro 1991).

Advocates for womens emancipation must guard against the self destruct sequence of equating gender only with women!!!. The kind of tendency to orchestrate blindly for 'more and better' development and the idea that the main task left is now just to master tools to achieve this objective must be sincerely reconsidered. When the struggle to create a just system for all is collapsed into a struggle against men in the biological sense, a fundamental misjudgement occurs in which advocates for women then fail to disaggregate forms and types of oppression and how these are manifested in different contexts. Another danger that could threaten advocacy is that connected with the issue of mandate. Instead of gaining their mandate from women's voices as to their total experiences which need not always be the tale of oppression by men, it would appear that in contemporary frameworks for 'gender sensitization' women's perceptions that do not fit within the framework of the 'universal oppression' are recorded as products of mistaken, distorted perception, the products most certainly, *of primitive feelings*. This usurping of cognitive authority from the women themselves, and arrogating it to experts has had the consequence that the role and process of schooling as well as the kind of development it reinforces are not brought out into critical focus. It has also led to regurgitative and superficial analyses as to parental attitudes in making various life choices, as well as their own understanding and expectations of the factory we call the school leading to a new dichotomization of behaviors that are passed as 'correct' and those that are 'evil'. Once more, researchers are doing to African parents (especially the poor) precisely the same thing that was done to the black community in the United States in the 1960s and to women;.......... analyze and scrutinize their behavior to pieces not in order to really understand the world as they see it, but to judge the extent to which they see it as we want them to; and of course, there is the factor of career opportunities.....We simply have got to do better.

African women educationalists and those working in the development industry have a responsibility first and foremost to the reconstruction of the African woman's identity as a full human being in her societal context, not some deficit image in relation to some western scale of progress. The have a responsibility and mandate to assist her figure her way through the intricate mechanisms by which the modern constructs of gender, based on experiences of gender in industrialized countries itself limits her self-assertion based on a power that may not derive from the western experience; and in particular the way that such a western construction of gender itself thrives on the subjugation of the 'Otherness' in her. They have a responsibility to assist the African woman to decipher and make sense of the process of enclosure and industrialization and in particular how the resultant dislocation of the individual from community ties and from ties to the land and landscape can even remotely be called a process of 'engendering development' that is more *humane*. This much we owe the 'primitive' African woman who should be set upon and schooled into development.

References

Altbach. P.G. 1982. Servitude of the Mind? Education, Dependency and Neo-Colonialism. In Altbach P.G; Arnove R.F; Kelly G.P. eds. *Comparative Education.* N.Y. MacMillan Publishing.

Ake C. 1988. Recovery in Africa: The Challenge for Development Cooperation in the 1990s. Stockholm, Ministry of Foreign Affairs.

Amman Declaration. June 1996. Education For All Mid-Decade Conference. Amman-Jordan.

Aronowitz S & Giroux H. 1985. Education Under Siege: The Conservative, Liberal and Radical Debate Over Schooling. South Hadley, Mass. Bergin & Garvey.

Bernard J. 1987. The Female World from a Global Perspective. Bloomington. Indiana University Press.

Boulding E. 1980. Woman. The Fifth World, New York: Foreign Policy Association Headline Series.

Brock-Utne 1989. Feminist Perspectives on Peace and Peace Education. Oxford, Pergamon Press.

Carmen R. 1994. The Logic of Economics vs the Dynamics of Culture: Daring to Re-Invent the Common Future. In Harcourt W. (ed). 1994. Feminist Perspectives on Sustainable Development. London. Zed Books.

Chung F. & Ngara E. 1985. Socialism, Education and Development: A Challenge to Zimbabwe. Zimbabwe publishing House.

Colclough c. & Lewin K. 1993 Educating All the Children: Strategies for Primary schooling in the South. Oxford University Press. Oxford.

Datta A. 1990 The Development of African Educational Research Capacity. Infrastructure and Methodology: Aspects of Educational Research in the SADC Region. In Mautle G. & Youngman F. 1990. Educational Research in the SADC Region. BERA-Gaborone.

Dias P. 1993. Democratization of education as a Political Challenge to Social Authoritarianism in India. Inword Sud Aktuell-Themen 2. Quartal 1993.

Dorsey B.J. 1996. Gender Inequalities in Education in the Southern African region. An Analysis of Intervention Strategies. UNESCO Sub-Regional Office for Southern Africa.

Durston S. 1996. Increasing education For All: Community Schools in Zambia. UNICEF-Zambia.

Ekins. P. 1992. A New World Order. Grassroots Movements for Social Change. London. Routledge.

Ekundayo Thompson J.D. 1995. Curriculum Development in Non-Formal Education. African association for Literacy and Adult Education. Nairobi.

Escobar Z. 1989. Examples of Special projects for Out of School Children. In Ranaweera A.M. 1989. Non Conventional Approaches to Education at the Primary Level. UNESCO Institute for Education Monographs No. 14. Hamburg.

Fanon. F. 1962. The Wretched of the Earth. Harmondsworth, Penguin Books.

French M. 1986. Beyond Power. On Women, Men, and Morals. London Abacus.

Foucault M. 1980. Power and Knowledge. Toronto. The harvester Press.

Fagerlind I. & Saha L. 1989. Education & National Development. London Pergamon Press.

Gramsci A. 1970. Prison Notebooks. New York. International Publishers.

Hanlon J. 1991. Mozambique, Who Calls the Shots? Indiana. James Currey.

Havelock R.G. & Huberman A.M. 1977. Solving Educational Problems. The Theory and Reality of Innovation in Developing Countries. UNESCO.

Hoppers W. & Komba D. 1995. Productive Work in Education and Training. A State of the Art in Eastern Africa. The Hague. CESO.

Hyde K.A.L. 1996. Girls Education in Eastern and Southern Africa: An Overview. Prepared for the Regional Mid Decade Review Towards Education For All Meeting. Johannesburg-South Africa. UNICEF-ESARO.

Ki-Zerbo J. 1990. Educate Or Perish: Africa's Impasse and Prospects. Paris. UNESCO.

Kuhn T.S. 1970. The Structure of Scientific revolutions. London, University of Chicago Press.

Lalonde H. 1996. Girls and Women's education in Africa. Recent experiences, Challenges and Strategies. CIDA Discussion Paper.

Mama. A. 1991. Shedding the Masks and Tearing the Veils: Towards a Gender Approach to African Culture. Paper presented for the workshop on 'Gender analysis and African Social Science'. Dakar Senegal.

Mbilinyi M; Mbughuni P.; Meena R; Olekambaine P.; 1991. Education in Tanzania With a Gender perspective. Stockholm. SIDA. Stockholm.

Moumouni A. 1968. Education in Africa. London. Andre Deutch Limited.

Namuddu K. 1992. Gender Perspectives in African Higher Education. Paper presented at the Senior Policy Seminar on African Higher Education, University of Zimbabwe.

Nyerere J.K. 1967. The Process of Liberation. In Nabudere D. W. 1989. The One Party state and Its Assumed Philosophical Roots. Unpublished seminar paper. Stockholm.

NORRAG News. 1996.

Obanya P. 1994. Patterns of Educational Reform in Africa. Keynote address at the Pan African Colloquium on Reforms in Post Colonial Africa. Cape Town-South Africa.

Odaga A. & Heneveld W. 1995. Girls and Schools in Sub-Saharan Africa: From analysis to action. AFTED-World bank. Washigton DC.

Odora C.A. 1993. Educating African Girls in a Context of Patriarchy and Transformation: A Theoretical and Conceptual Analysis. Institute of International Education. Stockholm University.

—1995. Women and Education: Beijing and After. An African Perspective. In Kehitys. Ministry of Foreign Affairs, Finland.

—1995. Public Policy Dialogue: Making It Work. Framework Document for the Establishment of the Division of Social and Public policy Dialogue at the Southern African Regional Institute for policy Studies. Harare-Zimbabwe.

——1996 (forthcoming). Education Policy and the International Context. A Study of power Relations and Constraints to Policy Formation in Africa in the 1990s.

Ouagadougou Declaration and Framework for Action 1993.

Pawar P. 1992. A letter from Africa: Education and development Through the Eyes of a critical Theory. Paper presented at the 20th anniversary of the Institute of International Education. Swedish Royal Academy of Sciences. Stockholm.

Samoff J. 1991. Defining What is, and What is Not an Issue: An Analysis of Assistance Agency Africa Educational Sector Studies. SIDA, Stockholm.

——1992. The Intellectual Financial Complex of Foreign Aid. In Review of African Political Economy No 53:60-87.

——1994 ed. Coping With Crisis. Austerity, Adjustment and Human Resources. UNESCO-ILO Task Force Report. UNESCO.

Ranaweera A.M. 1989. Non Conventional Approaches to Education at the Primary level. UNESCO Institute for Education Monographs No 14. Hamburg.

Segou Perspectives 1995. From Jomtien to The Segou Perspectives. Bamako-Mali.

Shapiro S. 1991. The End of Radical Hope? Post Modernism and the Challenge to Critical Pedagogy. In Education and Society, Vol. 9.No2 1991.

Stromquist N. 1987. The State and the Education of Women: Towards a Theoretical Understanding. CIES Annual Meeting, Washington D.C.

——1992. Macro and Micro Democracy: Towards a Theory of Convergence. In Odora C.A. (ed. forthcoming) 1996. Education and Development Revisited. Institute of International Education, Stockholm University.

Universalia 1995. Female Education in Africa and the Role of the NGOs. Vols I & II. Universalia-Montreal-Canada.

Weiler K. 1988. Women Teaching for Change. New York. Bergin & Garvey Publishers.

Weskott M. 1987. Feminist Criticism of the Social Sciences. In Havard Educational Review. Vol. 49 No. 4.

World Education Report 1995. UNESCO Publishing-Oxford.

Appendix 1. Non-Formal Approaches to Education at the Primary Level

Country	Targt Group	Altern. Struct.	Curriculum	Method Mater'ls	Evaluvation	Teachers
Bangladesh	out-of-sch.; ruralpoor; landless; slumdwellers	Sat.Sch; Sch for chd labourers; Mass educ. for illit; Girl's facilities	Specially designed by Govt. Learner-centered; Learnercentered Usual subj.+Social & human values; working skills; then voc. training	*....All cases....* Heterogeniety recognized & catered for; against rigidity & fixed entry/ exit approach of formalsystem; flexible exit/ entry; progress at own pace;	...see *footnote....*	*....All caases* NFE progs need personnel who understand the special prob -lems and circumstnce of learners; & who perceive th potencicities of the NF appraoch Must be sensi-tive and sympathetic to learners' disad-vantages;
Brazil	out-of-sch; Illit. youths; sch. drp-outs; rural poor.	State prov. Priv. insts; EDUCAR* Spec. MoE agency Fed., NLP	Specially designed using particip meth; link with cont. educ. at higher levels context senstivity			
China	out-of-sch; ec-underpriv.; nat. minorities	NF-teaching stations; Mobile, Multigr, & special classes;	usual subject + aesthetics and moral lessons; shorter dur.		Final exams; teacher evaluation by sup' visors; attempts at self eval by trs;	

Appendix 1. Non-Formal Approaches to Education at the Primary Level *(cont.)*.....

Colombia	cult. minority peasant chn.; cul. pushouts	NGO. structures; MoE*; INRAV*; INCORA; ICBF; Rel. grps	developed by learners; vetted for content relev for life-world		carried out w/r to learner achievment and prog. impact; particip. eval meant to foster the spirit of togeth. ness;	*...Cont...* Personel with expertise e.g.social and health workers are recognized as teachers;
Egypt	nomad. grps; urban poor;	One-class; trad & indig approaches e.g. Kahab	usual, but presented in integrated rather than as distinct disciplines categories	*....cont....* principles of life-long educ. e.g. self-learning inter-learning, and self-directed learning under gird the NF-approach;		Volunteers. retired person, students on holidays can be engaged thus.
Ethopia	nomad. grps: ec-underpriv; mount. coms;	NLP Villagiz.*	Usual		Eval mechnism through the NLP & other NGO	Prayer for a time when tr training can have specific space to train personnel for the NF appraoch.

Appendix 1. Non-Formal Approaches to Education at the Primary Level (*cont.*)....

India	out-of-sch; poor; illit girls	State-run NFE centres; girls facil.;	Curr. of Formal system; cond-ensed version of the same; integ-rated model; need-based; dev. model life-world.	against didactic approch of formal system teacher as facilitator of learning	Pupil eval.; Cumulative eval; specially devised gra-ding tools used to avoid exam stress	
Indonesia	mount. comes; cult. disinterest rural poor nomad. grps out-of-sch.: urban destitut: ment. handicpp	MoE-NFE supervisedp rogs incl: Learn. grps Inc.gen-learn -grps; appren-ticep rogs & Voluntary & Relilg. Grps	Rural bias		group & indiv evaluation; formative eval; No stand/dized instruments for testing achievemnt in 3Rs; external eval on prog & impact. Self-eval not tried.	Must be able to chart own course using innovative strategies to suit unique situations of learners. Teachers trained in formal system need familiarize themselves with the differece between formal and NF appraoch.
Kenya	street chn.; urban poor drop-outs out of-sch.;	No sepaarte structures	centrally developed usual subj; + usual voc subject.			
Liberia	drop-outs	Commun.	same as formal			

Appendix 1. Non-Formal Approaches to Education at the Primary Level *{ cont.}*.....

	non-west ed;	Facilities; City buildings				
Mexico	indig. grps cult. marg. ec. expolited out-of-sch.;	see Colombia	jointly developed with learners; community & commun. needs focus; local lang & culture.	*....cont....* materials= compatible culturally with context; materials= compatible culturally with context.	Periodic eval on general parti- cip. problems e.t.c, and result are used at once to improve conditions	
Nepal	illit: rural poor	MoE-NEF; Setti				
Pakistan	drop-out; rural pop rel. minorities: girls; sch. stay-aways	Nai Roshi;				
Philipines	ethn. minorities fishing grps.	Mobile tent sch; PRODED; MoE-NFE	Inter-ministerial collab.		Eval By Reg Dev Councils;	
Sri Lanka	rural poor; urban poor;	Learning Activity	centrally developed		D'centralized eval: curr.	

Appendix 1. Non-Formal Approaches to Education at the Primary Level *{ cont.}.....*

	migrant fam. sch. stay-aways conf-displaced slum-dwellers; dest & delinq. out-of-sch: drop-outs: illit.;	Centers; Lit. Centeres Communit. (open) Schools;			Eval by external team of evaluators to gauge attendance. adequacy of support services. and take corrective action.	
Syria	**********	Women's organiz; Workers unions Cult. dev, villages				
Zambia	**********	MoGenEd;	N/A		learners to sit nat. public exams	
Venezuela	*********	Adulteduc. progs: INCE*	academic (usual); and professional (tech. knowl & voc skills)	*.....cont....* joint dev of materials= common; teaching methods to conform with learner's needs;	Separate eval for *regular* attendants, and another for *occaasional* attendants; regular att. has	

Appendix 1. Non-Formal Approaches to Education at the Primary Level *{ cont.}.....*

				class/school time never to obstruct life-world activities; s'times progs. are compressed; against teacher-dominated oppressive atmosphere of formal system classrooms;	continuous assessment; occasional att. Is not oblig-atory but there is eval by a final exam at end of course.	

Collated, compressed and summarized from Ranaweera A.M. 1989. Non-Conventional Approaches to Education at the Primary Level. UNESCO Institute for Education-Hamburg and other sources from interviews.

* EDUCAR: National Foundation for Youth and Adult Education (Brazil)

*INRAVISION: National Radio and TV (Colombia)

*MOBRAL: National Linking and facilitating body between state and country services providing out of school education to those between 7-14 years of age (Brazil).

*Villagization in Ethiopia may not be in practice following the political changes there.

*PRODED: Is a Programme of Decentralized Educational Development of the Ministry of Education, Culture and Sports. The "Tent School" is its own innovation to cope with the out of school children and marginalized groups.

*INCE: The National Institute for Educational Cooperation is an autonomous institution in Venezuela that provides technical support to the national programes.

*About evaluations in general, it can be said that the NFE appraoch is clear that evaluations should not be measurement, but improvement or development oriented; providing insights to achieve better results rather than acting as a stumbling block and a threateing, impersonalized instrument for grading, or failing learners.

Appendix 2. NGO Activities in Support of Basic & Girl's Education: The Scope

Country	Natural & Thrust	Programmes & Limitations.
Burkina Faxo	* Improvement of living conditions *of their members* *more than 3000 women's groupings exist in BK's 30 provinces *Prof. Associations cater for womens rights in the workplace * 27NGOs work on women & chn *Few deal directly with formal ed. *AFED focus is reintegration of girl-child dropouts into formal *AFED focus is reintegration of girl-child dropouts into formal *Coordinated and facilated by BSONG *NGOs are an asset to a country's development. *70 local; and 121 international NGOs operating	* Training component of dev. activities. * Sensitization on health. rights, soc. issues: * Training: literacy, management. income generating activities. * Research /action on women related issues; *Advocacy & promotion of women's issues component; **Limitations:** *single issue/single sector * Island' syndrome; * sustainability & uncertaintly (due to financial base); * often volunteer staff
Guinea	* Arrival of international NGOs signalled by new liberalization policy * 318 national and 73 international NGOs; * Target is specific community *Local NGOs rely on one-person type leadership; * Survival is collab. with international NGOs; * Must sign technical agareements with govt viz their programmes * No country level NGO collective. SCIO is a coordination structure;	* Little link with formal education; * Main contribution is in school constr.; * No link with curricula dev. except in development related training; * Greater influence on profess. training * potential for intervention in 'reintegration' programmes. * Main asset lies in advocacy role **Limitations:** * acute mistrust horizontally

		* large gap between local and int. NOGs * Little dynamism, finance, HRD. infras.
Kenya	* Operating guidelines provided thru 'the NGO Act. * Avoidance of local politics is appreaciated; and careful attention is paid to this sector esp. in the context of existing multiparty politics; * Community based organizations have a weak resource base, and some have yet to develop clear visions; *More dialogue needed between NGOs, local communities and government; *Money alone, though an important factor, is NOT ENOUGH to resolve the profound issues surrounding gender, education and development.	* School construction, * Bursaries to disadv. Chn; * Support to Research & Training; * Advocacy & sensitization work * Review of text books & tr. materials **Limitations:** * dependency on external NGOs * limited territorially; * unable to grapple with actual socio cultural factors or economic issues other than amelioration
Senegal	* 254 registered organizations, the increase fuelled esp. by donor agency desire to channel funds directly to rural populations. * Cooperatives are coming up; * Coordination by Min of Women. Chn, and the Family. * Effort to integrate NGO activities with government initiatives through a consultative and policy dialogue process. * NGOs perceive the possibility of even greater involvement in both formal and girls education; *A broader knowledge of NGO capacities would help create a	* General avoidance of involvement with formal educ. due to perception that this is a state activity; acknowl. of the regidity, inflexibility and unresponsiveness of the formal educ. system. * New moves to test alternative school models: * Donor led interventions target school dropouts, & re-integration programmes * Literacy training; * skills training: management of groups & associa-
tions,	better basis for cooperation or assitance in strategic planning.	civic ed; health e.t.c. **Liminations:** * Overall pedagogy and curriculum dev. is unclear & fragmented; * Weak institutional dev; lack of strategic planning

Appendix 2. NGO Activities in Support of Basic & Girl's Education: The Scope *(Cont).....*

Tanzania	* NGOs represent a fast growing sector (N about 700); but 315 recorded as registered in 1994. * Scepticism in general perception towards NGO capabilities; * Most NGO agenda shifts with the wind (donor agenda); * Perception among most NGOs is that the problems affecting girls educ are overcrowding, few sec. schools (i.e. no apparent awareness of structural factors) * Consensus among stakeholders= of the needs for an efficient organism (organiz) which is less bureaucratic, more efficient and trustworthy, to facilitate the movement of funds and experiences as well as disseminate information.	* Few have concrete progs. for girls ed. * Some have projs. for practical skills * Research and documentation; * Empowerment & sensitization * Advocacy and awareness raising; * Scholarships; * Reading materials **Limitations:** Financial constraints; Competitiveness, self interest & lack of trust in even the coordinating bodies in which they are registered) * Weak leadership from coordinating bodies;
Zimbabwe	* 640 registered NGOs; project oriented, and often revolve around one person; * Coordinated by NANGO * Concern that aid money is 'by-passing' the government and going to NGOs. * The stronger they become. the more like government most of NGOs become:	* Scholarship programmes for girls; * Gender training; * training projects in survival skills; * Human resource Development; * Book publishing & Library resources * Esp churches: provision of single sex schools.

40

THE EXPERIENCE AND CHALLENGES OF VENTURING INTO A MALE DOMINATED PROFESSION AS THE FIRST WOMAN MEDICAL DOCTOR IN EAST AND CENTRAL AFRICA

I attended mission schools for my primary and secondary education during the pre-independence period. Coming from a low income family, though of highly committed parents, I managed to attain secondary school education by sitting for a special examination (in addition to the primary leaving examination) the passing of that exam entitled me to a full scholarship of one hundred shillings (100.00) a year, which was probably about seventy five (75.00) US dollars and which far exceeded my parents' income. When I learnt that I had passed, I informed my parents that I was going to an elite girl's secondary school and that I had secured a full scholarship, all they had to do was to provide me with the requirements for a boarding school. Even that was bit difficult for them but they were prepared to further my education.

The school was not very restrictive and did not conform to the stereotyped perceptions of what a girl's education should be, it was still very new with limited facilities for science subjects and poorly equipped laboratories.

After realising that I had a potential for higher education, the school looked for alternative options to enhance my potential. Arrangements were made for me and a fellow student to attend a boys' school for additional science classes and practical work. This was our first experience to study with boys, we did not know what to expect. At that time, girls were considered to be shy and inferior to boys in every respect. Our teachers told us that as ambassadors of our school we had to project a good image of educated girls and to try to demistify all the misconceptions. We also realised that boys had their own expectations about us, we therefore decided to demonstrate that we were cultured, well informed, had a clear vision, were academically competent and equal to the boys. We were, however, pleasant to the boys, answered all questions smartly and indulged in discussions whenever we had the opportunity. Although we never got a feed- back from the boys, our presence must have made individually or in groups. We also had a very good report from the Headmaster to our Headmistress when our study period expired. I should have mentioned that although we were about thirty five when we joined the secondary school, only two of us appeared for the 'O' level examination, the others mainly joined the various training institutions while a few joined the institution of marriage.

Towards the end of my secondary school education, I informed my parents of my intention to study medicine. My father remarked that it was a long and very difficult course, my mother who was a very humble woman made no comment. I told them that I was prepared to give it a try and probably I would succeed. Since there was no clear objection, I concluded that I had received my parents' blessing which was exhibited by their invaluable support from them onwards. Although my intention was to help the sick, I also anticipated that the remuneration would enable me to overcome poverty.

After my admission to Makerere University College (as it was called at that time) members of my village community were very excited that this would redeem our village which had never produced a Doctor. Simiarly, members of the general public were equally excited and rather surprised, they watched my progress with interest. There were many well wishers, there were also a few who doubted whether I would succeed since medicine was very difficult for men, it would be even more difficult for a woman, others believed that I would fall by the way side and opt for an easier alternative. Many women would say to me "Daughter/sister, we admire your courage for venturing into a male-dominated profession, we are very proud of you and we pray for your success". I should have mentioned that at that time many parents had reservations about sending girls to study with boys in a secular institution, they feared that this could make a negative influence on their morals and jeorpadise the chances of attaining their goals.

At the University I symbolised the long waited women's representation first at the Faculty of Science which substituted for the two years of 'A' level and later at the Medical School. In the anatomy dissecting room I was surprised to find out that women have exactly the same number of ribs as the men, contrary to what I had believed all long. My teachers were very supportive, they all wanted me to succeed so that I could be a role model and inspire other women to join the profession. At the Medical School there was a total of about fifty students from Kenya, Uganda and Tanzania, because we were so few, everyone knew everybody else, also, there was good interaction with the Faculty members. We were only seven in our class, all my colleagues treated me well and "ladies first" was a familiar phrase.

Sometimes we would have joint study sessions where we would try to comprehend some of the difficult areas of the course. However, once during the examination period I had reason to suspect that one of my colleagues was propably feeling *suspect that one of my colleagues was probably feeling* threatened, he remarked that I was reading up to the early hours of the morning because when he look at my window the previous night he noticed that my light was still on. Whether he had really checked or not, I had no proof, I brushed this aside as a joke to avoid ruining our cordial relationship.

As there were no provisions for women students during internship on the wards, I was first accommodated at the Nurses Hostel and later at the residence of a lady doctor from overseas who had hospital housing for her internship. I took my meals at the men's hostel.

When I graduated I became famous overnight, everyone congratulated me, the myth about women and medicine was dispelled, many people wanted to see me, I also had very wide media coverage. The Faculty of Medicine honored me with a reception and a present at the Dean's residence, the late Prof. Alexander Galloway, I was greatly touched by this very kind gesture which was unprecedented. I also had the honour to receiving my Licentiate in Medicine and Surgery in 1959 from the Queen Mother as the Chancellor of London University, to which Makerere University College was affiliated. This qualification was later converted to a Bachelor of Medicine and Bachelor of Surgery degrees when the University of East Africa was inaugurated.

Although the first few years were rough, I enjoyed working with fellow doctors from different parts of the world who were interning at Mulago Hospital. We had all experienced the same type of training, we were governed by the same code of ethics, had to make the right decisions at the right time and make referrals appropriately according to the standard procedures. All in all, I had excellent relationship with all my colleagues, both horizontally and vertically. Doctors of the same rank were equal in all respects, the issue of gender never arose.

Earlier, I had noticed that occasionally, while conducting ante-natal clinics, the number of mothers outside my consulting room tended to exceed that in the other rooms, I attributed this either to pure curiosity that they wanted to see the first African woman doctor or to their preference for a woman. In any case, we all shared the extra patients before we could leave the clinic.

During my internship and the first post-registration year, I noticed that although there was no shortage of drugs, the commonest medical problem were repetitive and preventable. They consisted mainly of anemia, diarrhoeal diseases, malaria, malnutrition, measles, whooping cough, pneumonia, worms, obstructed labour and others. This inspired me to study public Health at the Postgraduate level, a speciality which was not so popular and less prestigious than the other clinical disciplines, with a hope that I could perhaps help in preventing some of these conditions. I specialised in Maternal and child Health plus family Planning.

In 1962, after completing my studies overseas, I was appointed as the first Medical officer at Kasangati Teaching Health Centre for the Medical School. I had to provide a service to the community, teach medical students and conduct research. Since I had to go round the community with my staff and students, I sometimes had to drive an old-fashioned Landrover, which was difficult to manoeuvre. Knowing that I was the right person for the job, I decided not to complain to avoid any possible gender-related criticisms. When members of the community saw me driving, they would remark that despite being petite, I could manipulate a huge vehicle just like a man.

The community at Kasangati was a partner in the health care team, they participated fully in the various health activities which included Health Education, immunisation, environmental sanitation, including housing improvement and others, this facilitated sustainbility. We had some positive results, people became healthier, the attendances for treatment dropped while those for preventive services increased, the infant mortality rate also dropped.

As a lecturer at the Medical School, I religiously complied with the slogan of 'publish or perish' this enabled me to move up in the academic hierarchy from lecturer to professor and later Head of the Institute of Public Health, a position I held for several years.

Some of the many challenges I experienced were the combination of my career with motherhood and family life, plus other voluntary obligations, particularly during a very difficult period in the country with shortages of everything and of medical personnel. Very often I had to work for long hours before I could complete all my domestic and employment related tasks. Because maternity leave, which is a special need for women workers, had not been introduced, the coping strategy was to accumulate leave which was utilised just before delivery up to a few weeks after delivery. Also, periodically, I experienced problems with the baby sitter and had to take the baby to my mother's place before going to teach at the Medical School.

Joining the medical profession has been of great satisfaction to me, I have invaluable knowledge about health and diseases and I can alleviate suffering. I also believe that my success was an inspiration to women and contributed towards changing the attitude about women's higher education in the subregion. Several women have studied medicine and are in all areas of specialisation. As a Professor of Public Health, I have former students in many countries, both in Africa and beyond. I also had the honour to work for the World Health Organisation, first as a WHO Representative in Botswana and later as Director of Support for Health Services Development at the WHO Regional Office in Brazzaville, Republic of Congo where I was responsible for number of programmes for the fourty six (46) countries in the Region.

In conclusion, let me state that while education is the key to success for a woman to attain her potential she must overcome the numerous obstacles and constraints, in this process, she needs the support of her parents, her community, her teachers at all levels. Her peer group and where applicable her own family.

41

THE EMPOWERMENT OF WOMEN THROUGH THE EDUCATION OF GIRLS AND FUNCTIONAL LITERACY FOR WOMEN IN BOTSWANA

Introduction

Empowerment of individuals is making information and material resources available in order for them to improve their status and well being. The availability of information which is education leads to new ideas, a clear understanding of ones position or state, a change of out look questioning and challenging of rules and regulations in one's community which the individual feels threaten their very existence or well being.

Access to education in Botswana is recognised as a basic human right and a major contributor to both economic growth and a social process for achieving equality and sustainable development. Non-discriminatory education plays a major role in conferring equal opportunities in employment, productivity and personal development of both female and male.

In order to ensure full integration of women in development, there is need to start with the education of the Girl Child like is said "educate a woman you educate the nation and educate a man you educate an individual". The girl child therefore needs to acquire the skills necessary for active and effective participation in all levels of social, cultural, economic and political sphere. Those skills, ideas and energy of the Girl child are also vital for full attainment of the goals of **equality, development and peace**. There is therefore need to ensure that the Girl Child has the full enjoyment of education as a basic human right.

Education alone will not totally bring the necessary changes that the individual demands or needs, material resources also have to be made available as to give the individual a bargaining power.

Though it is said that "the hand that rocks the cradle is the one that rules the world" the woman is still powerless even among the people that she brought up. As soon as the boy child starts socialising he intellectually looks down on women including his mother. This is not surprising since the woman is left behind at home to do house work and other minibemal jobs while the man is economically employed outside the home because initially when she was a girl child she did not have the opportunity to go to school or even if she did she did not have the opportunity to finish her education or even to use knowledge she gained on economic employment. However, a few women complete their education and manage to get employment at low levels while still fewer women get to the top.

Accessibility

At primary schools the enrolment numbers for girls and boys are almost equal (as shown in tables 1 and 2).

Table 1
Primary School Enrolment by Standard and sex in Government and Government Aided schools

Sex	Year	1	2	3	4	5	6	7	Sped	Total
Boys	1994	25603	22067	21524	24867	20969	19584	17785	*(-)	152399
	1995	25764	22992	21517	24155	21006	20204	18103	147	153888
Girls	1994	25553	21258	21026	23569	21723	21071	19608	*(-)	152808
	1995	24240	22421	20859	22757	21473	21491	20085	98	153604
Total	1994	50156	43325	42550	48436	42692	40655	37393	(40)	305247
	1995	50184	45413	42376	46912	42479	41695	38188	24	307492

Table 2
Primary School Enrolment in Private School

Sex	1	2	3	4	5	6	7	Sped	Total
Boys	995	925	866	765	754	720	708	115	5848
Girls	903	860	859	764	749	746	832	113	5796
Total	1898	1785	1695	1529	1503	1466	1540	228	11644

Source : Department of Primary Education 1995 Annual Report.
SPED stands for Special Education.

According to the Botswana national population census of 1991, females constitute 52%. The 1993 literacy survey showed that Botswana literacy rate is 68.9% with 66.9% for males and 70.3% for females.

Though the statitistics favour females in the literacy rate, it must be noted however that literacy of most females is at a very low level.

The enrolment of girls starts declining at primary and this dropout rate increases at secondary in particular at forms 3, 4 and 5. The most common reason for dropout is pregnancy followed by others which includes withdrawal due to early marriages, poverty and academic performance particularly at form 5.

Table 3. Drop-outs in Secondary Schools by Sex and Reason. 1991.

Reason for Drop-out	Male (%)	Female (%)	Total (%)
Pregnancy	13	1083	1096
(%)	(2.9)	(67.8)	(53.5)
Expelled	18	12	30
(%)	(4.1)	(0.7)	(1.5)
Other	412	509	921
(%)	(93.0)	(31.7)	(45.0)
Total	443	1604	2047
(%)	(21.6)	(78.4)	(100.0)

Source: (CSO, 1992) Education Statistics 1991

Table 3 reveals that many more girls (78.4%) than boys (21.6%) drop out of secondary school and that pregnancy is the main reason for dropping out for girls but not for boys. Most pregnancy related expulsions occurred in the upper secondary years (form 3, 4 and 5). These figures suggest a crisis in female education at secondary school levels. A large number of females do not complete their secondary education and therefore are poorly equipped to compete alongside men in the better paying occupations. According to the boys-girls pregnancy drop out ratio, it is clear that most of the pregnancies are caused by adult males in the communities. This also has implications for STDs including HIV transmission. These figures suggest early and widespread sexual activity in secondary schools such that an aggresive approach to sex education is a greater requirement. As such initiatives such as the YWCA peer education project are required.

In academic achievement males seem to lead as evidenced by the number of male professionals in Science related fields and other highly place occupations. See Table 4.

Table 4.

Programme/ Gender		Year 1		Year 2		Year 3		Year 4		Overall	
		No	%	No	%	No	%	No	%	No	%
B.SC	Male	208	71	111	79	29	69	18	64	366	74
	Female	83	29	30	21	13	31	10	36	126	26
BA	Male	80	44	64	40	66	45	63	43	273	43
(Hum)	Female	108	56	97	60	80	55	82	57	362	57
B.ED	Male	-	-	27	84	16	70	27	79	70	79
(Hum)	Female	-	-	05	16	07	30	07	21	19	21

Source: University of Botswana- 1993/94 Academic Year.

Table 5.
Enrolment at Teacher Training Colleges by sex in 1995

	Year 1		Year 2	
Sex	Male	Female	Male	Female
Number	77	410	84	284
%	16	84	23	77

A look at teacher training colleges (TTCs) which are academically lower than the University shows a female enrolment of 84% and 16% male in 1995. If one considers the teachers in Technical/ Vocational institution, they are overwhelmingly male. Within the Brigades females tend to be concentrated in book-keeping, typing and textiles while building and carpentry are heavily male dominated. Thus the success of gender stereo-typing and socialisation are reflected in these statistics.

Despite the fact that education is the key to future but for girls "school is still a place of unequal opportunity" because of discrimination from teachers, gender-biased text books and exclusion from many male fields of study.

This view was echoed by the Botswana Education Commission of 1993 on Science related subjects in page 179 of the report. Another dimension of enrolment is that the girls have a far lower participation rate than boys in the Pure Science and Additional Mathematics. For example, in 1991, 876 boys and 391 girls took Physics and 218 Mathematics at COSC (Cambridge Ordinary level School Certificate).

Having realised that formal education is not accessible to all, the Government of Botswana through the Ministry of Education's Department of Non-formal Education launched the National Literacy Programme to complement the school education in 1980. Since its inception more females (13 773) than males (71 83) enroled in the National Literacy Programme (1995).

The National Literacy Programme curriculum though at a very low level (first four years of primary education) covers many subjects such as Agriculture, Health, Environmental Education, Moral Education etc. To improve the level of the National Literacy Programme the Botswana Government through the Revised Policy on Education of 1994 mandated the Department of Non-formal Education to "introduce primary education to provide adults with the equivalent of Standard Seven". (that is Primary School Leaving Certificate). To bring in the functionality of the Literacy Programme the Department also offers training on productive skills e.g. how to rear chickens, horticulture, making clothes etc. After the training the National Literacy Programme participatns are also encouraged to embark on income generating projects to improve their living standards. Some of the projects that exist are sewing, bakery, knitting, handicraft, poultry etc. As already mentioned that most of the national literacy programme participants are females they are more inclined to choose projects which are traditionally female oriented. The Department thus has to make extra effort to encourage women to engage in projects which are more profitable and have been dominated by men, and, bearing in mind that we live in a dynamic world where gender issues have to be dealt with, the Department of Non-formal Education is reviewing the literacy curriculum with a view to develop the curriculum which is gender sensitive and accommodating to the new developments. The 1994 Revised Education Policy has also stressed the need for all involved in the development of the informal sector to receive gender sensitive training.

In order to address the imbalance in the provision of education and in particular for girls, the Botswana Government had made provision for girls who fall pregnant to be admitted back into formal schools after a year of feeding the baby. However not all the girls manage to go back to school and one of the reasons why they don't is that they are not aware of this regulation.

The Government should make sure that the regulation on re-admission of girls after they have given birth is known by girls and ensure a certain quota of places for the affected girls. The year that the girls are expected to observe before going back to school is too long. Working mothers are allowed eighty-four days for maternity leave. Why should school-going girls be expected to go back to school after a year?

The YWCA in Botswana established a "Teenmother Programme." This Programme offers further education to girls who dropped out of school due to teenage pregnancy. When the mothers are in class their babies are looked after in a day care centre. The mothers are given time off to feed their babies during the school day. This Programme should be extended to other towns and villages or similar programmes started.

The Revised National Policy on Education committed itself through the following recommendations.

In relation to the participation of girls in science related subjects that:

> "Special measures should be developed to increase the participation and performance of girls in Science, Mathematics and Technology."

This should ensure not only participation but change of attitudes towards those subjects and participation in the traditionally male dominated fields.

Educators should be sensitised on issues of gender. Workshops should be conducted for educators who are already in the field. For those in Teacher Training Colleges and adult education training, a course on gender should be taught and made compulsory.

To Eliminate Gender Stereo-typing in the Schools Curricula

- Gender neutral books are recommended
- The number of female teachers for Science and Technology course should be increased
- Career- guidance seminars by Ministry of Education and gender-sensitise workshops be conducted
- Parents and teachers should be urged to encourage girls to take up Science and Technology courses.
- The NGO community and other bodies should also support the Government in this endeavour by material and financial assistance to encourage girls to participate in Science and Technology courses in schools.

Enforce Minimum Legal age for marriage

—this has been recommended at some fora in the country.

CONCLUSION

The Government has taken steps to address gender imbalances in education, but there is room for more improvement.

Functional literacy can go a long way in empowering women if all conserved women participate in the Progrmme. Functional literacy is a tool for poverty alleviation. As it is the women who are mostly affected by illiteracy and poverty, functional literacy can be the answer if these women come forward and are helped to gain the skills, that they need.

42

WOMEN AND GIRLS EDUCATION IN THE GAMBIA.

It is globally accepted that the education of girls is one of the most important investments that any developing country can make in its own future. In the long term, almost every other aspect of process, from nutrition to family planning from child health to women's rights is profoundly affected by whether or not a nation educate its women and girls. Therefore, it merit special attention in any formulation of socio-economic, cultural and political policies for women in the country.

As a result a lot of energy and resources have been utilised over the years towards initiative and activities for the advancement of women and girls especially in the field of education. The last decade has witnessed dramatic changes in girls and women education in the Gambia with the focus more directed towards the rural areas where the problem is more acute.

It is noteworthy to observe that problems and obstacles to girls education in the Gambia emanare more from the wider economic and socio-cultural setting than the education system which provides equal opportunities for both sexes. Some traditional beliefs coupled up with some economic and other related factors which will be discussed later in this paper militate against the education of girls and women.

In an era when the full potentials of female education is realised, efforts have to be made for orientation towards scientific, technical and vocational education to give this sector a new orientation and impetus. In the instances where women have had access to formal education they have held their own and have amply demohstrated that they can contribute their fair share in development.

The Inequitable distribution of labour and roles also has had a seroius effect in undermining the development of the full potential of women. The traditional attitude has been that women should concentrate on the upkeep of the home and the rearing of children. They are also considered to be suitable for only certain types of economic activities which were exclusively for them.

The result has been that their participation in the development of society as a whole has been below its full potential and more seriously, their actual contribution often went unrecorded. And unrecognised, their influence was limited.

The reason why women play secondary roles in society are not hard to find. What has been an old age problem of attitudes still lingers on in the present time. From the beginning, the female child is seen by the family and society as being less fortunate as her male counterpart. The female child is brought up to view herself as being subordinate to her brothers and unlike the other brother is not given the kind of training and orientation designed to make her an independent individual in adult life. Rather, she is trained to be good housewife, mother and obedient servant to society.

In the Gambian situation, illiteracy is widely associated with the fact that the value of formal education for all members of society has only been widely accepted recently by both rural and urban communities. It is recognised that the level of illiteracy and the general level of education, particularly female education is a major obstacle in people's participation in development.

In 1993 the literacy rate of males was 38.5% and for females 14.7% and a total literacy rate of about a third of the population. This indicates that nearly 60% of Gambians 10 years and over are illiterate. The 1992/93 SDA Household Economic Survey revealed that the literacy rate of females 10 years and above is 35% and 71% for males in the same age group. (The 1993 Census estimated literacy rate for male and female as about 27% and 55% respectively). The total literacy rate for the total population in the Gambia is just over 40% and 3.7% of The Gambian population did not list their literacy status.

Less than 1/3 of primary school teachers are women, out of this 1/3, just over half, 54%, were qualified in some way (Education Statistics 1992/93). Only a quater of middle school teachers are females, and less than 20% of them were qualified. In high schools 17% of the teachers were females. There were only 17% of both middle and high school female teachers who had some sort of qualification for this same period.

Currently (1993/94), 31% of primary school teachers are females and 42% are qualified. In middle school, less than a quarter (17%) of teachers were females and 63% of them were qualified. Female high school teachers constitute 15% of high school teachers and 95% of them have some form of qualification.

The education statistics (1991/92 and 1993/94) also show that the gap between male and female enrolment widens as the student progress to higher primary school grades, although this is most marked in the rural regions. The Education Statistics for 1992/93 peg the actual enrolment at 40,314 out of 97,262 pupils at the primary level, which is 41% of the total enrolment. The current education statistics reveals an enrolment of 61,099 and 44,372 for males and females, respectively. The total enrolment rate for primary level is 42% a 1% increase from 1992/93 statistics. From these figures one can see the disparity between male and female enrolments within geographical areas. The further one goes away from the capital and its immediate environs, the more female participation in education matters. The first three grades in all four educational regions have a relatively high per centage of female participation but female attrition sets in for the last three grades of which the end grade six of primary education has the lowest girls enrolment. The madrassas have a high rate of attendance. Therefore, there is need to critically review this alternative form education for females with a view to ascertaining its implications for girls' education.

The low rate of female participation in education can be attributed to a number of interdependent variables such as economic, social cultural and demographic.

Economically

Most families need child labour for commercial and non-commercial ventures. Girls are used for sibling care, street selling and domestic chores and for the average rural parent, these activities satisfy immediate basic needs while the benefits of schooling are more distant. This supports the above statistical figures where by enrolment is highest in urban areas such as Greater Banjul Area which records both the highest total pupils and also the enrolment of girls. Out of a total enrolment of 113, 419 (1994/95) nationally, the capital area (Banjul) registers a roll of 32,651 pupils of which 15,881 or 48%, is female. Comparatively, in rural regions where parents attitudes might be more removed from the benefits of formal schooling, female participation records 36%.

The Socio Economic Level of Parents

Seem to be a determining factor in the attendance rates of girls at any level of education n The Gambia. The higher social status of the parents the more likely that they will send their daughters to school and encourage them to continue to higher level. Though education is tuition-free and non-compulsory at the primary level some parents find it difficult to meet the cost of book rental fees, uniforms, furniture and other charges that the school may levy on the students.

Socio-Cultural Factors

Such as early marriages, teenage pregnancies and religion are also contributing factors. The practice of early marriage is a deterrent to girl's education. The widely held belief in The Gambia that "the place of the woman is in her husband's home"-renders formal education for women as irrelevant for a lot of people. It is also believed what a woman learns from early childhood to puberty is enough to help her manage a home. There is also the fear that exposure to education may develop attitudes and values contrary to tradition. With over 85% of the population being Muslim, misinterpretation of Islam affects girls access to and continuation in education.

Teenage Pregnancy

Is yet another obstacle for girls education. The envisaged risks of external influences and pressures have been noted to persuade protective parents to keep their daughters at home where it is hoped that such risks are minimal.

The attrition rate from school, though higher in the rural areas than in the urban, affects the country as a whole. From the figure of 48% the female enrolment as at 1994/95 dropped to 41% as one goes higher in the education ladder.

The basic problem of not educating girls stems from the attitude of parents and society towards western education and anything that is alien to local tradition. The fact that the mother or both parent are illiterate is a factor which does not help the situation. Quite often, the parent hold the belief their being exposed to western culture and in particular formal western schooling, is a recipe for alienation from indigenous culture and respect for traditional norms and values. An attitude of defence and challenge of parental and social authority could, as they see it, be derived from exposure to western education.

A. Intervention to Improve Girls Education in the Gambia.

The education of female has positive impact on total fertility and infant mortality rates and on health, nutrition and life expectancy. Girls education can also determine children's educational participation of future generations.

The government is fully aware of these facts and attaches great importance to the education of girls. The Education Policy has set out its goals and objectives to increase the primary enrolment rate from 65-71% by 1996 with special emphasis on increasing the participation of girls in education. In the light of this, government has institute a series of measures geared towards addressing the gender imbalances in education.

In 1988, a Women in Education Committee was set up to examined and determine the root causes of the problems affecting female education. In line with the regulations adopted at the Job-theme World Conference on Education for all in 1990 and the follow-up Conference on the Education of Girls in Ouagodougou in 1993, the ministry of Education initiated an 18 person Multi-sector Working Group on Girls Education. The working group task was to look into the effective improvement of girls education with the key objectives of prompting increase access to education at all levels and improvement in the quality of delivery systems. Some of the findings of the Women in Education committee were drawn on by subsequent bodies such as the Technical Working Group which has developed an action plan to foster community action towards increasing the enrolment of girls to at least 80% by the year 2000 which may be attainable given that The Gambia's donor partners have committed funding towards this venture.

Perhaps the greatest and most important achievement and efforts to improve the Education of girls was the National seminar on girls education held from the 4th- 7th April 1995 in which a plan of action for increasing the participation of girls in education was formulated. The plan presents a range of strategies for action with the understanding that no single strategy is by itself sufficient for the solution of the complex Social-Cultural and economic problems surrounding girls Education. A good number of activities in the plan of action are currently been implemented with the help of Government, UNICEF, World Bank and other donor agencies.

Teachers are being trained on gender analysis and in the elimentation of gender stereotyping in Schools. Both Gambia College- (an institute for training teachers) and the curriculum Research and development Unit are also addressing the problem. The recent posting policy developed by the Ministry is addressing the problem of using female teachers as role models in the rural areas. The building of separate toilets facilities for girls to address the problems of security and privacy had been competed in 21 Primary schools this year.

A series of community workshops to involved the community in designing and implementing strategies for improving girls Education had been organised in all the six Educational Regions.

The Non-Formal Education Services of the Ministry has also been implementing series of community base seminars and training programmes for girls and women to up grade and improve their participation in Education.

School fees have been reduced to increase girls Education as girls always suffer if the family income is low.

A project proposal for funding has been accepted by the World Bank to carry out participatory research Approach (PRA) to improve girls Education. A pilot study has been conduct in two Villages in the rural areas. Another study on girls retention is underway using schools countrywide. The girls Education programme has been evaluated this year with an aim to forge the way ahead. In trying to make the programme very formal a focal point for girls Education has been identified since may 1995 to coordinate all inputs.

Although NOGs such as Action Aid and Christian's Children Fund have made significant contributions in complementing government's interventions in formal education system, the NGO presence is more apparent in the vocational sector. Apart from the skills centres run by NGOs for girls dropping out of school for various reasons, most NGOs have been encouraging women's participation in training progrmmes which are geared towards enhancing their literacy and numeracy capabilities. These training programmes have been instrumental in enabling women to keep records and to run their business efficiently. In the formal sector, government has made some progress in enabling women and girls to access vocational and skills training. The government through its specialised agencies has directed considerable energies at positively influencing women's perceptions, values and behaviour in many aspects of life. These efforts are channelled through both formal and informal systems.

B. International Support for Women Education

International support in education is mainly for infra structural development, sensitization programme, provision of educational materials, human resource development through teacher training and fellowships and functional literacy. Organisations such as DANIDA, ADB, World Bank, IDA, UNESCO, ODA, and CODE have supported functional literacy programmes geared towards women's empowerment and skills development. Funding organisation of major interventions in education are the World Bank and ADB, NGO support largely compliments government's development efforts to sustain institutions as well as projects and programmes. Due to the recent political developments in the country most of the donors have suspended aid; some of them have indicated the possibility of committing funds through NGOs. The suspension has negative implications for the attainments of targets in the education of girls by the year 2000.

At present the future seems to be brought and with the untiring efforts pumped in improving the education of women and girls, it is envisaged that positive results will be achieved in the near future.

43

WOMEN EDUCATION IN GHANA

Introduction:

1.0 In Ghana girls and women's education is recognised as crucial to national development and throughout the ages attempts have been made to put girl's and women's education to the fore. The fact that one of the Girls schools established by the early missionaries is over one hundred and sixty years old buttresses the point. Again a Ghanaian educationist, Dr Kwegyir Aggrey of Africa, (one of the founders of Achimota College, the first co-educational institution in Ghana) emphasised the importance of Girls and Women's education to national development as he made a statement in 1927, as follow:

> "Educate a man and you educate an individual, educate a woman and you educate a nation".

Inspite of all the efforts being made, women still lag behind in literacy. The situation is a result of certain factors which are common to all of us in Africa-Negative attitude of parents to the education of girls, inhibiting cultural values and practices, religious values, poverty and early marriages, among others.

It must be noted, however, that education was in existence in Ghana in various traditional forms before the Europeans introduced the formal system. The traditional form of education also put girls and woman in the fore. Certain aspects of it, regrettably put women in subjugation.

2.0 Educational Policy

2.1 The educational policy as contained in our national Vision 2020 are as follows:--

— Achieve universal basic education and educate each individual to his or her maximum potential
— Eradicate adult illiteracy.
— Increase female enrolments and completion rates at all levels in the educational system.
— Increase school enrolments and reduce drop-out rates of rural populations at all levels of the educational system.
— Improve the quality of education and give greater emphasis to science and technology at all levels.
— Expand and increase access to secondary and tertiary education.

Training

Improve the technical proficiency of the Ghanaian Labour force through increased opportunities for technical and vocational training, including apprenticeship schemes.

- Inculcate awareness of the need for continuous training and retraining of workers in all categories and at all levels, including managerial.

3.0 Safety and Security for Girls in Schools

3.1 The safety and security for girls in schools are assured as our educational policy is geared towards universal primary/basic education and eradication of illiteracy. The current educational system has removed gender biased stereotypes of the former educational system. Text books and teaching aids currently in use are also free of gender biased stereotype. School hours are within the day time. For example, schools run at various times between 07.30 hours to 17.30 hours (GMT).

3.2 School Sessions

Currently, schools run one session. Due to inadequate accommodation and other school facilities a "shift system" was introduced in the late fifties and has continued to date. The shift system and the single session have enabled some girls to remain in school while they offer domestic service to their guardians.

3.3 Role of Female Teachers

Even though the overall per centage of female teachers is lower than that of males, at the basic level of education, the per centage of females are higher than that of men. This is very important as girls at this state need the guidance of females. The girls also see them as role models.

3.4 "Schooling" for Teenage Mothers

One of the reasons why some girls dropout of school is adolescent motherhood. All efforts are being made to encourage adolescent mothers to continue with their education. Family Life Education is one of the important components of the curricula in schools.

3.5 Scholarship for Girls

In the even of having to apportion family financies on the education of girls vis-a-vis that of a boy, the girl is nearly always at a disadvantage. To this end, it is being proposed that a scholarship scheme be set up to cater for girls under such a situation. It must be noted, however, that already, certain NGOs such as FAWE, Past Students Associations, and the District Assemblies (Local Councils) are offering scholarships to needy girls.

4.0 Alternative Approaches to Education

(Education has been noted as a key to empowerment and all attempts have been made now to get as many of our citizens, irrespective of gender, functionally literate). But due to factors which are already known, girls and women lag behind in all aspects of formal education except inadult education programmes. (Statistics Provided).

Various alternative forms of education have been introduced to ensure that women in particular make the best use of education.

4.1 Science Technology and Mathematics Education Clinic for Girls

Due to gender biased, stereotypes, girls and women have "Shyed" away from subjects like science and Mathematics. In addressing the latter, the Ghana Education Service has Instituted a programme to motivate and encourage more girls to go into science and technology. The programme is science, Technology and Mathematics Education clinic for Girls (STME).

4.2 Religion and Literacy

Religious organisations have a programme where they teach both young and old reading and writing in the local language to enable them read their holy books (the bible and the Quoran). Christians refer to the programme as Sunday Schools.

4.3 Sheperd Schools

In the Northern Sector of the country "Sheperd Schools" based on flexible hours of study was introduced to allow the children tend their animals and also to avail themselves for formal classes.

4.4 Extenssion Services

Agencies working with and for women provide extension services in Agriculture, Health and Nutrition, Simple Book Keeping, Civic Education and Legal Literacy among others.

4.5 NGO Programmes for Adolescent Mothers

Even though it is our policy to get adolescent mothers back to the formal school system, some fail to return due to various reasons. Concerned NGOs have put in place a programme to teach such girls skills and to get them to be self-supporting.

4.6 Vocational Training

For women to be self supporting, they need marketable skills. The country abounds with formal vocational schools and appreticeship programmes where both boys and girls are introduced to such skills as sewing/tailoring, confectionery and baking, plumbing and electrical/ auto mechanics and hair dressing.

4.7 In- Service Training

In-service training is offered to workers on the job and these are organised by employers of the unions of TUC.

4.8 Workers College/Distance Education

There are workers colleges throughout the country being run by institute of Adult Education, University of Ghana. They have a wide range of courses leading to award of school certificates and professional certificates. Since they are limited to regional capitals, only those who find themselves in the capital benefit from their courses. An alternative programme- Distance education-is being instituted for the benefit of those who for one reason or the other cannot leave their jobs and families "to go to school".

5.1 Functional Literacy

Functional literacy though a new concept has been carried on in different forms over the past five decades. Initially it was meant to teach adult non-literates reading and writing in local languages. The set-back to the programme was that there were insufficient reading materials in our local languages then and so the learners for want of reading materialsin no time lapsed into illiteracy. The new concept of functional literacy was started as a pilot programme in 1989. It was launched as a national programme in 1992.

5.2 The main objective of the programme is to eradicate illiteracy and poverty among the rural folks with special emphasis on women. It aims at improving the quality of life of the participants/Learners, their home, their community and the society as a whole. The socio-economic development of participants is carried out through lessons that cover, among others, the family and its related issues such as Family Planning, and Teenage Pregnancy, Health, the Environment, Income Generating Activities, Social Responsibilities and Rights and Legal Issues.

5.3 Facilitators are generally drawn from within the various communities and trained. Most of the participants/learners are women (statistics attached). Available figures also indicate that the drop out rate of men is higher than that of women.

5.4 Functional Literacy classes are held in the evening when learners have finished with their day's work or chores. Lighting poses a problem. To address the situation, the Non-formal Education Division (NFED) of the Ministry of Education provides kerosine lamps to the facilitators. Currently the Government is carrying out a rural electrification programme vigorously and a number of towns and villages have been connected to the national grid for the supply of electricity.

5.5 The NFED is the division responsible for functional literacy in the country. They however, work closely with NGOs and Government Departments for the effective implementation or their programmes. There is no programme without its inherent problems and limitations but what every they might be, functional literacy is on course. Women and girls who have pursued the programme to date are better equipped to lead a more satisfying life than before.

6.0 Conclusion:

Ghana as a nation is conscious of the fact that education is the key to empowerment and the empowerment of women is crucial to national development. Our constraints, not withstanding, we are moving steadily towards our goal.

Chapter 43: Education of the Girl-Child Kampala - 8 , 13 September, 1996

Country Highlights

Enrolment in Primary, Secondary and Tertiary levels of Education by Sex.

	1980/81 Proportions			1985/86 Proportions			1990/91 Proportions		
	Number '000	Female	Male	Number '000	Female	Male	Number '000	Female	Male
Primary	1378	44	56	1575	44	56	1803	45	55
Middle*	530	40	60	595	41	59	--	-	-
Junior Sec. School	-	-	-	-	-	-	569	41	59
Secondary School**	113	31	69	130	32	68	199	33	67
Senior Sec. School	-	-	-	-	-	-	50	32	68
Teacher Training	12	44	56	16	44	56	15	44	56
Vocational Institutes	11	10	90	14	8	92	17	9	91
Deiploma Awarding Institute	2	20	80	1	17	83	2	19	81
Polytechnics									
Part Time	3	19	81	3	28	72	6	32	68
Full Time	8	20	80	3	21	79	4	23	77
University	35	17	83	8	17	83	10	21	79

* Middle School Education was phased out in 1988/89

** Covers sixth form enrolment

Source: Ministry of Education

Teachaers in Primary, Secondary and Tertiary Levels of Education

Level of Teaching	1980/81 Proportions		1985/86 Proportions		1990/91 Proportions	
	Numb. r '000	Female	Number r '000	Female	Number r '000	Female
Primary						
Trained	26	43	35	44	-	-
Untrained	22	41	30	46	-	-
Total	48	42	65	45	-	-
Middle	16	25	21	40	-	-
Trained	7	17	11	23	-	-
Untrained						
Total	23	22	32	34	-	-
Junior Sec. Sch.						
Trained	-	-	-	-	23	29
Untrained	-	-	-	-	7	19
Total	-	-	-	-	31	27
Secondary School	6034	18	7769	19	9195	17
Teacher Training	698	23	953	21	952	21
Polytechnics	237	16	268	21	405	20
Diploma Awarding	173	17	174	11	192	15
Institutions	-	-	-	-	1115	4
Universities						

Source:Ministry of Education

* Dats refers to 1980/81 academic year

** Date refers to 1991/92 academic year.

44

EMPOWERING STRATEGY FOR DEALING WITH SEXUAL HARASSMENT AND ABUSE: A CASE STUDY FROM KENYA

Dr. Sheila, P. Wamahiu, Ms. Fatuma Chegu

1.0 Introduction:

A significant factor frustrating equal participation of girls in formal education in Africa is the that of sexual harassment and abuse. Sexual harassment and abuse, as suggested by newspaper reports and personal testimonies, not only occur outside the school, but often are carried into educational institutions and impact negatively on the educational participation of girls in three obvious ways. First, parental decision not to send their daughters to school, or defer their admission, may be influenced by a concern for their sexual and physical safety. The perceived threat to family honour and respectability, and relatively lower value for sexually abused daughters in the marriage market, further contribute to their non-enrolment or delayed entry into school. Second, the resulting stress on the psychological, emotional and physical health of the girl-victims affect their self-confidence and concentration, resulting in poor examination performance and educational aspirations. Finally, the trauma experienced by them may lead to premature exit from formal education.

Despite its significance to the achievement of gender equity and equality in education, the actual magnitude of the problems of sexual harassment and abuse, both forms of gender violence, may never be know. This situation stems partly from a conceptual confusion regarding definition of the terms 'sexual harassment' and 'sexual abuse', partly from the wall of silence that surrounds discussion of the issue, and partly because of an outright refusal by society to acknowledge the gravity of the offence committed. It is only the extreme cases of sexual abuse, such as the rape of

3. Staging the play; and
4. The workshop

3.1 Conducting Research:

The issue of safety of school-girls featured prominently on the agenda of WERK right from its inception in 1993. A sub-committee set up to focus on the issue decided to investigate the impact of commuting in public service vehicles (PSV) on the safety and security of secondary school-girls in Nairobi, the Kenya capital. A seed grant from the Royal Netherlands Embassy in Nairobi helped to cover basic research expenses.

Though the research included a quantitative dimension, it was possible to publish the preliminary findings of the qualitative component as the research group's contribution to the African Regional Preparatory Conference and NGO Forum on Women in November 1994. The publication cost was met through a grant made by the Kenya Office of UNICEF to FAWE as Chair of the NGO Regional Education Sub-Committee for the Fourth Women's Conference and Forum in Beijing. One thousand copies of the report, published and distributed in Dakar and Nairobi, generated intense discussion.

The report entitled *Getting to and from School in Nairobi: Girls and the Painful Matatu Ride*, was an expose of veiled and blatant sexual harassment and abuse of urban school-girls by PSV personnel and some members of the public as they commute to school daily. What was even more frightening was the apathy of other commuters, both men and women, towards these incidents! Though the study further highlighted the apparent passivity of the girls themselves in the face of harassment, it revealed them to be thinking beings, concerned about their situation and keen to change it. Within this context, perhaps one of the most significant contributions of the report was the set of recommendations made by girls who were interviewed during the course of the research. In their recommendations, they suggested practical measures that could be adopted to create a safe environment for them.

The matatu study identified factors like loud music and money that induce girls to fall prey to the sexual attention of the PSV personnel often leading to pre-marital sex, early pregnancies, absenteeism, poor performance and eventually exit from the education system. Other studies, conducted within Kenya educational institutions, confirmed the high incidence of sexual harassment and abuse of female students (Karanja, 1995). They also confirmed the negative impact on the self esteem, examination results and the persistence of girls in school (Deabstar, 1995).

3.2 Developing the Play:

Having conducted the research and disseminated its findings in a conventional way, albeit to a limited audience, the questions that the group posed to itself were: Is the traditional way of disseminating the research results sufficient? Did it fully meet the stated objectives of WERK? The objectives of WERK are to

a. Conduct creative research impacting on the education of women and girls in Kenya;
b. Disseminate research findings to educationists and non-educationists alike;
c. Link research to advocacy for the promotion of a gender equitable society;
d. Building female professionalism in educational research.

Members felt that while objectives a, b and d had been addressed by the research and dissemination procedure adopted, objective c was yet to be met. During a brainstorming session, members agreed that role play or theatre might be the most effective medium for advocating elimination of gender violence in, and outside, education. It was felt that the research findings, translated into a play, could form the basis of an interactive workshop aimed at conscientisation of the participants.

It was decided that professional help would be sought to translate the research into a play. The Mzizi Cultural Enterprises (MCE), a Nairobi-based group, was identified for the task. Its selection was influenced by its reputation for gender sensitivity, and for its commitment to taking theatre to the people. With funding from FAWE, WERK was able to pay a modest honorarium to MCE for writing the script and later, for helping to direct the play.

Once and initial draft was prepared, a half-day workshop was organised to critique its content, language and potential to elicit and sustain an interactive forum on sexual harassment and abuse. The workshop participants comprised university lecturers, theatre artists, gender trainers, youth representatives, and members of MCE and WERK. While participants were unanimous about the efficacy of the medium adopted to achieve the stated objectives, the frank and often sexually demeaning language used in the play provoked considerable debate. It was eventually agreed to retain the language used as it accurately portrayed the stressful, abusive and disempowering environment that girls are forced to operate in daily. There was also a consensus that the very shocking nature of the language employed would act as a powerful mechanism for breaking down the walls of silence surrounding discussion of the problem.

3.3 Staging the Play:

The play, entitled *With Our Eyes, in Our Own Voices*, utilises a minimum of props. The opening scene is set at a health clinic, where the four character meets and shares their experiences as they wait for the doctor. Their actual experiences take place at home, in school, in public transportation and in the community. The audience is expected to take an imaginative leap into the scenes and situations sketched by the characters.

While the play requires the characters to narrate the word exactly as scripted for maximum effect, identification with the roles portrayed have enabled the actresses to be flexible in their approach. As, and when required, summarised versions of the parts have been presented without losing their essence or impact.

A narrative style is adopted in the play. The play consists of the monologue and dialogue within monologue of four girls/young women recounting their experiences of, and different responses to, sexual harassment and abuse. It places their response firmly within the traditional and contemporary cultural contexts, revealing how gendered socialisation constructs a state of sexual vulnerability and powerlessness, and consequently, a situation of dehumanisation that involves not only the female gender, but the male as well.

The powerlessness and dehumanisation of the main characters are not absolute, however. The play shows each of them to be at a different conscientisation level. Characters One and Two portray girls brought up within cultural contexts that clearly undervalue them. Instead, males are glorified at the expense of females.

However, while Character One appears to accept her situation submissively, and prays "God, please take me bring me back a boy", Character Two a rural girl, rebels against her mother, comes to the bright lights of Nairobi, and mistakenly equates sexual freedom to be liberation:

> The streets of the city welcomed me. The city must have been waiting for me. I was the newest thing that had happened to me. I was the *manyanga*—the new one. Calls of *saree*—free rides—rent the air as I approached any matatu. I had learnt that all I needed to protect myself were a number of tablets. So I had bought myself a tin of 500 tablets of Aspirin. They were the cheapest, and I had been told that as long as the tabs were white the danger of messing up did not exist. (....) I had also learnt that if we did it

> standing the force of gravity would ensure that the sperms would not flow inside me....

Specific incidents in their lives spark off the beginning of self-examination, the very preliminary stage of conscientisation and empowerment. The voicelessness of female commuters in a matatu, including her own mother, to come to the defense of a woman who is harassed by a drunken passenger plants the seeds of doubt into the mind of Character One about the belief that women should be seen and not heard, that they should be passive and submissive. "Maybe I should have said something after all.......?" she asks herself at the end of the scene.

Character Two's realisation is prompted by her boyfriend's rejection of her when she tells him of she is bearing his baby. She recounts his reaction: "He chased me like a dog that is not wanted. I tried to think of things that would hurt but everyting I said was not cruel as the fact that he had slept with me almost at my instigation".

Character Three is the most controversial. Having lost her virginity to a catechism teacher at the age of thirteen, she learns to use her sexuality to "succeed" in life, right through primary and secondary school. The hidden curriculum of the school—both religious and secular, had taught her skills to manipulate men, skills that she applies most diligently in the world of work. She believes that she is empowered, that women "have the power over these fellows if only we know what to do".

Unlike Character One and Two, Character Four transcends her socialisation, and defies social norms, to defend herself physically when sexually harassed by a stranger in a bus. In the face of initial public apathy, and subsequent hostility towards her, she fights the man who ejaculates on her.

> No. No! This can't be real.....A man could bring himself to ejaculate on me.....in a bus. Dog! Maggot! My teeth clasped into each other.....I had it! I was not going to take it from anyone, not this man.....not anyone (....) It was a scene, my sisters! A scene! I got my share of my bruises but they were worth it.....I discovered my strength and dignity since that day and I have never looked back. So my sisters, I decided no more suffering. I no longer keep quiet in the face of male abuses.

To date, the play has been staged in several venues in Nairobi (ongoing since August 1995) Houairou (at the NGO Forum on Women, 1995) and Cape Town (August 1996). Venues have included universities in

Nairobi and Cape Town[1], and a secondary school, also in Cape Town. The play has been acted out in these venues by different sets of actresses, all of whom are amateurs and either university or high school students. In addition, a video of the first performance was used to provoke discussion during a campaign organised in November, 1995 by the Coalition against Gender Violence. Approximately 2,000 people have watched the play and participated in the discussions so far.

Advocacy and empowerment through the play medium has been supplemented by the distribution of low-cost posters. Carrying the message, "Sexual harassment dehumanises us all, stop it", they force visibility on an issue that society would rather remains invisible.

3.4 The Workshop:

The inter-active theater strategy adopted by WERK to deal with sexual harassment and abuse was stated to have four main objectives. These include facilitating the audience to recognise the problem, breaking the wall of silence and taking them through a journey of self-examination and problem solving.

The play draws attention to the interrelationship between gendered socialisation and discrimination; the hypocritical approach to the issues of sex, sexuality and sex education; the absence of safe transportation especially for girls; the lack of professional and human ethics by men; and a conspiratorial silence by women themselves, keen to be perceived as the guardians of "feminine virtues". In the discussion that follows, a facilitators guides the audience through an analysis of the characters and solution-finding exercise. In doing so, two major approaches have been adopted. If enough time is available, each character is discussed in turn. When time is more limited, a more general approach is taken. It is interesting to note the change in attitude in sections of the audience who begin by condemning the girls for their inaction in the face of abuse. Character Three draws the most condemnation, being initially viewed as an unrepentant temptress. However, this attitude of blaming the victims change to one of sympathy and a realisation that society, as a human construct, can, and should, be deconstructed and subsequently reconstructed in the face of dehumanising and disempowering practices.

Neither the facilitators and the performers refrain from offering solu-

---

[1] In Nairobi, the play was recently staged at Kenyatta University, and attended by a largely male audience. The three tertiary institutions where the play was performed, that is, the University of Western Cape, Peninsula Technicon and University of Cape Town, drew mixed crowds. The first performance of the play was at the University of Nairobi during the Mini-Beijing.

tion to the problems identified. Just before the end of the workshop, each of the performers are given time to articulate their own feeling about the character that they have portrayed. They also suggest what they would do differently if faced with the same situation.

4.0 CONCLUSIONS

The play empowers by breaking the wall of silence and initiating a process of dialogue. It empowers by promoting the sharing of experiences—and almost every female member of the audience, and some males, confess to having been subjected to sexual harassment and abuse during their life. More importantly, the play empowers individuals to realise that sexual harassment and abuse is dehumanising for all involved; that we *can* and *must* change the situation; and that true empowerment comes from within ourselves. Both the performers and members of the audience have come forward to state how the play has touched them personally and instilled a new perspective of life in them.

The strength of the play lies in its indigenous roots—researched, scripted, performed and discussed in Africa, it rings a familiar bell in the minds of local audiences. The incidents and events described in the play appear very real because they are real, and people of both genders. The voices of girls and young women, normally voiceless and powerless, are given expression in the play. The harassment and abuse experienced by them, are articulated in their voices, and seen through their eyes. This adds to the potency to the play.

The effectiveness of the play as an empowerment and advocacy tool is further demonstrated by the demand that it has generated, not only from Kenya but from outside the country as well. It is a tool that can be relatively easily replicated at little cost, but with plenty of commitment to creating a gender equitable society.

BIBLIOGRAPHY

Ayodele, B Rape....You Can Beat it Vintage Press. New York. 1995.

Chege, F "Report on Interactive Workshops on 'With Our Eyes, In Our Own Voices' A play on the effects of Sexual Harassment and Abuse on the Education of the Girl-Child' Women Educational Researchers of Kenya. 1995 (draft)

Chege, F., Z. Rimbui & W. Olembo Travelling to and from school in Nairobi: Girls and the Painful Matatu Ride Women Educational Researchers of Kenya (School Environment and Safety Sub-Group) Nairobi 1994

Deabstar, K "Seen and Not Heard: Girls Educational Barriers in Secondary Schools in Western Kenya" Seminar Paper presented at the Bureau of Educational Research. Kenyatta University. Nairobi. 1995

Hashim, L.S. "A Survey of Sexual Harassment in Dar-es-Salaam" Tanzania Media Women's Association. Dar-es-Salaam. 1990

Hyde, K.A.L. "Safety and Security of Girls in School: Creating an Enabling and Empowering Environment' Prepared for the OAU Conference on the Empowerment of Women September 8-13, 1996 Kampala (Draft)

Heise, L.L. with J. Pitanguy and A. Germain Violence against Women: The Hidden health burden World Bank Discussion Paper No. 255. The World bank. Washington. 1994.

Kameri-Mbote, P. "The Silent tragedy of Gender Violence" in Gender Review Vol 1 No. 3 Dec 1994 women and media Project. Nairobi. 1994.

Karanja, D. "Sexual Harassment in Campus" in We: The Women of Today Nairobi. March 1995

Kelkar. Govind Violence against Women in India: Perspectives and Strategies Asia Institute of Technology. Bangkok 1992

Kerr. J. (ed) Calling for Change: International Strategies to end Violence against Women Poverty and Development Cooperation Information Department of the Ministry of Foreign Affairs. The Hague. 1994.

Ng'weno, Hilary "Girls' Education in Africa' Key Note Address at the Seminar on Girls' Education in Anglophone Africa World Bank/ HEDCO/FAWE. Nairobi. 1994.

Njau, W. & S. P. Wamahiu Counting the Costs: School Drop-Outs and Adolescent Pregnancies" Paper presented at the Interministerial. Consultation Mauritius 1994. FAWE Working Paper Series No. 7. Nairobi. 1995.

Stein, N. "Sexual Harassment in School: The public Performance of Gendered Violence" Harvard Educational Review special issue on violence and gender Harvard. 1995.

United Nations "Violence against Women" in The Advancement of Women: Notes for Speakers Department of Public Information. United Nations Reproduction Section. New York. 1995

University of Cape Town Final Report of the Committee of Enquiry into Sexual Harassment Equal Opportunity Research Project. University of Cape Town. Protem. 1991.

Wamahiu, S.P. "The Pedagogy of difference: An African Perspective" in Effective Pedagogies? Educating Girls and Boys by Patricia Murphy (ed) UNESCO. Palmer Press. London. 1996 (in print)

Wamahiu, S.P. F.A. Opondo & G. Nyaggah "Educational Situation of the kenyan Girl-Child" Inter-Country Study on the Girl-Child: Educational Disparities: ERNIKE/

UNICEF. Nairobi. 1992

Wamahiu, S.P. G. Nyaggah & F.a. Opondo "Education Situation of the Kenyan Girl-Child: Profiles" Inter-Country Study on the Girl-Child. ERNIKE/UNICEF. Nairobi. 1992.

Wamahiu, S.P. & F. Chege "Girls, Schooling and a Democratic Culture: Towards Gender Equity in Kenya" Prepared for the Gender Assembly of the Association of African Women in Research and Development (AAWORD), Pretoria, April 7-11, 1995.

45

THE PROBLEM OF FEMALE SCHOOL DROP-OUT: THE ROLE OF TRADITIONAL AUTHORITIES

GHANA'S EXAMPLE

Barfuo Akwasi Abayie Boatenl

Introduction

> "These young girls do not seem to get much support from other older males in their society, including their fathers, church leaders, and traditional authorities. These elders turn their backs on the needs of the younger generation. They do not take any steps to protect the youth from the dangers of adolescent life. Instead they are prepared to risk the sexual and reproductive health of the youth to uphold their own principles" (Tumbo-Masabo & Rita Leljestrom 1994 p. 74).

This quotation sets the tone for the solution of the problem of drop-out adolescent girls from our schools, especially from out rural schools where the bulk of the incidence of drop-out occurs (Bleck, 1976).

Since the adolescent period of both boys and girls coincide with Ghana's Junior Secondary School (JSS) system, it is on this period that this search-light is fixed. The ages of these JSS students range between 12 and 17 with the upper limit being prevalent in rural areas. A research to determine the average ages of urban and rural JSS students of Cape Coast Municipality and Asebu Traditional area indicated that while the average age of Cape Coast JSS final year students was 14, that of Asebu was 17 years. This picture is true of town/city students and rural students throughout the country. The simple explanation is that the urbanized Ghanaians often take advantage of modern civilization as against the rural setting where ignorance is still prevalent, thus reflecting the difference between the average ages of the urban and rural students. The same thing is true of the attitudes of people from rural and urban areas concerning formal education.

How does Dropping-out of School by Girls Constitute a Problem?

To be able to address this querry properly we need to know what it means to drop-out of school. In Ghana the new Education Reforms (ER) have a basic education level of 6 years and 3 years, that is, 6 years primary schooling and 3 years junior secondary schooling after which the Basic Education Certificate Examination (BECE) is taken by all students. This is the first terminal point in the country's education system, hence its basic nature. It is known that if a child fails to take this Basic Examination, BECE then that child is said to have dropped from school. An individual who goes through this basic examination but fails to go to the Senior Secondary School, (SSS) cannot be said to have drop-out of school. The SSS is another terminal point which prepares the more ambitious candidates to university and other tertiary education programmes.

The training programme for the JSS prepares the candidates to understand the world around them, to be conversant with elementary mathematic and science as well as being able to handle simple tools of major crafts within a particular locality. This being the basic ultimate goal of education, should be the aspiration of all children in the country. Therefore, if an individual, for whatever reason(s), does not avail himself /herself of this inalienable right, then that individual is said to have dropped-out of school.

This phenomenon constitutes a big problem to the individual and to the society at large. For example (i) That person becomes a half-baked scholar. Most of his ideas on issues are baseless and therefore unuseable. He/She does not want to accept that he/she belongs to the class of illiterates-and by posing as a literate often causes serious blunders which boarder on deception. Such individual tends to be 'too known'.

(ii) The opposite of this extrovert is an individual who, as a result of dropping out of school, recoils into his/her shell. As an introvert he/she shuns the society in general; as a result he/she becomes a liability to the society. (iii) A few years after dropping-out of school the individual joins the army of illiterates by being unable to read and write properly. Unfortunately, such people do not have the illiterate's ability to understand the folk society well. In addition to this lack of indigenous knowledge she/he grown into the abyss of ignorance and superstition. (iv) A school drop-out who holds himself/herself in 'high esteem' would not take-up a job which is considered as menial. To be specific, farming as a vocation becomes an anathema. People in this category usually move from their roots to towns where, in most cases, they fail to secure jobs of their taste. The result is that some of the males often join gangs of thieves and thugs; while some of the females join the hordes of prostitutes. From my own investigation about the educational background of some prostitutes seventy per cent was found to be school drop-outs. This conclusion is confirmed by Akosua Adomako (1992) in a study of prostitutes of both Accra and Abidjan. I think the negative effect of such persons on themselves and the society at large is not difficult to discern. The sum total of their negativity to themselves and society is that they become misfits. The women often return to their rural roots debilitated with diseases and have to be cared for, sometimes for the rest of their lives. (v) Some of these unfortunate drop-out who find themselves in towns and cities take up simple economic activities such as being *chop-bar* attendants[2], house-help, simple petty-traders (sellers of bread and other confectionaries, cold water in plastic containers for thirsty travellers), street sweepers, cleaners of offices, carriers at market places known as *kayayei* (*Kayayo*: single), etc. A few of such people later branch into serious petty-trading, while others learn trades such as dress-making and hairdressing.[3] (vi) Among the groups mentioned above are those who fail to get accommodation in houses or simply decent accommodation, such individuals both male and female tend to live on the streets, (Abayie Boaten, 1995).

We have tried to demonstrate how an individual who drops out of school constitutes a problem and at times poses a danger to himself/herself in the society. Indeed, by losing their self-esteem and their sense of purpose such individuals lose their human touch and become "living dead".[4]

Causes of Drop-outs

Bleek (1976) states:

> "The school has become an institution promoting early sexual contacts and secondary school pupils in particular are favourable sexual partners". (p. 390)

It is in this setting that the young adolescents find themselves. This statement underscores the dangerous atmosphere which the school (by its constitution) creates. However, it is the same place where both boys and girls should gather to acquire skills and knowledge which eventually would help them to cope with life.

Several researches have been conducted into the causes of drop-out for both girls and boys. Kiram Campbell (1981) stated that about 30 per cent of girls drop out of Middle Schools in 70s and 80s and put the causes of this state of affairs as follows:

- cost of education
- economic roles of girls
- the assumption that higher education is primarily a male prerogative.

Walf Bleek (1976) who worked at rural Kwahu in Eastern Regional of Ghana gave the following as reasons for drop-out of girls:

- truancy
- transfers of parents
- pregnancy

While truancy is known to be mainly boys problem, absenteeism of girls which may be the result of pregnancy or ill-health due to abortion might have been recorded by Bleek as truancy.

Felix Odei Akuffo (1987) attributed drop-out of adolescent girls in school to the following reasons:

- teenage pregnancies
- financial constraints
- relative lack of achievement orientation.

Out of 125 girls she studied at a rural setting in Eastern Region of Ghana 45 dropped-out of school through pregnancies; 25 dropped out through financial constraints; while 20 pupils were withdrawn by parents for whatever reasons.

Tumbo-Masabo and Rita Leljestrom (1995) ed. in their work on *The Dilemma of Teenage Girls in Tanzania* opined that the main causes of girls dropping-out of school are:

- early pregnancies of girls
- lack of opportunities after primary school
- preference for boys education
- truancy (but girls who drop-out through pregnancies are often recorded as truancy).

My own research conducted in rural Kwabre District in Ashanti Region of Ghana revealed the following causes as reasons for girls dropping-out of schools. The research was conducted in fifteen Junior Secondary School.

Causes	No. of Schools
• pregnancy	14
• poverty of parents	7
• lack of parental care	7
• desire for money/trading	6
• academic weakness	4

• truancy	4
• broken homes	3
• lack of motivation	2
• bad friends/peer pressure	1

(Credit: Kwabre Education District Directorate)

Out of the fifteen schools, it was only one school which did not consider pregnancy as a problem since those girls who dropped-out do so not because of pregnancy.[5] (It appears that this traditional sanction has worked well). Even though the research indicated that girls drop-out from that school for lack of parental care, transfers, broken homes and poor academic performance.

As a result of the preponderance of pregnancy factor in girls dropping-out from school there is the crucial need to address this problem.

Factors of Pregnancy among J.S.S. Students

In order to solve the pregnancy syndrome among the teenage girls in our schools, there is the urgent need to look at the factors which encourage or aid this menace. (Mbilinyi *et al* 1991) The following factors predominantly appear among the rural communities in sub-Saharan African countries:

(a) Girls involvement in love relationship. This means that some girls emotionally get attracted to men; whose involvement in the sex act is physically based.

(b) As a result of parents' failure (Apewokin 1995) to cater for the educational needs of their female wards, there is the tendency for some of these girls to depend on older and richer men. Akuffo (1987 p. 160) agreed that the most significant reason of girls' possessing boy friends was financial. Most of the men who take these girls as love companions were in gainful employment. The girls used the monies provided for their school fees, school uniforms, other clothing and pocket money for breakfast and lunch. Ohene-Konadu (1994) in his study at craft centres in Kwabre District in Ashanti emphasized the lack of parental control of school pupils due to poor financial status of parents.

(c) Peer group influence or what people call "peer pressure" do affect a sizeable number of girls who drop-out of school through pregnancy. Girls who appear better-off economically due to their reliance on boy friends normally influence their less fortunate friends; who might not appreciate the intricacies of such relationships. They thus get attracted to the idea of picking boy friends. Usually because of ignorance of what the whole idea entails some of the girls become pregnant and thus drop-out of school.

(d) Research conducted among J.S.S. pupils in some selected schools in the same District in the Ashanti Region resulted in the factors below.
   (i) lack of effective communication between parents and girls-children as well as the boys,
   (ii) test for maturity-this is where due to curiousity girls play and behave like adults which often result in pregnancy,
   (iii) lack of parental care often the result of poverty and broken homes,
   (iv) due to the proliferation of electronic media, there is the widespread of bad films, such a pornographic and film with wild scenes. This conflict of cultures adversely affect the innocent children (see Mbiti 1967).

Problems Faced by Pregnant Students

Once girls become pregnant while still in school they seem to face series of problems which usually make them lose their sense of self-esteem. The following problems have been identified as relevant:

(a) Low social status-this results in lack of respect from both their peers and seniors.
(b) They develop sense of shame.
(c) They often become isolated; people just avoid them.
(d) In some extreme cases some of them are disowned by their enraged parents and are driven away from home.
(e) Quite often they are denounced by the men who were responsible for the pregnancies. The plight of the girls become more precarious when they mention more than one name as being responsible for the pregnancy.

In addition to the above problems are:

(a) the girls' inability to continue with their studies,
(b) expulsion from school,
(c) child/baby without any economic support,
(d) future expectation destroyed,
(e) psychologically disturbed,
(f) socially displayed,
(g) medically handicapped.

One can add many more problems which pregnancy bestows on these poor girls. Indeed, the result is an identity crisis which lead some of them to succumb to negative acts such as illegal abortion and suicide.

It is pertinent to note that the ordinary adolescent, especially those from the rural setting, often have no clear notion or are so ambiguous about what it means to realize oneself as "woman", even when they have none of the problems associated with pregnancy. Usually they face problems of how to handle standards of evaluation in their different personal relationship, especially with the opposite sex.

Preventing Teenage Pregnancies in Schools

Before we address the role the traditional authorities have to play to stop the several drop-out of school girls from school we need to look at the most fundamental measures that could be taken to prevent pregnancies. These measures are:

- avoiding sex at all cost,
- controlling one's desire for material and mundane things,
- listening to counselling from the elders,
- avoiding friendship with boys and men,
- concentrating on one's studies since the devil finds job (s) for an idle hand.

We have dwelt more extensively on drop-out caused by pregnancy because we see it as the most prevalent, though one that could easily be avoided if proper measures are taken. The problem is that in rural areas most girls appear less and less knowledgeable about sex and related matters, therefore, the boys and men use this as an advantage to demand sex from girls. This poses the greatest danger for the teenage girls.

Attempted Solutions to the Drop-out Syndrome

Out research indicated that though drop-out of girls in schools is seen as a social problem, indeed a phenomenon which undermines the very fabric of the society, not much concerted efforts are being undertaken to stop or to address the issue positively. This view often appears to be erroneous. Serious counselling through the activities of P.T.A. is going on in the schools and these seem to have positive effect in the school attendants. Attempted solutions to this problem will be discussed under the following headings:

(a) Parent, Teacher Association (PTA).

(b) Students/Pupils themselves and

(c) of most significant to this essay should be the role of the Traditional Authorities including the opinion leaders in the society.

(a) PTAs: These associations are known to be prevalent in all rural communities. The PTA is a forum which combines the efforts of teachers and parents in seeking the welfare of pupils and students. The Kwabre District research wanted to find our what the various PTAs have put in place to check the drop-out of girls from schools: the following came out:

- sex-education and counselling of students
- counselling of parents on the need to look after their wards and guard them through schooling
- provision of the needs of pupils while in school
- moral education both at home and in school.

These measure which are prevalent in the District are arranged in the order of priority. It is the belief of the respondents that it was because of such measures put in place in the schools which have seen the reduction of drop out of girls in schools.[6]

Statistics collected in the Kwabre District confirm the usually less number of girls dropping-out of JSS as compared with boys.

Name of the School	No. of Boys	No. of Girls
Mamponteng Catholic	7	9
Dumanafo	21	12
Wadie Adwumakase	96	82
Maase	45	19
Mpobi	29	15
Asonomaso	80	67
Aboabogya	34	39
Ahwiaa	16	16
Wonoo-Ahodwo	20	15
Ntonso	104	97
Afrancho	13	12
Kasaam	91	103

These figures which represent actuals in the school concerned, covered the period between 1985-1986 academic year to 1994-1995 academic year. Within the period under review 556 boys and 486 girls dropped-out of the JSS. We had previously held a notion that the few girls who enrolled in our school dropped-out of school while boys remained in school until they sat for their final examinations. We now know that this picture appears false.

(b) Counselling and guidance of students. These appear to be yielding some fruits among our female students. In the craft centres of Ntonso and Asonomaso there is a tendency among the boys to stop schooling to join the army of craftsmen in the manufacturing of Kente and Adinkra cloths. The general statistics indicate that there is still a large army of boys and girls in our rural schools who continue to drop-out of school to join the already large number of people who cannot be described as literates.

(c) Proposals to check drop-outs: In the research, a general question was put to the respondents to suggest proposals aimed at checking school drop-out. Quite interesting suggestions were made:

- District Assembly to enact a legislation to discourage early marriage of girls;
- District Assembly to put in place legislation to punish irresponsible parents.[7] (There are Family Tribunals to punish parents who wilfully neglect their children)
- Free Vocational Institutions. These institutions in each District will serve as a motivating factor to urge on some of the girls to remain in schools.
- Introduction of the traditional nubility rites. It is being suggested that a modernised form should be instituted when a girl is actually out of the JSS. Those who continue to the Senior Secondary School may have to go through these rites when they are in their second year. It is believed that at this period the girls are already highly motivated and knew what they wanted in life. Nubility rites ushers girls into the threshold of adulthood and therefore licence to marriage, hence the delay after JSS.
- District Assembly to enact by-laws by which teenage school girls and boys who are seen in the streets after 9 p.m. could be arrested and punished.

From the above proposals we realize the role the District Assemblies (DAs) are expected to play in the crusade against school drop-outs.

The Role of the Traditional Authorities

In this essay the traditional authorities are described as the chief and his elders including the queenmother as well as opinion leaders both male and females within the community (including church leaders). These elements as a group have not exerted any serious influence on the behaviour of those young ones who are in schools. It is so strange that the respect which the youth used to give to these elders are no longer in vogue (Mbiti

1967). The idea of disrespect of the youth is so high in all communities that the elders have shown lukewarm attitude in the training of the boys and girls. In times of social crisis the mob action exhibited by the teenage make them appear like people without any moral training. [8] For this reason these elders and other opinion leaders have lost interest in participating in the moral training of the young ones. In the course of this very research, an opinion leader opined that she as an individual was not prepared to undertake any advisory role of girls in her rural society because the teenage students do not have respect for the aged and do not care for the (so-called) wisdom which elders assume that they have.

This development, as apprehensive as it appeared, made us probe further into the question of possible rapport which should develop between the natural leaders and the teenagers. The problem was found to be deep seated. The young ones looked unto the elders and their institutions as anachronistic and moribund. They seemed to have lost faith and confidence in the older institutions such as chieftaincy, orthodox churches etc. These no longer appeal to the youth. Their peer leaders were found to be guided by vices such as drinking of alcoholic beverages, and smoking of marijuana called "wcc"; often they copied such antisocial behaviours from foreign film which are abundant on video tapes. These are found in all communities where there is a JSS. It is this schism which this essay seeks to bridge. This is because we think the elders have something useful to contribute to the training of these "innocent" ones.

Home Training

There are two *Twi* proverbs which should be evoked here: *Yebebo dam ą yebo fi fie and yebobo nkukuo a yebobo fi fie*, rendered freely "when you become mad you start from the house" and "when you want to break pots you commence from home". The import of these wise sayings are that home training should be the foundation upon which further moral training, admonishing and counselling should be based. It is here that the PTA should take it upon themselves to instill discipline in parents. There are instances where some parents had become offended and taken the law into their hands by brutally assaulting teachers who during their normal school duties had punished their wards. If parents do not want even teachers to punish their wards what about you outsiders. There is the need, a serious one, to counsel parents to exert parental control on their wards at home. It is quite evident that children with excellent home training behave differently and abhor violence once they leave home. "By their fruits you will know them' is a truism which exposes people/ youth from the type of home they come from, whether it is good home or a bad home.

Church Leaders: The church as a strong source of moral training in the times past has virtually lost its hold on the youth. The incident narrated below illustrates the weak position of the church today. "I was at a church service when the Reverend Minister asked for suggestions from the floor. A young girl, a teenager, suggested that the church elders should insist on seeing the fathers of the little ones at the church premises before those children were baptised. She added that by that omission the church was encouraging promiscuity as some of the young mothers were known to have no husbands or not properly married before having babies.

She, in fact, demanded some sanctions against such church members. The answer from the puipit was that the babies born should not be denied baptism. This gave a chance to the other girls who murmurred against the girl who made that suggestion". I was particularly saddened by the Priest's answer, because it failed to address the issues raised by the questioner. Firstly, the answer did not say how good or bad the act of having a baby without a recognised father is. Secondly, it did not address the issue of how that child should be brought up in the society since some of the babies have no fathers. We know, however, that one of the serious problems of child behaviour is the absence or the irresponsible nature of some men who fathered these children.

The church has lost its grip on the morals of the folk since by their actions and words the church leaders cannot serve as correct role models.

Traditional Leaders

This group also lost its grip on the youth long time ago. In certain societies in this country the chief is only recognised as a leader during festivals (Abayie Boaten, 1995). His power as an adjudicator and as a focal point of mobilization, is virtually eroded. The youth do not look up to them as sources of inspiration. Recently, the youth of Chiraa in Brong Ahafo Region, demanding what they called accountability, attacked their chief by taking the law into their own hands. In the meantime the traditional heritage which the chief is the custodian is regarded by the youth as a thing of the past. This idea of disregarding the cultural heritage appears to be the result of the in-roads made by the Western education. Unfortunately, while no British citizen will query the nature of the Queen's Crown, the youth and the educated in our society have the audacity to question the institution of chieftaincy which is the very fabric of our civilization.

It is this 'degraded' institution in the eyes of the youth that we are hoping should play a leading role in correcting a social cancer among our teenage girls. Whether or not the institution succeeds in this endeavour would depend on the interplay of several factors, two most important of them being:

(a) The behaviour of the natural leaders as role models. This means that the youth should accept the personality and the ideas of the chief without the latter losing his stance as a natural leader.
(b) The youth may have to learn to respect the traditional authority, since it is the foundation upon which the stability of our communities is built. The learning process should be through respect, humility and the acceptance of the way we as Africans do our things, since whatever we do by way of imitation of the whiteman can best be described as apeing.

The research wanted to find out if there were measures from the traditional view point to control school drop-out of girls. With the exception of one community, it was seen that the traditional authorities have not instituted any measures to stop this social evil. However, in the community where the traditional authority had outlawed teenage pregnancy in schools such a thing had ceased to occur. This means that with proper orientation, comportment and dignity on the part of the natural leaders serving as role models, they could exert some influence on the youth generally. What has happened in that community should not be regarded as contradiction to the fact that the traditional authorities have lost a grip on the youth. We would want to emphasis that with proper orientation, education, good example coupled with the idea that the chiefs, queenmothers and all elders would serve as good role models, the traditional authorities could serve as a fulcrum upon which a stronger moral foundation for the youth could be built.

The traditional authorities can embark on this crusade by being the leading proponents of the concept of "Community Participation in Education". We must give credit to our earlier rulers who embraced the Western education system. Perhaps if they knew the innovation they embraced wholeheartedly was going to have such negative effects in their domain, as we are experiencing today, they would probably have hesitated. In fact, these unlettered chief and their elders mobilised their people and constructed school buildings. The aged of Asonomaso township remember with nostalgia how the chiefs drove the inhabitants of Asonomaso Safo to construct, through communal labour, the block of buildings now housing the Presbyterian Primary and Junior Secondary School complex. It is a delight to see these buildings as we doff our hats for them.

interesting to note that over 80 per cent of these boys have an ambition to learn trades, such as auto-mechanism, carpentry, tailoring etc. at a future date after they have acquired some funds to pay for the apprenticeship fees which range between ¢ 70,000-¢120,000.

4. This is both spiritual and sociological. Since they have lost their spiritual identity or self-esteem, they resort to vices such as drug addiction, especially among prostitutes, liars etc. Socially some of them fail to cope with realities of life and finally commit suicide.
5. The Traditional Authority has put sanctions on any girl who drops out of school through pregnancy. The sanction goes against the girl, the boy/man who puts her in the family way and the parents of the boy or the girl involved.
6. We do not have figures for the years before 1985, yet observation from school authorities indicates that now more girls remain in schools than previously.
7. There are Family Tribunals to punish parents who wilfully neglect their children.
8. In chieftaincy matters, these teenagers join the older group of youths and inflict injuries, through stone throwing, assault and hurl insults against traditional authorities. This new phenomenon could not be thought of about two decades ago. Now it is all over Ghana.
9. A memorandum will be sent to the District Directorate on the idea of Community Participation in Education (CPE) for consideration and adoption in the Schools of the District. The author's community should be used for a pilot project.

Reference

Abayie Boaten	1994	Chieftaincy Institution: An Overview. I.A.S. Legon.
Abayie Boaten	1995	"Rural Poverty in Ghana: The failure of the call on the Youth to go back to the Land". Green Earth Organization, Accra.
Adomako, Akosua	1992	'I Own By Body, Do I' Paper Presented at Staff Seminar. I.A.S., Legon.
Akuffo, Felix Odei	1987	'Teenage Pregnancies and School Drop-outs. The Relevance of Family Life Education and Voca tional Training to Girls' in *Sex Roles Population and Development in West Africa* ed. Christine Oppong. James Currey LTD, London.
Apewokin,, Mrs. E. Yaa	Sept., 1995	"Empowerment of Women through Population Policy and Decision Making" *NCWD Workshop on Strengthening the Integration of Population* and *Family Welfare into Women's Activities*, Accra.
Bleek, Wolf	1976	*Sexual Relationships and Birth Control in Ghana*, University of Amsterdam.
Campbell, Kiram	1981	The Drop-out Rate Among Girls and Boys at the Primary, Middle and Secondary Levels of Educa tion in Selected School' ed. NCWD *Proceedings of the Seminar of Ghanaian Women in Development*, USAID/Ghana, Accra.

Kwabre District Directorate of Education. Research Questionnaire

Mbiti, Rev. J.S.	1967	*African Religions of Philosophy* Heinemann, London.
Mbilinyi, M.; Mbughuni F. Meena R.; Olekanbaine, P.	1991	'Education in Tanzania with Gender *Perspective' Education Division Documents* No. 53 Stockholme, Sweden.
Ohene Konadu	1994	"The Effects of Kente and Adinkra Industries in Kwabre District of Ashanti: A Study in Industrial Sociology" in *I.A.S. Research Review* NS Vol. 10 Nos. 1 & 2.
Tumbo-Masabo and Liljestrom Rita	1994	Chelewa The Dilemma of Teenage Girls, Nordiska Afrikains Insitutet.